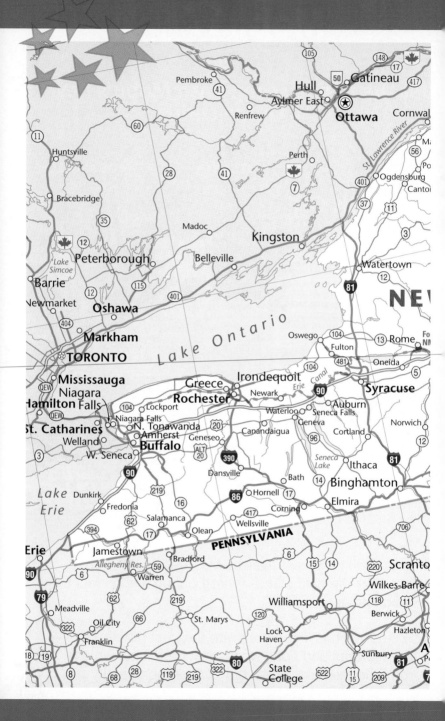

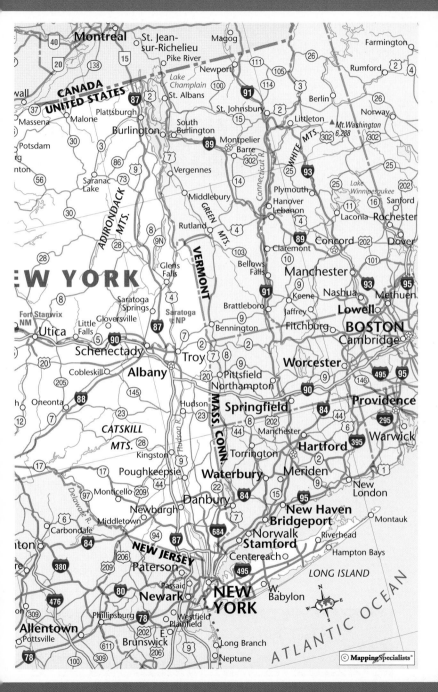

The Center for Hospitality Research

█████ Hospitality Leadership Through Learning

The Cornell School of Hotel Administration's
world-class faculty explores new ways
to refine the practice of hospitality
management.

Our research drives better results.
Better strategy.
Better management.
Better operations.

See our work at:
www.chr.cornell.edu

537 Statler Hall • hosp_research@cornell.edu • 607.255.9780

Cornell University
School of Hotel Administration

Mobil ★★★★★
Travel Guide®

NEW YORK

ACKNOWLEDGMENTS

We gratefully acknowledge the help of our representatives for their efficient and perceptive inspections of the lodging and dining establishments listed, the establishments' proprietors for their cooperation in showing their facilities and providing information about them, and the many users of previous editions who have taken the time to share their experiences. Mobil Travel Guide is also grateful to all the talented writers who contributed entries to this book.

Front and back cover images: ©iStockPhoto.com

All maps: created by Mapping Specialists

The information contained herein is derived from a variety of third-party sources. Although every effort has been made to verify the information obtained from such sources, the publisher assumes no responsibility for inconsistencies or inaccuracies in the data or liability for any damages of any type arising from errors or omissions.

Neither the editors nor the publisher assume responsibility for the services provided by any business listed in this guide or for any loss, damage or disruption in your travel for any reason.

ISBN: 9-780841-60864-1   Manufactured in Canada

10 9 8 7 6 5 4 3 2 1

TABLE OF CONTENTS

3

★ NEW YORK

★
★
★
★
★

Serials Section

WRITTEN IN THE STARS

Because time is precious and the travel industry is ever-changing, having accurate, reliable travel information at your fingertips has never been more important. With this in mind, Mobil Travel Guide has provided invaluable insight to travelers through its Star Rating system for more than 50 years.

The Mobil Corporation (known as Exxon Mobil Corporation since a 1999 merger) began producing the Mobil Travel Guide books in 1958 following the introduction of the U.S.-interstate highway system in 1956. The first edition covered only five Southwestern states. Since then, our books have become the premier travel guides in North America, covering all 50 states and Canada, and beginning in 2008, international destinations such as Hong Kong and Beijing.

Today, the concept of a "five-star" experience is one that permeates the collective conciousness, but few people realize it's one that originated with Mobil. We created our star rating system to give travelers an easy-to-recognize quality scale for choosing where to stay, dine and spa. Based on an objective process, we make recommendations to our readers that we believe will enhance the quality and value of their travel experiences. Our trusted Mobil One- to Five-Star rating system is the oldest and most respected lodging and restaurant inspection and rating program in North America. Most hoteliers, restaurateurs and industry observers favorably regard the rigor of our inspection program and understand the prestige and benefits that come with receiving a Mobil Star rating.

The Mobil Travel Guide process of rating each establishment includes unannounced inspections, incognito evaluations and a review of unsolicted comments from the general public. We inspect more than 500 attributes at each property we visit, from cleanliness to the condition of the rooms and public spaces, to employee attitude and courtesy. It's a system that rewards those properties that strive for and achieve excellence each year. And the very best properties raise the bar for those that wish to compete with them.

Only facilities that meet Mobil Travel Guide's standards earn the privilege of being listed in the guide. Properties are continuously updated, and deteriorating, poorly managed establishments are removed. We wouldn't recommend that you visit a hotel, restaurant or spa that we wouldn't want to visit ourselves.

★★★★★The Mobil Five-Star Award indicates that a property is one of the very best in the country and consistently provides gracious and courteous service, superlative quality in its facility and a unique ambience. The lodgings and restaurants at the Mobil Five-Star level consistently continue their commitment to excellence, doing so with grace and perseverance.

★★★★The Mobil Four-Star Award honors properties for outstanding achievement in overall facility and for providing very strong service levels in all areas. These award winners provide a distinctive experience for the ever-demanding and sophisticated consumer.

★★★The Mobil Three-Star Award recognizes an excellent property that provides full services and amenities. This category ranges from exceptional hotels with limited services to elegant restaurants with a less formal atmosphere.

★★The Mobil Two-Star property is a clean and comfortable establishment that has expanded amenities or a distinctive environment. These properties are an excellent place to stay or dine.

★The Mobil One-Star property is limited in its amenities and services but provides a value experience while meeting travelers' expectations. The properties should be clean, comfortable and convenient.

We do not charge establishments for inclusion in our guides. We have no relationship with any of the businesses and attractions we list and act only as a consumer advocate. We do the investigative legwork so that you won't have to.

Restaurants and hotels—particularly small chains and stand-alone establishments—change management or even go out of business with surprising quickness. Although we make every effort to continuously update information, we recommend that you call ahead to make sure the place you've selected is still open.

5

NEW YORK

★
★
★
★

STAR RATINGS

MOBIL RATED HOTELS

Whether you're looking for the ultimate in luxury or the best bang for your travel buck, we have a hotel recommendation for you. To help you pinpoint properties that meet your needs, Mobil Travel Guide classifies each lodging by type according to the following characteristics.

★★★★★The Mobil Five-Star hotel provides consistently superlative service in an exceptionally distinctive luxury environment. Attention to detail is evident throughout the hotel, resort or inn, from bed linens to staff uniforms.

★★★★The Mobil Four-Star hotel provides a luxury experience with expanded amenities in a distinctive environment. Services may include automatic turndown service, 24-hour room service and valet parking.

★★★The Mobil Three-Star hotel is well appointed, with a full-service restaurant and expanded amenities, such as a fitness center, golf course, tennis courts, 24-hour room service and optional turndown service.

★★The Mobil Two-Star hotel is considered a clean, comfortable and reliable establishment that has expanded amenities, such as a full-service restaurant.

★The Mobil One-Star lodging is a limited-service hotel, motel or inn that is considered a clean, comfortable and reliable establishment.

For every property, we also provide pricing information. The pricing categories break down as follows:

$ = Up to $150

$$ = $151-$250

$$$ = $251-$350

$$$$ = $351 and up

All prices quoted are accurate at the time of publication; however, prices cannot be guaranteed.

MOBIL RATED RESTAURANTS

Every restaurant in this book has been visited by Mobil Travel Guide's team of experts and comes highly recommended as an outstanding dining experience.

★★★★★The Mobil Five-Star restaurant offers one of few flawless dining experiences in the country. These establishments consistently provide their guests with exceptional food, superlative service, elegant décor and exquisite presentations of each detail surrounding a meal.

★★★★The Mobil Four-Star restaurant provides professional service, distinctive presentations and wonderful food.

★★★The Mobil Three-Star restaurant has good food, warm and skillful service and enjoyable décor.

★★The Mobil Two-Star restaurant serves fresh food in a clean setting with efficient service. Value is considered in this category, as is family friendliness.

★The Mobil One-Star restaurant provides a distinctive experience through culinary specialty, local flair or individual atmosphere.

Because menu prices can fluctuate, we list a pricing category rather than specific prices. The pricing categories are defined as follows, per diner, and assume that you order an appetizer or dessert, an entrée and one drink:

$ = $15 and under

$$ = $16-$35

$$$ = $36-$85

$$$$ = $86 and up

★
★★
★★
★

MOBIL RATED SPAS

Mobil Travel Guide's spa ratings are based on objective evaluations of hundreds of attributes. About half of these criteria assess basic expectations, such as staff courtesy, the technical proficiency and skill of the employees and whether the facility is clean and maintained properly. Several standards address issues that impact a guest's physical comfort and convenience, as well as the staff's ability to impart a sense of personalized service. Additional criteria measure the spa's ability to create a completely calming ambience.

★★★★★The Mobil Five-Star spa provides consistently superlative service in an exceptionally distinctive luxury environment with extensive amenities. The staff at a Mobil Five-Star spa provides extraordinary service beyond the traditional spa experience, allowing guests to achieve the highest level of relaxation and pampering. These spas offer an extensive array of treatments, often incorporating international themes and products. Attention to detail is evident throughout the spa, from arrival to departure.

★★★★The Mobil Four-Star spa provides a luxurious experience with expanded amenities in an elegant and serene environment. Throughout the spa facility, guests experience personalized service. Amenities might include, but are not limited to, single-sex relaxation rooms where guests wait for their treatments, plunge pools and whirlpools in both men's and women's locker rooms, and an array of treatments, including a selection of massages, body therapies, facials and a variety of salon services.

★★★The Mobil Three-Star spa is physically well appointed and has a full complement of staff.

INTRODUCTION

If you've been a reader of Mobil Travel Guides, you may have noticed a new look and style in our guidebooks. Since 1958, Mobil Travel Guide has assisted travelers in making smart decisions about where to stay and dine. Fifty-one years later, our mission has not changed: We are committed to our rigorous inspections of hotels, restaurants and, now, spas, to help you cut through all the clutter, and make easy and informed decisions on where you should spend your time and budget. Our team of anonymous inspectors are constantly on the road, sleeping in hotels, eating in restaurants and making spa appointments, evaluating hundreds of standards to determine a property's star rating.

As you read these pages, we hope you get a flavor of the places included in the guides and that you will feel even more inspired to visit and take it all in. We hope you'll experience what it's like to stay in a guest room in the hotels we've rated, taste the food in a restaurant or feel the excitement at an outdoor music venue. We understand the importance of finding the best value when you travel, and making the most of your time. That's why for more than 50 years, Mobil Travel Guide has been the most trusted name in travel.

If any aspect of your accommodation, dining, spa or sightseeing experience motivates you to comment, please contact us at Mobil Travel Guide, 200 W. Madison St., Suite 3950, Chicago, IL 60606, or send an email to info@mobiltravelguide.com Happy travels.

NEW YORK

THE LARGEST OF THE NORTHEASTERN STATES, NEW YORK STRETCHES FROM THE GREAT Lakes to the Atlantic. The glitter and glamour of New York City—from the sky-scrapers in Midtown to the beaches of Coney Island—make America's most populous city, a world capital. But New York state has much more to offer than just Gotham. Niagara Falls, Genesee Gorge, the Finger Lakes, the Thousand Islands of the St. Lawrence, the Catskills (where Rip Van Winkle is said to have slept for 20 years) the white-sand beaches of the Hamptons, the lakes and forested peaks of the Adirondacks and the stately bluffs along the Hudson are just a few of the features that attract millions of tourists every year.

When Giovanni da Verrazano entered New York Harbor in 1524, the Native Americans who lived there were at constant war with one another. Around 1570, under Dekanawidah and Hiawatha, they formed the Iroquois Confederacy (the first League of Nations) and began to live in peace. They were known as the Five Nations and called themselves the "Men of Men."

In 1609, Samuel de Champlain explored the valley of the lake that now has his name, and Henry Hudson sailed up the river that bears his name. New Amsterdam (later called New York City) was founded in 1625. Wars with the Native Americans and the French kept the area in turmoil until after 1763. During the Revolution, New York's eastern part was a seesaw of military action and occupation. After the war, George Washington was inaugurated as president in 1789 in the new seat of federal government, New York City.

Governor DeWitt Clinton envisioned a canal extending from the Hudson River at Albany to Buffalo in order to develop the state and give aid to its Western farmers. Started in 1817 and completed in 1825, the Erie Canal became the gateway to the West and was the greatest engineering feat of its time, reducing the cost of freight between Buffalo and New York City from $100 to $5 a ton. Enlarged and rerouted, it is now part of the New York State Canal system, 527 miles of waterways used mainly for recreational boating.

Industry grew in New York because water power was available; trade and farming grew because of the Erie Canal and its many branches. The state has given the nation four native-born presidents (Van Buren, Fillmore and both Roosevelts) and two who built their careers here (Cleveland and Arthur).

From the Big Apple to Niagara Falls, from the rolling hills near the Canadian border to the picturesque stretch of Long Island, New York has something for every traveler.

FUN FACTS

The New York Stock Exchange began in 1792 when 24 brokers met under a buttonwood tree facing 68 Wall Street.

In 1895, Gennaro Lombardi opened the country's first pizzeria in New York City.

As late as the 1840s, thousands of pigs roamed Wall Street to consume garbage—an early sanitation system.

Downtown Manhattan was the nation's first capital.

ALBANY

Albany is situated on the Hudson River where Henry Hudson ended the voyage of the *Half Moon* in 1609. It was settled by immigrants from Holland, Norway, Denmark, Germany and Scotland during the patronship of Kiliaen Van Rensselaer and was named in honor of the Duke of Kent and Albany when the British took over the city in 1664. Despite the French and Indian War, Albany was a thriving fur-trading center in 1754. Albany's General Philip Schuyler commanded the northern defenses in the Revolution and, according to Daniel Webster, was "second only to Washington in the services he performed for his country."

Albany has been a transportation center since American Indian trail days. Robert Fulton's steamboat, the *Clermont*, arrived here from Jersey City in 1807. The Erie Canal opened in 1825, and by 1831, 15,000 canal boats and 500 ocean-going ships crowded Albany's docks.

Politics is a colorful part of the business of New York's capital city. Located on the western bank of the Hudson River and at the crossroads of major state highways, Albany is now a hub of transportation, business, industry and culture.

Information: Albany County Convention and Visitors Bureau, 25 Quackenbush Square, Albany, 518-434-1217, 800-258-3582; www.albany.org

WHAT TO SEE AND DO
ALBANY INSTITUTE OF HISTORY & ART

125 Washington Ave., Albany, 518-463-4478; www.albanyinstitute.org
Hudson-Mohawk Valley paintings and sculpture; contemporary art; changing exhibits and programs promote fine arts as well as regional history. Admission: adults $10, seniors $8, students with ID $8, children 6 to 12 $6, children under 6 free. Wednesday-Saturday 10 a.m.-5 p.m., Sunday noon-5 p.m., Tuesday registered groups only; closed Mondays and major holidays.

AUSABLE CHASM

Route 9, Plattsburgh, 518-834-9990; www.ausablechasm.com
Located in the beautiful Champlain Valley, this chasm plummets 150 feet where the Au Sable River flows through the sandstone strata. Stroll through the Adirondack Forest, float along the river in a raft or tube or follow a guide into the chasm at dusk on the "lantern tour." Admission: adults $16, children under 13 $9. Mid-May to late October, daily.

CRAILO STATE HISTORIC SITE

9 1/2 Riverside Ave., Rensselaer, 518-463-8738; www.nysparks.state.ny.us
This 18th-century Dutch house is now a museum of Dutch culture in the Hudson Valley. Exhibits explain the history and development of Dutch settlements in America. Mid-April to October, Wednesday-Sunday 11 a.m.-5 p.m. Tours begin on the hour and half-hour. Last tour begins at 4 p.m; Also open on Tuesdays in June, July and August; November-March, Monday-Friday 11 a.m.-4 p.m by appointment only.

HISTORIC CHERRY HILL

523 1/2 S. Pearl St., Albany, 518-434-4791; www.historiccherryhill.org
This Georgian-style farmhouse was built in 1787 for Philip Van Rensselaer, a prominent merchant farmer, and was lived in by four generations of descendants until

★
★
★
★
★

1963. Nine period rooms contain original furnishings and personal belongings from the 18th to 20th centuries. Admission: adults $5, seniors $4, college students $4, children 6 to 17 $2. Tours: Closed January-March, Mondays and major holidays.

NEW YORK STATE MUSEUM

Cultural Education Center of the Empire State Plaza, Madison and State Streets, Albany, 518-474-5877; www.nysm.nysed.gov

Life-size dioramas, photo murals and thousands of objects illustrate the relationship between people and nature in New York State. Three major halls detail life in metropolitan New York, the Adirondacks and upstate New York. Special exhibits of photography, art, history, nature, science and American Indian history. Working carousel. Memorial to the World Trade Center. Open daily 9:30 a.m.-5 p.m. Closed Thanksgiving, Christmas and New Year's Day.

ADIRONDACK PARK

From Albany, take Route 9 north to Glens Falls and Lake George Village. Described as "the most queenly of American lakes," Lake George is 44 square miles of deep blue water dotted with 225 islands. Opportunities for water recreation abound in this vacation mecca while fresh powder awaits winter travelers north on Route 28 at the Gore Mountain Ski Area in North Creek.

Farther north on Route 28 is Adirondack Park, which is bordered by Lake Champlain on the east, the Black River on the west, the St. Lawrence River on the north and the Mohawk River valley on the south. At six million acres, Adirondack State Park is the largest U.S. park outside of Alaska (9,000 square miles—that's the size of New Jersey and Rhode Island combined). You could spend days here and not even scratch the surface of all there is to see and do. Whitewater raft on the Hudson, Moose or Black Rivers. Climb one of the 46 peaks in the Adirondack Range. Feeling adventurous? Have a go at Mount Marcy, also known as Cloud Splitter, which is the highest peak in the range at 5,344 feet. Not a climber? Try canoeing, fishing or mountain biking instead.

The next stop is Blue Mountain Lake. Take the three-mile trail to the summit of Blue Mountain (3,800 feet) for spectacular views of Adirondack Park. Then head to the Adirondack Museum for a taste of Adirondack history and modes of life. Housed in 20 buildings on 30 acres, the museum also showcases one of the best boat collections in the world, including sail canoes, steamboats and the famous Adirondack guide boat.

Head south on Route 28 back to Lake George. Take Route 9 north to Bolton Landing and Ticonderoga, home of Fort Mt. Hope and Fort Ticonderoga (circa 1755). Head south on 22 to Whitehall, then follow the Champlain Canal and Hudson River down Route 4. Stop in Saratoga Springs to visit Saratoga National Historical Park, the National Museum of Racing and Hall of Fame and Saratoga Spa State Park. Continue on Route 4 to return to Albany.

RENSSELAERVILLE

63 Huyck Road, Rensselaerville, 518-797-3783; www.rinstitute.org

A village established in 1787, this area has restored homes, inns, churches and a grist-mill. Also here is the Rensselaerville Institute, which offers cultural programs and a conference center for educational and business meetings.

SCHUYLER MANSION STATE HISTORIC SITE

32 Catherine St., Albany, 518-434-0834; www.nysparks.state.ny.us

This Georgian mansion, built in 1761, was the home of Philip Schuyler, a general of the Revolutionary War and U.S. Senator. Alexander Hamilton married Schuyler's daughter Elizabeth here in 1780, and other prominent early leaders visited here. Tours begin on the hour. Mid-April-October, Wednesday-Sunday 11 a.m.-5 p.m. Last tour begins at 4 p.m. Also open on Tuesdays June-August. November to March, by appointment only, Monday-Friday, 10 a.m.-4 p.m. Group tours by appointment year-round.

SHAKER HERITAGE SOCIETY

875 Watervliet Shaker Road, Albany, 518-456-7890; www.shakerheritage.org

Located on the site of the first Shaker settlement in America. Grounds, 1848 Shaker Meeting House, orchard and cemetery where founder Mother Ann Lee is buried. Tours.

STATE CAPITOL

Empire State Plaza, State and Swan Streets, Albany, 518-474-2418;
www.assembly.state.ny.us

The New York State capitol is a $25,000,000 granite "French" chateau. Legislative session begins on the Wednesday after the first Monday in January. Guided tours daily.

HOTELS

★★BEST WESTERN SOVEREIGN HOTEL-ALBANY

1228 Western Ave., Albany, 518-489-2981, 888-963-7666; www.bestwestern.com

192 rooms. Wireless Internet access. Complimentary full breakfast. Restaurant, bar. **$**

★★COURTYARD BY MARRIOTT ALBANY AIRPORT

168 Wolf Road, Albany, 518-482-8800, 866-541-6400; www.marriott.com/albca

78 rooms. High-speed Internet access. Airport transportation available. **$$**

★★CENTURY HOUSE HOTEL

997 New Loudon Road, Latham, 518-785-0931, 888-674-6873;
www.thecenturyhouse.com

68 rooms. Wireless Internet access. Complimentary full breakfast. Restaurant, bar. Tennis. Laundry. **$**

★★★CROWNE PLAZA HOTEL ALBANY-CITY CENTER

State and Lodge Streets, Albany, 518-462-6611, 877-227-6963;
www.ichotelsgroup.com

Catering to business travelers and politicos, this hotel is located in historic downtown Albany, across from the Capitol Building and near Empire State Plaza and the Pepsi Arena, and is within walking distance of the city's top sights and attractions. 384 rooms. Wireless Internet access. Two restaurants, bar. Airport transportation available. **$$**

★★★DESMOND HOTEL AND CONFERENCE CENTER

660 Albany Shaker Road, Albany, 518-869-8100, 800-448-3500;
www.desmondhotels.com

With indoor courtyards and elegantly decorated rooms, this hotel offers Old World charm within minutes of downtown. 323 rooms. High-speed Internet access. Two restaurants, two bars. Airport transportation available. **$$**

★★★GREGORY HOUSE COUNTRY INN

3016 Highway 43, Averill Park, 518-674-3774; www.gregoryhouse.com

This country inn, located near Albany and Troy, offers 12 rooms and a restaurant that specializes in high-end Italian fare. The inn is the perfect accommodation for guests who plan to visit nearby Tanglewood in Lenox, Massachusetts, the summer home of the Boston Symphony. 12 rooms. Complimentary continental breakfast. Restaurant, bar. **$**

★HAMPTON INN

10 Ulenski Drive, Albany, 518-438-2822, 800-426-7866; www.hamptoninn.com

153 rooms. Wireless Internet access. Complimentary continental breakfast. Pool. Business center. Airport transportation available. **$**

★★HOLIDAY INN ALBANY

205 Wolf Road, Albany, 518-458-7250, 888-465-4329; www.holiday-inn.com

153 rooms. Wireless Internet access. Restaurant, bar. Airport transportation available. Fitness center. Pool. Business center. Pets accepted. **$$**

★★★MARRIOTT ALBANY

189 Wolf Road, Albany, 518-458-8444, 800-443-8952; www.marriott.com

Convenience is king at this seven-story brick hotel: It is within two miles of the Albany International Airport; downtown Albany is approximately 10 miles away; and Sarasota Springs is a 30-minute drive to the north. 359 rooms. Wireless Internet access. Restaurant, bar. Airport transportation available. Fitness center. Pool. **$$**

SPECIALTY LODGINGS

MANSION HILL INN & RESTAURANT

115 Philip St., Albany, 518-465-2038, 888-299-0455; www.mansionhill.com

Eight rooms. Wireless Internet access. Complimentary full breakfast. Restaurant. **$$**

THE MORGAN STATE HOUSE

393 State St., Albany, 518-427-6063, 888-427-6063;
www.statehouse.com

Six rooms. Wireless Internet access. Complimentary full breakfast. **$$**

RESTAURANTS

★BONGIORNO'S RESTAURANT

23 Dove St., Albany, 518-462-9176; www.thebongiornosrestaurant.com

Italian menu. Lunch, dinner. Closed Sunday; holidays. Bar. Business casual attire. Outdoor seating. **$$**

★★★JACK'S OYSTER HOUSE

42 State St., Albany, 518-465-8854; www.jacksoysterhouse.com

This downtown landmark—a two-block walk from the State Capitol and just across from the city's former 19th-century train station—has been dishing out seafood to local politicians, businessmen and families since 1913. Enormous photos of historic Albany look down upon black-leather booths and elegant tables topped with flowers and candles. Renowned for its oyster selection, Jack's also serves terrific steaks. American menu. Lunch, dinner. Bar. Children's menu. Casual attire. Reservations recommended. $$$

★★★LA SERRE

14 Green St., Albany, 518-463-6056; www.laserrealbany.com

Located inside a beautiful historic building that dates to the 1840s, La Serre features vintage-looking light fixtures and a gas fireplace in the main dining room that add punch to the elegant décor. The continental-styled menu features standouts such as Angus beef and New Zealand lamb. Continental menu. Lunch, dinner. Closed Sunday; holidays. Bar. Business casual attire. Reservations recommended. Outdoor seating. $$$

★★★MANSION HILL

115 Philip St., Albany, 518-465-2038, 888-299-0455; www.mansionhill.com

This charming inn bills itself as Albany's best-kept secret, and indeed meals at this downtown bed and breakfast are top notch. The menu, which might include homemade ravioli, pan-roasted half duckling or chicken tenderloins, mirrors the relaxed-elegant décor—lots of wood and fresh flowers. American menu. Breakfast, dinner. Closed Sunday; holidays. Business casual attire. Reservations recommended. Outdoor seating. $$$

★★★SCRIMSHAW

660 Albany-Shaker Road, Albany, 518-452-5801, 800-448-3500;
www.desmondhotels.com

Servers dress in period costumes at this elegant, 18th-century-styled eatery within the Desmond Hotel where the fish—trucked in daily from Boston—takes center stage. Standouts include oysters on the half shell and cedar-plank salmon, the numerous surf-and-turf options and the signature "Scrimshaw Potato," whipped potatoes served within a puff pastry shell. American menu. Dinner. Closed Sunday; holidays. Bar. Children's menu. Business casual attire. Reservations recommended. $$

ALEXANDRIA BAY

The resort center of the Thousand Islands, Alexandria Bay overlooks a cluster of almost 1,800 green islands divided by intricate waterways. The island ranges in size from a few square inches (a handful of rocks with a single tree) to several miles in length.
Information: Chamber of Commerce, 7 Market St., Alexandria Bay, 315-482-9531,
800-541-2110; www.alexbay.org

WHAT TO SEE AND DO

BOLDT CASTLE

Collins Landing, Alexandria Bay, 315-482-9724, 800-847-5263; www.boldtcastle.com

George C. Boldt came from Prussia in the 1860s and became the most successful hotel magnate in America by managing the Waldorf-Astoria in New York City and owning the Bellevue-Stratford in Philadelphia. The castle was a $2.5-million present to his wife, who died in 1904; the building was never completed. The structure and grounds are now being restored. Admission: adults $6.50, children 6 to 12 $4. May 10-October 5 daily 10 a.m.-6:30 p.m.; July and August, daily 10 a.m.-7:30 p.m.; October 6-13, 18-19 10 a.m.-5:30 p.m.

WELLESLEY ISLAND
44927 Cross Island Road, Fine View, 315-482-2722, 800-456-2427;
www.wellesleyisland.net/stateparks.htm
Wellesley Island State Park is 2600-plus acres of family fun. There is a marina with boat rentals, four boat launch sites, a swimming beach and picnic area, concession, natural sand beach and a lot of beautiful shoreline. There are also more than 430 campsites.

HOTELS
★★BONNIE CASTLE RESORT
Holland Street, Alexandria Bay, 315-482-4511, 800-955-4511;
www.bonniecastle.com
128 rooms. Restaurant, bar. Airport transportation available. $

★★EDGEWOOD RESORT
Edgewood Park Drive, Alexandria Bay, 315-482-9923; www.theedgewoodresort.com
125 rooms. Restaurant, bar, café. Outdoor pool. $

★LEDGES RESORT MOTEL
71 Anthony St., Alexandria Bay, 315-482-9334; www.ledgesresort.com
27 rooms. Closed mid-October-early May. Complimentary continental breakfast. $

★★PINE TREE POINT RESORT
70 Anthony St., Alexandria Bay, 315-482-9911; www.pinetreepointresort.com
96 rooms. Closed November-April. Restaurant, bar. $

★★★RIVEREDGE RESORT HOTEL
17 Holland St., Alexandria Bay, 315-482-9917, 800-365-6987; www.riveredge.com
Situated on the St. Lawrence River, this resort offers many rooms—outfitted with floral wallpaper and country-style wooden furnishings—with scenic river views as well as casual and fine dining. 129 rooms. Restaurant, bar. $$

RESTAURANTS
★★CAVALLARIO'S STEAK & SEAFOOD HOUSE
24 Church St., Alexandria Bay, 315-482-9867; www.thousandislands.com/cavallarios
American menu. Dinner. Closed early November-mid-April. Bar. Children's menu. Valet parking. $$$

★★★THE CRYSTAL DINING ROOM
31 Holland St., Alexandria Bay, 315-482-451; www.bonniecastle.com
Located in the Bonnie Castle Resort and overlooking the St. Lawrence River, the Crystal Dining Room serves a simple menu heavy on seafood options. A mirrored baby grand piano accentuates the Vegas-like atmosphere of this elaborately adorned (think

fountains and chandeliers) restaurant. American menu. Breakfast, lunch, dinner. Closed holidays. Bar. Children's menu. Outdoor seating. No handicapped accessibility. **$$**

AMAGANSETT

This small town in the Hamptons offers all the natural beauty of the region. Enjoy bay and ocean beaches as well as charming restaurants and shops.

Information: East Hampton Chamber of Commerce, 42 Gingerbread Lane,
East Hampton, 631-324-0362; www.easthamptonchamber.com

WHAT TO SEE AND DO
MISS AMELIA'S COTTAGE MUSEUM
Montauk Highway 27A and Windmill Lane, Amagansett, 631-267-3020

This original home, built in 1725, is part of the history of Amagansett, a quaint village in the Hamptons near the end of the South Fork. Mary Amelia Schellinger, was a descendant of Jacob Schellinger, the founder of Amagansett. She was the last of her family to live in the house, and went without electricity and running water for years. The cottage features its original colonial furnishings. June-September, Friday-Sunday 9 a.m.-1 p.m.

TOWN MARINE MUSEUM
301 Bluff Road, Amagansett, 631-267-6544; www.easthamptonhistory.org

This museum gives a history lesson on Long Island's East End community and its relationship with sea through artifacts, photographs, models and displays. There are three floors of exhibits to explore. Memorial Day weekend-Columbus Day weekend, Saturday 10 a.m.-5 p.m., Sunday 12-5 p.m. or by appointment; Open Friday and Monday 10 a.m.-5 p.m. in July and August.

HOTEL
★SEA CREST ON THE OCEAN
2166 Montauk Highway, Amagansett, 631-267-3159, 800-732-3297;
www.duneresorts.com

74 rooms. Tennis. Swimming pool. Picnic and Barbecue Area. Handball, shuffleboard and basketball courts. **$$$**

RESTAURANTS
★LOBSTER ROLL
1980 Montauk Highway, Amagansett, 631-267-3740; www.lobsterroll.com

Seafood menu. Lunch, dinner. Closed November-April. Children's menu. Casual attire. Outdoor seating. **$$**

★TED'S GRILL
195 Main St., Amagansett, 631-267-2200

American menu. Breakfast, lunch, dinner. Casual attire. **$$**

AMENIA

On the Connecticut border, Amenia offers a picturesque setting about 90 miles north of New York City. The town gets its name from the Latin word *amoena*, meaning "lovely or pleasant"—a fitting moniker for this pretty little town.

Information: www.amenia-cofc.com

17

NEW YORK

★
★
★
★
★

RESTAURANT

★★CASCADE MOUNTAIN WINERY & RESTAURANT

835 Cascade Road, Amenia, 845-373-9021; www.cascademt.com

American menu. Lunch, dinner. Casual attire. Reservations recommended. Outdoor seating. $$

AMSTERDAM

Located on the Mohawk River and New York Barge Canal, this city manufactures clothing, novelties, toys and electronic equipment.

Information: Montgomery County Chamber of Commerce, 12 South Bridge St., Fonda, 518-853-1800, 800-743-7337; www.montgomerycountyny.com

WHAT TO SEE AND DO

ERIE CANAL

Highway 5 South, Amsterdam, 518-842-8200, 800-743-7337; www.nyscanals.gov

Opened in 1825, the Erie Canal was an engineering marvel of the 19th century, and it proved to be the key that unlocked an enormous series of social and economic changes in the young nation. The Canal spurred the first great westward movement of American settlers, gave access to the rich land and resources west of the Appalachians and made New York the preeminent commercial city in the United States.

GUY PARK STATE HISTORIC SITE

Canal Lock 11, Route 5 W., Evelyn St., Amsterdam, 518-842-8200, 800-743-7337; www.montgomerycountyny.com

This was the former home of Guy Johnson, Superintendent of Indian Affairs, who remained loyal to King George III during the revolution. Johnson abandoned the house in 1775 and it served as a tavern for many years. Exhibits detail the history of the area. Monday-Friday 8:30 a.m.-dusk; closed holidays.

SCHOHARIE CROSSING STATE HISTORIC SITE AND VISITORS CENTER

129 Schoharie St., Fort Hunter, 518-829-7516; www.nysparks.state.ny.us/sites

Learn a bit more about the preservation and interpretation of the Erie Canal as one of the 19th century's greatest commercial and engineering projects. The Visitor Center exhibit shows the history of the Erie Canal and its impact on the growth of New York State and the nation. Visitor Center: May 3-29, Wednesday-Saturday 10 a.m.-5 p.m. and Sunday 1-5 p.m.; May 31-October, Wednesday-Monday 10 a.m.-5 p.m. Closed Tuesdays. Grounds open daily dawn to dusk, weather permitting.

HOTEL

★★AMERICA'S BEST VALUE INN

10 Market St., Amsterdam, 518-843-5760, 888-315-2378; www.bestvalueinn.com

125 rooms. Restaurant, bar. $

RESTAURANT

★★★RAINDANCER STEAK PARLOUR

4582 State Highway 30, Amsterdam, 518-842-2606; www.raindancerrestaurant.com

Settle in for casual American food at this rustic, friendly environment that has been family owned for more than 20 years. The varied menu features fish, chicken, pastas and a well-regarded prime rib dinner and salad bar. Lunch, dinner. Closed holidays. Bar. Children's menu. $$$

AQUEBOGUE

On the east end of Long Island, near Flanders Bay, Aquebogue will delight visitors who want to enjoy the water.

Information: Riverhead Chamber of Commerce, 542 East Main Street-Suite 2 Riverhead, 631-727-7600; www.riverheadchamber.com

RESTAURANT

★MEETING HOUSE CREEK INN

177 Meeting House Creek Road, Aquebogue, 631-722-4220; www.meetinghousecreekinn.com

American menu. Dinner, Sunday brunch. Bar. Children's menu. Outdoor seating. No handicapped access. $$

AUBURN

On Owasco Lake, Auburn is one of the largest cities in the Finger Lakes region. Harriet Tubman, whose home was a link in the Underground Railroad, lived here.

Information: Cayuga County Office of Tourism, 131 Genesee St., Auburn, 315-258-9820, 877-343-0002; www.tourauburnny.com

WHAT TO SEE AND DO

CAYUGA MUSEUM/CASE RESEARCH LAB MUSEUM

203 Genesee St., Auburn, 315-253-8051; www.cayuganet.org/cayugamuseum

The Cayuga Museum is housed in a Greek Revival Willard-Case Mansion built in 1836; 19th-century furnishings; local industrial history; Bundy Monumental clock; Civil War exhibit. The Case Research Lab Museum is the restored lab where T. W. Case and E. I. Sponable invented sound film; permanent exhibits of lab, Fox Movietone and sound studio. Cayuga Museum: Tuesday-Sunday noon-5 p.m. Case Research Lab: Tuesday-Sunday noon-4:30 p.m. Closed Mondays and major holidays. Closed January.

CAYUGA MUSEUM IROQUOIS CENTER

203 Genesee St., Auburn, 315-253-8051; www.cayuganet.org/cayugamuseum

Featuring permanent and changing exhibits on traditional North East Woodlands Native-people's arts and culture, this museum focuses on Iroquois cultures of central New York. June: weekends; July-August: Wednesday-Sunday.

FORT HILL CEMETERY

19 Fort St., Auburn, 315-253-8132

Fort Hill Cemetery was incorporated on May 15, 1851 under its official name: "Trustees of the Fort Hill Cemetery Association of Auburn." The original portion of the Cemetery consisted of 22 acres and was dedicated on July 7, 1852. Today the cemetery has 83 acres. In 1951, the Jewish section of the cemetery was created, and in 1998, the Oak View section opened with space for new burials.

HARRIET TUBMAN HOME

180-182 South St., Auburn, 315-252-2081; www.nps.gov

Born as a slave, Harriet Tubman escaped in 1849 and rescued more than 300 slaves via the Underground Railroad. She assisted the Union Army during the Civil War and, after settling in Auburn after the war, continued to pursue other humanitarian endeavors. Tuesday-Friday 11 a.m.-4 p.m., Saturdays by appointment; closed holidays.

SEWARD HOUSE

33 South St., Auburn, 315-252-1283; www.sewardhouse.org

This structure was the home of William Henry Seward, governor of New York, U.S. Senator, and Abraham Lincoln and Andrew Johnson's secretary of state, who was instrumental in purchasing Alaska. Civil War relics, original Alaskan artifacts, costumes, furnishings. February-late June, Mid-October-late December: Tuesday-Saturday 1-4 p.m.; July-mid-October: Tuesday-Saturday 10 a.m.-4 p.m., Sunday from 1 p.m.; closed holidays.

WILLARD MEMORIAL CHAPEL AND WELCH MEMORIAL BUILDING

17 Nelson St., Auburn, 315-252-0339; www.willardchapel.org

These gray-and-red stone Romanesque Revival buildings were once part of the Auburn Theological Seminary. The chapel's interior was designed and handcrafted by the Tiffany Glass and Decoration Company and is the only complete and unaltered Tiffany chapel known to exist. Tiffany Concert Series in the chapel take place in July and August, Wednesday noon. Open Regular Hours: Tuesday-Friday, 10 a.m.-4 p.m.; also Sunday 1-4 p.m. in summer; closed on holidays.

HOTELS

★★★AURORA INN

391 Main St., Aurora, 315-364-8888, 866-364-8808; www.aurora-inn.com

A perfectly charming 1833 red-brick structure perched on the banks of Cayuga Lake, this Finger Lakes-area inn offers recently renovated rooms with beds topped with Frette linens and contemporary touches such as flat-screen TVs and whirlpool baths. The onsite restaurant is a local favorite and features a large outdoor patio with views of the lake for memorable dining in warm weather. 10 rooms. Wireless Internet access. Restaurant. $$

★★HOLIDAY INN

75 North St., Auburn, 315-253-4531; www.holiday-inn.com

165 rooms. Restaurant, bar. Fitness center, indoor pool. Wireless Internet access. $

★★SPRINGSIDE INN

6141 W. Lake Road, Auburn, 315-252-7247; www.springsideinn.com

78 rooms. Complimentary continental breakfast. Restaurant. $

RESTAURANTS

★★★AURORA INN DINING ROOM

391 Main St., Aurora, 315-364-8888, 866-364-8808; www.aurora-inn.com

Located in the recently renovated Aurora Inn, this comfortable spot offers perfectly prepared versions of American classics in a lakefront setting. Dishes include traditional recipes such as lobster Newburg, Waldorf salad and traditional pot roast, slow-cooked and served with roasted fingerling potatoes and vegetables. American menu. Breakfast, lunch, dinner. $$

★★LASCA'S
252 Grant Ave., Auburn, 315-253-4885; www.lascas.com
Italian, American menu. Dinner. Closed Monday; holidays; also first two weeks in February. Bar. Children's menu. $$

★★SPRINGSIDE INN
6141 W. Lake Road, Auburn, 315-252-7247
Dinner, Sunday brunch. Closed holidays. Bar. Children's menu. $$

AVERILL PARK
Along the Hudson River, Averill Park is in a region beloved for its scenic towns, rural-landscapes and opportunities for "agritourism," which give visitors opportunities to participate in rural farm life. Ask about the area's farmers' markets, trek along the miles of quiet trails or shop for antiques. This region has a little something for everyone.
Information: www.renscochamber.com

RESTAURANT
★★LA PERLA
3016 Highway 43, Averill Park, 518-674-3774; www.gregoryhouse.com
Italian menu. Lunch, dinner. Closed Monday-Tuesday. Bar. Reservations recommended. $$

BAINBRIDGE
Four rivers roll through the hills surrounding Bainbridge, making it a scenic spot for a stroll or a drive.
Information: Chamber of Commerce, Bainbridge, 607-967-8700; www.bainbridgeny.org

SPECIAL EVENT
GENERAL CLINTON CANOE REGATTA
Highway 7, Bainbridge, 607-967-8700; www.canoeregatta.org
World championship flatwater canoe race, arts and crafts show, midway, entertainment. One week in late May.

HOTEL
★SUPER 8
4 Mang Drive, Sidney, 607-563-8880; www.super8.com
39 rooms. Free superstart breakfast. Wireless Internet access. No pets. $

RESTAURANT
★JERICHO TAVERN
4 N. Main St., Bainbridge, 607-967-5893
Lunch, dinner. Closed Monday-Tuesday; holidays Bar. Children's menu. $$

BATAVIA

Established at the crossing of two Native American trails by Joseph Ellicott, an agent of the Holland Land Company, which purchased 3.3 million acres from Robert Morris, Batavia was named for a province of the Netherlands. The brisk rate of sales of this Western New York State land is said to have inspired the phrase "doing a land-office business." Batavia today is a lively farm area producing potatoes, onions, fruit and dairy products. The New York State School for the Blind is located here.

Information: Genesee County Chamber of Commerce, 210 E. Main St.,
Batavia, 585-343-7440, 800-622-2686; www.geneseeny.com

WHAT TO SEE AND DO

BATAVIA DOWNS RACE TRACK
8315 Park Road, Batavia, 585-343-3750; www.batavia-downs.com
The oldest par-mutuel harness track in North America. Clubhouse, open-air and enclosed grandstands. Early August-late November, daily.

HOLLAND LAND OFFICE MUSEUM
131 W. Main St., Batavia, 585-343-4727; www.hollandlandoffice.com
This was the building from which deeds to the lands in the Holland Purchase were issued. This 1815 stone office was built by land agent Joseph Ellicott. Local American Indian and pioneer artifacts, period furniture and costumes; Civil War, medical and surgical collections. Tuesday-Saturday 10 a.m.-4 p.m.; From Memorial Day to Labor Day, open Monday-Saturday 10 a.m.-4 p.m.

IROQUOIS NATIONAL WILDLIFE REFUGE
Highway 63, Alabama, 585-948-5445; www.fws.gov/northeast/iroquois
The refuge is one of more than 500 national wildlife refuges in the United States. The National Wildlife Refuge System is the only network of federal lands dedicated specifically to wildlife conservation. Migratory waterfowl, especially geese, visit here in large numbers during the spring migration. Overlooks, trails, illustrated talks (reservation); fishing, hunting (in-season). Monday-Friday 7:30 a.m.-4 p.m. except holidays, Saturday-Sunday 9 a.m.-5 p.m.

LEROY HOUSE
23 E. Main St., Le Roy, 716-768-7433; www.jellogallery.org
Early 19th-century house with furnishings of the period; nine rooms open to the public. Also home of Le Roy Historical Society. The Jell-O Gallery has a large new exhibit that reflects Bill Cosby's influence over 30 years. Admission: adults $4, children 6-11 $1.50, children 5 and under free. January 1-March 31, Monday-Friday 10 a.m.-4 p.m.; April 1-December 31, Monday-Saturday 10 a.m.-4 p.m., Sundays 1 p.m.-4 p.m. closed Thanksgiving, Christmas, New Year, Easter.

HOTEL

★★RAMADA LIMITED
8204 Park Road, Batavia, 585-343-1000, 800-272-6232; www.ramada.com
75 rooms. Restaurant, bar. Free continental breakfast. Wireless Internet access. Fitness center. Pets accepted. **$**

BAYVILLE

Plentiful beaches and views of the water make Bayville a popular place to live and play on Nassau County's North Shore.

Information: www.bayvillevillagehall.com

RESTAURANT

★★STEVE'S PIER ONE

33 Bayville Ave., Bayville, 516-628-2153; www.pieronerestaurant.com

Lunch, dinner, brunch. Bar. Children's menu. Valet parking. Outdoor seating. On Long Island Sound. $$

BEACON

In the last decade, Beacon has undergone a renaissance. Many of its historic buildings have been restored to their original splendor. The area's antique shops are popular among visitors searching for that perfect piece of furniture or art to take home.

Information: cityofbeacon.org

RESTAURANT

★PIGGY BANK

448 Main St., Beacon, 845-838-0028; www.piggybankrestaurant.com

American, BBQ menu. Lunch, dinner. Bar. Casual attire. Outdoor seating. $$

BELLPORT

Marked by Long Island charm and a quaint downtown area, Bellport has adopted a motto: "It's all here." Indeed, visitors will find plenty of activities, restaurants and shops to keep them busy for days.

RESTAURANTS

★★BELLPORT

159 S. Country Road, Bellport, 631-286-7550

Dinner. Closed Tuesday. Bar. $$

★BELLPORT CHOWDER HOUSE

19 Bellport Lane, Bellport, 631-286-2343; www.bellportchowderhouse.com

Lunch, dinner, Sunday brunch. Bar. Outdoor seating. No handicapped accessibility. $$

BEMUS POINT

This village is on the shore of Lake Chautauqua, and across the lake visitors will find the famous Chautauqua Institution.

Information: www.bemuspt.com

WHAT TO SEE AND DO

LONG POINT STATE PARK ON LAKE CHAUTAUQUA

4459 Route 430, Bemus Point, 716-386-2722; www.nysparks.state.ny.us

Swimming, fishing, boating (marina); snowmobiling, ice fishing, cross-country skiing, picnicking. Day use; Open all year.

HOTEL

★★LENHART HOTEL
20 Lakeside Drive, Bemus Point, 716-386-2715; www.hotellenhart.com
53 rooms. Closed September-May. Complimentary continental breakfast. Restaurant, bar. Airport transportation available. $

RESTAURANT

★★YE HARE 'N HOUNDS INN
64 Lakeside Drive, Bemus Point, 716-386-2181; www.harenhounds.com
International menu. Dinner. Children's menu. Casual attire. Outdoor seating. No handicapped. $$$

BINGHAMTON

Largest of the Triple Cities (Johnson City and Endicott branched off later), Binghamton lies at the junction of the Chenango and Susquehanna rivers. Completion of the Chenango Canal in 1837 made it an important link between the coal regions of Pennsylvania and the Erie Canal.
Information: Broome County Convention and Visitors Bureau, 49 Court St., Binghamton, 607-772-8860, 800-836-6740; www.binghamtoncvb.com

WHAT TO SEE AND DO

BINGHAMTON ZOO AT ROSS PARK
60 Morgan Road, Binghamton, 607-724-5461; www.rossparkzoo.com
The zoo officially opened in 1875, and it is the fifth oldest zoological institution in the country behind ones in Philadelphia, Chicago, Cincinnati and Buffalo. The 90-acre plot was donated to the city of Binghamton by a wealthy businessman, Erastus Ross. April-November, daily 10 a.m.-5 p.m. Playground, picnicking.

DAY OF A PLAYWRIGHT
The Forum, 236 Washington St., Binghamton, 607-778-2480; www.binghamtoncvb.com/visitors/rodserling.aspx
"Day of a Playwright" is the name of the permanent display at the Forum Theatre for the Performing Arts. This theater has an exhibit honoring Syracuse-born Rod Serling, who grew up in Binghamton and created *The Twilight Zone* TV series. It includes photos and documents highlighting his career in TV and films. Monday-Friday and during Forum performances.

DISCOVERY CENTER OF THE SOUTHERN TIER
60 Morgan Road, Binghamton, 607-773-8661; www.thediscoverycenter.org
Kids can learn about arts, science and the humanities at this center for intellectual, physical and emotional exploration. Exhibits change regularly. Admission: adults $5, children 1-16 $6, children under 1 free. Tuesday-Friday 10 a.m.-4 p.m., Saturday 10 a.m.-5 p.m., Sunday noon-5 p.m.

ROBERSON MUSEUM AND SCIENCE CENTER
30 Front St., Binghamton, 607-772-0660, 888-269-5325; www.roberson.org
Roberson Memorial, Inc. was established by the will of Alonzo Roberson in 1934 to create an educational center. Opened to the public in 1954 in the Roberson Mansion.

An addition in 1966 provided galleries, a theatre, the Link Planetarium and offices. The A. Ward Ford wing, added in 1984, houses modern vaults and collections preparation space, and now holds the Decker Life Science Center. Wednesday-Thursday noon-5 p.m., Friday noon-9 p.m., Saturday-Sunday noon-5 p.m.

HOTELS

★★CLARION COLLECTION GRAND ROYALE HOTEL
80 State St., Binghamton, 607-722-0000, 888-242-0323; www.grandroyalehotel.com
61 rooms. Complimentary full breakfast. Restaurants. Business center. Bar. **$$**

★DAYS INN
65 Front St., Binghamton, 607-724-2412, 800-329-7466; www.daysinn.com
106 rooms. Complimentary continental breakfast. Wireless Internet access. No pets allowed. **$**

★★HOLIDAY INN
2-8 Hawley St., Binghamton, 607-722-1212; www.holidayinnbinghamton.com
240 rooms. Restaurant, bar. Wireless Internet access. Fitness center. Pool. **$**

RESTAURANTS

★ THE NEW ARGO
117 Court St., Binghamton, 607-724-4692; www.thenewargo.com
Italian, Greek menu. Breakfast, lunch, dinner. Closed holidays. Children's menu. **$$**

★★NUMBER FIVE
33 S. Washington, Binghamton, 607-723-0555; www.number5restaurant.com
American, seafood menu. Dinner. Closed holidays. Bar. Children's menu. **$$**

★SPOT
1062 Upper Front St., Binghamton, 607-723-8149
American, Greek menu. Breakfast, lunch, dinner, late-night. Bar. Children's menu. **$$**

BLUE MOUNTAIN LAKE
This central Adirondack resort village has mountain trails, splendid views, interesting shops, water sports and good fishing and hunting.
Information: www.indian-lake.com

WHAT TO SEE AND DO

ADIRONDACK LAKES CENTER FOR THE ARTS
Route 28, Blue Mountain Lake, 518-352-7715; www.adk-arts.org
This community center hosts concerts, films, theatrical performances, art and photography exhibits and workshops. Gallery hours: Tuesday, Thursday-Saturday 10 a.m. -4 p.m., Sunday noon-4 p.m.

BLUE MOUNTAIN
Blue Mountain Lake
Three-mile trail to 3,800-foot summit; 35-foot observation tower overlooks Adirondack Park. The Blue Mountain Lake Association has maps of the possible trails.

HOTEL

★★HEMLOCK HALL HOTEL

Maple Lodge Road, Blue Mountain Lake, 518-352-7706; www.hemlockhall.com
22 rooms. Closed November-late May. Restaurant. Beach. **$**

BOLTON LANDING

Bolton Landing, on the shores of Lake George, has been home to musicians, artists and authors. Today, most of the estates are resorts, but the cultural atmosphere lives on.
Information: Chamber of Commerce, Lakeshore Drive, Bolton Landing, 518-644-3831; www.boltonchamber.com

HOTELS

★★MELODY MANOR RESORT

4610 Lakeshore Drive, Bolton Landing, 518-644-9750; www.melodymanor.com
40 rooms. Closed November-April. Restaurant, bar. Beach. **$$**

★★★THE SAGAMORE

110 Sagamore Road, Bolton Landing, 518-644-9400, 866-385-6221; www.thesagamore.com
This historic resort reigns over its own private 72-acre island in Lake George. From golf, tennis and water sports to myriad winter activities, this resort is a year-round destination. Two types of accommodations offer visitors the choice of the comfortable rooms at the historic hotel or the appealing cabin decor of the spacious lodges. Dining always comes with a view at the six restaurants; meals are even served aboard the resort's own replica of a 19th-century training vessel. 350 rooms. High-speed Internet access. Eight restaurants, two bars. Spa. Beach. Airport transportation available. **$$$**

RESTAURANTS

★FREDERICK'S RESTAURANT

4970 Lake Shore Drive, Bolton Landing, 518-644-3484; www.fredericksrestaurant.com
Mexican, seafood menu. Lunch, dinner. Bar. **$$**

★★★TRILLIUM

110 Sagamore Road, Bolton Landing, 518-644-9400; www.thesagamore.com/dining/trillium.php
This restaurant boasts some of the most majestic views of Lake George in the area, only to be matched by a casual, stylish atmosphere and a staff that provides unsurpassed professional service. Organic and local ingredients fill the imaginative menu and the wine list is extensive. American menu. Dinner. Casual attire. Reservations recommended. Valet parking. **$$$**

★★VILLA NAPOLI

4608 Lakeside Drive, Bolton Landing, 518-644-9047; www.melodymanor.com/villanap.htm
Italian menu. Breakfast, dinner. Closed mid-October-mid-May. Bar. Children's menu. Casual attire. Reservations recommended. Outdoor seating. **$$**

BREWSTER

Sixty miles north of Manhattan, Brewster and the surrounding villages are home to a number of important historic buildings, including the Walter Brewster House, former home of the town's namesake.

Information: Chamber of Commerce, 845-279-2477; www.brewsterchamber.com

WHAT TO SEE AND DO

SOUTHEAST MUSEUM

67 Main St., Brewster, 845-279-7500; www.southeastmuseum.org

Step back in time to the early years of the American Circus, the Harlem Line Railroad and the birth of the Town of Southeast at this museum established in 1963. Even the location is historic: It is in the 1896 Old Town Hall of Southeast. The museum presents various changing exhibits, drawing on its extensive collection of antique farm and household implements, quilts, clothing and assorted Americana reflecting 19th-century material culture. April-December, Tuesday-Saturday 10 a.m.-4 p.m.

THUNDER RIDGE SKI AREA

137 Birch Hill Road, Patterson, 845-878-4100; www.thunderridgeski.com

Located in the rolling hills of Patterson, Thunder Ridge offers acres of skiing and snowboarding for all ages and skill levels. The facilities include ski schools for the kids and equipment rentals. The longest run is one mile. Cafeteria, bar. Vertical drop 500 feet. Night skiing. December-March, daily; closed holidays. Half-day rates.

RESTAURANT

★★★ARCH

Route 22, Brewster, 845-279-5011; www.archrestaurant.com

Named for its windows—which overlook lush, manicured gardens—Arch offers a spiffy, four-course prix fixe dinner of classic European cuisine and delicious game entrées. Service is attentive and friendly. French menu. Lunch, dinner, Sunday brunch. Bar. Children's menu. Outdoor seating. $$$$

BRIDGEHAMPTON

Not surprisingly, Bridgehampton is a community in the tony Hamptons. It hosts the Hampton Classic, an annual summer horse show. It's also home to several palatial homes, wineries and a polo team.

Information: www.southhamptonchamber.com

WHAT TO SEE AND DO

BRIDGEHAMPTON COMMONS

Montauk Highway, Bridgehampton, 631-537-2174

Get out the credit cards and shop at retail outposts such as Banana Republic, Victoria's Secret and Williams-Sonoma.

CHANNING DAUGHTERS WINERY

1927 Scuttlehole Road, Bridgehampton, 631-537-7224; www.channingdaughters.com

This 30-acre winery produces a host of wines, such as pinot grigio, cabernet franc, merlot and chardonnay. Although small, South Fork's Channing Daughters has some special features such as its unique wine club (which offers a variety of discounts on a host of wines) and its wood-sculpture garden showcasing the art of owner Walter Channing. Once a potato farm, the winery offers special wine tasting classes all year round, as well as festivals and parties. May-September, Daily 11 a.m.-5 p.m.; October-April, Thursday-Monday 11 a.m.-5 p.m., closed Tuesday-Wednesday.

WÖLFFER ESTATE VINEYARD

139 Sagg Pond Road, Sagaponack, 631-537-5106; www.wolffer.com

This Tuscan-style winery is more reminiscent of an enchanted European estate than a vineyard in the Hamptons, but the harvests are decidedly American. The local soil acts as the perfect host for Wölffer's slow-growing vines, and the cool climate, thanks in part to the close proximity of the Atlantic, allows for late harvests and strong, natural acidity. A visit to the estate is a special affair: immaculately manicured grounds and a trickling, circular fountain greet you as you make your way into the impressive 12,000-square-foot winery. While the winemaking facilities make their home on the lower level, the main floor impresses with terracotta tiling, antique stained-glass windows and massive French doors that open onto the vineyards. Sit, imbibe on a glass of crisp chardonnay and take in the spectacular view and you'll forget that you're farther from Italy than it seems. Winter: Sunday-Wednesday 11 a.m.-5 p.m., Twilight Thursdays 11 a.m.-7:30 p.m., Friday and Saturday 11 a.m.-6 p.m. Summer: Sunday-Wednesday 11 a.m.-6 p.m., Twilight Thursdays 11 a.m.-7:30 p.m., Friday and Saturday 11 a.m.-7 p.m.

SPECIAL EVENT
HAMPTON CLASSIC HORSE SHOW

240 Snake Hollow Road, Bridgehampton, 631-537-3177; www.hamptonclassic.com

Horse show jumping event. Celebrities, food, shopping, family activities. Last week August. Admission: adults $10, children under 6 free.

RESTAURANTS
★★★ALISON

95 School St., Bridgehampton, 631-324-5440; www.alisonrestaurant.com

Special emphasis is placed on the local cuisine and wines of the Hamptons at this always-hopping spot. Seafood is the star of the menu, with dishes like sautéed striped bass or Atlantic salmon making regular appearances. American, seafood menu. Dinner. Bar. **$$**

★★BOBBY VAN'S STEAKHOUSE

2393 Montauk Highway, Bridgehampton, 631-537-0590; www.bobbyvans.com

Seafood, steak menu. Lunch, dinner. Closed holidays. Bar. **$$$**

BRONX (NEW YORK CITY)

Jonas Bronck, a Swedish settler, bought 500 acres of land from the Dutch in 1639, lending his name to the future borough. Locally, it is always referred to as "the Bronx," never just "Bronx." It is the only borough in New York City on the North American continent (the others are all on islands).

Information: Chamber of Commerce, 1200 Waters Place, Bronx, 718-828-3900; www.bronxchamber.org

WHAT TO SEE AND DO

BARTOW-PELL MANSION MUSEUM

895 Shore Road, Bronx, 718-885-1461; www.bartowpellmansionmuseum.org

This Greek Rivival stone mansion, built between 1836 and 1842, has been functioning as a museum since 1946 and exemplifies the type of country living that existed in the Pelham Bay Park area in the early 19th century. Educational programs are run year-round for children and adults. Mansion: Wednesday, Saturday and Sunday noon-4 p.m. Gardens and Grounds: open daily from 8:30 a.m. to dusk.

BRONX MUSEUM OF THE ARTS

1040 Grand Concourse, Bronx, 718-681-6000; www.bxma.org

Changing exhibits focus on contemporary art and current cultural subjects pertaining to the Bronx. Concerts, family workshops and special events. Museum open: Monday, Thursday, Saturday and Sunday 11 a.m.-6 p.m. Friday 11 a.m.-8 p.m. Museum will be closed on Thanksgiving, Christmas and New Year.

BRONX ZOO

Fordham Road and Bronx River Parkway, Bronx, 718-367-1010; www.bronxzoo.com

See endangered snow leopards, come nose to nose with a gorilla and encourage your kids to ride a camel at the imaginative children's zoo. This is the largest urban zoo in the United States and the heart of the Wildlife Conservation Society's efforts to save animals and wild places. The superb and cutting-edge exhibits re-create naturalistic habitats for many of the zoo's more than 4,000 animals. Be sure to see the Congo Gorilla Forest and the new habitat, Tiger Mountain. Daily.

CITY ISLAND

Off the southeast coast of the Bronx mainland, Bronx, 718-829-4111; www.cityisland.com

Considered a slice of New England in the city, City Island is devoted to shipping and shipbuilding. Seafood restaurants abound, and the City Island Historical Nautical Museum is also located here.

EDGAR ALLAN POE COTTAGE

East Kingsbridge Road and Grand Concourse, Bronx, 718-881-8900;
www.bronxhistoricalsociety.org/poecottage.html

The last years of Edgar Allan Poe's life, 1846 to 1849, were spent in the Bronx at Poe Cottage. The small wooden cottage built in 1812 once boasted amazing views of the rolling Bronx hills and the Long Island sound. It was a bucolic setting in which Poe penned many of his greatest works, including "Annabel Lee," "The Bells" and "Eureka." Admission: adults $5, seniors, students and children $3. Poe Cottage hours: Saturday 10 a.m.-4 p.m., Sunday 1-5 p.m., Monday-Friday 9 a.m.-5 p.m. Guided group tours: by appointment.

FORDHAM UNIVERSITY

Rose Hill Campus Bronx, 718-817-1000; www.fordham.edu

All four original Gothic structures of the Rose Hill campus are designated landmarks: University Chapel (St. John's Church), St. John's Residence Hall, the Administration Building and the Alumni House. A second campus is at 60th and Columbus Avenue, across from the Lincoln Center for the Performing Arts.

★
★
★
★
☆

ARTHUR AVENUE

Old World charm abounds in this section of the Bronx, which has been the home of generations of Italian families for more than a century. Seven square blocks make up the Arthur Avenue Retail Market, an Italian-American food oasis. One of the last indoor markets in New York and opened by Mayor Fiorello LaGuardia in the 1940s, it thrives to this day as a bustling cacophony of sights, sounds and smells. Shoppers entering through the rickety doors can only think of the possibilities lined up before them as they begin to scan the stands. Perhaps some roasted peppers? What about some cardoon fritters? The market is a mecca for serious cooks. The crowded storefronts of mom-and-pop shops sell everything from fine Italian wines and homemade pastas to imported cheeses and meats to gifts and cookware.

And then there are the abundant restaurants, pizza parlors and pastry shops—some dating to the 1920s—to entice your palate. If you are lucky enough to have a garden and are looking for heirloom seed varieties, see **Joe Liberatore's Garden of Plenty** (*2344 Arthur Avenue, 718-733-7960*) located inside the market. They carry seeds ideal for the Italian kitchen, difficult to find elsewhere. The fresh, locally made (farm and production in Pennsylvania) cheeses and velvety ricotta at **S. Calandra & Sons** (*2314 Arthur Avenue, 718-365-7572*) are alluring, as is the pungent scent at **Calabria Pork Store** (*2338 Arthur Ave., 718-367-5145*). The bread sold at **Terranova Bakery** (*691 E 187th St., 718-733-3827*) is a feast in itself. And **Marie's Roasted Coffee** (*2378 Arthur Avenue, 718-295-0514*) will turn you off Starbucks.

Many of the nearly 200 shops around this densely packed area do not take credit cards, so have plenty of cash on hand. If all the shopping has made you hungry, one of the best restaurants for enjoying an Italian-American meal is **Roberto's** (*632 E. 186th St., 718-733-9503*). And if you desire a little culture to finish off the day, there's a small repertory theater, the Belmont Playhouse, dedicated to works by Italian writers. Additionally, the Italian Cultural Center, part of the New York Library, has an amazing collection of Italian books, newspapers and films.

The most fascinating part of this historic market's evolution is that although the products sold and the dishes served are primarily consumed by Americans of Italian descent, the area serves a non-distinct community. Fordham University students prowl at all hours for sustenance; families coming from or going to the nearby Bronx Zoo or Botanical Garden stop by to stock up on fare for their picnics or their dining tables back in Manhattan. And any foodie in the area worth his or her salt makes a regular pilgrimage.

THE HALL OF FAME FOR GREAT AMERICANS

University Avenue and West 181st St., Bronx, 718-289-5161;
www.bcc.cuny.edu/hallofFame/

A 630-foot open-air colonnade provides the framework for bronze busts of great Americans; exhibits. The Hall of Fame is open to the public for tours daily between the hours of 10 a.m. and 5 p.m.

THE NEW YORK BOTANICAL GARDEN

200th Street and Kazimiroff Boulevard, Bronx, 718-817-8700; www.nybg.org

One of the largest and oldest in the country, this botanical garden consists of 250 acres of natural terrain and 50 gardens. The garden also contains the last 50 acres of the forest that once covered New York City. The Enid A. Haupt Conservatory has 11 distinct plant environments with changing exhibits and permanent displays, including the Fern Forest, Palm Court and Desert Houses. Tours. Tuesday-Sunday 10 a.m.-6 p.m.; to 5 p.m. from November-March; closed holidays.

NEW YORK YANKEES (MLB)

Yankee Stadium, 161st Street and River Avenue, Bronx, 718-293-6000; www.yankees.com

If you're a baseball fan visiting New York City during the summer, you owe it to yourself to catch a Yankees game. Watching the Bronx Bombers is the quintessential New York experience. Get tickets as early as you can, because these legendary pinstripers are popular with locals and tourists alike. The annual games between the Yankees and the New York Mets sell out quickly. The 2009 season is the first to be held in the new stadium, a block away from the historic original.

PELHAM BAY PARK

East of the Hutchinson River, Bronx, 718-430-1832; www.nycgovparks.org

Stretching out over 2,700 acres, Pelham Bay Park is New York City's largest park and takes advantage of the sprawling space. The expansive public park includes Orchard Beach, 13 miles of shoreline, fishing, an 18-hole and miniature golf course, a wildlife refuge, an environmental center, a nature trail, a visitor center, tennis courts, ball fields, a running track, riding stables and bridle paths and picnicking.

VAN CORTLANDT GOLF COURSE

Van Cortlandt Park South and Bailey Avenue, Bronx, 718-543-4595; www.nycgovparks.org

The Van Cortlandt Golf Course was the nation's first public course when it opened in 1895. The Golf Clubhouse, built in 1902, is situated on the lake and contains equipment rental facilities, lockers and a snack shop. Subway riders can get there by walking east from the IRT Nos. 1 and 9 terminal. Drivers can enter the park off Bailey Avenue and Van Cortlandt Park South, adjacent to the northbound entrance to the Major Deegan Expressway.

VAN CORTLANDT HOUSE MUSEUM

Broadway and 246th Street, Bronx, 718-543-3344; www.vancortlandthouse.org

This 1748 Georgian house is furnished in the 18th-century Dutch-English manner. Tuesday-Friday 10 a.m.-3 p.m., Saturday-Sunday 11 a.m.-4 p.m.; closed holidays.

WAVE HILL

West 249th Street and Independence Avenue, Bronx, 718-549-3200; www.wavehill.org

This Hudson River estate was, at various times, home to notables such as Mark Twain, Teddy Roosevelt and Arturo Toscanini. It's now a public garden and cultural center featuring Wave Hill House built in 1843, gardens, four greenhouses, nature trails, woods and meadows. The grounds consist of 28 acres overlooking the Hudson. Special events include concerts, dance programs, art exhibits and education and nature workshops. Admission: adults $6, seniors and students $3, children over 6 $2, children under 6 free; free admission Tuesday and Saturday mornings. Spring-summer: Tuesday-Sunday 9 a.m.-5:30 p.m., Wednesday until 9 p.m.; fall-winter: Tuesday-Sunday 9 a.m.-4:30 p.m.; closed holidays.

HOTEL

★★★LE REFUGE INN
586 City Island Ave., Bronx, 718-885-2478; www.lerefugeinn.com
Located on Long Island Sound with views of Manhattan, this Victorian house features individually decorated rooms with numerous antiques. The inn overlooks the bustling waterfront at City Island, home to a bevy of seafood restaurants. Seven rooms. Restaurant, bar. $

RESTAURANTS

★BLACK WHALE
279 City Island Ave., Bronx, 718-885-3657; www.dineatblackwhale.com
American menu. Lunch, dinner, Sunday brunch. Bar. Children's menu. Casual attire. $$

★★EMILIA'S
2331 Arthur Ave., Bronx, 718-367-5915; www.emiliasrestaurant.com
Italian menu. Lunch, dinner. Closed Monday; holidays. Bar. $$

★FEEDING TREE
892 Gerard Ave., Bronx, 718-293-5025
Caribbean menu. Breakfast, lunch, dinner. Children's menu. Casual attire. $$

★★★LE REFUGE INN
586 City Island Ave., Bronx, 718-885-2478; www.lerefugeinn.com
Le Refuge Inn is, as its name suggests, a splendid escape. Surrounded by the waters of the Long Island Sound, this 19th-century Victorian manor house on historic City Island is a cozy retreat of warmth, peace and romance—perfect for decompressing. The elegant antique-filled dining room is the setting for meals that include classic dishes such as bouillabaisse and duck a l'orange. French menu. Dinner. Closed Monday. Bar. Children's menu. Jacket required. Reservations recommended. Outdoor seating. $$

★★LOBSTER BOX
34 City Island Ave., Bronx, 718-885-1952; www.lobsterbox.com
Seafood menu. Lunch, dinner. Bar. Casual attire. Valet parking. $$

★★ROBERTO'S TRATTORIA
603 Crescent Ave., Bronx, 718-733-9503; www.roberto089.com
Italian menu. Lunch, dinner. Closed Sunday. Casual attire. Outdoor seating. $$

★VENICE RESTAURANT AND PIZZERIA
772 E. 149th St., Bronx, 718-585-5164; www.venicerestaurant149.com
Italian menu, pizza. Lunch, dinner. Children's menu. Casual attire. $$

BROOKLYN (NEW YORK CITY)

Many of the novels, plays, films and television shows about New York City—ranging from *Death of a Salesman* to *The Honeymooners*—are set in Brooklyn rather than Manhattan, perhaps because of the widely differing characters of these two boroughs. While Manhattan is world-class in sophistication and influence, Brooklyn is more grounded and quintessentially American, famous for things such as the hot dogs on Coney Island.

Yet there is much more to Brooklyn than popular stereotypes. Manhattanites flock to performances at the renowned Brooklyn Academy of Music, and the Egyptology collection at the Brooklyn Museum is on par with those in London and Cairo. Brooklyn's beautiful Prospect Park was designed by Olmsted and Vaux, who considered it more beautiful than another park they designed—Central Park in Manhattan.

The most heavily populated borough, Brooklyn also handles about 40 percent of New York City's vast shipping industry. It was pieced together from 25 independent villages and fought valiantly before allowing itself to be taken into New York City in 1898.

Information: Brooklyn Historical Society, 128 Pierrepont St., Brooklyn, 718-222-4111; www.brooklynhistory.org; NYC Convention and Visitors Bureau, 212-484-1200

WHAT TO SEE AND DO

ATLANTIC AVENUE
Atlantic Avenue, Brooklyn

Imagine a colorful shopping bazaar in downtown Cairo, and you've just pictured Atlantic Avenue. This area has a mix of more than 30 antiques and gift shops, ethnic food and bread stores, and savory Middle Eastern restaurants. If you crave real falafel, kebabs and hummus at value prices, this is the neighborhood to visit. You can also enjoy a mild day by wandering around nearby Brooklyn Heights, with its quaint brownstone apartments and quiet streets.

BROOKLYN ACADEMY OF MUSIC
30 Lafayette Ave., Brooklyn, 718-636-4100; www.bam.org

Founded in 1859, BAM is the oldest performing arts center in America, presenting original productions in contemporary performing arts. In the Next Wave Festival each fall, BAM opens its stage to noted national and international theater, dance and opera companies, and classical and contemporary music programs.

BROOKLYN BOTANIC GARDEN
1000 Washington Ave., Brooklyn, 718-623-7200; www.bbg.org

For a peaceful respite away from Manhattan, hop the 1 or 2 subway to Eastern Parkway in Brooklyn and enjoy a natural wonder: the 52-acre Brooklyn Botanic Garden. It features a gorgeous Japanese garden; the Steinhardt Conservatory, which has several greenhouses filled with a variety of plants; and the Fragrance Garden, designed specifically for the blind. There are rose gardens, the annual cherry blossom festival, a terrific alfresco café and many other beautiful sights. Tuesday-Friday: 8 a.m.-6 p.m., weekends and holidays:10 a.m.-6 p.m. Weekends and holidays: 10 a.m.-6 p.m. Closed Monday (but open holiday Mondays).

★
★★
★★
★★
★

BROOKLYN CHILDREN'S MUSEUM

145 Brooklyn Ave., Brooklyn, 718-735-4400; www.bchildmus.org

Founded in 1899, this is the world's oldest children's museum, featuring interactive exhibits, workshops and special events. Wednesday-Friday 1-6 p.m., Saturday-Sunday 10 a.m.-6 p.m.; also open during school holidays.

BROOKLYN HEIGHTS PROMENADE

Columbia Heights and Middagh Street, Brooklyn, 718-965-8900

For a peaceful stroll and a great view of Manhattan, visit this 1/3-mile-long waterfront area, stretching from Orange Street on the north to Remsen Street on the south. Pack a lunch, claim a bench and enjoy the sights of the city skyline, Ellis Island and Statue of Liberty. The promenade is lined with lovely homes and is a popular outdoor hangout for Brooklyn Heights yuppies during the summer. If you're in town over Independence Day weekend, this is usually a great place to view the Fourth of July fireworks. Daily.

BROOKLYN HISTORICAL SOCIETY

128 Pierrepont St., Brooklyn Heights, 718-222-4111; www.brooklynhistory.org

Brooklyn was originally the commercial and cultural center of Long Island, which explains why this society was originally founded in 1863 as the Long Island Historical Society. During World War I, BHS contributed to the war effort by transforming its 600-seat auditorium into a Red Cross headquarters. Programs include performances, readings, lectures and activities for children. Wednesday-Saturday 10 a.m.-5 p.m.; Sunday noon-5 p.m.; Closed July 4, Thanksgiving Day, Christmas Day and New Year's Day.

BROOKLYN MUSEUM OF ART

200 Eastern Parkway, Brooklyn, 718-638-5000; www.brooklynmuseum.org

Housed in a 560,000-square-foot Beaux-Arts building, this is one of the oldest and largest art museums in the country. The permanent collections include ancient Egyptian masterpieces alongside contemporary art, and represent a wide range of cultures. The "First Saturday" series (the first Saturday of every month, 5-11 p.m.) featuring free concerts, performances, films, dances and dance lessons. Wednesday-Friday 10 a.m.-5 p.m., Saturday-Sunday 11 a.m.-6 p.m.; closed holidays.

CONEY ISLAND

1208 Surf Ave., Brooklyn, 718-372-5159; www.coneyisland.com

Although it has become a bit frayed, you can still experience a bit of old New York along Coney Island's beachfront boardwalk. Take a ride on the legendary Cyclone roller coaster at Astroland Amusement Park (*www.astroland.com*). Afterward, grab the perfect hot dog, waffle fries and a lemonade at Nathan's Famous. For some really cheesy thrills, experience the nearby circus sideshow shown on weekends in summer.

DYKER BEACH GOLF COURSE

86th St. and Seventh Ave., Brooklyn, 718-836-9722; www.dykerbeach.americangolf.com

Few would believe that this beautiful 18-hole championship golf course sits just below the shadows of the Verrazano Narrows Bridge in Brooklyn. Built just before the turn of the 20th century and redesigned in the 1930s, Dyker Beach offers a few nice views and just a few trees. Easily accessible via public transit, the course is inexpensive and should be playable for almost any golfer. Open year-round, it can get crowded.

GATEWAY NATIONAL RECREATION AREA

Kings Highway and Flatbush Avenue, Brooklyn, 718-354-4606; www.nps.gov/gate

This sprawling collection of urban recreation areas consists of approximately 26,000 acres of land and water covering parts of two states, New York and New Jersey. Jamaica Bay Wildlife Refuge in Broad Channel, Queens (9,000 acres) offers wildlife observation and hiking trails. Floyd Bennett Field in Brooklyn has nature observation opportunities. Jacob Riis Park in Queens, with a mile-long boardwalk, offers beach and waterfront activities. Fort Tilden in Queens offers exhibits, nature walks, guided and self-guided tours of old defense batteries, sporting events and fishing. Canarsie Pier in Brooklyn offers free weekend summer concerts and restaurants.

NEW YORK AQUARIUM

West Eighth Street and Surf Avenue, Brooklyn, 718-265-3474; www.nyaquarium.org

A varied collection of marine life that includes sharks, beluga whales, seals, seahorses, jellyfish, penguins, sea otters and walruses. Visitors can watch dolphin feedings (April-October, outdoors) and sea lion shows daily. Restaurant. Opens daily at 10 a.m.; closing times vary by season.

NEW YORK TRANSIT MUSEUM

Boerum Place at Schermerhorn Street, Brooklyn Heights, 718-694-1600;
www.mta.nyc.ny.us/museum

Exhibits on the history of the New York City transit system are displayed within a 1930s subway station, including photographs, maps, antique turnstiles and subway cars dating back to 1903. Tuesday-Friday 10 a.m.-4 p.m., Saturday-Sunday noon to 5 p.m.

PROSPECT PARK

95 Prospect Park West, Brooklyn, 718-965-8951; www.prospectpark.org

Prospect Park is a 585-acre masterpiece of famed landscape architects Frederick Law Olmsted and Calvert Vaux, who also designed Central Park. It holds Brooklyn's only forest and a 60-acre lake. There is also the nation's first urban Audubon Center, the Prospect Park Zoo, and the Celebrate Brooklyn. Daily.

SHEEPSHEAD BAY

2575 Coney Island Ave., Brooklyn,718-627-6611; www.nycgovparks.org

This area boasts all the advantages of an ocean fishing community: seafood restaurants, clam bars, tackle shops, fishing boats and some lovely views.

HOTEL

★★★NEW YORK MARRIOTT AT THE BROOKLYN BRIDGE

333 Adams St., Brooklyn, 718-246-7000, 888-436-3759;
www.brooklynmarriott.com

Located in downtown Brooklyn, this hotel features spacious guest accommodations with wonderful amenities—luxurious bedding, massaging showerheads, plush bathrobes and in-room video games. A large indoor lap pool with a whirlpool and Jacuzzi, and complimentary guest access to Eastern Athletic Club provide ways to stay fit while on the road. 637 rooms. High-speed Internet access. Restaurant, bar. Business center. $$$

RESTAURANTS

★★AL DI LA TRATTORIA
248 Fifth St., Brooklyn, 718-636-8888
Italian menu. Dinner. Closed Sunday. Bar. Casual attire. Reservations recommended. Valet parking. $$$

★★ALMA
187 Columbia St., Brooklyn, 718-643-5400; www.almarestaurant.com
Mexican menu. Dinner, Saturday-Sunday brunch. Bar. Business casual attire. Reservations recommended. Valet parking. Outdoor seating. $$

★★BLUE RIBBON BROOKLYN
280 Fifth Ave., Brooklyn, 718-840-0404; www.blueribbonrestaurants.com
American menu. Breakfast (Sunday), dinner, late-night. Children's menu. Casual attire. $$

★★BLUE RIBBON SUSHI
278 Fifth Ave., Brooklyn, 718-840-0408; www.blueribbonrestaurants.com
Japanese, sushi menu. Dinner, late-night. Closed Monday. Children's menu. Casual attire. $$$

★★BONITA
338 Bedford Ave., Brooklyn, 718-384-9500; www.bonitanyc.com
Mexican menu. Lunch, dinner, Saturday-Sunday Brunch. Bar. Casual attire. Valet parking. $$

★★CHESTNUT
271 Smith St., Brooklyn, 718-243-0049; www.chestnutonsmith.com
American menu. Dinner, Sunday brunch. Closed Monday. Bar. Casual attire. Reservations recommended. Outdoor seating. $$

★★CONVIVIUM OSTERIA
68 Fifth Ave., Brooklyn, 718-857-1833; www.convivium-osteria.com
Mediterranean menu. Dinner. Casual attire. Outdoor seating. $$

★DINER
85 Broadway, Brooklyn, 718-486-3077; www.dinernyc.com
American menu. Lunch, dinner, late-night, Saturday and Sunday brunch. Casual attire. $$

★GRIMALDI'S PIZZERIA
19 Old Fulton St., Brooklyn, 718-858-4300; www.grimaldis.com/brooklyn.htm
Pizza menu. Lunch, dinner. Bar. Children's menu. Casual attire. $

★★★THE GROCERY

288 Smith St., Brooklyn, 718-596-3335; www.thegroceryrestaurant.com

When husband-and-wife team Charlie Kiely and Sharon Patcherchef—veterans of the New York restaurant scene—opened The Grocery, an intimate spot with a leafy back patio and yard, they had no idea that they would inspire a cult following. This stylish, earth-toned dining room has a serene vibe, and the delicious food coming out of the tiny kitchen makes the 13-table space all the more exquisite. Star dishes include brook trout with spinach and bacon-flecked spaetzle, ratatouille-stuffed squid, roasted beets with goat cheese ravioli, duck confit with roasted quince sauce and pork loin with sweet potatoes and roasted pears. American menu. Dinner. Closed Sunday. Bar. Casual attire. Outdoor seating. $$$

★★M SHANGHAI BISTRO & DEN

129 Havenmeyer St., Brooklyn, 718-384-9300; www.mshanghaiden.com

Chinese menu. Lunch, dinner, late-night. Closed Monday. Bar. Casual attire. $$

★★PATOIS

255 Smith St., Brooklyn, 718-855-1535

French menu. Dinner, Sunday brunch. Closed Monday. Casual attire. Outdoor seating. $$

★★★PETER LUGER STEAK HOUSE

178 Broadway, Brooklyn, 718-387-7400; www.peterluger.com

This renowned landmark restaurant has served porterhouse steaks since 1887 and is still one of the city's top tables. But don't expect elegant surroundings with your expertly charred dry-aged slab of beef. This place is bare bones, with exposed beamed ceilings, worn tables and chairs, and waiters who are as well seasoned as the beef. Do expect a hefty check when all is said and done. In addition to the marbled steaks, there are sides like German-fried potatoes and creamed spinach. If you make it over for lunch, try New York's best burger, made from fresh ground beef and served with slices of tearjerker raw onion and a thick beefsteak tomato. Steak menu. Lunch, dinner. Bar. Casual attire. Reservations recommended. $$$

★★RELISH

225 Wythe Ave., Brooklyn, 718-963-4546; www.relish.com

American menu. Lunch, dinner. Bar. Casual attire. $$

★★★RIVER CAFÉ

1 Water St., Brooklyn, 718-522-5200; www.rivercafe.com

Located on the Brooklyn waterfront with an unmatched view of the East River and the twinkling Manhattan skyline, this elegant old timer has always been a favorite for celebrating special occasions. The kitchen prepares sophisticated, artistically plated New American fare such as lobster, rack of lamb and duck. The wine list is award winning, and the service is unobtrusive. American menu. Lunch, dinner. Bar. Jacket required. Reservations recommended. Valet parking. Outdoor seating. $$$

★★SAUL
140 Smith St., Brooklyn, 718-935-9844; www.saulrestaurant.com
American menu. Dinner, Sunday brunch. Bar. Casual attire. **$$**

★★SEA
114 N. Sixth St., Brooklyn, 718-384-8850; www.seathairestaurant.com
Thai menu. Lunch, dinner, late-night. Bar. Casual attire. Reservations recommended. **$$**

★★SUPERFINE
126 Front St., Brooklyn, 718-243-9005
American menu. Lunch, dinner, Sunday brunch. Closed Monday. Bar. Casual attire. **$$**

BUFFALO

Buffalo, at the eastern end of Lake Erie, is New York's second-largest city and one of the largest railroad centers in America. Fifteen freight depots and one passenger terminal handle more than 25,000 trains annually.

Planned by Joseph Ellicott (agent of the Holland Land Company) in 1803, the city was modeled after Washington, D.C., which was laid out by his brother, Major Andrew Ellicott. Buffalo radiates from Niagara Square, dominated by a monument to President William McKinley, who was assassinated here while attending the Pan-American Exposition in 1901.

In 1679, when Buffalo was claimed by the French, La Salle built the first boat to sail the Great Lakes, the wooden *Griffon*. During the War of 1812, Buffalo was set ablaze by the British, but its 500 citizens returned a few months later and rebuilt. In 1816, *Walk-on-the-Water*, the first steamboat to ply the Great Lakes, was launched here. The opening of the Erie Canal in 1825 made Buffalo the major transportation hub between the East and West and brought trade and prosperity. Joseph Dart's 1843 invention of a steam-powered grain elevator caused Buffalo's grain-processing industry to boom. Since completion of the St. Lawrence Seaway in 1959, Buffalo has been one of the top Great Lakes ports in import-export tonnage.

Buffalo has a $7 million city hall and state and federal buildings. The Buffalo Philharmonic Orchestra, Albright-Knox Art Gallery and many nightclubs cater to the varied interests of residents and visitors. The city is ringed with 3,000 acres of parks, which offer swimming, boating, tennis, golf and riding.

Information: Buffalo Niagara Convention and Visitors Bureau, 617 Main St., Buffalo, 716-852-0511, 888-228-3369; www.buffalocvb.org

WHAT TO SEE AND DO
ALBRIGHT-KNOX ART GALLERY
1285 Elmwood Ave., Buffalo, 716-882-8700; www.albrightknox.org
One of the oldest arts organizations in the United States, the gallery has a varied collection, including extensive works from 18th-century English, 19th-century French and 20th-century American and European painters. Works by Picasso, Matisse, Monet, Renoir and Van Gogh are on display, we well as sculpture from 3000 BC to present. Changing exhibits. Admission: adults $10, seniors and students 14-18 $8, children under 14 free. Saturday-Sunday 10 a.m.-5 p.m., Thursday-Friday 10 a.m.-10 p.m., Wednesday 10 a.m.-5 p.m. Closed Monday, Tuesday and holidays.

ALLENTOWN
Allen Street, Buffalo
Historic preservation district containing Victorian-era structures of every major style. Many restaurants, antique stores, art galleries and boutiques.

BUFFALO AND ERIE COUNTY BOTANICAL GARDENS
Olmsted's South Park, 2655 S. Park Ave., Buffalo, 716-827-1584; www.buffalogardens.com
Boasting a Victorian conservatory and outdoor gardens, this 156-acre park is teeming with plants in its eleven greenhouses and desert, rainforest and Mediterranean collections. It often hosts seasonal shows. Monday-Tuesday, Thursday-Friday 9 a.m.-4 p.m., Wednesday 9 a.m.-6 p.m., Saturday-Sunday 9 a.m.-5 p.m.; closed holidays.

BUFFALO & ERIE COUNTY HISTORICAL SOCIETY
25 Nottingham Court, Buffalo, 716-873-9644; www.bechs.org
Explore the history of Western New York, see an exhibition about pioneer life and view a street scene from 1870 in this Pan-American Exposition building from 1901. Pan-Am Building Tuesday-Saturday 10 a.m.-5 p.m., Sunday noon-5 p.m. Closed Monday. Resource Center (459 Forest Avenue) Wednesday-Saturday 1-5 p.m., separate admission fee.

BUFFALO AND ERIE COUNTY NAVAL & MILITARY PARK
One Naval Park Cove, Buffalo, 716-847-1773; www.buffalonavalpark.org
This is the largest inland naval park in the nation and displays multiple ships, aircraft and tanks, including cruiser *USS Little Rock*, destroyer USS *The Sullivans* and submarine *USS Croaker*. Video presentations and a gift shop are inside. April-October, daily 10 a.m.-5 p.m.; November, Saturday-Sunday 10 a.m.-4 p.m.; Guided tours April-October, Monday-Saturday 10 a.m. and 12:30 p.m.

BUFFALO MUSEUM OF SCIENCE
1020 Humboldt Parkway, Buffalo, 716-896-5200, 866-291-6660; www.buffalomuseumofscience.org
Explore exhibits on astronomy, botany, geology, zoology, anthropology and natural sciences in one of the region's premier museums, which contains a research library. A Discovery Room is available for children. Lectures. Admission: adults $7, seniors $6, military and students $5, children 3-18 $5, children under 3 free. June 21-August 31, Monday-Saturday 10 a.m.-5 p.m., closed Sunday; September 2-June 20, Wednesday-Saturday 10 a.m.-5 p.m., Sunday noon-5 p.m., Monday closed, Tuesday reserved for school groups.

BUFFALO ZOOLOGICAL GARDENS
Delaware Park, 300 Parkside Ave., Buffalo, 716-837-3900; www.buffalozoo.org
More than 2,200 animals roam in this 23½-acre park. It features indoor and outdoor exhibits, a gallery of Boehm wildlife porcelains, a tropical gorilla habitat, outdoor lion and tiger exhibits and a children's zoo. July-August, daily 10 a.m.-5 p.m.; September-June, daily 10 a.m.-4 p.m.; closed holidays.

39

NEW YORK

★
★
★
★
☆

CITY HALL/OBSERVATION TOWER
65 Niagara Square, Buffalo, 716-851-4200; www.ci.buffalo.ny.us
Enjoy panoramic views of Western New York, Lake Erie, and Ontario, Canada from the observation deck. Monday-Friday; closed holidays.

FRANK LLOYD WRIGHT HOUSES
Buffalo
The famed American architect designed several buildings in Buffalo. They include the Darwin D. Martin house (125 Jewett Parkway); George Barton House (118 Summit); Gardener's Cottage (285 Woodward); Walter V. Davidson House (57 Tillinghast Place) and the William Heath House (76 Soldiers Place).

PRUDENTIAL BUILDING
28 Church St., Buffalo, 716-829-3543
Designed by Dankmar Adler and Louis Sullivan and completed in 1896, the Prudential (formerly Guaranty) Building is an outstanding example of Sullivan's ideas of functional design and terra-cotta ornament and one of America's great skyscrapers.

QRS MUSIC ROLLS
1026 Niagara St., Buffalo, 800-247-6557; www.qrsmusic.com
Enjoy an effortless performance at the world's largest and oldest manufacturer of player-piano rolls. Tours offered Monday-Friday 10 a.m., 2 p.m.

SHEA'S PERFORMING ARTS CENTER
646 Main St., Buffalo, 716-847-1410; www.sheas.org
Broadway shows, theater, dance, opera, music and family programs.

STUDIO ARENA THEATRE
710 Main St., Buffalo, 716-856-8025, 800-777-8243; www.studioarena.org
This regional professional theater presents world premieres, musicals, classic dramas and contemporary works. September-May, Tuesday-Sunday evenings.

THEODORE ROOSEVELT INAUGURAL NATIONAL HISTORIC SITE
641 Delaware Ave., Buffalo, 716-884-0095; www.nps.gov/thri
Theodore Roosevelt was inaugurated in this classic Greek Revival house in 1901 following the assassination of President McKinley. Victorian herb garden. Self-guided, two-mile architectural walking tours. Admission: adults $5, seniors and students $3, children 6-14 $1, children under 4 free. Monday-Friday 9 a.m.-5 p.m., Saturday-Sunday noon-5 p.m.

SPECIAL EVENTS
BUFFALO PHILHARMONIC ORCHESTRA
Kleinhans Music Hall, 370 Pennsylvania St., Buffalo, 716-885-5000; www.bpo.org
Classical and pop concert series; children's and family programs. Summer season also. July.

TASTE OF BUFFALO

Main Street, Buffalo, 716-831-9376; www.tasteofbuffalo.com

Hosting more than 50 local restaurants, this annual event represents some 15 ethnic and regional varieties of food, including Greek, Italian, Indian, Chinese, Middle Eastern, Mexican and Southwestern, as well as traditional American favorites, local specialties and all manner of desserts. More than 450,000 people attend annually. Mid-July.

HOTELS

★★★ASA RANSOM HOUSE

10529 Main St., Clarence, 716-759-2315, 800-841-2340; www.asaransom.com

This charming inn surrounded by gardens, offers nine rooms, each with its own distinct character and charm. Rooms are furnished with antiques and period reproductions, and several have both fireplace and private balconies. Nine rooms. Closed January. Complimentary full breakfast. Restaurant. $$

★BEST WESTERN INN - ON THE AVENUE

510 Delaware Ave., Buffalo, 716-886-8333, 800-780-7234; www.innontheavenue.com

61 rooms. Complimentary continental breakfast. High-speed Internet access. $

★★★BUFFALO MARRIOTT NIAGARA

1340 Millersport Highway, Buffalo, 716-689-6900, 800-334-4040;
www.buffaloniagaramarriott.com

Although situated in a quiet suburban location, the Buffalo Marriott Niagara is close to Buffalo Airport, downtown Buffalo and Niagara Falls. Rooms are bright, elegant and spacious. Amenities include a complimentary airport shuttle, indoor/outdoor pool and 24-hour health club. 356 rooms. High-speed Internet access. Restaurant, bar. Fitness center. Pool. $$$

★COMFORT SUITES

901 Dick Road, Buffalo, 716-633-6000, 877-424-6423; www.comfortsuites.com

100 rooms, all suites. Complimentary continental breakfast. Whirlpool. Pool. Airport transportation available. $

★★SUITES DOWNTOWN

601 Main St., Buffalo, 716-854-5500, 877-424-6423; www.comfortsuites.com

146 rooms. Complimentary continental breakfast. Wireless Internet access. Restaurant, bar. Airport transportation available. $

★★★HYATT REGENCY BUFFALO

Two Fountain Plaza, Buffalo, 716-856-1234; www.buffalo.hyatt.com

This hotel is located downtown and connected to the Buffalo Convention Center and is on the metro rail and within walking distance of shopping, restaurants, theaters, cultural and sports entertainment and other attractions. 396 rooms. High-speed Internet access. Two restaurants, two bars. Fitness center. Pool. Full-service business center. $$

RESTAURANTS

★★★ASA RANSOM HOUSE

10529 Main St., Clarence, 716-759-2315, 800-841-2340; www.asaransom.com

Sample fare like the Asa chicken potpie loaded with home-grown vegetables or the grilled apple butter salmon at this romantic, country-style retreat. Enjoy a stylish meal in the formal Ransom Room, or head for the more casual Clarence Hollow Room should you wish to leave the sportcoat behind. American menu. Breakfast, lunch, dinner. Closed Christmas; also January-mid-February. Children's menu. Outdoor seating. $$$

★★★SALVATORE'S ITALIAN GARDENS

6461 Transit Road, Buffalo, 716-683-7990, 800-999-8082; www.salvatores.net

One of Buffalo's finest Italian eateries, Salvatore's is renowned for its "dinner for two" meals as well as its seafood medley and several varieties of veal. American, Italian menu. Dinner. Closed holidays. Bar. Children's menu. Casual attire. $$$

CAIRO

At the foot of the Catskills, Cairo is a town of charming streets, outdoor recreation, historic paths (such as the Mohican Trail) and pretty old buildings.

WHAT TO SEE AND DO

DURHAM CENTER MUSEUM

Highway 145 and East Durham, Cairo, 518-239-8461

View relics from the Catskill Valley's past in this renovated schoolhouse, used from 1825 to 1940, including folk art, American Indian artifacts, fossils, minerals, railroad and turnpike relics, antiques and household and business equipment. Memorial Day-Columbus Day, Thursday-Sunday 1 p.m.-4 p.m.; other times by appointment.

HOTEL

★★WINTER CLOVE INN ROUND TOP

Winter Clove Road, Round Top, 518-622-3267; www.winterclove.com

40 rooms. Closed first three weeks of December. Conference center, dining, restaurant (public by reservation). Children's activity center. $

SPECIALTY LODGING

GREENVILLE ARMS 1889 INN

Routes 32 and 81, Greenville, 518-966-5219, 888-665-0044; www.greenvillearms.com

Built in 1889, this inn is bursting with antiques. Many rooms have private baths and air conditioning and some have canopied beds or a private porch from which to enjoy the view of the grounds. The original artwork reflects the natural beauty of the Catskill Mountains. 16 rooms. Closed November-April. Children over 12 years only. Complimentary full breakfast. $

CAMILLUS

A 20-minute drive from Syracuse, this town is a center of outdoor recreation and rich in history, with five museums in its vicinity.

Information: townofcamillus.com

RESTAURANT

★★★INN BETWEEN

2290 State Route 5, Camillus, 315-672-3166; www.inn-between.com

Located outside Syracuse, this 1880 country house sits on the outskirts of central New York wine country and boasts standout dishes such as crispy roast duckling with an herb-filled stuffing. Day trips to local wineries and special wine festivals in the fall are among the unique activities. American menu. Lunch, dinner. Closed Monday; holidays. Bar. Children's menu. $$

CANANDAIGUA

Located on the westernmost of the Finger Lakes, this resort city is close to scores of attractions, galleries and wineries.

Information: Chamber of Commerce, 113 S. Main St., Canandaigua, 585-394-4400; www.canandaiguachamber.com

WHAT TO SEE AND DO

BRISTOL MOUNTAIN SKI & SNOWBOARD RESORT

5662 State Route 64, Canandaigua, 585-374-6000; www.bristolmt.com

Two quad, two triple, double chairlifts; tow rope; patrol, school, rentals; snowmaking; cafeteria, bar. Longest run two miles, vertical drop 1,200 feet. Mid-November-April, daily.

GRANGER HOMESTEAD

295 N. Main St., Canandaigua, 585-394-1472; www.grangerhomestead.org

Namesake and previous resident Gideon Granger was Postmaster General under presidents Jefferson and Madison. The 10-acre site includes nine restored rooms with original furnishings and a carriage museum in two buildings with more than 50 antique horse-drawn vehicles including coaches, cutters, surreys, sleighs and hearses. Admission: adults $6, seniors $5, students $2, preschoolers free. Tours by appointment, June-September, Tuesday-Sunday 1-5 p.m.; late May-mid-October, Tuesday-Friday 1-5 p.m.

SONNENBERG GARDENS

151 Charlotte St., Canandaigua, 585-394-4922; www.sonnenberg.org

A 50-acre Victorian garden estate, complete with an 1887 mansion and conservatory, is ringed with nine formal gardens, including Italian, Japanese, colonial, rock, rose and blue and white pansy. Visitors can also sample local vintages at the Finger Lakes Wine Center. Tours. May 26-September 1, daily 9:30 a.m.-5:30 p.m.; May 10-25 and September 2-October 13, daily 9:30 a.m.-4:30 p.m.

SPECIALTY LODGING

1795 ACORN INN

4508 Highway 64, Canandaigua, 585-229-2834, 888-665-3747; www.acorninnbb.com

Built in 1795, the Acorn Inn was originally a stagecoach stop and has rooms designed in the Federal style. Four rooms. Children over 14 years only. Complimentary full breakfast. $

CANASTOTA

In 1820, when the first packet boat run was established on the Erie Canal from here to Rome, Canastota became a canal town. Some of the original structures still exist along the canal, which bisects the village.

Information: www.canastota.org

WHAT TO SEE AND DO

CANASTOTA CANAL TOWN MUSEUM

122 Canal St., Canastota, 315-697-3451; www.canastota.com

This quaint museum's displays trace the growth of the Erie Canal and its effect on Canastota and Western New York. It's adjacent to a state park. Admission: adults $3, children under 13 free. May-June, noon-3 p.m.; July-August, 11 a.m.-3 p.m.; September-October noon-3 p.m.; closed Sunday and Monday.

CHITTENANGO LANDING CANAL BOAT MUSEUM

7010 Lake Port Road, Chittenango, 315-687-3801;
www.chittenangolandingcanalboatmuseum.com

Located on a remaining section of the Erie Canal, this historic site is dedicated to the preservation of a 19th-century boat building and repair industry. It offers guided and self-guided walking tours, excavations, interpretive center, hands-on activities and exhibits. May-June, Saturday-Sunday 1-4 p.m.; July-August: daily 10 a.m.-4 p.m.; September-October, Saturday-Sunday 1-4 p.m.; closed holidays.

INTERNATIONAL BOXING HALL OF FAME

One Hall of Fame Drive, Canastota, 315-697-7095; www.ibhof.com

A paean to pugilism, this site preserves boxing heritage and honors those who have excelled in boxing. Monday-Friday 9 a.m.-5 p.m., Saturday-Sunday 10 a.m.-4 p.m.; closed holidays.

OLD ERIE CANAL STATE PARK

8729 Andrus Road, Kirkville, 315-687-7821; www.nysparks.com

This 35-mile strip of canal runs from Dewitt to Rome, with canoe launches and picnicking in the Cedar Bay Area. Many features of the original canal remain, including a towpath, aqueducts, change bridges and culverts. Fishing, canoeing; hiking, bicycling, horseback riding, snowmobiling.

CANTON

Canton, which lies on the Grass River, was settled in the early 1800s by Vermonters. Canton College of Technology is located here.

Information: Chamber of Commerce, Municipal Building, Canton, 315-386-8255;
www.cantonnychamber.org

WHAT TO SEE AND DO

SILAS WRIGHT HOUSE AND MUSEUM

3 E. Main St., Canton, 315-386-8133; www.slcha.org

This Greek Revival house, once the residence (1832-1844) of the U.S. Senator and New York Governor Silas Wright, currently houses the St. Lawrence County Historical

Association, a library, archives and a museum. The first floor has been restored to the 1830-1850 period, and the second-floor gallery is set aside for temporary exhibits on local history. Tuesday-Saturday noon-4 p.m., Friday noon-8 p.m.; closed holidays.

ST. LAWRENCE UNIVERSITY

23 Romoda Drive, Canton, 315-229-5011, 800-285-1856; www.stlawu.edu

The Griffiths Arts Center, Gunnison Memorial Chapel, Owen D. Young Library and Augsbury-Leithead Physical Education Complex are all on campus. Campus tours.

HOTEL

★★BEST WESTERN UNIVERSITY INN

Route 11, 90 E. Main St., Canton, 315-386-8522, 888-386-8522;
www.bestwestern.com

99 rooms. High-speed Internet access. Restaurant, bar. Fitness center. Pool. **$**

RESTAURANT

★MCCARTHY'S

5821 Highway 11, Canton, 315-386-2564

Breakfast, lunch, dinner, Sunday brunch. Closed holidays. Bar. Children's menu. **$$**

CARLE PLACE

Long a rural town sustained by its local farms, Carle Place is now an affluent community on Long Island.

Information: www.westburycarleplacechamber.com

RESTAURANT

★★RIALTO

588 Westbury Ave., Carle Place, 516-997-5283; rialtorestaurantli.com

Italian menu. Lunch, dinner. Closed August; Monday; holidays. Bar. Casual attire. Reservations recommended. **$$$**

CATSKILL

This is the eastern entrance to the Catskill Mountains resort area. The town is at the west end of the Rip Van Winkle Bridge, across the Hudson River from the manufacturing town of Hudson. The legendary Rip is said to have slept for 20 years near here.

Information: Greene Tourism, Catskill, 518-943-3223, 800-355-2287;
www.greenetourism.com

HOTELS

★CARL'S RIP VAN WINKLE MOTOR LODGE

810 Route 23B, Leeds, 518-943-3303; www.ripvanwinklemotorlodge.com

68 rooms. Wireless Internet access. Closed mid-November-mid-April. **$**

★★WOLFF'S MAPLE BREEZE RESORT

360 Cauterskill Road, Catskill, 518-943-3648, 800-777-9653;
www.wolffsresort.com

42 rooms. Closed November-April. Restaurant, bar. Children's activity center. **$**

NEW YORK
★
★
★
★
★

★★FRIAR TUCK RESORT AND CONVENTION CENTER
4858 Highway 32, Catskill, 518-678-2271, 800-832-7600; www.friartuck.com
500 rooms. Restaurant, bar. Spa. Children's activity center. Theater. **$**

CAZENOVIA
Located in central New York on the shores of Cazenovia Lake, this town has worked
to preserve its historical buildings and the stories that go with them.
Information: www.cazenovia.com

WHAT TO SEE AND DO
CHITTENANGO FALLS STATE PARK
2300 Rathbun Road, Cazenovia, 315-655-9620; www.nysparks.com/parks
Glaciers carved out this picturesque area millions of years ago, sculpting a landscape
filled with hiking trails, rivers for fishing and a 167-foot waterfall. The park grounds
include a picnic area, playground and tent and trailer sites. Daily.

LORENZO STATE HISTORIC SITE
17 Rippleton Road, Cazenovia, 315-655-3200; www.lorenzony.org
This elegant 1807 Federal-period mansion built by John Lincklaen has retained its
original furnishings along with a garden and arboretum. Admission: adults $5, seniors
and students $4, children under 12 free. May 13-October 26, Tuesday-Sunday 10
a.m.-4:30 p.m.

TOGGENBURG SKI CENTER
Toggenburg Road, Fabius, 315-683-5842, 800-720-8644; www.skitog.com
Triple, double chairlifts; two beginners' lifts, two T-bars; patrol, ski school, rentals;
snowmaking; cafeteria, bar; nursery. Night skiing. December-early April, daily. Cross-
country trails in Highland Forest, approximately two miles west on Highway 80.

HOTELS
★★★BREWSTER INN
6 Ledyard Ave., Cazenovia, 315-655-9232; www.thebrewsterinn.com
Built in 1890 as the summer home of financier Benjamin B. Brewster, the inn overlooks the calming waters of Cazenovia Lake and offers a carefree and relaxed setting.
Guests may choose to stay in rooms in the main house or in the renovated carriage
house. Massage therapists are on hand to offer a variety of experiences, from Swedish massages to medical massages. 17 rooms. Complimentary continental breakfast.
Restaurant, bar. **$**

★★★LINCKLAEN HOUSE
79 Albany St., Cazenovia, 315-655-3461; www.lincklaenhouse.com
Since the turn of the 20th century, this property has provided fine dining and lodging for luminaries like former president Grover Cleveland and John D. Rockefeller.
Rooms are elegantly decorated, as is the main floor dining room. 23 rooms. Complimentary continental breakfast, lunch and dinner. **$**

★★BRAE LOCH INN

5 Albany St., Cazenovia, 315-655-3431; www.braelochinn.com

American menu. Dinner, Sunday brunch (September-June). Closed holidays. Bar. Children's menu. **$$**

★★★BREWSTER INN

6 Ledyard Ave., Cazenovia, 315-655-9232; www.thebrewsterinn.com

This gourmet restaurant at the historic Brewster Inn offers an elegant atmosphere and house specialties such as New Zealand rack of lamb, crispy boneless duck and the Brewster Inn veal "Atlantis"—lightly sautéed veal topped with lobster served on a bed of tender greens and finished with a tarragon beurre blanc. American, French menu. Dinner, Sunday brunch. Closed holidays; open on Thanksgiving. Bar. Outdoor seating. **$$**

CHATHAM

On the north edge of the Hudson River Valley, Chatham is a stretch of land marked by Colonial homes and rolling hills. Visitors and residents enjoy the slower pace of life in this charming town.

RESTAURANT

★★BLUE PLATE

1 Kinderhook St., Chatham, 518-392-7711; www.chathamblueplate.net

American menu. Lunch, dinner. Bar. Casual attire. **$$**

CHAUTAUQUA

The Chautauqua Institution is a lakeside summer center for the arts, education, religion and recreation. Programs are offered to adults and children. The summer population swells to more than 10,000. The community began as a Sunday school teachers' training camp and developed into a cultural center that started nationwide book clubs and correspondence schools. It has provided a platform for presidents and political leaders, as well as great musical artists and popular entertainers.

Information: www.tourchautauqua.com

WHAT TO SEE AND DO

CHAUTAUQUA AMPHITHEATER

Bowman St. and Roberts Ave., Chautauqua, 716-357-6200, 800-836-2787;
www.ciweb.org

This 5,000-seat amphitheater built in 1893 is the home of the Chautauqua Symphony Orchestra. It also hosts recitals, ballet, opera, lectures and special popular musical events.

CHAUTAUQUA BELLE

78 Water St., Mayville, 716-269-2355; www.chautauquabelle.com

A replica of a 19th-century paddlewheel steamboat, the Chautauqua Belle cruises around the lake all summer on various trips and themed cruises, including wine tasting events and Fall Foliage tours. Memorial Day-Labor Day, daily.

47

NEW YORK

★
★
★
★
★

THE CHAUTAUQUA INSTITUTION

1 Ames St., Chautauqua, 716-357-6200, 800-836-2787; www.ciweb.org

This famous center for arts, education, religion and recreation, offers relaxing and revitalizing summer programs that touch on everything from pop culture to politics. The nine-week season (late June-late August, daily) features a lecture platform as well as performing arts events.

NORTON MEMORIAL HALL

Chautauqua

Each season, the Chautauqua Opera Company presents four full-length English-language operas in this unique performance space.

HOTELS

★★WEBB'S LAKE RESORT

115 West Lake Road Route 394, Mayville, 716-753-2161; www.webbsworld.com

52 rooms. High-speed Internet access. Continental breakfast. Restaurant, bar. Indoor pool. Pets accepted. Miniature golf. **$**

★★★WILLIAM SEWARD INN

6645 S. Portage Road, Westfield, 716-326-4151; www.williamsewardinn.com

Southwest Chautauqua County is the perfect setting for this 1837 country inn with its nearby attractions such as ski areas, Chautauqua Lake and the well-known Chautauqua Institution. Rooms are comfortable and overstuffed with rich fabrics and comfortable furnishings. Sample the black olive-crusted salmon or apricot-stuffed quail in the two dining rooms. 12 rooms. Children over 12 years only. Complimentary full breakfast. Restaurant. **$$**

RESTAURANT

★★★ATHENAEUM

South Lake Drive, Chautauqua, 716-357-4444, 800-821-1881; www.athenaeum-hotel.com

This grand Victorian hotel has been serving guests since 1881 and is now listed on the National Historic Register. Head here for the formal, five-course dinner or stellar Sunday brunch. American menu. Breakfast, lunch, dinner, Sunday brunch. Closed September-May. Children's menu. Jacket required. Reservations recommended. Valet parking. Outdoor seating. **$$**

CLAYTON

Clayton juts into the St. Lawrence River in the midst of the Thousand Islands resort region and serves as the home for numerous pleasure boats that line the waterfront docks.

Information: Chamber of Commerce, 517 Riverside Drive, Clayton, 315-686-3771, 800-252-9806; www.thousandislands.com/claytonchamber

WHAT TO SEE AND DO

ANTIQUE BOAT MUSEUM

750 Mary St., Clayton, 315-686-4104; www.abm.org

This nautical museum showcases more than 200 antique boats, including canoes, sailboats, hydroplanes and cruisers, as well as artifacts related to boating. The museum also sponsors educational programs about boat building and boater safety. Mid-May-mid-October, daily 9 a.m.-5 p.m.

CEDAR POINT STATE PARK
36661 Cedar Point State Park Drive, Clayton, 315-654-2522; www.nysparks.state.ny.us/parks
Cedar Point State Park, one of the oldest state parks in New York, is a popular spot, offering excellent camping, fishing, boating and swimming. The beach is sheltered and sandy, there are docks for boats, a fishing pier and picnic grounds. Swimming beach, bathhouse, fishing, boating; picnicking, playground, recreation programs, camping. Mid-May-mid-October.

GRASS POINT STATE PARK
42247 Grassy Point Road, Clayton, 315-686-4472; www.nysparks.state.ny.us/parks
On the West side of the beach is Grass Point cottage, a two-story lodging with a bathroom shower and full kitchen. Bedding, pillows and linens are also provided. The screened-in porch has outstanding views of the river and sunsets. Swimming beach, bathhouse, fishing, boating, picnicking, playground, camping. Mid-May-late September.

THOUSAND ISLANDS MUSEUM
312 James St., Clayton, 315-686-5794; www.timuseum.org
The rich history of the Thousand Islands is reflected inside the museum, which, despite being founded in the 1960s, has become the driving force behind numerous annual events, including the Decoy Show and Christmas Festival of Trees. Mid-May-Labor Day, daily.

UNCLE SAM BOAT TOURS
45 James St., Alexandria Bay, 315-482-9611, 800-253-9229; www.usboattours.com
A variety of cruises are offered by this local boat company, which takes trips around the Thousand Islands, through Canadian and American waters and up the St. Lawrence Seaway, with stops at Boldt Castle and Alexandria Bay. Late April-October, daily.

SPECIAL EVENT
ANTIQUE BOAT SHOW
Antique Boat Museum, 750 Mary St., Clayton, 315-686-4104; www.abm.org
The show features more than 125 restored antique craft in addition to the museum's 200 antique boats, as well as sailing skiff races, a boat parade and an auction of boats. First weekend in August.

HOTEL
★FAIR WIND LODGE
38201 Highway 12 E., Clayton, 315-686-5251, 800-235-8331; www.fairwind.us
24 rooms. Closed mid-October-mid-May. $

RESTAURANTS
★★CLIPPER INN
126 State St., Clayton, 315-686-3842; www.clipperinn.com
American menu. Dinner. Closed November-March. Bar. Children's menu. $$

49

NEW YORK

★
★
★
★
★

★★THOUSAND ISLANDS INN

335 Riverside Drive, Clayton, 315-686-3030, 800-544-4241; www.1000-islands.com

American, seafood menu. Breakfast, lunch, dinner. Closed October-mid-May. Bar. Children's menu. **$$$**

COLD SPRING

If you're searching for the quintessential small-town atmosphere, Cold Spring on the Hudson River is a good choice. The Main Street shopping district attracts shoppers and visitors who just want to stroll the pretty streets. The surrounding area offers opportunities for outdoor recreation, including hiking, boating and kayaking. Don't miss the unique Hudson Fjord.

WHAT TO SEE AND DO
FOUNDRY SCHOOL MUSEUM

63 Chestnut St., Cold Spring, 845-265-4010; www.pchs-fsm.org

Visitors can learn a lot from this old-fashioned schoolroom, which contains West Point Foundry memorabilia, paintings, Native American artifacts and antiques. Maintained by the Putnam County Historical Society, the museum contains a genealogy and historical research library and rotating exhibits. Admission: adults $5, seniors and children 7-12 $2, children under 7 free. Wednesday-Sunday, 11 a.m.-5 p.m.; closed Monday-Tuesday.

HOTEL
★★★HUDSON HOUSE INN

2 Main St., Cold Spring, 845-265-9355; www.hudsonhouseinn.com

This circa-1832 country inn on the banks of the Hudson River offers 11 guest rooms and two suites. After settling in, head downstairs to dine in the country-styled restaurant or sup alfresco on the front porch with its terrific vistas out over the river and West Point. 11 rooms, two suites. Lunch, dinner, complimentary continental breakfast. Two restaurants, bar. **$$**

RESTAURANTS
★★★BRASSERIE LE BOUCHON

76 Main St., Cold Spring, 845-265-7676

This adorable French restaurant is as authentic as it gets. The menu reads like a greatest hits compilation of classic French cooking, from escargot kissed with garlic butter to hearty cassoulet. French menu. Dinner. Bar. Business casual attire. Reservations recommended. Outdoor seating. **$$**

★★HUDSON HOUSE INN

2 Main St., Cold Spring, 845-265-9355; www.hudsonhouseinn.com

Lunch, dinner. Closed holidays. Bar. Children's menu. Reservations recommended. **$$$**

★★★PLUMBUSH INN

1656 Route 9D, Cold Spring, 845-265-3904; www.plumbushinn.net

Just across the Hudson River from West Point, this Victorian inn offers elegant dinners in a romantic waterfront setting. The chef applies creative flair to the menu's appetizers while offering classic entrées such as venison stew served with roasted potato and vegetables. American menu. Lunch, dinner, Sunday brunch. Closed Monday-Tuesday. Bar. Valet parking. $$$

COLD SPRING HARBOR

John Lennon, Lindsay Lohan and Meg Whitman (CEO of eBay) have called Cold Spring Harbor home, and Billy Joel's first album was titled *Cold Spring Harbor*. Its cover featured a photo of Joel in front of a local beach.

Information: www.huntingtonchamber.com

WHAT TO SEE AND DO

COLD SPRING HARBOR WHALING MUSEUM

147 Main St., Cold Spring Harbor, 631-367-3418; www.cshwhalingmuseum.org

Fully equipped 19th-century whale boat from the brig *Daisy* is on display. Marine paintings, scrimshaw, ship models, changing exhibit gallery. Admission: adults $5, seniors and students 5-18 $4, children under 5 free. Tuesday-Sunday 11 a.m.-5 p.m.

RESTAURANT

★★INN ON THE HARBOR

105 Harbor Road, Cold Spring Harbor, 631-367-3166; www.105harbor.com

French menu. Lunch, dinner, Sunday brunch. Closed holidays. Bar. Valet parking. $$

CONGERS

Who would guess that you can enjoy the pastoral Hudson River Valley only 16 miles from Manhattan? Leisure activities here range from golf and boating to shopping and dining.

Information: www.rockland.org

RESTAURANT

★★★RESTAURANT X AND BULLY BOY BAR

117 N. Route 303, Congers, 845-268-6555; www.xaviars.com

Chef/owner Peter Kelly started off strong, opening the nationally praised Xavier's at Garrison at the young age of 23. Now, more than 15 years and three restaurants later, he wins kudos at this contemporary American restaurant in the woods of Rockland County. American menu. Lunch, dinner, Sunday brunch. Closed Monday; holidays. Bar. Casual attire. Reservations recommended. $$$

COOPERSTOWN

Founded by James Fenimore Cooper's father, Judge William Cooper, Cooperstown is in the center of "Leatherstocking" country. Here in 1839, on the south end of Otsego Lake, legend has it that Abner Doubleday devised modern baseball. The National Baseball Hall of Fame and Museum is located on Main Street.

Information: Chamber of Commerce, 31 Chestnut St., Cooperstown, 607-547-9983; www.cooperstownchamber.org

WHAT TO SEE AND DO

THE FARMERS' MUSEUM AND VILLAGE CROSSROADS

5775 State Highway 80, Cooperstown, 607-547-1450, 888-547-1450; www.farmersmuseum.org

An outdoor museum of rural life, this sprawling site showcases craftspeople presenting printing, weaving and blacksmithing in an historic setting. A village of historic buildings and a barn are filled with exhibits. The famous "Cardiff Giant," a 10-foot statue presented to the public in 1869 as a petrified prehistoric man, is here. April-October, daily.

FENIMORE ART MUSEUM

5798 State Highway 80, Cooperstown, 607-547-1400, 888-547-1450;
www.fenimoreartmuseum.org

This museum doubles as the headquarters of the New York State Historical Association and is filled with exhibits of American Indian art and artifacts, James Fenimore Cooper memorabilia, academic and decorative arts of the Romantic Era, a research library and a large American folk art collection. April-mid-May, Tuesday-Sunday 10 a.m.-4 p.m.; mid-May-mid-October, daily 10 a.m.-5 p.m.; mid-October-December: Tuesday-Sunday 10 a.m.-4 p.m.; closed holidays. Inquire about combination ticket with Farmers' Museum and/or National Baseball Hall of Fame.

GLIMMERGLASS STATE PARK

1527 County Highway 31, Cooperstown, 607-547-8662; www.nysparks.com/parks

The same Glimmerglass mentioned in James Fenimore Cooper's *Leatherstocking Tales*, this park overlooks Ostego Lake. Plenty of outdoor activities are available, including swimming, fishing, hiking, biking, cross-country skiing and picnicking. The park also has a bathhouse, playground and tent and trailer sites. Hyde Hall, the Clarke family mansion with a view of Otsego Lake, is nearby. Daily; closed holidays.

NATIONAL BASEBALL HALL OF FAME AND MUSEUM

25 Main St., Cooperstown, 607-547-7200, 888-425-5633;
www.baseballhalloffame.org

This nationally known museum is dedicated to the game and its players. The Hall of Fame Gallery contains plaques honoring the game's all-time greats. The museum features displays on baseball's greatest moments, the World Series, All-Star Games, ballparks and a complete history of the game. The theater presents a special multimedia show. Early September-late May: daily 9 a.m.-5 p.m.; late May-early September: daily 9 a.m.-9 p.m.; closed holidays.

SPECIAL EVENTS

AUTUMN HARVEST FESTIVAL

The Farmers' Museum and Village Crossroads, Lake Road, Cooperstown,
607-547-1450, 888-547-1450; www.farmersmuseum.org

Crafts, food and entertainment. Mid-September.

GLIMMERGLASS OPERA

Alice Busch Opera Theater, 7300 State Highway 80, Cooperstown, 607-547-2255;
www.glimmerglass.org

A great place to start a career, Glimmerglass Opera offers internships in production, administration and artistic administration. Our well-known internship program provides the opportunity for young professionals and students to experience firsthand the fast-paced world of repertory opera. Four productions, 28 performances. July-late August.

A BASEBALL KIND OF TOWN

Cooperstown is best known as the home of the Baseball Hall of Fame, and anyone who has an affinity for the game will love being immersed in it here. Not a baseball fan? Don't worry—the town also offers a variety of entertaining historic sites, activities, shops and restaurants.

Start by picking up a copy of the self-guided walking tour at the information kiosk in the **Chamber of Commerce** office (*31 Chestnut Street*). From there, turn right and walk into the heart of town. At the corner of Chestnut and Main is the Cooper Inn, which was built in 1813 and is surrounded by its own pocket park. Peek at the entrance hall and lobby, highlighted by paintings from the Fenimore Art Museum. Return to Main Street and walk east. On the right is Doubleday Field where, if your timing is right, a baseball game might be in progress.

Both sites of Main Street are lined with shops, many of which have baseball themes. Among these are **Cooperstown Bat Company** (*66 Main Street*), **America's Game** (*75 Main Street*), **National Pastime** (*81 Main Street*), **Third Base** (*83 Main Street*), **Where It All Began Bat Company** (*87 Main Street*), **The Cap Company** (*108 Main Street*), **Collector's World** (*139 Main Street*) and **Grand Slam Collectibles** (*134 Main Street*). Other Main Street shops of note are the **Cooperstown General Store** (*45 Main Street*) and **Cooperstown Kid Co.** (*131 Main Street*). Take a left onto alley-like Hoffman Lane, and visit the **Cooperstown Book Nook** (*1 Hoffman Lane*). Stop in next door for a meal at Hoffman Lane Bistro, a modern café with outdoor dining.

Return to Main Street, turn left and visit the **National Baseball Hall of Fame** (*25 Main Street*). The nearby **Doubleday Café** (*93 Main Street*) serves up good homemade food in a real small-town atmosphere. After lunch, head north on First Street and follow it to the end for nice views of Otsego Lake.

Go west on Lake Street for two blocks to Lake Front Park at the foot of Pioneer Street—a good spot for a picnic. From there, walk about two more blocks to the Otesaga Resort Hotel—it's the huge building on your right with the three-story columns guarding the entry portico. The lobby is immense and filled with fine art. Peek into the ballroom, decorated with circa-1910 murals by Blendon Campbell and a lounge on the back veranda overlooking the lake. The food here is excellent, too.

Continue walking—or hop on the village trolley—up Lake Street (now Highway 80) for about ½ mile, where the **Fenimore Art Museum** appears on the right and the **Farmers Museum** is on the left. You can spend between one and three hours in each of these venues. The Art Museum contains an outstanding collection of New York State-based art, excellent works from the Hudson River School and an American Indian Wing. The Farmers Museum is a 19th-century living history installation and working farm. Ride the village trolley back to town and visit the art galleries on Pioneer Street: the **Smithy-Pioneer Gallery** and the **Leatherstocking Brush** and **Palette Club**.

HOTELS

★BEST WESTERN INN AND SUITES AT THE COMMONS

50 Commons Drive, Cooperstown, 607-547-7100; www.bestwestern.com

62 rooms. Complimentary continental breakfast. Fitness center. High-speed Internet access. Pool. $

★HICKORY GROVE MOTOR INN

6854 Highway 80, Cooperstown, 607-547-9874, 877-547-9874;
www.hickorygrovemotorinn.com

12 rooms. Closed mid-October-mid-April. $

★★LAKE FRONT MOTEL

10 Fair St., Cooperstown, 607-547-9511; www.lakefrontmotelandrestaurant.com

45 rooms. Daily boat tours, Restaurant, bar. $

★★★OTESAGA RESORT

60 Lake St., Cooperstown, 607-547-9931, 800-348-6222; www.otesaga.com

The elegant accommodations and lovely surroundings of this grand lakeside resort have been a draw for visitors since 1909. The Federalist-style building, with its large wood-columned portico and stunning veranda that overlooks Lake Otsego, is part of the Historic Hotels of America. Spacious guest rooms feature a charming, antique feel, yet include amenities such as wireless high-speed Internet access. The championship 18-hole Leatherstocking Golf Course is adjacent, and tennis, fishing, jogging, biking and horseback riding are available. 136 rooms. Closed December-mid-April. Complimentary continental breakfast. High-speed Internet access. Two restaurants, two bars.

SPECIALTY LODGING

THE INN AT COOPERSTOWN

16 Chestnut St., Cooperstown, 607-547-5756; www.innatcooperstown.com

This former annex to the Fenimore Hotel was built in 1874 and features Victorian furnishings. The Inn offers clean, comfortable lodging just a short stroll from the National Baseball Hall of Fame, shopping and fine dining. Luxury suite with two fireplaces, a spa bath, flatscreen televisions. 17 rooms. Complimentary continental breakfast. High-speed Internet access. $$

RESTAURANT

★★PEPPER MILL

5418 State Highway 28, Cooperstown, 607-547-8550; www.cooperstownpeppermill.com

Dinner. Restaurant. Closed holidays; January-March. Bar. Children's menu. $$

CORNING

This world glassmaking center began to grow when completion of the Chemung Canal brought in shipments of Pennsylvania anthracite, a type of coal. In 1868, lower fuel and materials costs attracted the Brooklyn Flint Glass Works, incorporated in 1875 as the Corning Glass Works. Mass production of bulbs for Thomas A. Edison's electric light soon began. The city's central shopping district has been restored to its 1890s appearance.

Information: Chamber of Commerce, 1 West Market St., Corning, 607-936-4686;
www.corningny.com

WHAT TO SEE AND DO

BENJAMIN PATTERSON INN MUSEUM COMPLEX

59 W. Pulteney St., Corning, 607-937-5281; www.pattersoninnmuseum.org

The central attraction at this complex is a restored and furnished 1796 inn, originally built to encourage settlement in Genesee Country. The two-story structure includes a public room and kitchen on the first floor and a ballroom and two bedrooms on the second floor. The DeMonstoy Log Cabin (circa 1785), Browntown one-room schoolhouse (1878), Starr Barn with agricultural exhibit (circa 1860) and blacksmith shop (circa 1820) are also on site. Monday-Friday, 10 a.m.-4 p.m.; June-August, Saturday 10 a.m.-2 p.m.

CORNING MUSEUM OF GLASS

One Museum Way, Corning, 607-937-5371, 800-732-6845; www.cmog.org

More than 25,000 objects are on display in this real-life glass menagerie, including outstanding pieces of both antique and modern Steuben glass and an 11-foot-high leaded glass window designed by Tiffany Studios in 1905. The library has the most complete collection of materials on glass in the world. The Steuben Factory, the only factory in the world that produces Steuben crystal, features skilled craftsmen transforming hot molten glass into fine crystal. Memorial Day-Labor Day: daily 9 a.m.-8 p.m.; rest of year: daily 9 a.m.-5 p.m.; closed holidays.

ROCKWELL MUSEUM OF WESTERN ART

111 Cedar St., Corning, 607-937-5386; www.rockwellmuseum.org

Along with antique firearms and changing exhibits, this museum contains the largest collection of American Western art in the East, including paintings by Remington, Russell, Bierstadt, Catlin and others. The museum also offers a combination ticket in conjunction with the Corning Glass Museum. Memorial Day-Labor Day: daily 9 a.m.-8 p.m.; rest of year: daily 9 a.m.-5 p.m.

HOTELS

★COMFORT INN

66 W. Pulteney St., Corning, 607-962-1515, 877-424-6423; www.comfortinn.com

62 rooms. Wireless Internet access. Fitness center. Complimentary continental breakfast. $

★★DAYS INN

23 Riverside Drive, Corning, 607-936-9370, 800-329-7466; www.daysinn.com

56 rooms. Wireless Internet access. Complimentary continental breakfast. Pool. Pets not accepted. $

★GATE HOUSE MOTEL

11409 E. LPGA Drive, Corning, 607-936-4131

20 rooms. Restaurant. $

★★RADISSON HOTEL CORNING

125 Denison Parkway E., Corning, 607-962-5000, 800-333-3333; www.radisson.com

177 rooms. High-speed Internet access. Pool. Restaurant, bar. Pets accepted $

SPECIALTY LODGING
ROSEWOOD INN
134 E. First St., Corning, 607-962-3253; www.rosewoodinn.com

An ideal place for antique lovers, this elegant Victorian house sits among other period homes and is a short walk from downtown Corning. From the moment the owner greets you at the door (in full Victorian attire, no less), to the antique linens and lace in each room, to the full, formal breakfast served each morning, a stay at this inn is memorable. Seven rooms. Complimentary full breakfast. **$$**

RESTAURANT
★★LONDON UNDERGROUND CAFE
69 E. Market St., Corning, 607-962-2345; www.londonundergroundcafe.biz

American menu. Lunch, dinner. Closed Sunday; holidays. Children's menu. Casual attire. Outdoor seating. **$$**

CORONA
Paul Simon immortalized this area of Queens in his 1972 song *Me and Julio Down by the Schoolyard* when he sang, "Goodbye to Rosie, the queen of Corona."
Information: www.queenschamber.org

RESTAURANT
★★PARK SIDE
107-01 Corona Ave., Corona, 718-271-9274; www.parksiderestaurant.com

Italian menu. Lunch, dinner. Bar. Valet parking. Outdoor seating. **$$**

CORTLAND
Cortland lies in the midst of rich farming country and is the home of the State University College at Cortland.
Information: Cortland County Convention and Visitors Bureau, 37 Church St., Cortland, 607-753-8463, 800-859-2227; www.cortlandtourism.com

WHAT TO SEE AND DO
1890 HOUSE MUSEUM
37 Tompkins St., Cortland, 607-756-7551; www.1890house.org

Built in a style known as Victorian chateauesque, the former mansion of industrialist Chester F. Wickwire has four stories and 30 rooms adorned with hand-carved cherry and oak woodwork, stained- and painted-glass windows, parquet floors and elaborate stenciling. The house remained in the Wickwire family until 1974. Friday-Saturday 1-4 p.m.; closed holidays.

CORTLAND COUNTRY MUSIC PARK
1804 Route 13, Cortland, 607-753-0377; www.cortlandcountrymusicpark.com

The self-proclaimed "Nashville of the Northeast," this Hall of Fame museum and park has an Opry Barn with a large dance floor, an outdoor stage and a memorial garden. It hosts concerts, dinner theater, dance classes and bingo.

FILLMORE GLEN STATE PARK

1686 Highway 38, Cortland, 315-497-0130; www.nysparks.com/parks

This park is home to a replica of President Millard Fillmore's birthplace cabin. The park itself offers a full-service cottage located on the shore of Cayuga Lake at Long Point. Cottage amenities include a full kitchen and bath, hot water, electricity, sleeping arrangements, furniture, dining table with chairs, a wood stove, boat dock, picnic table and a fire ring and grill. Flow through natural pool, bathhouse; hiking trails, picnicking, playground area, cross-country skiing, snowmobiling, tent and trailer sites, cabins. Mid-May-mid-October.

GREEK PEAK MOUNTAIN RESORT

2000 Highway 392, Cortland, 607-835-6111, 800-995-2754; www.greekpeak.net

Eight chairlifts, one tubing lift; patrol, school, adaptive ski program, rentals; snowmaking; cafeteria, restaurants, lounges; ski shop, nursery. Lodging (year-round), longest run 1½ miles; vertical drop 952 feet. Cross-country trails. December-April, daily, depending on weather conditions.

LABRADOR MOUNTAIN

Highway 91, Truxton, 607-842-6204, 800-446-9559; www.labradormtn.com

Triple, two double chairlifts; T-bar; snowboarding; two ski shops, patrol, school, rentals; snowmaking; cafeterias, restaurant, bar; nursery. Longest run 1½ miles; vertical drop 700 feet. Twenty-four slopes. December-March, daily; closed holidays.

SONG MOUNTAIN

1 Song Mountain Road, Tully, 315-696-5711; www.songmountain.com

Double and triple chairlifts, two T-bars, J-bar; patrol, school, rentals; snowmaking; restaurant, cafeteria, bar. Longest run one mile; vertical drop 700 feet. December-March, daily. Summer: 3,000-foot Alpine Slide. Mid-June-Labor Day: daily; late May-mid-June and rest of September: weekends only.

SUGGETT HOUSE MUSEUM AND KELLOGG MEMORIAL RESEARCH LIBRARY

25 Homer Ave., Cortland, 607-756-6071; www.cortland.org/ent/museums

Headquarters of the Cortland County Historical Society, the museum houses vignettes of home arts from 1825 to 1900, including an 1882 kitchen. The circa 1880 building also contains military memorabilia, local art, a children's room and changing exhibits. The library has local history and genealogy material. Tuesday-Saturday 1-4 p.m.; library to 5 p.m.; other times by appointment; closed holidays.

SPECIAL EVENTS
CENTRAL NEW YORK MAPLE FESTIVAL

42 Front St., Marathon, 607-849-3812; www.maplefest.org

A variety of events showing the process of making maple syrup; also arts and crafts, hay rides and entertainment. Early April.

CORTLAND REPERTORY THEATRE

Dwyer Memorial County Park Pavilion Theatre, 37 Franklin St., Cortland,
607-753-6161, 800-427-6160; www.cortlandrep.org

The Cortland Repertory Theatre performs musicals, comedies and dramas in the Edward Jones Playhouse of the Little York Pavilion, a former trolley park pavilion now listed on the National Historic Register. Tuesday-Sunday evenings. Mid-June-early-September.

HOTELS

★★★BENN CONGER INN

206 W. Cortland St., Groton, 607-898-5817; www.benncongerinn.com

This property is located near downtown Ithaca, wineries, antique shops, horseback riding and more. The inn, a Greek Revival mansion and former home of Benn Conger, the founder of Smith Corona, features large rooms with custom mattresses and imported linens. A five-course breakfast is included. 10 rooms. Complimentary breakfast. Restaurant, bar. Airport transportation available. **$$$**

★COMFORT INN

2 1/2 Locust Ave., Cortland, 607-753-7721; www.comfortinn.com

66 rooms. Complimentary continental breakfast. Restaurant. Wireless Internet access. Children's activity center. **$**

★HAMPTON INN

26 River St., Cortland, 607-662-0007; www.hampton-inn.com

111 rooms. Complimentary continental breakfast. High-speed Internet access. Business center. Fitness center. **$**

CROWN POINT

Located on a peninsula that forms the northernmost narrows of Lake Champlain, the Point was a strong position from which to control the trade route between New York and Canada during the French and Indian War.

Information: Ticonderoga Area Chamber of Commerce, 94 Montcalm, Ticonderoga,
518-585-6619; www.ticonderogany.com

WHAT TO SEE AND DO

CROWN POINT RESERVATION STATE CAMPGROUND

784 Bridge Road, Crown Point, 518-597-3603; www.dec.ny.gov/outdoor

Fishing, boating, camping. Mid-April-mid-October.

CROWN POINT STATE HISTORIC SITE

739 Bridge Road, Crown Point, 518-597-3666; www.nysparks.com/sites

Preserved ruins of fortifications occupied by French, British and American forces during the French and Indian and Revolutionary wars: Fort St. Frederic (1734) and Fort Crown Point (1759). Site museum with exhibits on history of area. Self-guided tours; events. Grounds: May-October, daily 9 a.m.-dusk; Museum: Monday, Wednesday-Sunday 9 a.m.-5 p.m.

PENFIELD HOMESTEAD MUSEUM

703 Creek Road, Crown Point, 518-597-3804; www.penfieldmuseum.org

A museum of local history built around the Adirondack iron industry, Penfield offers self-guided tour through the ironworks ruins and is the site of the first industrial use of electricity in the United States. June-October, Thursday-Sunday 11 a.m.-4 p.m.

HOTELS

★★CANOE ISLAND LODGE

3820 Lakeshore Drive, Diamond Point, 518-668-5592; www.canoeislandlodge.com

65 rooms. Breakfast, dinner. Closed mid-October-mid-May. Restaurant, bar. Children's activity center. Beach. **$$$**

★TREASURE COVE RESORT MOTEL

3940 Lake Shore Drive, Diamond Point, 518-668-5334; www.treasurecoveresort.com

Swimming, motor boat. 50 rooms. Closed mid-October-April. Children's activity center. Beach. **$**

DOVER PLAINS

Small-town appeal abounds in Dover Plains, which is surrounded by lush hills in Eastern New York.

Information: www.townofdover.us

RESTAURANT

★★★OLD DROVERS INN

196 E. Duncan Hill Road and Old Route 22, Dover Plains, 845-832-9311;
www.olddroversinn.com

This elegant inn built in 1750 is located near vineyards, the Hudson Valley and the Berkshires. Visitors here can explore the nearby Vanderbilt Mansion, the Culinary Institute of America, the Franklin D. Roosevelt Home or enjoy riverboat tours on the Hudson. The very chic, candlelit Tap Room prepares specialties such as pan-seared Long Island duck with figs and dates and turkey hash with sautéed spinach. Lunch, dinner. Closed Wednesday; Christmas. Bar. Outdoor seating. **$$**

DUNKIRK

A pleasant city southwest of Buffalo on the shores of Lake Erie about 35 miles from the Pennsylvania border, Dunkirk was the birthplace of author-historian Samuel Hopkins Adams.

Information: Northern Chautauqua Chamber of Commerce, 212 Lakeshore Drive W., Dunkirk, 716-366-6200; www.tourchautauqua.com

WHAT TO SEE AND DO

DUNKIRK LIGHTHOUSE

1 Lighthouse Point Drive, Dunkirk, 716-366-5050; www.dunkirklighthouse.com

Built in 1875; 10 rooms in lighthouse with a room dedicated to each branch of the military service; also a lighthouse keeper's room; Victorian furnishings in kitchen and parlor. Guided tour includes tower and history of the Great Lakes. June-September: daily; April-June and September-October: Monday-Tuesday and Thursday-Saturday.

EVANGOLA STATE PARK

10191 Old Lake Shore Road, Irving, 716-549-1802; www.evangolastatepark.com

This 733-acre park opened in 1954. It was formerly a farmland; the land was used to grow tomatoes, beans and corn. Since the very beginning, Evangola's major attraction has been its arc-shaped shoreline and natural sand beach. The park has a variety of habitats (including lakeshore, woodland, meadow and wetlands), and wildlife such as white-tailed deer, raccoons, turkey and red-tailed hawks call Evangola home. The park receives more than 100,000 visitors each year. Swimming, 4,000-foot sand beach, bathhouse, lifeguards, fishing; nature trails, hiking, cross-country skiing, snowmobiling, picnicking, playground, game areas, tent and trailer sites.

HISTORICAL MUSEUM OF THE DARWIN R. BARKER LIBRARY

7 Day St., Fredonia, 716-672-8051; www.barkerlibrary.org

Period furniture, 1880s parlor; exhibits on Fredonia and Pomfret; documents, photos, portraits and genealogical material; children's museum, education programs. Tuesday, Thursday-Saturday 2:30 p.m.-4:30 p.m.

SPECIAL EVENT
CHAUTAUQUA COUNTY FAIR

1089 Central Ave., Dunkirk, 716-366-4752; www.chautauquacountyfair.org

The Chautauqua County Fair has been going on for more than 127 years. Expect rides, games and food in the fair's midway. Last week in July.

HOTELS
★★DAYS INN

10455 Bennett Road, Fredonia, 716-673-1351; www.daysinn.com

135 rooms. Complimentary continental breakfast. High-speed Internet access. Commercial services. Tennis. Fitness center. Restaurant, bar. Pets accepted. $

★★★THE WHITE INN

52 E. Main St., Fredonia, 716-672-2103, 888-373-3664; www.whiteinn.com

This inn has all the comfort and charm of a country manor and offers eloquently decorated rooms and suites and fine dining, as well as a location close to cultural, historical and recreational attractions. 23 rooms. Complimentary full breakfast. Restaurant, bar. $$

EAST AURORA

East Aurora lies very close to the large industrial center of Buffalo. In the early 1900s, Elbert Hubbard, author of *A Message to Garcia,* lived here and made it the home of the Roycroft, a handicraft community known for making fine books, copper and leather ware and furniture. The Roycroft campus is still operating, and it is the only continuous operation of its kind in America today. East Aurora is also the headquarters of Fisher-Price toys. The Baker Memorial Methodist Church, which has hand-signed Tiffany windows, is located here.

Information: Greater East Aurora Chamber of Commerce, 431 Main St.,
East Aurora, 716-652-8444, 800-441-2881; www.eanycc.com

WHAT TO SEE AND DO

THE ELBERT HUBBARD MUSEUM

363 Oakwood Ave., East Aurora, 716-652-4735; www.roycrofter.com

This five-bedroom, 1910 Craftsman period home built by and for the Roycrofters is a testament to their handiwork. It contains Roycroft furniture, modeled leather, hammered metal, leaded glass, books, pamphlets and other artifacts from 1895 to 1938. There's also material on Elbert Hubbard, author of the famous essay *A Message to Garcia*. June-October, Wednesday, Saturday-Sunday 1-4 p.m.; tours by appointment.

KISSING BRIDGE SKI AREA

10296 State Road, Glenwood, 716-592-4963; www.kbski.com

This bridge area has two quad, four double chairlifts, two T-bars, J-bar and handle tow. Moreover, it has a school and snow-gear rentals. Longest run 3,500 feet; vertical drop 550 feet. Night skiing. December-March, daily.

MILLARD FILLMORE MUSEUM

24 Shearer Ave., East Aurora, 716-652-8875

This is the house President Millard Fillmore built for his wife in 1825. It contains memorabilia, furnishings and a 1830s herb and rose garden. The Carriage house, built in 1830 of lumber from the former Nathaniel Fillmore farm, contains antique tools and a Fillmore sleigh. June-October: Wednesday, Saturday-Sunday 1-4 p.m.; rest of year: by appointment.

SPECIAL EVENT

TOYFEST

636 Girard Ave., East Aurora, 716-687-5151; www.toytownusa.com

This annual celebration commemorates Fisher-Price Toy Company's establishment here in the 1930s. Last weekend in August.

HOTEL

★★★ROYCROFT INN

40 S. Grove St., East Aurora, 716-652-5552, 800-267-0525; www.roycroftinn.com

Visit this birthplace of the New York Arts and Crafts movement, located just 30 minutes from Buffalo. The grounds, called the Roycroft Campus, originally housed 500 craftsmen and their shops and now are a national landmark. Rooms are breathtaking showcases of original furniture and fixtures. 22 rooms. Complimentary continental breakfast. Restaurant, bar. $$

RESTAURANTS

★★OLD ORCHARD INN

2095 Blakeley Corners Road, East Aurora, 716-652-4664; www.oldorchardny.com

A century-old rustic country inn, this former hunting lodge offers hearty food in a warm atmosphere. During the summer months, enjoy its covered patio seating or wander through the property's 25 woodsy acres. American menu. Lunch, dinner. Closed Monday-Tuesday; also January-April. Bar. Casual attire. Outdoor seating. $$$

★★★ROYCROFT INN

40 S. Grove St., East Aurora, 716-652-5552; www.roycroftinn.com

This inn originally opened in 1905 to accommodate the thousands of visitors to the thriving Roycroft Arts and Crafts Community, a large, self-contained group of writers and craftspeople. Now a National Landmark that has been restored to early 1900s Arts and Crafts style, the inn preserves this history in its original and reproduction furnishings. A popular gathering place for locals, the restaurant serves creative and fresh cuisine with continental influences, including French onion soup au gratin, rack of lamb and sesame-encrusted tuna. American menu. Lunch, dinner, Sunday brunch. Bar. Children's menu. Casual attire. Reservations recommended. Outdoor seating. $$

EAST BLOOMFIELD

This small town in the Finger Lakes region of New York has historic buildings that date back to 1794. Stop by for a stroll of the village center and its antique shops.

RESTAURANT

★★★HOLLOWAY HOUSE

29 State St., East Bloomfield, 585-657-7120; www.thehollowayhouse.com

Housed in an 1808 stagecoach tavern, this seasonal restaurant has been owned by the Wayne family for more than 47 years and serves comfort fare such as seafood Newburg and sautéed chicken breast stuffed with cranberries. American, seafood menu. Lunch, dinner. Closed Monday; also late December-March. Bar. Children's menu. $$

EAST HAMPTON

East Hampton is an old Long Island village founded in 1648 by a group of farmers. Agriculture was the main livelihood until the mid-1800s, when the town began to develop into a fashionable resort. Today, the town glitters in the summer months when celebrities and wealthy Manhattanites escape to their palaces by the sea.

Information: East Hampton Chamber of Commerce, 79 A Main St.,
East Hampton, 631-324-0362; www.easthamptonchamber.com

WHAT TO SEE AND DO

GUILD HALL MUSEUM

158 Main St., East Hampton, 631-324-0806; www.guildhall.org

Regional art exhibits; changing shows. Art and poetry lectures, classes. Library covering art and artists of the region. June-September: Monday-Saturday 11 a.m.-5 p.m. Sunday from noon; rest of year: Thursday-Saturday 11 a.m.-5 p.m. Sunday from noon; closed holidays.

HISTORIC CLINTON ACADEMY

151 Main St., East Hampton, 631-324-6850; www.easthamptonhistory.org

The first preparatory school in New York is now a museum housing a collection of Eastern Long Island artifacts. Late May-mid-October, Saturday 10 a.m.-5 p.m., Sunday noon-5 p.m.; July-August, Friday 10 a.m.-5 p.m.

HISTORIC MULFORD FARM

10 James Lane, East Hampton, 631-324-6850; www.easthamptonhistory.org

This living history museum and farm features 18th-century New England architecture, colonial history, period rooms and costumed interpretation. Late May-mid-October, Saturday 10 a.m.-5 p.m., Sunday noon-5 p.m.; July-August, Friday 10 a.m.-5 p.m.

HOME, SWEET HOME HOUSE

14 James Lane, East Hampton, 631-324-0713; www.easthampton.com/homesweethome

Named after the popular 19th-century song, *Home, Sweet Home*, written by John Howard Payne, this house was originally owned by Payne's grandfather, Aaron Isaacs (the first Jewish person to settle in the area). The historic house features beautiful antiques and china and is dedicated to Payne, who was also an actor, playwright and diplomat. Monday-Saturday 10 a.m.-4 p.m., Sunday 2-4 p.m.

JOHN DREW THEATER AT GUILD HALL

158 Main St., East Hampton, 631-324-0806; www.guildhall.org

A 382-seat theater for films, plays, concerts, lectures and children's performances.

POLLOCK-KRASNER HOUSE AND STUDY CENTER

830 Fireplace Road, East Hampton, 631-324-4929; www.naples.cc.sunysb.edu/CAS

Abstract Expressionist artist Jackson Pollock's studio and house, plus a reference library on 20th-century American art, are open to the public. May, September-October: Saturday, by appointment only; June-August: Thursday-Saturday, by appointment only.

HOTELS

★★★THE 1770 HOUSE

143 Main St., East Hampton, 631-324-1770; www.1770house.com

This restored 18th-century house boasts antique furnishings and a prime location close to East Hampton's stellar shopping and restaurants. The rooms are sumptuous and elegant with Frette linens and flatscreen televisions. Seven rooms. Children over 12 years only. Restaurant, bar. $$$

★★★MAIDSTONE ARMS

207 Main St., East Hampton, 631-324-5006; www.maidstonearms.com

The Osborne family built this estate as a private residence in the 1750s, and the terrifically situated property has been operating as an inn since the 1870s. Enjoy the bustle of the Hamptons during the summer months or settle in by the fireplaces during cozy winter stays. 19 rooms. Complimentary full breakfast. Restaurant, bar. $$$

SPECIALTY LODGING

THE BAKER HOUSE 1650

181 Main St., East Hampton, 631-324-4081; www.bakerhouse1650.com

This stuccoed English Tudor house in the Hamptons has been refurbished into a quaint inn. Enjoy a relaxing afternoon in the cottage's living room—a perfect spot to sit and read a book. Five rooms. High-speed Internet access. Spa. $$$

ART IN THE HAMPTONS

The history of art in the Hamptons can be traced back to the Montauket and Shinnecock Indians, who transformed seashells into wonderful wampum they traded with 17th-century colonists. By the 1870s, the area's luminous light, fertile farmlands and sandy shores lured painters to a rural countryside that reminded them of Europe. The artists—Winslow Homer, Edwin Austin Abbey, John Twachtman and William Merritt Chase—called themselves "The Tile Club" and created what became the second-oldest art colony in America.

As time passed, artists continued to move eastward. Childe Hassam arrived in the 1920s. In the 1940s, Jackson Pollock and Lee Krasner, Willem and Elaine de Kooning and Robert Motherwell reinterpreted the landscape according to their individual sensitivities. Abstract Expressionism attracted more artists and the first of dozens of art galleries opened. (This first gallery is now known as the **Elaine Benson Gallery and Sculpture Garden**, *2317 Montauk Highway, Bridgehampton; 631-537-3233*.) Artists from the New York School displayed their work and exhibitions, including pop artist Larry Rivers, cubist Fernand Leger, abstract painter Harry Kramer, glass artist Dale Chihuly, sculptor Louise Nevelson, ceramist Toshiko Takaezu and jeweler David Yurman.

Most of the art galleries are found in the villages of Southampton, Westhampton Beach and East Hampton. On just one tiny passageway between Main Street and the public parking lot in East Hampton, art lovers can stop in to **Vered** (*68 Park Place, 631-324-3303*) and see work by Marc Chagall, Pablo Picasso, Henri Matisse, Ben Shahn, David Hockney and Louise Nevelson. The **Wallace Gallery**, across the Passage (*37A Main Street, 631-329-4516*), displays a retrospective of local landscapes and seascapes that reflect the authentic history of the region, including work by east-end artists Edward Lamson Henry, Thomas Moran and Childe Hassam.

Guild Hall (*158 Main Street, East Hampton, 631-324-0806*) provides exciting lectures, films, music and live theatrical performances at the John Drew Theater. Its fine art exhibitions often focus on regional artists. The **Parrish Art Museum** (*25 Job's Lane, Southampton, 631-283-2118*) has the largest public collection of the works of William Merritt Chase and Fairfield Porter. This leading cultural institution offers changing exhibitions, lectures, films and concerts, as well as children's events. Its sculpture garden and arboretum provide a pleasant refuge from the shops on Job's Lane. Art aficionados flock to the **Ossorio Foundation** (*164 Mariner Drive, Southampton, 631-287-2020*) and to the **Pollock-Krasner House and Study Center** (*830 Fireplace Road, East Hampton, 631-324-4929*).

RESTAURANTS

★★★ALISON AT THE MAIDENSTONE ARMS

207 Main St., East Hampton, 631-324-5440; www.alisonrestaurant.com

Alison is frequently visited by celebrities such as Scarlett Johannson, Christy Turlington, Ed Burns, Julianne Moore, Shirley MacLaine, Betsey Johnson, and more. The restaurant is housed inside a charming white clapboard inn with striped awnings.

The real attraction is on the plates, though: the restaurant serves a range of hearty and light contemporary dishes. Wrap up dinner with a cigar and a game of backgammon in the Water Room Lounge. American menu. Breakfast, lunch, dinner. Bar. $$$$

★★★DELLA FEMINA
99 N. Main St., East Hampton, 631-329-6666; www.dellafemina.com
This happening eatery boasts a sunken bar area complete with caricatures of famous regulars like Martha Stewart. On the menu, you'll find such favorites as yellowfin tuna tartare, maple-soy pork loin chops, roasted chicken with rosemary jus and pan-roasted day boat halibut. The sizable wine list includes many premium wines and a number of boutique and hand-crafted selections. American menu. Dinner. Closed Wednesday in the off-season. Bar. Casual attire. Outdoor seating. $$$

★★★EAST HAMPTON POINT
295 Three Mile Harbor Road, East Hampton, 631-329-2800;
www.easthamptonpoint.com
With stunning waterfront and sunset vistas, East Hampton Point serves dishes such as roasted Scottish salmon with asparagus and morel risotto and a truffle-leek sauce, and Maine halibut with black olives, tomatoes, fennel and baby artichokes. American menu. Lunch, dinner. Closed September-March. Bar. Children's menu. Casual attire. Reservations recommended. Valet parking. Outdoor seating. $$$

★★MICHAEL'S
28 Maidstone Park Road, East Hampton, 631-324-0725
Seafood, American menu. Dinner. Casual attire. $$

★★NICK & TONI'S
136 N. Main St., East Hampton, 631-324-3550; www.nickandtonis.com
Mediterranean menu. Dinner, Sunday brunch. Bar. Casual attire. Reservations recommended. $$$

★★PALM
94 Main St., East Hampton, 631-324-0411; www.thepalm.com
Seafood, steak menu. Dinner. Bar. Casual attire. $$$

EAST NORWICH
In Nassau County on Long Island, East Norwich offers beautiful views of the water.
Information: www.visitoysterbay.com

EAST SYRACUSE
This aptly named town is about five miles east of Syracuse. It offers small-town amenities near this metropolitan hub.
Information: Greater Syracuse Chamber of Commerce, 572 South Salina St.,
Syracuse, www.syracusechamber.com

HOTEL
★★HILTON GARDEN INN
6004 Fair Lakes Road, East Syracuse, 315-431-4800; www.hiltongardeninn.com
100 rooms. High-speed Internet access. Restaurant, bar. Business center. No pets. $

★★JUSTIN'S GRILL

6400 Yorktown Circle, East Syracuse, 315-437-1461; www.justins-grill.com
Steak menu. Lunch, dinner. Closed Sunday; holidays. Bar. Children's menu. $$

EASTCHESTER

This small town about 20 miles north of New York City was settled in 1664. U.S. President John Adams lived here for a short time during his presidency when a yellow fever epidemic broke out in Philadelphia. During that time, the White House was temporarily located here at Adams' daughter's house.

Information: www.eastchester.org

RESTAURANT
★★PINOCCHIO

309 White Plains Road, Eastchester, 914-337-0044
Italian menu. Dinner. Closed Monday. Bar. Casual attire. Reservations recommended. Outdoor seating. $$

ELLENVILLE

Center of the Ulster County resort area, Ellenville offers abundant scenic beauty. Hang gliding is popular here.

Information: Chamber of Commerce, 81 North Main St., Ellenville, 845-647-7080; www.ellenvilleny.org

HOTELS
★★HUDSON VALLEY RESORT AND SPA

400 Granite Road, Kerhonkson, 845-626-8888, 888-948-3766; www.hudsonvalleyresort.com
296 rooms. Restaurant, bar. Golf. Children's activity center. Ski in/ski out. $

★★NEVELE GRANDE RESORT

1 Nevele Road, Ellenville, 800-647-6000; www.nevele.com
900 rooms. Restaurant, bar. Children's activity center. Spa. Ski in/ski out. $

ELMIA

Elmira is on both shores of the Chemung River—it's located on a site where, in 1779, the Sullivan-Clinton expedition found an American Indian village. By the mid-19th century, railroads and canals were opening new fields of industry here; first lumber, later metalworking and textiles. Samuel Clemens (Mark Twain) spent more than 20 summers at Quarry Farm, the Elmira country home of his wife's sister, Susan Crane. Elmira also is the birthplace of noted filmmaker Hal Roach, fashion designer Tommy Hilfiger and astronaut Eileen Collins, the first woman to pilot a space shuttle.

Information: Chemung County Chamber of Commerce, 400 E. Church St., Elmira, 607-734-5137, 800-627-5892; www.chemungchamber.org

WHAT TO SEE AND DO

ARNOT ART MUSEUM

235 Lake St., Elmira, 607-734-3697; www.arnotartmuseum.org

An 1833 mansion with a three-story wing. Includes 17th- and 19th-century European paintings displayed in 1880 gallery; 19th-century American gallery; also changing exhibits. Tuesday-Sunday 10 a.m.-5 p.m., Sunday from 1 p.m.; closed holidays.

CHEMUNG VALLEY HISTORY MUSEUM

415 E. Water St., Elmira, 607-734-4167; www.chemungvalleymuseum.org

The Chemung Valley History Museum goes over the history of the Chemung River Valley region by showcasing a collection of artifacts that focuses on the Southern Tier of New York State and neighboring Northern Pennsylvania. Local history displays. Mark Twain exhibit, research library; special events. Tuesday-Saturday, 10 a.m.-5 p.m.; Sunday 1-5 p.m.; closed holidays.

ELMIRA COLLEGE

1 Park Place, Elmira, 607-735-1941; www.elmira.edu

Coeducational since 1969, Elmira College was the first to grant women degrees equal to those of men in 1855. The Mark Twain Study was presented to the college by the Langdon Family in 1952. Clemens did much of his writing here, including *The Adventures of Huckleberry Finn*. The Mark Twain exhibit in Hamilton Hall has memorabilia. Study and exhibit, summer: Monday-Saturday; rest of year: by appointment.

HARRIS HILL PARK

557 Harris Hill Road, Elmira, 607-732-1210; www.harrishillamusements.com

High above the valley, this park offers picnicking, a playground, swimming pools, grills and summertime amusements including batting cages, miniature golf and go-karts. Birthday room available, picnic area and pool.

NATIONAL SOARING MUSEUM

51 Soaring Hill Drive, Elmira, 607-734-3128; www.soaringmuseum.org

Features a large collection of soaring planes that depict the history of this type of motorless flight. The simulator is a good place to test what soaring feels like before signing up for the real thing. Daily 10 a.m.-5 p.m.

WINGS OF EAGLES DISCOVERY CENTER

Elmira-Corning Regional Airport, 17 Aviation Drive, Horseheads, 607-739-8200; www.wingsofeagles.com

Dedicated to preserving the planes, engines and memories of those who molded aviation heritage. Museum houses interactive displays, exhibits, aircrafts. November-April, Wednesday-Saturday 10 a.m.-4 p.m., Sunday noon-4 p.m.; May-October, Monday-Saturday 10 a.m.-4 p.m., Sunday noon-4 p.m.; closed holidays.

HOTELS

★BEST WESTERN MARSHALL MANOR

3527 Watkins Road, Horseheads, 607-739-3891, 800-780-7234; www.bestwestern.com

40 rooms. Complimentary continental breakfast. Restaurants. Outdoor pool. High-speed Internet access. Pets accepted. $

★
★
★
★
☆

★★HOLIDAY INN

760 E. Water St., Elmira, 607-734-4211; www.holidayinn.com

149 rooms. Restaurant, bar. Fitness center. High-speed Internet access. Pool. **$**

RESTAURANT

★★HILL TOP INN

171 Jerusalem Hill Road, Elmira, 607-732-6728, 888-444-5586; www.hill-top-inn.com

American menu. Dinner. Closed Sunday; also November-February. Bar. Children's menu. Business casual attire. Reservations recommended. Outdoor seating. **$$**

FINGER LAKES

Scientists say glaciers scooped out the Finger Lakes, resulting in one of the most delightful landscaping jobs in America. There are 11 lakes in all, and Canandaigua, Keuka, Seneca, Cayuga, Owasco and Skaneateles are the largest. The smaller lakes also have the characteristic finger shape. Seneca is the deepest at 630 feet and Cayuga the longest at 40 miles. The region has many glens and gorges with plunging streams. Hundreds of recreation spots dot the shores, offering every imaginable sport. The famous New York State wine grapes grow in the many miles of vineyards in the area.

Information: www.fingerlakes.org

FISHKILL

In the Hudson River Valley, this area is a great place to commune with Mother Nature, brush up on your American history or just enjoy a day strolling along its historic streets.

Information: Dutchess County Tourism Promotion Agency, 3 Neptune Road, Poughkeepsie, 914-463-4000, 800-445-3131; www.dutchesstourism.com

WHAT TO SEE AND DO

BRANTON WOODS GOLF COURSE

178 Stormville Road, Hopewell Junction, 845-223-1600; www.brantonwoodsgolf.com

About 70 miles from New York City in tiny Hopewell Junction is Branton Woods, a course that makes good use of the natural wildlife. Each fairway has plenty of undulations, and golfers have three lakes to contend with from time to time. Elevation changes force difficult shots into elevated greens, and the back-to-back par-fives at 14 and 15 are quite a challenge (the 15th alone is 600 yards long). The course is beautifully manicured, and twilight golf starts early (2 p.m.), so play then, as the rates go down significantly and there's still plenty of daylight left to get in a leisurely round.

MADAM BRETT HOMESTEAD

50 Van Nydeck Ave., Beacon, 845-831-6533

The oldest standing structure in Dutchess County, this 1709 house has period furnishings from seven generations, from Dutch Colonial through the Federal and Victorian eras. Garden. Occupied by the same family from 1709 to 1954. May-December, first Sunday every month, afternoons or by appointment.

MOUNT GULIAN HISTORIC SITE

145 Sterling St., Beacon, 845-831-8172; www.mountgulian.org

This is the headquarters of Baron von Steuben during the final period of the Revolutionary War. It's also the birthplace of the Order of the Society of Cincinnati, the first veteran's organization. There's a Dutch barn and restored garden on the grounds. Mid-April-December, Wednesday-Sunday 1-5 p.m.; also by appointment.

VAN WYCK HOMESTEAD MUSEUM

Junction of Highway 9 and I-84, Fishkill, 845-896-9560

During the revolution, the Continental Army requisitioned this house as headquarters and issued orders from here. It was also the site of court-martials, including that of Enoch Crosby, counterspy for the American forces. Washington, Lafayette and von Steuben visited here. Collection of Hudson Valley Folk Art; also changing exhibits. Memorial Day-October, Saturday and Sunday 1-4 p.m., also by appointment.

HOTEL

★RAMADA FISHKILL-POUGHKEEPSIE

20 Schuyler Blvd., Fishkill, 845-896-4995, 800-272-6232; www.ramada.com

82 rooms. Wireless Internet access. Complimentary continental breakfast. Bar. $

RESTAURANT

★★HUDSON'S RIBS & FISH

1099 Highway 9, Fishkill, 845-297-5002, www.hudsonsribsandfish.com

Seafood menu. Dinner. Bar. Children's menu. $$

FLORAL PARK

John Lewis Childs started a florist and seed business here in the 1870s. He planted the village with acres of flowers, even lining the railroad tracks for more than a mile, and had the town's name changed from East Hinsdale to Floral Park.

Information: www.fpvillage.org

HOTEL

★FLORAL PARK MOTOR LODGE

30 Jericho Turnpike, Floral Park, 516-775-7777, 800-255-9680; www.floralparkmotorlodge.com

107 rooms. Business center. Wireless Internet access. Complimentary continental breakfast. $

RESTAURANTS

★★ARTURO'S

246-04 Jericho Turnpike, Floral Park, 516-352-7418; www.arturorestaurant.com

Italian menu. Lunch, dinner. Closed holidays. Bar. $$

★KOENIG'S

86 S. Tyson Ave., Floral Park, 516-354-2300; www.koenigsrestaurant.com

German, Continental menu. Lunch, dinner. Bar. Children's menu. Casual attire. Reservations recommended. $$

FLUSHING

This town in north Queens is an ethnically diverse community, whose claim to fame is the U.S. Open tennis tournament, which brings tennis greats to Flushing each year.
Information: www.queenschamber.org

SPECIAL EVENT
U.S. OPEN TENNIS
Flushing Meadows-Corona Park, USTA National Tennis Center, Flushing, 718-760-6200; www.usopen.org

Scores of tennis fans descend upon the U.S. Open tennis tournament each September. You can see your favorite players, the stars of tomorrow and a host of celebrities in the audience at this upper-crust sporting event. Tickets go on sale in late May or by the beginning of June, and matches held closer to the finals sell out first. Buying a ticket to the Arthur Ashe Stadium, the main court, gives you admission to all the other courts on the grounds. Late August-early September.

RESTAURANTS
★KUM GANG SAN
138-28 Northern Blvd., Flushing, 718-461-0909; www.kumgangsan.net
Korean menu. Lunch, dinner, late-night. Casual attire. $$

★★SICHUAN DYNASTY
135-32 40th Road, Flushing, 718-961-7500
Chinese menu. Lunch, dinner. Casual attire. $$

FREDONIA

On Lake Erie, Fredonia is a small town with charming streets and a storied history.
Information: fredoniachamber.org

RESTAURANT
★★★THE WHITE INN
52 E. Main St., Fredonia, 716-672-2103; www.whiteinn.com
This stately country manor with its impressive columned portico and authentic Victorian décor serves a spiffy rack of lamb rubbed with Dijon mustard and bone-in chicken breast seared in olive oil and pan roasted. Steak menu. Breakfast, lunch, dinner. Bar. Outdoor seating. $$

FREEPORT

This Long Island village has a prime waterfront spot, and anglers, boaters and swimmers will enjoy its easy access to the water. Residents of the Big Apple come here in the summer for the beaches, great seafood and lively ambiance.
Information: www.freeportny.com

WHAT TO SEE AND DO
NAUTICAL MILE
Woodcleft Ave., Freeport
A stroll along Freeport's Nautical Mile on a warm, summer afternoon cannot be beat. This revitalized stretch of walkway in the seaport village offers a mix of restaurants,

clam bars, knickknack shops, ice cream parlors, a seaport museum and boats for sale. Start off by eating shrimp or clams outdoor at one of the many ultra-causal restaurants (some have live bands on the weekends in summer), stroll nearby and enjoy Ralph's Ices (the best around), admire a few boats and take in the atmosphere. Finish off the day by sitting on the scenic pier at the end of the avenue and enjoying the waterfront view.

RESTAURANT

★★SCHOONER

435 Woodcleft Ave., Freeport, 516-378-7575; www.theschooner.com

Seafood, steak menu. Lunch, dinner. Closed second and third weeks in January. Valet parking. $$

GARDEN CITY

Established in 1869 by merchant millionaire Alexander Turney Stewart, Garden City was one of the country's first planned communities. Wide streets, lots of vegetation and handsome buildings still distinguish this town.

Information: Chamber of Commerce, 230 Seventh St., Garden City,
516-746-7724; www.gardencitychamber.org

WHAT TO SEE AND DO

CRADLE OF AVIATION MUSEUM

Charles Lindbergh Blvd., Garden City, 516-572-4111; www.cradleofaviation.org

With an emphasis on Long Island's important and colorful history in the field of aviation, the museum offers exhibits on World War I, World War II, the Jet Age and Space Travel, to name a few. There also is an IMAX Theater. Open Tuesday-Sunday 9:30 a.m.-5 p.m.

LONG ISLAND CHILDREN'S MUSEUM

Mitchell Center, 11 David Blvd., Garden City, 516-224-5800; www.licm.org

This popular museum located in a former military base offers many hands-on interactive exhibits. Some include a bubble machine, climbing ramps and a beach exhibit that lets kids shape their own sand dunes. There are performances on weekends and programs held during the week. Wednesday-Sunday 10 a.m.-5 p.m.; also Tuesday in July-August.

HOTEL

★★★THE GARDEN CITY HOTEL

45 Seventh St., Garden City, 516-747-3000; www.gardencityhotel.com

This hotel, which was built in 1874, features sophisticated accommodations and service that have attracted notable families such as the Kennedys and Vanderbilts. Spacious guest rooms feature antique desks, Wireless Internet access, fully stocked bars and luxury bath amenities. Room service is available 24 hours a day, but the hotel offers a number of other dining options, including the Polo Restaurant, Rein Bar and Bistro and the Atrium Café. 272 rooms. Wireless Internet access. Two restaurants, two bars. Airport transportation available. $$$

RESTAURANTS

★★AKBAR
2 South St., Garden City, 516-357-8300; www.theakbar.com
Indian menu. Lunch, dinner, Sunday brunch. Reservations recommended. **$**

★★ORCHID
730 Franklin Ave., Garden City, 516-742-1116
Chinese menu. Lunch, dinner. Bar. Reservations recommended. **$$**

GENEVA
In the 19th century, Geneva attracted large numbers of retired ministers and spinsters and became known as "the saints' retreat and old maids' paradise." Located at the foot of Seneca Lake, the deepest of the Finger Lakes, the town is surrounded by rich farmland.
Information: Chamber of Commerce, 35 Lakefront Drive, Geneva,
315-789-1776; www.genevany.com

WHAT TO SEE AND DO

GENEVA HISTORICAL SOCIETY MUSEUM
543 S. Main St., Geneva, 315-789-5151; www.genevahistoricalsociety.com
Prouty-Chew House, built in 1829, is a Federal-style home with items of local history and changing exhibits. The collections contain 30,000 historical photographs, as well as furniture, decorative art, costumes, textiles, fine art, tools and equipment. July and August: Tuesday-Sunday; rest of year: Tuesday-Saturday; closed holidays.

RED JACKET ORCHARDS FRUIT OUTLET
957 Canandaigua Road, Geneva, 315-781-2749, 800-828-9410;
www.redjacketorchards.com
Apples, apricots, peaches, plums, strawberries, raspberries and even rhubarb are among the fruits offered at this outlet. The company also serves up fresh-squeezed juices and ciders. Look for the big red building.

ROSE HILL MANSION
E. Lake Road, Geneva, 315-789-3848; www.genevahistoricalsociety.com
This elegant 1839 country estate has Greek Revival architecture and Empire furnishings. Guided tours. May-October, Monday-Saturday, 10 a.m.-4 p.m., also Sunday afternoons 1-5 p.m.

SENECA LAKE STATE PARK
1 Lakefront Drive, Geneva, 315-789-2331; www.nysparks.state.ny.us/parks
Swimming beach, bathhouse, fishing, boating, picnicking, playground. Open 1st April-23rd October.

SMITH OPERA HOUSE FOR THE PERFORMING ARTS
82 Seneca St., Geneva, 315-781-5483; www.thesmith.org
Alternates films with theater, concerts, children's shows. Tours. Monday-Friday.

HOTEL

★★★GENEVA ON THE LAKE

1001 Lochland Road, Geneva, 315-789-7190, 800-343-6382;
www.genevaonthelake.com

Situated in the Finger Lakes Wine District on Seneca Lake, this villa-like hotel offers a 70-foot pool, volleyball, 18- and 9-hole golf courses within a mile and romantic dining overlooking the scenic formal gardens and waterfront. The comfortable, traditionally styled rooms are decorated with overstuffed upholstery and rich fabrics. 130 rooms. Complimentary continental breakfast. **$$**

SPECIALTY LODGING

BELHURST CASTLE

4069 Route 14 S., Lochland Road, Geneva, 315-781-0201; www.belhurstcastle.com

This castle offers a unique stay thanks to its dramatic architecture and views of Seneca Lake. Six guest rooms are in the castle and some rooms even have their own Jacuzzi. 14 rooms. Restaurant, bar. **$$**

RESTAURANT

★★BELHURST CASTLE

4069 Route 14 S., Geneva, 315-781-0201; www.belhurstcastle.com

American menu. Breakfast, lunch, dinner, Sunday brunch. Bar. Children's menu. **$$**

GLENS FALLS

The Iroquois called this town "Chepontuc," a word meaning "a difficult place to get around." Surrounded by the Adirondack Mountains and adjacent to the 60-foot drop in the Hudson River, the area was settled by Abraham Wing.

Information: Adirondack Regional Chambers of Commerce, 5 Warren St.,
Glens Falls, 518-798-1761; www.adirondackchamber.org

WHAT TO SEE AND DO

CHAPMAN HISTORICAL MUSEUM

348 Glen St., Glens Falls, 518-793-2826; www.chapmanmuseum.org

Victorian/Second Empire home (1868). Major portion redecorated as a period home reflecting 1865 and 1910. Gallery with rotating exhibits on Glens Falls, Queensbury and the southern Adirondacks. Large photographic library featuring collection of Seneca Ray Stoddard. Hours: Tuesday-Saturday, 10 a.m.-4 p.m., Sunday, noon-4 p.m.

HYDE COLLECTION

161 Warren St., Glens Falls, 518-792-1761; www.hydecollection.org

Art museum in original collector's home. Emphasis on 15th-20th-century art, including Rembrandt, Rubens, Picasso, El Greco; sculptures, antique furniture; films and lectures. Tuesday-Saturday 10 a.m.-5 p.m., Sunday, 12-5 p.m.; closed Mondays and all national holidays.

WEST MOUNTAIN SKI RESORT

59 West Mountain Road, Glen Falls, 518-793-6606; www.skiwestmountain.com

Triple, two double chairlifts; two rope tows; night skiing; patrol, school, rentals; snowmaking; cafeterias, bar; shop, lodge. Longest run approximately 1½ miles; vertical drop 1,010 feet. December-April, daily.

HOTELS

★LAKE GEORGE BUDGET INN
932 Lake George Road, Queensbury, 518-792-9576; www.brownswelcomeinn.com
20 rooms. Closed mid-October-mid-May. **$**

★★RAMADA GLENS FALLS/LAKE GEORGE AREA
1 Abbey Lane, Queensbury, 518-793-7701; www.glensfallsramadainn.com
110 rooms. Restaurant, bar. Wireless Internet access. Pool. **$**

★★QUEENSBURY HOTEL
88 Ridge St., Glens Falls, 518-792-1121, 800-554-4526; www.queensburyhotel.com
125 rooms. Restaurant, bar. Pool. Fitness center. Business center. **$**

GREAT NECK

Consisting of nine villages and an unincorporated area, the population of this area is approximately 41,500.
Information: Chamber of Commerce, 643 Middle Neck Road, 516-487-2000; www.greatneckchamber.org

WHAT TO SEE AND DO

U.S. MERCHANT MARINE ACADEMY
300 Steamboat Road, Kings Point, 516-773-5000; www.usmma.edu
The American Merchant Marine Museum houses an extensive collection of marine art, ship models and nautical artifacts. A Memorial Chapel honors war dead. Daily; closed holidays and July.

HOTEL

★★★INN AT GREAT NECK
30 Cutter Mill Road, Great Neck, 516-773-2000; www.innatgreatneck.com
Located on Long Island's Gold Coast, this is an elegant inn with Art Deco-inspired décor. The rooms and suites are comfortably sophisticated and offer updated technology. The Giraffe Room Lounge and Restaurant serves American cuisine punctuated with colorful Latin flavors. 85 rooms. Wireless Internet access. Restaurant, bar. **$$**

RESTAURANT

★★BEVANDA RISTORANTE
570 Middle Neck Road, Great Neck, 516-482-1510; www.bevandarestaurant.com
Italian menu. Lunch, dinner. Bar. Reservations recommended. **$$**

GREENE

This town is a great place to hunt for your next conversation starter: The shops are full of unusual antiques and works of art.
Information: www.greenenys.com

RESTAURANT

★★SILO RESTAURANT & CARRIAGE HOUSE
203 Moran Road, Greene, 607-656-4377; www.thesilorestaurant.com
Seafood menu. Dinner, Sunday brunch. Closed holidays. Bar. **$$**

GREENPORT

Greenport is a bit of New England on Long Island's North Fork. There are clean, uncrowded beaches as well as several wineries. This nautical, artsy, harborside village exudes charm, offering a mix of craft shops, art galleries, antique stores, restaurants, ice cream parlors and candy shops. Stroll by the water and stop for some clams or buy some one-of-a-kind nautical knickknacks. Take your time and take in the old-world atmosphere, especially on a warm, sunny day. Walk a little bit off Main Street and you can admire some of the old Victorian houses.

Information: www.greenport.cc

WHAT TO SEE AND DO

EAST END SEAPORT AND MARITIME MUSEUM

North Ferry Dock, Third Street, Greenport, 631-477-2100; www.eastendseaport.org

The maritime history of Long Island's East End is depicted through exhibits that include actual yachts used during World War II, a small aquarium and submarine mock-ups. Lectures on nautical history are offered, and there are special exhibits in summer when the area really comes to life. There also is a maritime festival held in late September that offers a parade and various other events. Mid-May-June, Saturday-Sunday 11 a.m. -5 p.m.; July-August, Monday, Wednesday-Friday 11 a.m.-5 p.m., Saturday-Sunday 9:30 a.m.-5 p.m.; September, Saturday-Sunday 11 a.m.-5 p.m.

ORIENT POINT, N.Y. NEW LONDON, CONN. FERRY

41720 Highway 25, Orient Point, 631-323-2525; www.longislandferry.com

Ninety-minute crossing. Daily. One-day round trips. Reservations required for vehicle.

SPECIAL EVENT

GREENPORT MARITIME FESTIVAL

Main Street, and Highway 48, Greenport

Wooden boat regatta, fishing tournament, whale boat race; clam chowder tasting contest. Late September.

HOTELS

★★SOUND VIEW INN

58775 North Road, Greenport, 631-477-1910; www.soundviewinn.com

49 rooms. Wireless Internet access. Closed January-early March. Restaurant, bar. $

★SUNSET MOTEL

62005 Route 48, Greenport, 631-477-1776; www.sunsetgreenport.com

18 rooms. Closed January-March. $

RESTAURANT

★★CLAUDIO'S

111 Main St., Greenport, 631-477-0627; www.claudios.com

Seafood, steak menu. Lunch, dinner. Closed January-mid-April. Bar. Outdoor seating. $$

GREENWICH

A short jaunt from Lake George, the Adirondacks and southern Vermont, Greenwich offers plenty of outdoor activities in a beautiful, pastoral setting.

Information: www.greenwichny.org

BENNINGTON BATTLEFIELD STATE HISTORIC SITE

Highway 67, Walloomsac

Battlefield where militiamen under Brigadier General John Stark stopped a force of British sharpshooters, mercenaries, Loyalists and American Indians in August 1777. Hilltop view; relief map, picnic tables. View of monument in Vermont. May-Labor Day: daily 10 a.m.-7 p.m.; Labor Day-mid-November: Saturday-Sunday 10 a.m.-7 p.m.

WILLARD MOUNTAIN SKI AREA

Highway 40, Greenwich, 518-692-7337, 800-457-7669; www.willardmountain.com

Chairlift, T-bar, pony lift; patrol, school, rentals; snowmaking; bar, cafeteria, snack bar; ski shop. Longest run 3,500 feet; vertical drop 550 feet. Night skiing. Early December-late March, daily; closed holidays.

RESTAURANT

★ONE ONE ONE

111 Main St., Greenwich, 518-692-8016; www.111mainstreet.net

American menu. Dinner. Closed Monday. $

GROTON

In the Finger Lakes Region of the state, Groton is surrounded by scenic terrain and working farms.

Information: townofgrotonny.org

RESTAURANT

★★★BENN CONGER INN

206 W. Cortland St., Groton, 607-898-5817; www.benncongerinn.com

The elegant restaurant in the Benn Conger Inn offers a wide selection of beautifully prepared Mediterranean-inspired cuisine accompanied by an award-winning wine list. Mediterranean menu. Dinner. Closed Monday. Bar. Children's menu. Reservations recommended. $$$

HAMILTON

Colgate University, one of the country's celebrated liberal arts colleges, is in Hamilton. This college town also offers great biking and running—if you consider hills great—and in the winter, visitors and locals ski in the nearby Adirondacks.

Information: www.hamiltonny.com

WHAT TO SEE AND DO

COLGATE UNIVERSITY

13 Oak Drive, Hamilton, 315-228-1000; www.colgate.edu

This handsome campus has buildings dating from 1827. The Charles A. Dana Arts Center, designed by Paul Rudolph, houses the Picker Art Gallery (academic year, daily; closed holidays).

ROGERS ENVIRONMENTAL EDUCATION CENTER

2721 Highway 80, Sherburne, 607-674-4017; www.dec.ny.gov/education/1831.html

On 600 acres; trout ponds; visitor center, 350 mounted birds, outdoor exhibits, six miles of nature trails, cross-country skiing, observation tower, picnicking. Daily; closed holidays.

HOTEL

★★COLGATE INN

1 Payne St., Hamilton, 315-824-2300; www.colgateinn.com

45 rooms Complimentary continental breakfast. Restaurant, bar. Guests can use the recreational facilities of Colgate University. **$**

RESTAURANT

★★THE TAP ROOM

1 Payne St., Hamilton, 315-824-2300; www.colgateinn.com

Seafood, steak menu. Lunch, dinner, Sunday brunch. Bar. Children's menu. Outdoor seating. **$**

HAMMONDSPORT

Located at the southern tip of Keuka Lake, this is the center of the New York State wine industry. The grape growers are mainly of German and Swiss origin and have more than a century of viticulture in New York State behind them, dating from 1829, when the Reverend William Bostwick planted the first vineyard. Glenn H. Curtiss, a pioneer aviator, was born here; most of his early experimental flights took place in this area.

Information: Chamber of Commerce, 47 Shethar St., Hammondsport,
607-569-2989; www.hammondsport.org

WHAT TO SEE AND DO

GLENN H. CURTISS MUSEUM

8419 State Route 54, Hammondsport, 607-569-2160; www.glennhcurtissmuseum.org

Like the Wright brothers, local aviator Glenn H. Curtiss owned a bicycle shop. His invention of the first flying boat, which took off over Lake Keuka, gave him the nickname "the father of naval aviation." The museum displays the Curtiss bicycle shop and a Dawn of Aviation Gallery. November-April: Monday-Saturday 10 a.m.-4 p.m., Sunday 10 a.m.-4 p.m.; rest of year: Monday-Saturday 9 a.m.-5 p.m., Sunday 10 a.m.-5 p.m.; closed holidays.

WINE AND GRAPE MUSEUM OF GREYTON H. TAYLOR

8843 Greyton H. Taylor Memorial Drive, Hammondsport, 607-868-4814;
www.bullyhill.com

Vineyard equipment, exhibits on early champagne, wine and brandy production; presidential wine glass collection; barrel-making houses in old-area winery. Tours. May-October, daily.

HOTEL

★DAYS INN

330 W. Morris, Bath, 607-776-7644; www.daysinn.com

104 rooms. High-speed Internet access. Pool. Complimentary continental breakfast. **$**

★
★
★
★
★

AMITY ROSE BED AND BREAKFAST

8264 Main St., Hammondsport, 607-569-3402, 800-982-8818;
www.amityroseinn.com
Four rooms. Closed January-March. Complimentary continental breakfast. **$**

HAMPTON BAYS

This hamlet in the Hamptons has fresh fish and seafood markets, a great spot on Shinnecock and Tiana bays and great shopping and dining options.
Information: www.hamptonbayschamber.com

RESTAURANT

★★VILLA PAUL

162 W. Montauk Highway, Hampton Bays, 631-728-3261
American, Italian menu. Dinner. Bar. Children's menu. Casual attire. **$$**

HARTSDALE

This hamlet on the Bronx River is about 20 miles north of New York City.
Information: www.greenburghny.com

RESTAURANT

★★HARRY'S OF HARTSDALE

230 E. Hartsdale Ave., Hartsdale, 914-472-8777; www.harrysofhartsdale.com
Seafood, Steak menu. Lunch, dinner. Closed holidays. Bar. Casual attire. Reservations recommended. Outdoor seating. **$$**

HEMPSTEAD

This township is the country's largest, with 762,000 people, more than 65 parks and marinas and nearly 2,600 miles of roads. It is also one of the nation's oldest—Hempstead was founded in 1644.
Information: Hempstead Chamber of Commerce, 1776 Nicholas Court,
Hempstead, 516-483-2000; www.hempsteadchamber.org

WHAT TO SEE AND DO

AFRICAN-AMERICAN MUSEUM

110 N. Franklin St., Hempstead, 516-572-0730; www.aamoflongisland.org
Depicts the scope and depth of the story of African-American people on Long Island and their contributions to the development of its history. Collection of African-American artifacts; changing exhibits. Tuesday-Saturday 10 a.m.-5 p.m.; closed holidays.

EISENHOWER PARK

Hempstead Turnpike, East Hempstead, 516-572-0200
This centrally located Central Park of Nassau County features an Olympic-sized pool, tennis courts, running tracks, a roller rink, batting cages, golf, miniature golf, a gourmet restaurant and catering hall and a baseball field. Free concerts are held in summer.

HOFSTRA UNIVERSITY

1000 Fulton Ave., Hempstead, 516-463-6600; www.hofstra.edu

The Hofstra Museum presents exhibitions in the Emily Lowe Gallery, David Filderman Gallery, Hofstra's Cultural Center, and in nine other areas on campus. Daily; closed holidays.

NASSAU VETERANS MEMORIAL COLISEUM

1255 Hempstead Turnpike, Hempstead, 516-794-9300; www.nassaucoliseum.com

This major sports and entertainment complex in the center of Nassau County offers a little bit of everything for just about every kind of taste and interest. Hockey lovers can cheer on the New York Islanders here, their venue for all home games. The Coliseum also hosts special events, fairs and trade shows throughout the year in its exhibit hall.

HERKIMER

Herkimer is a town that takes pride in its history. General Nicholas Herkimer marched from the fort here to the Battle of Oriskany, one of the Revolutionary War's bloodiest, which took place August 4, 1777. The Gillette trial, the basis for Theodore Dreiser's *An American Tragedy*, was held in the Herkimer County Courthouse.

Information: Herkimer County Chamber of Commerce, 28 W. Main St., Mohawk, 315-866-7820; www.herkimercountychamber.com

WHAT TO SEE AND DO

★★BEST WESTERN LITTLE FALLS MOTOR INN

20 Albany St., Little Falls, 315-823-4954; www.bestwesternlittlefalls.com

56 rooms. Restaurant, bar. $

HERKIMER HOME STATE HISTORIC SITE

200 State Route 169, Little Falls, 315-823-0398;
www.nysparks.state.ny.us/sites/info.asp?siteID=12

General Nicholas Herkimer lived in this 1764 house, which features 18th-century furnishings, a family cemetery and a General Herkimer Monument. Mid-May-October, Tuesday-Saturday 10 a.m.-5 p.m., Sunday 1-5 p.m. July-August,Tuesday 10 a.m.-5 p.m.

HOTEL

★HERKIMER MOTEL

100 Marginal Road, Herkimer, 315-866-0490, 877-656-6835; www.herkimermotel.com

60 rooms. Wireless Internet access. Pets accepted. $

RESTAURANT

★★CANAL SIDE INN

395 S. Ann St., Little Falls, 315-823-1170; www.canalsideinn.com

Located in historic Canal Place near the Erie Canal, this restaurant offers classic French cuisine in a modest, wood-paneled dining room. Visiting for historic sightseeing or antiquing? Retire to the upstairs guest suite for a night. French menu. Dinner. Closed Sunday-Monday; holidays; also February-mid-March. Bar. $$

HILLSDALE

Hillsdale's Columbia County is a stretch of land from the Berkshire foothills to the Hudson River. If you're here to spend a little quality time with Mother Nature, you'll find plenty of places to hike, boat, fish, snow ski and golf. If you're searching for a quiet place to spend an afternoon, consider visiting the local boutiques or one of the area's wineries.

Information: Columbia County Tourism Department, 401 State St., Hudson, 800-724-1846; www.bestcountryroads.com

WHAT TO SEE AND DO

CATAMOUNT SKI AREA

3200 State Highway 23 Hillsdale, 518-325-3200, 800-342-1840; www.catamountski.com
Four double chairlifts, tow, J-bar; patrol, school, rentals; snowmaking; cafeteria, bar; nursery. Longest run two miles; vertical drop 1,000 feet. Night skiing. December-March, daily. Half-day rates.

TACONIC STATE PARK

Route 344 Hillsdale, 518-789-3993; www.nysparks.com/parks/info.asp?parkID=137
More than 4,800 acres. Bash Bish Stream and Ore Pit Pond are in the park. Swimming beach, bathhouse, fishing; hiking, picnicking, cross-country skiing, tent and trailer sites. At Rudd Pond, also boating; ice-skating.

HOTELS

★★★SIMMONS' WAY VILLAGE INN

Main Street, Route 44, Millerton, 518-789-6235; www.simmonsway.com
This inn offers Victorian elegance near the Berkshire Foothills. Rooms feature antiques, fireplaces and porches. Each room is uniquely decorated, and there is also a wonderful dining room, Martha's, that puts a spin on classics like baked salmon and roast rack of spring lamb. Nine rooms. Complimentary full breakfast. Restaurant. $$

★★SWISS HUTTE

Highway 23, Hillsdale, 518-325-3333; www.swisshutte.com
The Swiss Hutte is an old farmhouse built in the mid-1800's by the Nicholson Family. It has been under continuous operation as an inn for the past 50 years. In the mid-1970's a second building was added to the property with a total of 12 rooms. The property includes the main building or the old inn, the second building as mentioned with two stories each with six rooms for a total of 12. There is an outdoor pool area with a 25 x 45 swimming pool, a maintenance building and a brook-fed pond with a shaded deck, all surrounded by beautiful gardens, large trees, and the Berkshire Hills in a hidden valley. 12 rooms. Restaurant, bar. Tennis. Pool. Pets accepted. $

RESTAURANT

★★★SIMMONS' WAY

Main Street, Route 44, Millerton, 518-789-6235; www.simmonsway.com
Guests travel many miles for the elegant country fare found at this restored Victorian inn. The formal dining room, Martha's—complete with a cathedral ceiling and Oriental rugs—is the perfect setting for connoisseurs to sample the restaurant's fine wines and complex dishes. International menu. Dinner, Sunday brunch. Closed Monday-Tuesday. Bar. Outdoor seating. $$$

HOPEWELL JUNCTION

Hopewell Junction is a small town in the Hudson River Valley, near Poughkeepsie.

Information: www.dutchesscountyregionalchamber.org

RESTAURANTS

★★BLUE FOUNTAIN

826 Route 376, Hopewell Junction, 845-226-3570; www.thebluefountain.com

Italian menu. Lunch, dinner. Closed Monday. Bar. Business casual attire. Reservations recommended. **$$**

★★★LE CHAMBORD

2737 Route 52, Hopewell Junction, 845-221-1941; www.lechambord.com

French menu. Lunch, dinner. Bar. Business casual attire. Reservations recommended. Outdoor seating. **$$**

HORNELL

Also known as the "Maple City," Hornell is a scenic and popular gateway to the Finger Lakes Region. Fishing, hunting and outdoor recreation contribute to the town's offerings. Fall foliage is especially brilliant in September and October in and around Hornell.

Information: Hornell Area Chamber of Commerce, 40 Main St., Hornell, 607-324-0310; www.hornellny.com

WHAT TO SEE AND DO

STONY BROOK STATE PARK

10820 Route 36 South, Dansville, 585-335-8111; www.nysparks.state.ny.us/parks

Swimming beach, bathhouse; hiking, tennis, cross-country skiing, picnicking, playground, concession, tent and trailer sites. May-mid October.

SWAIN SKI CENTER

Main Street and Highway 24, Swain, 607-545-6511; www.swain.com

Three quad, double chairlifts; patrol, school, rentals; snowmaking; restaurants, cafeteria, bar. Longest run one mile; vertical drop 650 feet. Night skiing. November-March, daily.

HOTELS

★COMFORT INN

1 Canisteo Square, Hornell, 607-324-4300, 800-424-6423; www.comfortinn.com

62 rooms. Complimentary continental breakfast. Indoor pool. Fitness center. No pets allowed. **$**

★SAXON INN

1 Park St., Alfred, 607-871-2600; www.alfred.edu/saxoninn

26 rooms. Complimentary continental breakfast. **$**

HOWES CAVE

This community near Albany in upstate New York got its name from Lester Howe, the man who discovered the caves that attract visitors today.

Information: www.schohariechamber.com

WHAT TO SEE AND DO

HOWE CAVERNS

255 Discovery Drive, Howes Cave, 518-296-8990; www.howecaverns.com

Elaborately developed series of caverns with underground river and lake, unique rock formations 160-200 feet below the surface; reached by elevators; 52 F in caverns. July-Labor Day: daily 8 a.m.-8 p.m.; September-June: 9 a.m.-6 p.m.; closed holidays.

OLD STONE FORT MUSEUM COMPLEX

Highway 7, Schoharie, 518-295-7192; www.schohariehistory.net/OSF.htm

Church built in 1772 was fortified against raids by Tories and American Indians during the Revolutionary War and became known as Lower Fort. Major attack came in 1780; building restored to house of worship in 1785; now houses exhibits on Revolutionary War and Schoharie Valley history; firearms, American Indian artifacts and period furniture; local historical and genealogical library. Badgley Museum and Carriage House, annex built in style of fort. July-August: daily; May-October: Tuesday-Sunday.

SECRET CAVERNS, HOWES CAVE

Secret Caverns Road, Howes Cave, 518-296-8558; www.secretcaverns.com

Cave with natural entrance, 100-feet underground waterfalls, fossilized sea life; 50 F in caverns. June-August, daily 9 a.m.-6 p.m.; May-September, daily 10 a.m.-4:30 p.m.; mid-late April, October-November, daily 10 a.m.-4 p.m.

HOTEL

★★BEST WESTERN INN OF COBLESKILL

121 Burgin Drive, Cobleskill, 518-234-4321; www.bestwestern.com

76 rooms. Restaurant, bar. $

HUDSON

Green pastures, meandering trails, fresh air—this area has it all. It's the gateway to the scenic Hudson Valley and its many charming small towns.

Information: Columbia County Tourism Department, 401 State St., Hudson, 12534. 800-724-1846; www.bestcountryroads.com

WHAT TO SEE AND DO

AMERICAN MUSEUM OF FIREFIGHTING

117 Harry Howard Ave., Hudson, 518-828-7695, 877-347-3687; www.fasnyfiremuseum.com

Antique firefighting equipment including 1725 Newsham fire engine; memorabilia, art gallery. Daily 10 a.m.-5 p.m.; closed holidays.

CLERMONT STATE HISTORIC SITE

1 Clermont Ave., Germantown, 518-537-4240; www.nysparks.com/sites

The ancestral home of Robert R. Livingston, one of five men elected to draft the Declaration of Independence, who later as chancellor of New York administered the oath of office to George Washington. Lived in by seven generations of the Livingston family, the grounds and mansion retain their 1930 appearance, illustrating 200 years of changing tastes. Centerpiece of a 485-acre estate on the eastern shore of the Hudson River, the home features period furnishings, restored gardens, guided tours, nature trails and special events. April-October, Tuesday-Sunday 11 a.m.-5 p.m.; November-late March, Saturday-Sunday 11 a.m.-4 p.m. Grounds open all year for hiking, riding, cross-country skiing, picnicking.

JAMES VANDERPOEL HOUSE

16 Broad St., Kinderhook, 518-758-9265; www.cchsny.org
Federal period house built around 1820, now a museum with 19th-century furnishings and art. Maintained by the Columbia County Historical Society. Late May-early September: Thursday-Saturday 11 a.m.-5 p.m., Sunday 1-5 p.m.

LUYKAS VAN ALEN HOUSE

Highway 9H, Kinderhook, 518-758-9265; www.cchsny.org
Restored 1737 house is a museum of Dutch domestic culture during the 18th century. Late May-early September, Thursday-Saturday 11 a.m.-5 p.m., Sunday 1-5 p.m.

MARTIN VAN BUREN NATIONAL HISTORIC SITE

1013 Old Post Road, Kinderhook, 518-758-9689; www.nps.gov/mava
This is the retirement house of America's eighth president. The estate, Lindenwald, was purchased by Van Buren from General William Paulding in 1839. On 20 acres, the house contains 36 rooms. Tours, schedule varies. Grounds: daily, dawn-dusk; mid-May-October, daily 9 a.m.-4:30 p.m.

OLANA STATE HISTORIC SITE

5720 Highway 9G, Hudson, 518-828-0135; www.nysparks.state.ny.us/sites
A 250-acre 1870 hilltop estate with views of the Hudson River and Catskill Mountains, includes Persian/Moorish mansion and grounds landscaped in Romantic style, all designed by Hudson River School artist Frederic Edwin Church as a multidimensional work of art. Five miles of carriage roads for walking with views planned by the artist. Grounds daily. House Museum: entrance by guided tour only. Reservations recommended. April-October, daily 10 a.m.-5 p.m.; November, daily 10 a.m.-4 p.m.; December-March, Saturday-Sunday by appointment.

SHAKER MUSEUM AND LIBRARY

88 Shaker Museum Road, Old Chatham, 518-794-9100;
www.shakermuseumandlibrary.org
One of the largest collections of Shaker culture; 26 galleries in three buildings. Exhibits include furniture, crafts, basketry, agricultural and industrial tools. Library by appointment only. Picnic area, cafe. Late April-October: Monday, Wednesday-Sunday.

HOTEL

★★ST. CHARLES HOTEL

16-18 Park Place, Hudson, 518-822-9900; www.stcharleshotel.com
34 rooms. Complimentary continental breakfast. Restaurant, bar. $

RESTAURANTS
★EARTH FOODS
523 Warren St., Hudson, 518-822-1396
American menu. Breakfast, lunch. Closed Tuesday. Children's menu. Casual attire. $

★★MEXICAN RADIO
537 Warren St., Hudson, 518-828-7770; www.mexrad.com
Mexican menu. Lunch, dinner. Bar. Casual attire. Reservations recommended. $$

HUNTER
Hunter is in the area known as "the mountaintop"—a stretch of land in the picturesque northern Catskills.
Information: Greene County Promotion Department, 518-263-4900, 800-355-2287; www.hunterchamber.org

WHAT TO SEE AND DO
HUNTER MOUNTAIN SKI RESORT
Highway 23A, Hunter, 518-263-4223, 800-486-8376; www.huntermtn.com
Three quad, two triple, five double chairlifts. Offers 53 slopes and trails. Patrol, school, rentals; snowmaking; bar, restaurant, cafeteria; nursery. Longest run two miles; vertical drop 1,600 feet. Early November-late April, daily.

HOTEL
★★★SCRIBNER HOLLOW LODGE
Main St., Hunter, 518-263-4211, 800-395-4683; www.scribnerhollow.com
This resort has a classical mountain lodge atmosphere with modern hotel conveniences. The lodge has custom-decorated rooms and suites, a restaurant and a unique underground pool with seven waterfalls, Jacuzzi and saunas. 37 rooms. Closed April-mid May. Restaurant, bar. Tennis. Pool. $$

SPECIALTY LODGINGS
EGGERY COUNTRY INN
288 Platt Clove Road, Tannersville, 518-589-5363, 800-785-5364; www.eggeryinn.com
This restored farmhouse inn was built in 1900 and boasts stunning views of nearby Hunter Mountain. 15 rooms. Complimentary full breakfast. $

HUNTER INN
7433 Main St., Hunter, 518-263-3777, 800-270-3992; www.hunterinn.com
42 rooms. Complimentary continental breakfast. Whirlpool. $

HUNTINGTON
Although the expanding suburban population of New York City has reached Huntington, 37 miles east on Long Island, the town still retains its rural character. Huntington is a township of 17 communities, in which there are more than 100 industrial plants. The area has five navigable harbors and 51 miles of shorefront.
Information: Huntington Township Chamber of Commerce, 164 Main St., Huntington, 631-423-6100; www.huntingtonchamber.com

WHAT TO SEE AND DO

DAVID CONKLIN FARMHOUSE

2 High St., Huntington, 631-427-7045; www.huntingtonhistoricalsociety.org

Four generations of the Conklin family lived at this circa 1750 house. Thursday, Friday and Sunday 1-4 p.m.; closed holidays.

HECKSCHER MUSEUM OF ART

Heckscher Park, 2 Prime Ave., Huntington, 631-351-3250; www.heckscher.org

Permanent collection of European and American art dating from 16th century; changing exhibits. Tuesday-Friday 10 a.m.-5 p.m. Saturday-Sunday 1-5 p.m. First Friday of each month open until 8:30 p.m. Open on Monday holidays from 10 a.m.-5 p.m.

HUNTINGTON TRADE SCHOOL

209 Main St., Huntington, 631-427-7045

School building houses the offices of the Huntington Historical Society and a history research library. Tuesday-Friday.

SUNKEN MEADOW STATE PARK

Route 25A and Sunken Meadow Parkway, Northport, 631-269-4333;
www.nysparks.com/parks

Swimming beach, bathhouse, fishing (all year); nature, hiking and biking trails; three nine-hole golf courses. Picnicking, playground, concession. Cross-country skiing.

TARGET ROCK NATIONAL WILDLIFE REFUGE

12 Target Rock Road, Huntington, 631-286-0485; www.fws.gov/Refuges/profiles

An 80-acre refuge with hardwood forest, pond and beach. Fishing; photography, nature trail, wildlife nature study and environmental education. Daily.

WALT WHITMAN BIRTHPLACE STATE HISTORIC SITE

246 Old Walt Whitman Road, Huntington Station, 631-427-5240;
www.waltwhitmanbirthplace.org

Streets and malls are named for the famous American author. This simple home, which features 19th-century furnishings (including Whitman's schoolmaster's desk), offers a tour, as well as an exhibit that tells the story of Whitman's life. There is also a recording available of the author himself reading one of his poems. June 15-Labor Day, Monday-Friday 11 a.m.-4 p.m., Saturday-Sunday 11 a.m.-5 p.m.; Winter hours, Wednesday-Friday 1-4 p.m., Saturday-Sunday, 11 a.m.-4 p.m.

SPECIAL EVENTS

HUNTINGTON SUMMER ARTS FESTIVAL

Heckscher Park Amphitheater, 213 Main St., Huntington, 631-271-8423;
www.huntingtonarts.org

Local, national and international artists perform dance, folk, classical, jazz, theater and family productions. Late June-mid-August.

NEW YORK

LONG ISLAND FALL FESTIVAL AT HUNTINGTON

164 Main St., Huntington, 631-423-6100; www.lifallfestival.com

Entertainment, carnival, sailboat regatta, food, wine tasting, family activities. Mid-October.

HOTELS

★HUNTINGTON COUNTRY INN

270 W. Jericho Turnpike, Huntington Station, 631-421-3900, 800-739-5777;
www.huntingtoncountryinn.com

63 rooms. Complimentary continental breakfast. Fitness center. Business center. $

★★★HILTON LONG ISLAND/HUNTINGTON

598 Broad Hollow Road, Melville, 631-845-1000; www.hiltonlongisland.com

Guests enter the Hilton to find an atrium lobby with running waterfalls and a tropical setting. Rooms are comfortable, and the location is perfect for exploring Long Island's so-called "Gold Coast" and its numerous attractions. 302 rooms. Two restaurants, bar. Children's activity center. Whirlpool. Tennis. Fitness center. Pool. High-speed Internet access. $$

HURLEY

The English and Dutch settled this area in the mid-1600s, and buildings from the 18th and 19th centuries remain. History buffs can wander through Hurley and its neighboring towns and glimpse relics from early American life.

Information: Chamber of Commerce of Ulster County; www.ulsterchamber.org

HYDE PARK

Hyde Park was named for Edward Hyde, Lord Cornbury, provincial governor of New York, who in 1705 presented a parcel of land along the river to his secretary. Hyde's name was given to an estate on that property and later to the town itself. The area, noted for the varying scenery—from rock outcroppings to scenic water views—is best known as the site of Springwood, the country estate of Franklin Roosevelt.

Information: Dutchess County Tourism Promotion Agency, 3 Neptune Road,
Poughkeepsie, 845-463-4000, 800-445-3131; www.dutchesstourism.com

WHAT TO SEE AND DO

ELEANOR ROOSEVELT NATIONAL HISTORIC SITE AT VAL-KILL

56 Val-Kill Park Drive, Hyde Park, 845-229-9115, 800-967-2283;
www.nps.gov/elro

Dedicated as a memorial to Eleanor Roosevelt on October 11, 1984, the 100th anniversary of her birth, Val-Kill was her country residence from the 1920s until her death. The original house on the property, Stone Cottage, is now a conference center. Her second house at Val-Kill was originally a furniture and crafts factory that Roosevelt sponsored in an effort to stimulate rural economic development. After closing Val-Kill Industries, she had the factory remodeled to reflect her tastes and humanitarian concerns. She used the space to entertain family, friends and heads of state from around the world. May-October, daily 9 a.m.-5 p.m.; November-April, Thursday-Monday 9 a.m.-5 p.m.; closed holidays. Grounds daily until sunset.

FRANKLIN D. ROOSEVELT PRESIDENTIAL LIBRARY AND MUSEUM

4079 Albany Post Road, Hyde Park, 845-486-7770, 800-337-8474;
www.fdrlibrary.marist.edu

First of the public presidential libraries, it has exhibits covering the private lives and public careers of Franklin and Eleanor Roosevelt. Research library contains family artifacts and documents and presidential archives. Library, museum and home. November-April, daily 9 a.m.-5 p.m.; May-October, daily 9 a.m.-6 p.m.

HOME OF FRANKLIN D. ROOSEVELT NATIONAL HISTORIC SITE

4097 Albany Post Road, Hyde Park, 845-229-9115; www.nps.gov/hofr

This Hyde Park estate, Springwood, was President Roosevelt's birthplace and lifelong residence. The central part of the building and oldest section dates from about 1826. The house was bought in 1867 by FDR's father and was extensively remodeled and expanded in 1915 by FDR and his mother, Sara Delano Roosevelt. At that time, the frame Victorian house took on its present brick and stone, neo-Georgian form. The interior is furnished exactly as it was when FDR died. Roosevelt and his wife's graves are in the rose garden. Home, library and museum. Buildings daily 9 a.m.-5 p.m. Grounds daily 7 a.m.-sunset.

MILLS MANSION STATE HISTORIC SITE

Highway 9 and Old Post Road, Staatsburg, 845-889-8851; www.staatsburgh.org

Built for Ogden Mills in 1895-1896 by prominent architect Stanford White, this Greek Revival mansion includes 65 rooms furnished in Louis XIV, Louis XV and Louis XVI styles, with tapestries, art objects, marble fireplaces and gilded plasterwork. Park overlooks the Hudson. January-March, Saturday and Sunday 11 a.m.-4 p.m.; April-October, Tuesday-Saturday 10 a.m.-5 p.m., Sunday 12 a.m.-5 p.m.

MILLS-NORRIE STATE PARK

Highway 9 and Old Post Road, Staatsburg, 845-889-4646;
www.nysparks.state.ny.us/parks

Fishing, boat basin (marina, dock, launch); nature and hiking trails, 18-hole golf, cross-country skiing, picnicking; tent and trailer sites, cabins. Environmental education programs, concert series. Camping. May-late October.

VANDERBILT MANSION NATIONAL HISTORIC SITE

Highway 9, Hyde Park, 845-229-9115; www.nps.gov/vama

Beaux-Arts mansion (1898) designed by McKim, Mead & White for Frederick W. Vanderbilt is a prime example of the mansions typical of the period. The interior retains most of the original furnishings as designed by turn-of-the-century decorators. The grounds offer superb views up and down the Hudson River; many ancient trees; restored formal Italian gardens. Mansion daily 9 a.m.-5 p.m. Grounds daily 7 a.m.-sunset.

RESTAURANTS

★★AMERICAN BOUNTY

433 Albany Post Road, Hyde Park, 845-471-6608; www.ciachef.edu/restaurants/bounty
American menu. Lunch, dinner. Closed Sunday-Monday; holidays; also three weeks in July, two weeks in December. Bar. Business casual attire. $$

★★★THE ESCOFFIER
433 Albany Post Road, Hyde Park, 845-471-6608; www.ciachef.edu/restaurants/escoffier
Student chefs of the Culinary Institute of America prepare dishes that their peers serve in this classic French eatery that serves a lighter, more contemporary take on the cooking of Auguste Escoffier (think Asian-style braised veal cheeks with gratin potatoes). French menu. Lunch, dinner. Closed Sunday-Monday; holidays; also three weeks in July, two weeks in December. $$

★★★RISTORANTE CATERINA DE MEDICI
433 Albany Post Road, Hyde Park, 845-471-6608;
www.ciachef.edu/restaurants/caterina
With its five distinct dining areas—from the more casual to the formal—the Culinary Institute of America's flagship restaurant will carry you to Tuscany thanks to dishes like marinated pork, pancetta and mushroom skewers with spring vegetable or beef carpaccio with baby arugula, lemon vinaigrette, Parmesan shavings and truffle oil. American menu. Lunch, dinner. Closed Saturday-Sunday. Bar. Casual attire. Reservations recommended. $$$

★★ST. ANDREW'S CAFÉ
433 Albany Post Road, Hyde Park, 845-471-6608;
www.ciachef.edu/restaurants/standrews
American menu. Lunch, dinner. Closed Saturday-Sunday; holidays; also three weeks in July, two weeks in December. Bar. Outdoor seating. $$

IRVINGTON
This pretty spot on the Hudson River attracts stars and civilians alike, who come to see its stately homes, historic buildings and cute shops.
Information: www.hudsonriver.com

RESTAURANTS
★★THE RED HAT BISTRO ON THE RIVER
1 Bridge St., Irvington, 914-591-5888; www.redhatbistro.com
American menu. Lunch, dinner, brunch. Bar. Casual attire. Reservations recommended. $$

★★RIVER CITY GRILLE
6 S. Broadway, Irvington, 914-591-2033; www.rivercitygrille.com
American menu. Lunch, dinner. Bar. Casual attire. Reservations recommended. $$

ITHACA
Ithaca climbs from the plain at the head of Cayuga Lake up the steep slopes of the surrounding hills. Creeks flow through town and cut picturesque gorges with cascading waterfalls. Named for Grecian Ithaca by Simeon De Witt, surveyor general under Washington, Ithaca is a center of inland water transportation and an educational nexus of New York State.
Information: Ithaca/Tompkins County Convention and Visitors Bureau,
904 East Shore Drive, Ithaca, 607-272-1313, 800-284-8422; www.visitithaca.com

SMALL-TOWN NEW YORK

Ithaca combines the best of small-town America with a college-town sophistication, as well as the spectacular natural sites of **Cayuga Lake** and a variety of gorges and waterfalls. This walk explores Ithaca's center with a stroll to nearby falls. For those who really love to hoof it, other options include the **Cornell University Plantations**, an arboretum and botanical gardens, and, on the other end of town, **Stewart Park** along Cayuga Lakes shoreline.

Start on Green Street and walk west to Cayuga Street. City Hall is on the right. Turn right and walk a half block to the **Commons**, home to a wide variety of shops, restaurants, cafés and a gallery. Duck into the **Susan Titus Gallery** and ask about the Ithaca Arta guide to galleries and artists' studios throughout the region. Other shops of interest at the Commons are **Autumn Leaves, Ithaca Books**, **Angelheart Designs**, **Hand block** and **Harold's Army Navy** and **The Outdoor Store**. **The Home Dairy Bakery** is a great place to grab a snack. Here, too, begins the **Sagan Planet Walk**. Named after astronomer Carl Sagan, this is an outdoor, scale model of the solar system that stretches ¾ mile from the Commons to the Sciencenter on Second Street.

Leaving the west end of the Commons, turn right on Cayuga. The **Clinton House Art Space** is located at *116 Cayuga*, and **DeWitt Mall** is on the next block on the right. More shopping and eating await here. Highlights include the famous **Moosewood Restaurant, Calhoun's Antiques** and the **Sola Gallery**. Continue up Cayuga past DeWitt Park and turn left on Cascadilla Street. Go four blocks and turn right onto First Street. After two more blocks, you will reach the **Sciencenter**, an imaginative hands-on science exploratorium. Return along First Street and go left on Adams, which eventually merges to the right with East Lewis Street. Follow East Lewis three blocks to Tioga and turn left. The walk travels here through a pleasant residential neighborhood. After three blocks, turn right onto Falls Street, and walk two blocks to Lake Street to arrive at **Ithaca Falls and Fall Creek Gorge**.

These falls stand almost as high as Niagara. Pause for a picnic, play on the rocks in the stream or just admire the view. The energetic can follow the hiking trail into the upper areas of Fall Creek Gorge and onto the **Cornell University** campus, where a variety of trails lead to several waterfalls and Beebe Lake.

Return to Falls Street and, for diversity's sake, follow Aurora Street back into the town center. Just two blocks before arriving back at the Commons sits the **William Henry Miller Inn**, a circa-1880 historic home turned bed-and-breakfast at the corner of Buffalo Street. Turn left onto Court Street, and follow the trail in **Cascadilla Glen** (where Court meets Linn Street and University Avenue), an uphill clamber that will yield several waterfalls and views. For a more serene walk, drive west on Seneca Street (Highway 79), turn right onto Highways 34/13, and head into Stewart Park where miles of paths skirt Cayuga Lake. Or simply return to the Commons for a rest and some food.

WHAT TO SEE AND DO

ALLAN H. TREMAN STATE MARINE PARK

Highway 89, Ithaca, 607-273-3440; nysparks.state.ny.us/parks

Fishing, boating (launch, marina); picnicking. April-late October.

BUTTERMILK FALLS

105 Enfield Falls Road, Ithaca, 607-273-5761; www.nysparks.state.ny.us/parks

Swimming, bathhouse; hiking trails, picnicking, playground, concession, tent and trailer sites, cabins. Mid-May-Columbus Day.

CORNELL UNIVERSITY

159 Sapsucker Woods Road, Ithaca, 607-254-2473; www.cornell.edu

This 745-acre campus of 20,000 students overlooks Cayuga Lake and includes Beebe Lake, gorges and waterfalls. Founded both as a land-grant and privately endowed college by Ezra Cornell (1807-1874) and Andrew Dickson White (1832-1918). There are 13 colleges, four of which are state supported; 11 schools and colleges are in Ithaca, two in New York City.

DEWITT HISTORICAL SOCIETY & MUSEUM

401 E. State St., Ithaca, 607-273-8284; www.thehistorycenter.net

Local historical exhibits; large photography collection; local history library. Tuesday, Thursday and Saturday 11 a.m.-5 p.m.; closed holidays.

ITHACA COLLEGE

953 Danby Road, Ithaca, 607-274-3011; www.ithaca.edu

Liberal arts and professional programs. Music, art exhibits, drama, lectures and athletic programs. Handwerker Gallery. Campus overlooks city, Cayuga Lake. Tours of campus.

ROBERT H. TREMAN STATE PARK

105 Enfield Falls Road, Ithaca, 607-273-3440; www.nysparks.state.ny.us/parks

Swimming, bathhouse; hiking trails, picnicking, playground, cabins, recreation programs, tent and trailer sites. Daily.

SAGAN PLANET WALK

Sciencenter, 601 First St., Ithaca, 607-272-0600; www.sciencenter.org/saganpw

This scale model of the solar system was built in remembrance of Ithaca resident and Cornell Professor Carl Sagan. Daily.

SCIENCENTER

601 First St., Ithaca, 607-272-0600; www.sciencenter.org

There are 200 hands-on interactive science exhibits and an outdoor science park here. Tuesday-Saturday 10 a.m.-5 p.m., Sunday noon-5 p.m.; closed holidays, Mondays in July and August.

SIX MILE CREEK VINEYARD

1551 Slaterville Road, Ithaca, 607-272-9463, 800-260-0612; www.sixmilecreek.com

Family-operated winery. Tours, tasting. Open daily or by appointment May-October 10 a.m.-5:30 p.m.; November-April 11 a.m.-5:30 p.m.

TAUGHANNOCK FALLS
Taughannock State Park, 2221 Taughannock Park Road, 607-387-6739;
www.taughannock.com
The falls have a drop of 215 feet, one of the highest east of the Rockies. The park also features swimming, a bathhouse, fishing, boating, nature trails, hiking trails, cross-country skiing, ice skating, picnicking, playground.

SPECIAL EVENTS
APPLE HARVEST FESTIVAL
Downtown Ithaca Commons, 171 E. State St., Ithaca, 607-277-8679;
www.downtownithaca.com
This annual event features apples, cider, a craft fair and entertainment. First weekend in October.

FINGER LAKES ANTIQUE SHOW
Women's Community Building, 100 W. Seneca St., Ithaca, 607-272-1247;
www.lightlink.com/womens
First weekend in October.

GRASSROOTS FESTIVAL
Trumansburg Fairgrounds, 59 E. Main St., Trumansburg, 607-387-5098;
www.grassrootsfest.org/festival
This four-day concert features approximately 60 bands performing on four stages. Second to last weekend in July.

HANGAR THEATRE
116 N. Cayuga St., Ithaca, 607-273-8588; www.hangartheatre.org
Professional summer theater in park setting adjacent to Treman Marina. Five main stage productions; dramas, comedies and musicals. Tuesday-Saturday evenings, also Saturday and Wednesday afternoons; children's theatre Thursday-Saturday mornings, Late June-Labor Day weekend.

ITHACA FESTIVAL
215 N. Cayuga Street, Ithaca, 607-273-3646; www.ithacafestival.org
This four-day event features food, a parade and more than 1,000 local musicians and performers. First weekend in June.

HOTELS
★BEST WESTERN UNIVERSITY INN
1020 Ellis Hollow Road, Ithaca, 607-272-6100, 800-780-7234;
www.bestwesternuniversityinnithaca.com
101 rooms. Complimentary continental breakfast. Wireless Internet access. Airport transportation available. Pets accepted. $

★★HOLIDAY INN
222 S. Cayuga St., Ithaca, 607-272-1000, 800-465-4329; www.hiithaca.com
181 rooms. Wireless Internet access. Indoor heated pool and fitness Center. Restaurant, bar. Airport transportation available. $

NEW YORK

★
★
★
★
★

★★★LA TOURELLE RESORT & SPA

1150 Danby Road, Ithaca, 607-273-2734, 800-765-1492; www.latourelle.com

Offering guests a beautiful countryside setting and panoramic views of Cayuga Lake and its surrounding hill country, this inn is adjacent to state park lands with hiking trails and fishing ponds. Perfect for a romantic getaway, the inn evokes the feel of a far-flung French country estate. The inn is convenient to Ithaca College and Cornell University. 54 rooms. High-speed Internet access. Restaurant. Spa. Tennis. $$

★★★STATLER HOTEL AT CORNELL UNIVERSITY

130 Statler Drive, Ithaca, 607-257-2500, 800-541-2501; www.statlerhotel.cornell.edu

Because this well-appointed hotel serves as the main teaching facility for Cornell's prestigious School of Hotel Administration, no detail here has been overlooked. Boasting breathtaking views of the hills and dells of the campus's picturesque Finger Lakes location, each luxurious guest room features pillow-top mattresses and turndown service. Fresh flowers and rich wood floors are found throughout the hotel's open spaces. 153 rooms. High-speed Internet access. Restaurant, bar. Airport transportation available. $$

RESTAURANTS

★★★JOHN THOMAS STEAKHOUSE

1152 Danby Road, Ithaca, 607-273-3464; www.johnthomassteakhouse.com

John Thomas Steak House, an 1850s-era former farmhouse with lamp-lit white-clad tables beside a blazing fire, serves sophisticated cuts of meat like a porterhouse for two and 25-ounce T-bone steak paired with sides like German fried potatoes and creamed spinach. Steak menu. Dinner. Closed holidays. Bar. Business casual attire. Reservations recommended. $$$

★★MAHOGANY GRILL

112 N. Aurora St., Ithaca, 607-272-1438; www.mahoganygrill.com

American menu. Lunch, dinner, Sunday brunch. Bar. Children's menu. Casual attire. Reservations recommended. Outdoor seating. $$

★MOOSEWOOD RESTAURANT

215 N. Cayuga St., Ithaca, 607-273-9610; www.moosewoodrestaurant.com

Vegetarian menu. Lunch, dinner. Bar. Children's menu. Casual attire. Outdoor seating. $$

JAMESTOWN

Jamestown made its mark early in the 19th century with the manufacturing of metal products and furniture. These industries still flourish in this city located at the southern end of Chautauqua Lake. Tourism and farming are important to the economy as well.

Information: Chamber of Commerce, 101 W. Fifth St., Jamestown,
716-488-9401; www.jamestownchamber.org

WHAT TO SEE AND DO

FENTON HISTORICAL CENTER

67 Washington St., Jamestown, 716-664-6256; www.fentonhistorycenter.org

Home of post-Civil War governor; memorabilia of Chautauqua Lake area, Fenton family, Victorian era; re-created Victorian drawing room. Archival and genealogical library; Swedish and Italian heritage, Civil War exhibit. Monday-Saturday 10 a.m.-4 p.m.; also Sunday 1-4 p.m. from late November-early January; closed holidays.

LUCILLE BALL-DESI ARNAZ CENTER

10 W. Third St., Jamestown, 716-484-0800; www.lucydesi.com

Interactive exhibits provide a look into the lives and careers of Lucille Ball and Desi Arnaz. May-October Monday-Saturday 10 a.m.-5:30 p.m., Sunday 1-5 p.m.; November-April, Saturday 10-5:30 p.m., Sunday 1-5 p.m.

PANAMA ROCKS PARK

11 Rock Hill Road, Panama, 716-782-2845; www.panamarocks.com

Massive rock outcrop (25 acres) of a primeval seashore formation; cliffs, caves, crevices and passages. Rare mosses, wildflowers, ferns; unusually shaped tree roots. Self-guided tours; hiking trail; picnicking. May-late-October, daily 10 a.m.-5 p.m.

HOTEL

★COMFORT INN

2800 N. Main St. Extension, Jamestown, 716-664-5920, 800-453-7155; www.comfortinn.com

101 rooms. Complimentary continental breakfast. High-speed Internet access, Fitness center. Bar. **$**

RESTAURANTS

★★HOUSE OF PETILLO

382 Hunt Road, Jamestown, 716-664-7457

Italian menu. Dinner. Closed Sunday-Monday; holidays; two weeks at Easter. Bar. Casual attire. **$$**

★★IRONSTONE

516 W. Fourth St., Jamestown, 716-487-1516; www.ironstonerestaurant.net

Italian menu. Lunch, dinner. Business center. Closed Sunday; holidays. Bar. Children's menu. Casual attire. **$$$**

JERICHO

This village on Long Island is in the town of Oyster Bay, which stretches from the Atlantic Ocean on the south shore to the Long Island Sound on the northern edge.

RESTAURANTS

★★FRANK'S STEAKS

4 Jericho Turnpike, Jericho, 516-338-4595; www.frankssteaks.com

Seafood, steak menu. Lunch, dinner. Closed holidays. Bar. **$$$**

★★THE MAINE MAID INN

4 Old Jericho Turnpike, Jericho, 516-935-6400; www.themainemaidinn.com

American menu. Lunch, dinner, Sunday brunch. Closed Monday; holidays. Bar. Children's menu. Valet parking. **$$$**

585 N. Broadway, Jericho, 516-931-2201; www.milleridge.com
American menu. Lunch, dinner, Sunday brunch. Children's menu. $$

JOHNSTOWN

A center of leather tanning and related industries, Johnstown often is called a twin city to Gloversville, which it adjoins. A Revolutionary War battle was fought here six days after Cornwallis surrendered at Yorktown. Women's rights pioneer Elizabeth Cady Stanton was born here in 1815.

Information: Fulton County Regional Chamber of Commerce and Industry,
2 N. Main St., Gloversville, 518-725-0641, 800-676-3858; www.fultoncountyny.org

WHAT TO SEE AND DO
JOHNSON HALL STATE HISTORIC SITE
Highway 29 West and Hall Avenue, Johnstown, 518-762-8712;
www.nysparks.state.ny.us/sites
This house was the residence of Sir William Johnson, first baronet of New York colony. American Indians and colonists held meetings here. Site includes hall with period furnishings; stone blockhouse; interpretation center; dioramas depicting history of the estate; tours; special events. Mid-May-October, Wednesday-Saturday, also Sunday afternoons.

HOTEL
★★**HOLIDAY INN**
308 N. Comrie Ave., Johnstown, 518-762-4686, 800-465-4329; www.holiday-inn.com
99 rooms. Restaurant, bar. High-speed Internet access. Outdoor pool. Fitness center. $

RESTAURANT
★★**UNION HALL INN**
2 Union Place, Johnstown, 518-762-3210; www.unionhallinnrestaurant.com
American menu. Lunch, dinner. Closed Sunday-Monday; holidays. Bar. $$

KINGSTON

In more than 300 years, Kingston has had several names, including Esopus and Wiltwyck, and has been raided, burned and fought over by Native Americans, Dutch, British and Americans. It was the first capital of New York. The Delaware River and Hudson Canal and then the railroads brought prosperity. A huge cement industry bloomed and died on Rondout Creek harbor in the 19th century.

Information: Chamber of Commerce of Ulster County, 1 Albany Ave.,
Kingston, 845-338-5100; www.ulsterchamber.org

WHAT TO SEE AND DO
HUDSON RIVER MARITIME MUSEUM
50 Rondout Landing, Kingston, 845-338-0071; www.hrmm.org
Models, photographs and paintings depict era of river commerce; outdoor area features steam tug and a variety of antique and modern pleasure boats. Mid-May-mid-October, daily 11 a.m.-5 p.m.

OLD DUTCH CHURCH

272 Wall St., Kingston, 845-338-6759; www.olddutchchurch.org

With a congregation established in 1659, this is a 19th-century church. Buried on the grounds is George Clinton, first governor of New York and vice president under Madison and Jefferson. Church and museum tours by appointment.

SENATE HOUSE STATE HISTORIC SITE

296 Fair St., Kingston, 845-338-2786; www.nysparks.state.ny.us/sites

Stone residence in which the first New York State Senate met in 1777. Furnished in 18th-century Dutch style; delft tiles, Hudson Valley furniture. Paintings by John Vanderlyn and others in adjacent museum; boxwood garden. Also library of regional history, displays, special events. Mid-April-late October, Monday, Wednesday-Saturday 10 a.m.-5 p.m., Sunday 11 a.m.-5 p.m.

ULSTER PERFORMING ARTS CENTER

601 Broadway, Kingston, 845-339-6088; www.upac.org

Historic Vaudeville theater presents professional Broadway touring companies, dance, contemporary music, comedy and children's productions.

HOTEL

★★HOLIDAY INN

503 Washington Ave., Kingston, 845-338-0400, 800-465-4329; www.holiday-inn.com

212 rooms. Restaurant, bar. Whirlpool. Pool. $

RESTAURANTS

★★DOWNTOWN CAFÉ

1 W. Strand St., Kingston, 845-331-5904; www.downtowncafekingston.com

American menu. Lunch, dinner, brunch. Bar. Casual attire. Reservations recommended. Outdoor seating. $$

★HICKORY BBQ SMOKEHOUSE

743 Highway 28, Kingston, 845-338-2424; www.hickoryrestaurant.com

American menu. Lunch, dinner. Closed Wednesday. Bar. Children's menu. Casual attire. Reservations recommended. Outdoor seating. $$

★★LE CANARD ENCHAINÉ

276 Fair St., Kingston, 845-339-2003; www.le-canardenchaine.com

French menu. Lunch, dinner. Bar. $$$

LAKE GEORGE

This area near the Adirondack Mountains is a traveler's dream: You'll find everything from lakeside fun to quiet mountain retreats. Early explorers and settlers knew Lake George as Lac du St. Sacrement—the name it was given when it was a Jesuit mission. In the foothills of the Adirondacks, the area is a center for winter as well as summer sports; there are many miles of snowmobile trails.

Information: www.visitlakegeorge.com

WHAT TO SEE AND DO
FORT WILLIAM HENRY MUSEUM
48 Canada St., Lake George, 518-668-5471; www.fwhmuseum.com
A 1755 fort rebuilt from original plans; French and Indian War relics; military drills, musket firings, bullet molding and cannon demonstrations. Replica of the fort used in filming of the movie *Last of the Mohicans*. Daily 9 a.m.-6 p.m.

THE GREAT ESCAPE AND SPLASHWATER KINGDOM FUN PARK
1172 State Route 9, Queensbury, 518-792-3500; www.sixflags.com/parks/greatescape
New York's largest theme park has more than 120 rides, live shows and attractions, including numerous roller coasters, Raging River Raft Ride, All-American High-Dive Show, Storytown-themed children's area. Splashwater Kingdom water park features a giant wave pool, water slides, Adventure River and kiddie pools. Memorial Day-Labor Day, daily, hours vary.

LAKE GEORGE BATTLEFIELD PICNIC AREA
139 Beach Road, Lake George Village, 518-668-3352
Site of Battle of Lake George ruins of Fort George. Picnic tables, fireplaces, charcoal grills, water. (Mid-June-Labor Day: daily; May-mid-June: weekends)

SPECIAL EVENTS
AMERICADE
Canada Street, Lake George; www.tourexpo.com
This annual motorcycle touring rally includes seminars, exhibits, shows, social events and guided scenic tours. The event attracts 50,000 motorcycle enthusiasts each year. First full week in June.

FAMILY FESTIVAL
Shepard Park, Canada Street, Lake George, 518-668-5771
Craft show, family entertainment, game booths, music, food. Third week in August.

JAZZ FESTIVAL
Shepard Park Bandstand, Canada St., Lake George Village
Regional jazz bands; lawn seating. Mid-September.

WINTER CARNIVAL
Highway 9 and Lake George Village, Lake George Village, 518-668-5755; www.lakegeorgewintercarnival.com
Annual winter festival including food, winter sports, balloon rides and snowmobile skip.

HOTELS
★BEST WESTERN OF LAKE GEORGE
Exit 21 and I-H 87 Lake George, 518-668-5701, 800-582-5540; www.bestwestern.com
87 rooms. Complimentary continental breakfast. Children's activity center. Whirlpool. Airport transportation available. $$

★COLONEL WILLIAMS MOTOR INN

Highway 9, Lake George, 518-668-5727, 800-334-5727;
www.colonelwilliamsresort.com
40 rooms. Indoor and outdoor heated pools, kiddie pool, sauna. Fitness center.
Wireless Internet access. $

★★DAYS INN

1454 Highway 9, Lake George, 518-793-3196, 800-329-7466;
www.daysinnlakegeorge.com
104 rooms. Restaurant, bar. Wireless Internet access. Indoor heated pool and hot tub.
Fitness center. Restaurant, bar. Business center. $

★★DUNHAM'S BAY LODGE

2999 Highway 9L, Lake George, 518-656-9242, 800-795-6343; www.dunhamsbay.com
50 rooms. Restaurant, bar. Whirlpool. Business center. Pool, hot tub. Fitness
center. $$

★★★FORT WILLIAM HENRY RESORT

48 Canada St., Lake George, 518-668-3081, 800-234-6686; www.fortwilliamhenry.com
A spectacular setting in the Adirondacks—along with courteous service and elegant accommodations—has attracted visitors to this Lake George resort, the oldest in the area. Guest rooms vary by size and, depending on type, include king beds, full-size sleeper sofas, microwaves, refrigerators, whirlpool tubs and executive desks with workstations. Sup at resort's onsite restaurants, the White Lion, where breakfast is served among a spectacular lake view, and J.T. Kelly's Steak and Seafood, a casually elegant spot serving classic American and Italian cuisines. 193 rooms. Two restaurants, bar. Children's activity center. Whirlpool. Airport transportation available. $$

★★THE GEORGIAN

384 Canada St., Lake George, 518-668-5401, 800-525-3436; www.georgianresort.com
165 rooms. Restaurant, two bars. Beach. Airport transportation available. $$

★THE HERITAGE OF LAKE GEORGE

419 Canada St., Lake George, 518-668-3357, 800-883-2653;
www.heritageoflakegeorge.com
39 rooms. Pool. Closed mid-October-mid-May. $

★★HOLIDAY INN

2223 Route 9 Canada St., Lake George, 518-668-5781, 888-465-4329;
www.holiday-inn.com
105 rooms. High-speed Internet access. Restaurant, bar. Whirlpool. $

★★HOWARD JOHNSON TIKI RESORT

2 Canada St., Lake George, 518-668-5744, 888-843-8454; www.tikiresort.com
110 rooms. Closed November-April. Two restaurants, bar. Children's activity center. $$

★LAKE CREST MOTEL

366 Canada St., Lake George, 518-668-3374; www.lakecrestmotel.com
40 rooms. Pool. Closed late October-late April. Restaurant. Beach. **$$**

★★MOHICAN MOTEL

1545 Highway 9, Lake George, 518-792-0474; www.mohicanmotel.com
43 rooms. Restaurant. Pool. Jacuzzi. Whirlpool. **$**

★★NORDICK'S MOTEL

2895 Lake Shore Drive, Lake George, 518-668-2697, 800-368-2697;
www.nordicks.com
21 rooms. Wireless Internet access. Closed late October-April. Restaurant, bar. **$**

★★ROARING BROOK RANCH & TENNIS RESORT

Route 9N South, Lake George, 518-668-5767, 800-882-7665;
www.roaringbrookranch.com
142 rooms. Closed March-mid-May and November-December. Restaurant, bar.
Children's activity center. **$**

RESTAURANTS

★★LOG JAM

1484 Highway 9, Lake George Village, 518-798-1155; www.logjamrestaurant.com
American menu. Lunch, dinner. Bar. Children's menu. Casual attire. Reservations
recommended. Valet parking. **$$**

★★★MONTCALM

1415 Highway 9, Lake George Village, 518-793-6601; www.menumart.com/montcalm
Rich American classics such as roast rack of lamb and Veal Oscar are the mainstay of
this resort-town restaurant where the reasonable prices attract a loyal following. Salads are prepared tableside by an attentive wait staff. American menu. Lunch, dinner.
Closed holidays. Bar. Children's menu. Casual attire. Reservations recommended. **$$**

LAKE LUZERNE

Lumber and papermaking formed the economic background of Lake Luzerne, now an
all-year resort. In addition to its location on the small lake for which it is named, this town
is near Great Sacandaga Lake, another popular area for summer and winter sports.
Information: Chamber of Commerce, 37 Main St., Lake Luzerne,
518-696-3500; www.lakeluzernechamber.org

WHAT TO SEE AND DO

BOW BRIDGE

Lake Luzerne, 518-696-3500
Parabolic bridge spans the Hudson and Sacandaga rivers. The only remaining semi-
deck lenticular iron truss bridge, typical of the late 19th-century iron bridges in New
York State.

HOTEL

★★SARATOGA ROSE INN AND RESTAURANT

4136 Rockwell St., Hadley, 518-696-2861, 800-942-5025; www.saratogarose.com
Six rooms. Children over 10 years only. Complimentary full breakfast. Restaurant. **$**

SPECIALTY LODGING

LAMPLIGHT INN BED AND BREAKFAST

231 Lake Ave., Lake Luzerne, 518-696-5294, 800-262-4668; www.lamplightinn.com
Built in 1890, this comfortable inn offers rooms in the main house, the Brookside
House and the Carriage House, all decorated in the Victorian style. The inn features
chestnut woodwork and a chestnut keyhole staircase crafted in England. The property
boasts gardens and hiking and biking trails on its 10 acres. 17 rooms. Children over
12 years only. Complimentary full breakfast. Restaurant. **$$**

RESTAURANTS

★CIRO'S

1439 Lake Ave., Lake Luzerne, 518-696-2556; www.menumart.com/ciros
Italian, American menu. Dinner. Closed holidays Bar. Children's menu. **$$**

★WATERHOUSE

85 Lake Ave., Lake Luzerne, 518-696-3115; www.menumart.com/waterhouse
Seafood, steak menu. Lunch, dinner. Closed holidays. Bar. Children's menu. Outdoor
seating. **$$**

LAKE PLACID

Mount Marcy, the highest mountain in New York State (5,344 feet), rises in the
Adirondack peaks that surround the town. On Lake Placid, the village also partly sur-
rounds Mirror Lake. This is one of the most famous all-year vacation centers in the
East and the site of the 1932 and 1980 Winter Olympics. The Intervale Olympic Ski
Jump Complex has 229-foot and 296-foot ski jumps constructed for the 1980 games,
now open to the public and used for training and competition.
Information: Essex County Visitors Bureau, Olympic Center, 216 Main St., Lake Placid,
518-523-2445, 800-447-5224; www.lakeplacid.com

WHAT TO SEE AND DO

JOHN BROWN FARM HISTORIC SITE

115 John Brown Road, Lake Placid, 518-523-3900;
www.nysparks.state.ny.us/sites/info.asp?siteID=14
Brown's final home; graves of the noted abolitionist, two sons and 10 others who
died in the struggle to end slavery. Grounds daily. Admission: adults $2.00, New York
senior citizens and children $1.00, children under 12 free. May-October, Wednesday-
Monday 10 a.m.-5 p.m.; Closed on Tuesday. Grounds open all year. Also open Inde-
pendence Day.

LAKE PLACID CENTER FOR THE ARTS

17 Algonquin Drive, Lake Placid, 518-523-2512; www.lakeplacidarts.org
Concerts, films, art exhibits. Gallery fall and spring, Tuesday-Saturday 1-5 p.m.;
summer, Tuesday-Friday 10 a.m.-5 p.m., Saturday-Sunday 1-5 p.m.; winter, Tuesday-
Thursday 1-5 p.m., Friday 1-9 p.m.

NEW YORK

★
★
★
★

OLYMPIC ARENA AND CONVENTION CENTER

218 Main St., Lake Placid, 518-523-1655; www.orda.org

Built for the 1932 Winter Olympics and renovated for the 1980 winter games. Winter and summer skating shows, family shows, hockey; public skating, concerts.

OLYMPIC SPORTS COMPLEX (MOUNT VAN HOEVENBERG RECREATION AREA)

Highway 73, Lake Placid, 518-523-1655; www.orda.org

Site of 1980 Winter Olympic Games. Bobsled, luge, cross-country, biathlon events. Championship bobsled and luge races most weekends in winter. Cross-country trails (33 miles) open to the public when not used for racing. Bobsled rides mid-December-early March, Tuesday-Sunday; luge rides mid-December-early March, weekends; fee.

HOTELS

★★ADIRONDACK INN BY THE LAKE

2625 Main St., Lake Placid, 518-523-2424, 800-556-2424; www.adirondack-inn.com

50 rooms. Beach. Indoor pool. Sauna, Jacuzzi, fitness room, game room. Restaurant. Wireless Internet access. $

★ART DEVLIN'S OLYMPIC MOTOR INN

2764 Main St., Lake Placid, 518-523-3700; www.artdevlins.com

44 rooms. Wireless Internet access. Pets accepted. Pool. $

★★CROWNE PLAZA RESORT AND GOLF CLUB LAKE PLACID

101 Olympic Drive, Lake Placid, 518-523-2556, 877-570-5891; www.lakeplacidcp.com

245 rooms. Wireless Internet access. Four restaurants, bar. Beach. Ski in/ski out. Pets accepted. Fitness center. Pool. Golf. Tennis. $

★★GOLDEN ARROW LAKESIDE RESORT

2559 Main St., Lake Placid, 518-523-3353, 800-582-5540; www.golden-arrow.com

150 rooms. High-speed Internet access. Three restaurants, two bars. Beach. Pets accepted. Fitness center. Pool. $$

★★★MIRROR LAKE INN RESORT AND SPA

77 Mirror Lake Drive, Lake Placid, 518-523-2544; www.mirrorlakeinn.com

Located on a hilltop at the edge of Lake Placid's downtown, this resort overlooks Mirror Lake as well as a stunning mountain range on the horizon. The lake can be seen from many of the guest rooms and the resort's restaurants where the décor mixes a Mission-style sensibility with walnut floors, marble, antiques and stone fireplaces. 129 rooms. Wireless Internet access. Three restaurants, two bars. Spa. Beach. Whirlpool. Fitness center. Pool. Tennis. $$$

SPECIALTY LODGING

THE BARK EATER INN

124 Alstead Hill Lane, Keene, 518-576-2221, 800-232-1607; www.barkeater.com

This former stagecoach stop was built in the early 1800s and features rustic rooms filled with antiques. 19 rooms. High-speed Internet access, Conference space. Complimentary full breakfast. Restaurant. $

★★★LAKE PLACID LODGE

Whiteface Inn Road, Lake Placid, 518-523-2700; www.lakeplacidlodge.com

At this much-lauded restaurant located in a cozy cottage, guests will find anything from duck consommé to lobster and sweetbread ravioli paired with stunning lake vistas. American menu. Breakfast, lunch, dinner. Bar. Business casual attire. Reservations recommended. Outdoor seating. $$$$

LARCHMONT

Just outside of the New York City metro area, Larchmont is on the shore of the Long Island Sound.

Information: www.villageoflarchmont.org

RESTAURANTS

★★★LUSARDI'S

1885 Palmer Ave., Larchmont, 914-834-5555; www.lusardislarchmont.com

Sample top-flight Northern Italian dishes such as grilled artichokes with oil and parsley and rigatoni with ground sausages, prosciutto and cream paired with cosseting service at this elegant, warm eatery. Italian menu. Dinner. Bar. Business casual attire. Reservations recommended. $$$

★★WATERCOLOR CAFÉ

2094 Boston Post Road, Larchmont, 914-834-2213; www.watercolorcafe.net

American menu. Lunch, dinner. Bar. Casual attire. Reservations recommended. $$

101

LATHAM

Latham is a hamlet in Colonie, not far from Albany. You'll know you're nearby when you see the red-and-white checkered water towers.

Information: www.colonie.org

RESTAURANT

★★DAKOTA STEAKHOUSE

579 Troy-Schenectady Road, Latham, 518-786-1234; www.steakseafood.com

American menu. Lunch, dinner, brunch. Bar. Children's menu. Casual attire. Reservations recommended. Outdoor seating. $$

LETCHWORTH STATE PARK

Within this 14,344-acre park are 17 miles of the Genesee River Gorge, sometimes called the Grand Canyon of the East. Sheer cliffs rise 600 feet at some points, and the river roars over three major falls, one of them 107 feet high. The park has a variety of accommodations, including an inn and a motel, a 270-site tent and trailer camping area and 82 camping cabins ranging from one room to family size.

The park offers plenty of amenities and activities, including swimming pools with bathhouses, fishing, whitewater rafting, hot air ballooning, nature and hiking trails and outstanding fall foliage. The William Pryor Letchworth Museum, the grave of Mary Jemison and a restored Seneca Indian Council House are also in the park.

1 Letchworth State Park, Castile, 585-493-3600; www.nysparks.state.ny.us

NEW YORK

★
★
★
★

RESTAURANT

★★GLEN IRIS INN

7 Letchworth State Park, Letchworth State Park, 585-493-2622; www.glenirisinn.com
American menu. Breakfast, lunch, dinner. Closed first weekend in November-Easter. Children's menu. **$$**

LEWISTON

This historic town is on the Canada-U.S. border, about 15 miles from Niagara Falls. The town offers a peek at dramatic scenery and a dose of American history.
Information: www.northofthefalls.com

RESTAURANTS

★★CLARKSON HOUSE

810 Center St., Lewiston, 716-754-4544; www.theclarksonhouse.com
Seafood, steak menu. Dinner. Bar. Children's menu. Reservations recommended. **$$$**

★VILLA COFFEE HOUSE

769 Cayuga St., Lewiston, 716-754-2660
Breakfast, lunch, dinner. Closed holidays. Children's menu. **$**

★★WATER STREET LANDING

115 S. Water St., Lewiston, 716-754-9200; www.waterstreetlanding.com
Built 1871; riverboat atmosphere. Lunch, dinner. Bar. Children's menu. Outdoor seating. **$$**

LIBERTY

Near the junction of the Willowemoc and Beaverkill rivers and on the edge of the Catskill Forest Preserve, this area offers good hunting and trout fishing, camping, hiking and sightseeing.
Information: Chamber of Commerce, Liberty, 845-292-1878

HOTELS

★★DAYS INN

52 Sullivan Ave., Liberty, 845-292-7600; www.daysinn.com
120 rooms. Business center. High-speed Internet access. Meeting space. Pool. Complimentary continental breakfast. Restaurant, bar. **$**

★★LANZA'S COUNTRY INN

839 Shandelee Road, Livingston Manor, 845-439-5070; www.lanzascountryinn.com
Eight rooms. Restaurant, bar.**$**

LIVERPOOL

This small community—it covers about one square mile—is on the shores of Onondaga Lake.
Information: www.villageofliverpool.org

SCOTTISH GAMES

Long Branch Park, Liverpool Parkway and Highway 370, Liverpool
Mid-August.

HOTEL
★HOMEWOOD SUITES

275 Elwood Davis Road, Liverpool, 315-451-3800; www.homewood-suites.com
102 rooms, all suites. Complimentary full breakfast. **$**

LOCKPORT

The town was originally settled around a series of locks of the Erie Canal, now the
New York State Barge Canal.
Information: Chamber of Commerce, 151 W. Genesee St., Lockport, 716-433-3828;
www.lockport-ny.com

WHAT TO SEE AND DO
CANAL BRIDGE

Cottage Street, Lockport
Claimed to be one of the widest single-span bridges (399½ feet) in the world. View
of the locks' operation, raising and lowering barges and pleasure craft more than
60 feet.

COLONEL WILLIAM BOND HOUSE

143 Ontario St., Lockport, 716-434-7433; www.niagarahistory.org
Pre-Victorian home was built with bricks made on site. Restored, with 12 furnished
rooms; of special interest are the kitchen and the children's garret. March-December,
Thursday, Saturday-Sunday afternoons.

KENAN CENTER

433 Locust St., Lockport, 716-433-2617; www.kenancenter.org
Art gallery and recreation/sports arena. Gallery September-May: daily; June-August:
Monday-Friday and Sunday; Taylor Theater; garden and orchard, herb garden.

NIAGARA COUNTY HISTORICAL CENTER

215 Niagara St., Lockport, 716-434-7433; www.niagarahistory.org
An 1860 brick house with antiques; Erie Canal artifacts. Pioneer Building contains
American Indian collection, pioneer artifacts; Washington Hunt Law Office (1835);
Niagara Fire Company No.1, with 1834 and 1836 pumpers. 19th-century farming
equipment. Thursday-Sunday; closed holidays.

HOTEL
★LOCKPORT MOTEL

315 S. Transit Road, Lockport, 716-434-5595; www.lockportmotel.com
90 rooms. Fireplaces and Jacuzzi suites. Wireless Internet access. Valet dry cleaning.
Pool. **$**

103

NEW YORK

★
★
★
★
★

RESTAURANT
★GARLOCK'S
35 S. Transit Road, Lockport, 716-433-5595; www.garlocksrestaurant.com
Seafood, steak menu. Dinner. Closed holidays. Bar. Children's menu. Casual attire. **$$**

LOCUST VALLEY
A hamlet of Oyster Bay, Locust Valley boasts swanky homes, several pristine golf courses and an elegant downtown shopping district.
Information: www.locustvalley.com

RESTAURANT
★★BARNEY'S RESTAURANT
315 Buckram Road, Locust Valley, 516-671-6300; www.barneyslv.com
American menu. Dinner. Closed Monday. Bar. Casual attire. Reservations recommended. **$$$**

LONG ISLAND
Long Island stretches 118 miles east by northeast from the edge of Manhattan to the lonely dunes of Montauk. Much of the island is ideal resort country, with vast white beaches, quiet bays, coves and woods.

At the eastern tip, Montauk Light stands on its headland. On the southwestern shore is Coney Island. New York City sprawls over the whole of Long Island's two westernmost counties—Queens and Kings (the boroughs of Queens and Brooklyn).

Nassau County, adjoining the city, is made up of suburbs filled with residential communities. Eastward in Suffolk County, city influence eases. Potatoes and the famous Long Island duck are still raised here alongside farms for horse breeding and the vineyards producing Long Island wines.

Long Island has many miles of sandy barrier beaches along the south shore, with swimming and surf casting. The bays behind these make natural small-boat harbors. On the more tranquil waters of the north shore is a series of deeper harbors along Long Island Sound, many of them with beaches and offering good sailing opportunities.

The island has played a major role in U.S. history from the early 17th century, and the record of this role is carefully preserved in many buildings, some 300 years old. Few regions offer such varied interests in so small an area. The Long Island Railroad conducts tours to points of interest on the island from late May to early November.
Information: www.licvb.com

LONG ISLAND CITY
The western-most neighborhood in Queens, Long Island City has experienced a resurgence in recent years thanks to commuters who work in Manhattan.
Information: www.licnyc.com

WHAT TO SEE AND DO
P. S. 1 CONTEMPORARY ARTS CENTER—WARM UP MUSIC SERIES
22-25 Jackson Ave., Long Island City, 11101, 718-784-2084; www.ps1.org
This new-wave community arts center in Queens attracts the hippest of DJs and crowds to its Saturday afternoon/evening outdoor dance parties in its courtyard. You won't see dance parties like these anywhere else. All ages are welcome. July-August; Saturday evenings.

ESCAPE TO LONG ISLAND

Long Island is a world unto itself—especially off the Long Island Expressway. A mix of city sophistication and rural simplicity, Long Island is a playground for New Yorkers, who find the state parks, wildlife sanctuaries and small towns refreshing. From New York City, take Southern Parkway 27 to Freeport, then Meadowbrook Parkway south. Stop and visit the beautiful white beaches of Jones Beach State Park. Unwind by swimming in the cool waters of the Atlantic, fishing, boating, exploring the nature and bike trails, golfing, or playing softball or shuffleboard. Then continue East on the Parkway along the Atlantic Ocean to **JFK Wildlife Sanctuary, Cedar Beach** in **Gilgo Beach State Park** and **Oak Beach**.

Cross over Robert Moses Bridge for a trip to **Robert Moses State Park**, located on the western end of **Fire Island National Seashore**. The pristine white-sand beach located here features such amenities as rest rooms, showers, lifeguards, concession and picnic areas. Camping is available farther East at **Watch Hill**. Ranger-led interpretive canoe programs and nature walks begin at the Watch Hill visitor center. Stop in at the picturesque **Fire Island Light Station** to visit the ground-floor museum, which houses exhibits on shipwrecks and offshore rescues. The lighthouse can be toured if reservations are made in advance. From there, backtrack across the bridge to **Robert Moses Causeway**. Take State Route 27A East to Bay Shore to visit 690-acre **Bayard Cutting Arboretum**. Continue through Islip and East Islip back to 27 (Sunrise Expressway), connecting with 27A again to **Shinnecock Indian Reservation** and **Southampton**.

One of the oldest English settlements in New York, Southampton was settled in 1640 by colonists from Massachusetts. Today, it is a blue-blood resort, with old established homes lining the shady lanes as well as swanky boutiques and numerous restaurants. Tour the **Old Halsey House**, the oldest English frame house in New York. The **Parrish Art Museum** features 19th- and 20th-century American art, as well as Japanese woodblock prints and changing exhibits. The **Southampton Historical Museum** includes a fantastic collection of Indian artifacts.

Continue on to **East Hampton**, a very chic resort town with terrific shopping and restaurants. Take a guided tour of the 1806 windmill at **Hook Mill** or visit the **Guild Hall Museum** for a look at regional art. Explore **Historic Mulford Farm**, a living history museum with costumed interpreters or make an appointment to tour artist Jackson Pollock's home and studio. The nearby town of Amagansett is home to the **Town Marine Museum**—sure to be a hit with anglers. Exhibits explore commercial and sport fishing, whaling, fishing techniques and underwater archeology. At the very tip of Long Island is **Montauk**, home to **Hither Hills State Park** and **Montauk Point State Park**. Be sure to tour the **Montauk Point Lighthouse Museum** before taking Montauk Highway to the Long Island Expressway and then back to Manhattan.

NEW YORK

★
★
★
★
★

LONG ISLAND WINERIES

When Moses Fournier planted his French grapes during the pre-colonial period, he couldn't have imagined that vintners and visitors would be drawn to the region hundreds of years later for the same qualities that lured him: sunshine and fertile soil. Today, wine tastings and winery tours are popular in the Hamptons, particularly in the fall and on rainy weekends. Winemaking dates back almost 30 years on Long Island, and the region received a special designation as an American Viticultural Area on July 16, 2001. This assures that the grape-growing region has specific, ideal winemaking characteristics, including the right climate and soil conditions. Though there are fewer South Fork wineries than North Fork ones, visiting these wineries is always a pleasant way to spend an afternoon. **Channing Daughters Winery** (*1927 Scuttle Hole Road, Bridgehampton, 631-537-7224*), one of the newer wineries, opened its tasting room in 1998. A large chateau is the home of **Duck Walk Vineyards** (*231 Montauk Highway, Water Mill, 631-726-555*) where Dr. Herodotus Damianos of Pindar Vineyards grows local grapes and produces wine. **Wolffer Estate Vineyard** (*139 Sagg Road, Sagaponack, 631-537-5106*), formerly known as Sagpond Vineyards, was the first winery to produce estate-bottled wines. The estate's owner, Christian Wölffer, has built a stunning winery where tasting and sales take place under soaring ceilings.

Visitors willing to spend an extra hour (each way) traveling to Long Island's Wine Country on the **North Fork** will find the experience more than worthwhile. (Of course, this trip can take much longer on busy summer days.) The North Fork's two main roads run for 30 miles west to east, but there are a number of wineries near Greenport. Follow the grape cluster signs on Main Road (Route 25) and on Sound Avenue (North Road/Route 48). Among the top Main Road wineries are **Bedell Cellars**, **Bidwell Vineyards**, **Corey Creek Vineyards**, **Gristina Vineyards**, **Lenz Winery**, **Paumonok Vineyards**, **Pellegrini Vineyards** and **Pindar Vineyards**. **Pugliese Vineyards** is on Bridge Lane in Cutchogue, one of the many short north/south roads that connect the two east/west arteries. On Sound Avenue, **Hargrave Vineyards** and **Palmer Vineyards** offer award-winning selections.

RESTAURANTS

★★MANDUCATIS

1327 Jackson Ave., Long Island City, 718-729-4602; www.manducatis.com
Italian menu. Lunch, dinner. Closed holidays; also the last two weeks in August. Bar. $$

★★TOURNESOL

50-12 Vernon Blvd., Long Island City, 718-472-4355; www.tournesolnyc.com
French menu. Lunch, dinner, brunch. Bar. Casual attire. Reservations recommended. Outdoor seating. $$

★CASA MIA
2040 Goshen Turnpike, 211 E., Middletown, 845-692-2323
Italian, American menu. Dinner. Closed Monday, holidays. Bar. Children's menu. **$$**

MILLBROOK

Hunting for your next Louis XVI chair? A rare first-edition book? How about a hard-to-find print? Millbrook might be the perfect place to begin (and end) your search. Antiquing here is great, and there are plenty of restaurants that will sustain you between shopping sprees.
Information: www.millbrooknyonline.com

RESTAURANTS
★★CAFE LES BAUX
152 Church St., Millbrook, 845-677-8166; www.cafelesbaux.com
French menu. Lunch, dinner, brunch. Closed Tuesday; holidays. Casual attire. Reservations recommended. **$$**

★★CHARLOTTE'S
4258 Route 44, Millbrook, 845-677-5888; www.charlottesny.com
American menu. Lunch, dinner, Sunday brunch. Closed Tuesday. Bar. Children's menu. Outdoor seating. **$$**

★MILLBROOK CAFÉ
Franklin Avenue, Millbrook, 845-677-6956
American menu. Lunch, dinner. Closed Monday, children's menu. Casual attire. Reservations recommended. **$$$**

MINEOLA

Mineola has a long and storied relationship with aviation. The Wright Brothers, Igor Sikorsky, Capt. Rene Fonck and Clarence Chamberlain and his partner Bert Acosta all tested their various flying apparatuses here, an appealing place of rolling hills and good breezes. Charles Lindbergh took off from nearby Roosevelt Field on May 20, 1927 for his historic solo flight to Paris.
Information: www.mineola-ny.gov

RESTAURANT
★★CHURRASQUEIRA BAIRRADA
144 Jericho Turnpike, Mineola, 516-739-3856; www.churrasqueira.com
Portuguese steak menu. Lunch, dinner. Closed Monday. Bar. **$$**

MONTAUK

This is a lively, somewhat honky-tonk fishing town at the far eastern end of Long Island, with a big business in deep-sea fishing (tuna, shark, marlin, striped bass and other varieties). Boats can be rented, and there are miles of uncrowded sandy beaches

109

NEW YORK

for sunning and surfing. Of course, there is also a glittering summer community here, too, but residents like Ralph Lauren tend to be more low-key than the denizens of other nearby Hamptons communities.

Information: Chamber of Commerce, Montauk, 631-668-2428; www.montaukchamber.com

WHAT TO SEE AND DO
HITHER HILLS STATE PARK
50 S. Fairview Ave., Montauk, 631-668-2554; www.nysparks.state.ny.us/parks/info.asp?parkid=48

Swimming beach, bathhouse, lifeguards, fishing; nature and hiking trails, picnicking, playground, concession, tent and trailer sites; mid-April-November; reservations required.

MONTAUK LIGHTHOUSE
Montauk Point, Montauk, 631-668-2544; www.montauklighthouse.com

You've come as far east as you can on Long Island. In fact, Montauk Point is called "The End" by locals. What better way to end a trip on Long Island than with a visit to this historic lighthouse that was commissioned by George Washington and completed in 1796? It's the oldest lighthouse in the state, featuring 137 winding narrow steps to the top and views of the ocean from any angle. The lighthouse beacon still rotates and can be seen for 19 nautical miles. Mid-May-October from 10:30 a.m.; closing times vary.

MONTAUK POINT STATE PARK
50 S. Fairview Ave., Montauk, 631-668-3781; www.nysparks.state.ny.us/parks

Barren moor with sea-view Montauk Lighthouse; museum, tours (summer weekends), fishing; hiking, biking, picnicking, concession.

HOTELS
★★★GURNEY'S INN RESORT AND SPA
290 Old Montauk Highway, Montauk, 631-668-2345, 800-445-8062; www.gurneys-inn.com

This sprawling resort facing the Atlantic Ocean offers a peaceful escape. Once here, head to the beautiful beach, take a sunrise walk or participate in activities like volleyball or yoga. The Seawater Spa offers body wraps and scrubs, massage therapy, facials and salon services. The indoor heated pool, which features seawater drawn from the resort's own wells, has views from its floor-to-ceiling windows. Contemporary elegance is the theme of guest rooms. 109 rooms, all suites. Three restaurants, bar. Spa. Beach. **$$$**

★★★MONTAUK YACHT CLUB
32 Star Island Road, Montauk, 631-668-3100, 800-692-8668; www.montaukyachtclub.com

The resort's 60-foot lighthouse replica, built in 1928, is still a focal point at this elegant retreat overlooking Lake Montauk. The numerous activities include volleyball, charter fishing, the La Bella Vita Spa and a fitness center with saunas. 107 rooms. Closed December-March. Two restaurants, two bars. Children's activity center. Beach. **$$**

SPECIALTY LODGING

BURCLIFFE BY THE SEA

397 Old Montauk Highway, Montauk, 631-668-2880;
www.montauklife.com/h-burrcliff/burcliff.html

Seven rooms. Closed December-mid-January. **$$**

RESTAURANTS

★★CROW'S NEST RESTAURANT & INN

4 Old West Lake Drive, Montauk, 631-668-2077; www.crowsnestinn.com

American menu. Lunch, dinner. Bar. Children's menu. Casual attire. **$$**

★★DAVE'S GRILL

468 W. Lake Drive, Montauk, 631-668-9190; www.davesgrill.com

Seafood menu. Dinner. Closed Wednesday; also November-April. Bar. Casual attire.
Outdoor seating. **$$**

★★GOSMAN'S RESTAURANT

500 W. Lake Drive, Montauk, 631-668-5330; www.gosmans.com

Seafood menu. Lunch, dinner. Closed mid-October-mid-April. Bar. Children's menu.
Casual attire. Outdoor seating. **$$**

★★HARVEST

11 S. Emery St., Montauk, 631-668-5574; www.harvest2000.com

Mediterranean menu. Dinner. Closed February; also holidays. Bar. Business casual
attire. Outdoor seating. **$$$**

★MONTAUKET

88 Firestone Road, Montauk, 631-668-5992

American menu. Lunch, dinner. Bar. Children's menu. Casual attire. Outdoor seating. **$$**

★★SECOND HOUSE TAVERN

161 Second House Road, Montauk, 631-668-2877; www.secondhousetavern.com

Dinner. Bar. Children's menu. Outdoor seating. **$$**

★SHAGWONG RESTAURANT

774 Main St., Montauk Highway, Montauk, 631-668-3050; www.shagwong.com

American, seafood menu. Lunch, dinner, late-night, Sunday brunch. Bar. Children's
menu. Casual attire. Outdoor seating. **$$**

MOUNT KISCO

About 35 miles north of New York City, Mount Kisco is a hub in Westchester County.
Information: Chamber of Commerce, 3 N. Moger Ave., Mount Kisco,
914-666-7525; www.mtkisco.com

WHAT TO SEE AND DO

CARAMOOR CENTER FOR MUSIC AND THE ARTS

149 Girdle Ridge Road, Mount Kisco, 914-232-5035; www.caramoor.org

European-style villa built during 1930s. Collections of Chinese art, Italian Renaissance furniture; European paintings, sculptures and tapestries dating from the Middle

Ages through the 19th century; formal gardens. Martha Stewart's farm is just across the street. Tours June-mid-November: Thursday, Saturday and Sunday afternoons, also Wednesday, Friday by appointment; rest of year: by appointment. Also Summer Music Festival late June-mid-August.

JOHN JAY HOMESTEAD STATE HISTORIC SITE
400 J St., Katonah, 914-232-5651; www.johnjayhomestead.org
Estate of the first chief justice of the United States and four generations of his descendants; period furnishings, American portrait collection, gardens, farm buildings and grounds. Visits by guided tour only. April-October, Tuesday-Saturday 10 a.m.-5 p.m., Sunday 11 a.m.-5 p.m.; November-March, Tuesday-Saturday 10 a.m.-4 p.m., Sunday 11 a.m.-4 p.m.

HOTEL
★★HOLIDAY INN
1 Holiday Inn Drive, Mount Kisco, 914-241-2600, 888-452-5771; www.holiday-inn.com
122 rooms. High-speed Internet access. Restaurant, bar. $

RESTAURANTS
★★BISTRO 22
391 Old Post Road, Bedford Village, 914-234-7333
American, French menu. Lunch, dinner. Bar. Business casual attire. Reservations recommended. $$$

★★★CRABTREE'S KITTLE HOUSE
11 Kittle Road, Chappaqua, 914-666-8044; www.kittlehouse.com
This impressive historic restaurant serves the likes of slow-cooked wild Alaskan salmon with Jerusalem artichokes, and acorn and butternut squash risotto with toasted pumpkin seeds in a romantic, country-style setting. American menu. Lunch, dinner. Bar. Business casual attire. Reservations recommended. Outdoor seating. $$$

★★★LA CAMELIA
234 N. Bedford Road, Mount Kisco, 914-666-2466
This Spanish gem is located high upon a hilltop and is the perfect spot for a romantic dinner date. Share any of the wonderful tapas selections—like the piquillo peppers stuffed with cod or the traditional gazpacho Andaluz—paired with a bottle of a rioja or albarino wine. Spanish menu. Lunch, dinner, Sunday brunch. Closed Monday; holidays. Bar. Casual attire. Reservations recommended. Outdoor seating. $$

★★LE JARDIN DU ROI
95 King St., Chappaqua, 914-238-1368; www.lejardinchappaqua.com
French menu. Breakfast, lunch, dinner, brunch. Casual attire. Outdoor seating. $$

★★★TRAVELER'S REST
Route 100, Ossining, 914-941-7744; www.thetravelersrest.com
Serving continental-German food since the 1800s, this restaurant prepares seafood, beef and poultry specialties such as beef Wellington and baked stuffed fillet of sole in an old-world setting surrounded by formal gardens. Continental, German menu.

Dinner, brunch. Closed Monday-Tuesday. Bar. Children's menu. Casual attire. Reservations recommended. Outdoor seating. **$$$**

MOUNT TREMPER

This getaway in the Catskills is not far from the free love and artists' haven of Woodstock.

Information: woodstockchamber.com

HOTELS

★★★EMERSON RESORT & SPA

5340 Route 28, Mount Tremper, 877-688-2828; www.emersonresort.com

A country retreat with a Zen feel, rooms at this resort are available in the rustic lodge or the adults-only inn, which has 25 luxury suites with fireplaces and whirlpool tubs. The Phoenix restaurant serves sophisticated dishes with an Asian flair, while the Spa Café delivers food as soothing and delicious as a day at the resort's onsite spa. Restaurant. Spa.

★★KATE'S LAZY MEADOW MOTEL

5191 Highway 28, Mount Tremper, 845-688-7200; www.lazymeadow.com

Seven rooms, all suites. High-speed Internet access. Whirlpool. **$$**

RESTAURANT

★SWEET SUE

Route 28 Main St., Phoenicia, 845-688-7852

American menu. Breakfast, lunch, brunch. Closed Tuesday. Children's menu. Casual attire. Outdoor seating. **$**

SPA

★★★★THE EMERSON SPA

5340 Route 28, Mount Tremper, 877-688-2828; www.emersonresort.com

This Indian-influenced upstate spa features 10 treatment rooms perfect for sampling a variety of eastern-inspired treatments. Indian head massage, Dosha balancing massage and Abhyanga massage, involving two therapists in unison, are some of the bodywork offerings, while shirodhara and bindi herbal body treatments round out the Ayurvedic menu. From aromatherapy facials and sea salt body scrubs to warm mud wraps, many of the treatments use natural ingredients for cleansing, detoxifying, and healing the skin.

NAPLES

At the south end of Canandaigua Lake, one of the Finger Lakes, Naples is the center of a grape-growing, winemaking area. Many of its residents are descendants of Swiss and German winemakers.

Information: www.naplesvalleyny.com

WHAT TO SEE AND DO

CUMMING NATURE CENTER OF THE ROCHESTER MUSEUM & SCIENCE CENTER

6472 Gulick Road, Naples, 585-374-6160; www.rmsc.org

A 900-acre living museum; nature trails, natural history programs; conservation trail with operating sawmill; cross-country skiing (rentals) and snowshoeing. Visitors' building with theater and exhibit hall. Late December-mid-November, Wednesday-Sunday.

WIDMER'S WINE CELLARS
1 Lake Niagara Lane, Naples, 585-374-6311; www.widmerwine.com
Tours, wine tasting; daily, afternoons.

SPECIALTY LODGING
THE VAGABOND INN
3300 Sliter Hill Road, Naples, 585-554-6271, 877-554-6271; www.thevagabondinn.com
Secluded in the Bristol Mountains in the picturesque Finger Lakes region, this inn is a quiet hideaway close to wineries, ski areas and the Finger Lakes Performing Arts Center. Five rooms. Children over 13 years only. Complimentary full breakfast. Whirlpool. **$**

RESTAURANT
★★NAPLES HOTEL
111 S. Main St., Naples, 585-374-5630; www.naplesinnandsuites.com
German menu. Lunch, dinner. Bar. Children's menu. **$$**

NEW PALTZ
New Paltz was founded by a dozen Huguenots who were granted land by the colonial governor of New York. The town is surrounded by the fertile farmlands of the Wallkill River Valley, with apple orchards and vineyards.
Information: Chamber of Commerce, 124 Main St., New Paltz, 845-255-0243; www.newpaltzchamber.org

WHAT TO SEE AND DO
HUGUENOT STREET OLD STONE HOUSES
New Paltz, 914-255-1660
Six original stone dwellings (1692-1712), a reconstructed French church (1717); Jean Hasbrouck House (1694) of medieval Flemish stone architecture. All houses furnished with heirlooms of descendants. May-October, Tuesday-Sunday.

LOCUST LAWN
400 Highway 32 S., New Paltz, 845-255-1660; www.huguenotstreet.org
Federal mansion of Josiah Hasbrouck (1814). Includes smokehouse, farmers' museum; Terwilliger Homestead (1738); bird sanctuary. By appointment.

SPECIAL EVENTS
APPLE FESTIVAL/CRAFTS FAIR
Huguenot Street, New Paltz, 845-255-6340; www.newpaltzchamber.org
Second Saturday in October.

STONE HOUSE DAY
Highway 32 N. and Broadhead Avenue, New Paltz, 845-331-4121; www.stonehouseday.org
Tour of eight privately owned colonial stone houses, led by costumed guides; Hurley Reformed Church and old burial ground; antique show; re-creation of Revolutionary War military encampment; country fair. Second Saturday in July.

HOTEL

★★ROCKING HORSE RANCH RESORT

600 Highway 44-55, Highland, 845-691-2927, 800-647-2624; www.rhranch.com
120 rooms. Bar. Children's activity center. Spa, whirlpool. **$$**

RESTAURANTS

★★★DEPUY CANAL HOUSE

Route 213, High Falls, 845-687-7700; www.depuycanalhouse.net
Located in a charming, 18th-century stone house, the DePuy Canal House creates culinary fireworks like the quarter-braised duck with pierogies and quail and duck sfogliatelle on a whole button mushroom sauce. There are also a handful of charming guest rooms should you wish to stay longer than dinner or Sunday brunch. American menu. Dinner, brunch. Closed Monday-Wednesday. Bar. Business casual attire. Reservations recommended. Outdoor seating. **$$$**

★MAIN STREET BISTRO

59 Main St., New Paltz, 845-255-7766; www.mainstreetbistro.com
American, Vegetarian menu. Lunch, dinner, brunch. Closed holidays. Casual attire. Outdoor seating. **$$**

★★ROSENDALE CAFE

434 Main St., Rosendale, 845-658-9048; www.rosendalecafe.com
Vegetarian menu. Lunch, dinner. Casual attire. Reservations recommended. Outdoor seating. **$$**

★YANNI

51 Main St., New Paltz, 845-256-0988
Greek/Mediterranean menu. Breakfast, lunch, dinner. Bar. Casual attire. Reservations recommended. Outdoor seating. **$$**

NEW ROCHELLE

New Rochelle was founded in 1688 by a group of Huguenot families. Prior to European settlement, the area was home to the Siwanoys, a tribe of Mohegans stemming from the Algonquins. Boat building was the trade of many of the early settlers, who used these boats to carry goods to and from New York City and other towns and ports on the coast.
Information: Chamber of Commerce, 459 Main St., New Rochelle, 914-632-5700; www.newrochellechamber.org

WHAT TO SEE AND DO

THOMAS PAINE NATIONAL HISTORICAL ASSOCIATION

983 North Ave., New Rochelle, 914-632-5376; www.thomaspaine.org
Museum containing original writings and artifacts of Thomas Paine, author of *Common Sense;* also histories of the Huguenots and New Rochelle. Friday-Sunday, also by appointment; closed winter.

THOMAS PAINE COTTAGE

20 Sicard Ave., New Rochelle, 914-632-5376; www.thomaspainecottage.org
Located on the last two acres of the original 320 given to Thomas Paine by New York State in 1784, you will find Thomas Paine's second cottage (rebuilt after a fire claimed

★
★
★
★
★

the first one in 1793), and the Sophia Brewster One-Room Schoolhouse. The Thomas Paine Cottage contains a few of the artifacts still in existence that were once owned by Thomas Paine: a simple chair and a cast-iron Franklin Stove given to Paine by Benjamin Franklin himself.

RESTAURANTS

★COYOTE FLACO

273 North Ave., New Rochelle, 914-636-7222; www.mycoyoteflaco.com
Mexican menu. Lunch, dinner. Closed Monday. Bar. Casual attire. Outdoor seating. **$$**

NEW YORK

New York is the nation's most populous city, the capital of finance, dining, business, communications, theater, fashion, beauty—the list goes on from there. It may or may not be the center of the universe—native New Yorkers swear it is—but the metropolis does occupy a central place in the world's imagination.

Giovanni da Verrazano was the first European to glimpse Manhattan Island in 1524, but the area was not explored until 1609, when Henry Hudson sailed up the river that was later named for him searching for a passage to India. The Dutch West Indian Company established the first trading post in 1615. Peter Minuit is said to have bought the island from American Indians for $24 worth of beads and trinkets in 1626, when New Amsterdam was founded—the biggest real estate bargain in history.

In 1664, the Dutch surrendered to a British fleet and the town was renamed New York in honor of the Duke of York. One of the earliest tests of independence occurred here in 1734 when John Peter Zenger, publisher and editor of the *New York Weekly Journal*, was charged with seditious libel and jailed for making anti-government remarks. Following the Battle of Long Island in 1776, the British occupied the city through the Revolution until 1783.

On the balcony of Federal Hall at Wall Street, April 30, 1789, George Washington was inaugurated as the first president of the United States, and for a time New York was the country's capital.

When the Erie Canal opened in 1825, New York City expanded as a port. In 1898, Manhattan merged with Brooklyn, the Bronx, Queens and Staten Island. In the next half-century several million immigrants entered the United States through New York, providing the city with the supply of labor needed for its growth. Each wave of immigrants has brought new customs, culture and lifestyles, which make New York City the varied metropolis it is today.

The city was changed permanently on September 11, 2001 when terrorists hijacked two commercial airliners and flew them into the World Trade Center towers, which later collapsed. Nearly 3,000 people were killed in the towers, the planes and on the ground. The emotional and physical scars left by these attacks were profound. The area where the World Trade Center and many of its surrounding buildings has since been cleared, and plans for a memorial and rebuilding in the area are under way. Many visitors now make a pilgrimage to the Lower Manhattan site to better understand the events and implications of this tragic event.

Since 2001, New York has revitalized its image as the Big Apple, attracting more than 39 million visitors each year. Most of its many attractions are centered in Manhattan; however, do not overlook the wealth of sights and activities the other boroughs have to offer. Brooklyn has Coney Island, the New York Aquarium, the superb Brooklyn History Museum, Brooklyn Botanic Garden, Brooklyn Children's Museum and the famous Brooklyn Bridge. The Bronx is noted for its excellent Botanical Garden and Zoo and Yankee Stadium. Flushing Meadows-Corona Park, in Queens, was the site of two World's Fairs; nearby is Shea Stadium, home of the New York Mets. Uncrowded Staten Island has Richmond Town Restoration, a re-creation of 18th-century New York, rural farmland, beaches, salt marshes and wildlife preserves.

Information: New York City Convention & Visitors Bureau, 810 Seventh Ave., New York, 212-484-1200; www.nycvisit.com

NEIGHBORHOODS

CHINATOWN

The only truly ethnic neighborhood still thriving in Manhattan, Chinatown has streets teeming with crowds, bustling restaurants, exotic markets and prosperous shops. Once limited to a small enclave contained in the six blocks between the Bowery and Mulberry Street, Canal and Worth streets (now known as "traditional" Chinatown), it has burst these boundaries in recent years to spread north of Canal Street into Little Italy and east into the Lower East Side.

Chinatown is the perfect neighborhood for haphazard wandering. In traditional Chinatown, every twist or turn of the small, winding streets brings mounds of shiny fish (live carp, eels and crabs), piles of fresh produce (cabbage, ginger root, Chinese broccoli) or displays of pretty, colorful objects (toys, handbags, knickknacks). Bakeries selling everything from moon cakes and almond cookies to cow ears (chips of fried dough) and pork buns are everywhere, as is the justifiably famous Chinatown Ice Cream Factory (65 Bayard Street, near Mott) selling ice cream in flavors such as ginger and mango.

Chinese men, accompanied by only a handful of women, began arriving in New York in the late 1870s. Many were former transcontinental railroad workers who came to escape the persecution they were experiencing on the West Coast. They weren't especially welcomed on the East Coast either, and soon thereafter, the violent tong wars between criminal Chinese gangs helped lead to the Exclusion Acts of 1882, 1888, 1902 and 1924, forbidding further Chinese immigration. Chinatown became a bachelor society, almost devoid of women and children—a situation that continued until the lifting of immigration quotas in 1965.

Today, Chinatown's estimated population of 100,000 is made up of two especially large groups—the well-established Cantonese community that has been in New York for more than a century, and the Fujianese community, a much newer and poorer group who come from the Fujian Province on the southern coast of mainland China. The Cantonese own many of the prosperous shops and restaurants in traditional Chinatown, whereas the Fujianese have set up rice-noodle shops, herbal medicine shops and outdoor markets along Broadway and neighboring streets between Canal Street and the Manhattan Bridge.

To learn more about the history of Chinatown, visit the Museum of Chinese in the Americas (70 Mulberry Street, at Bayard). To get a good meal, explore almost any street; Mott Street—the neighborhood's main thoroughfare—has an abundance of restaurants. Pell Street is especially known for its barber and beauty shops and for its Buddhist Temple (4 Pell Street). The neighborhood's biggest festival is Chinese New Year, celebrated between mid-January and early February. During that time, the streets come alive with dragon dances, lion dances and fireworks.

TRIBECA

Short for *Tri*angle *Be*low *Ca*nal, Tribeca is a former industrial district encompassing about 40 blocks between Canal, Chambers and West Streets, and Broadway. Like Soho, its more fashionable cousin to the north, the neighborhood discarded its working-class roots years ago and now has its share of expensive restaurants and boutiques. Upper-middle-class residents have replaced factory workers, and avant-garde establishments have replaced sweatshops.

Nonetheless, Tribeca is much quieter than Soho—and many other sections of Manhattan—and, in parts, still retains its 19th-century feel, complete with cobblestone streets. After dark much of the area seems close to deserted.

Tribeca's main thoroughfares are Broadway, West Broadway and Church Street, three wide roads comfortable for strolling. West Broadway was originally built to relieve the congestion of Broadway and is home to a few art galleries, including the Soho Photo Gallery (15 White Street at W. Broadway), a cooperative gallery featuring the work of 100-plus members. At Church and Walker Streets reign the sleek Tribeca Grand, the neighborhood's first upscale hotel.

Also well known is the Tribeca Film Center, housed in the landmark Martinson Coffee Company warehouse (375 Greenwich Street). Actor Robert De Niro started the center in 1989. He wanted to create a site where filmmakers could talk business, screen films and socialize. Today, the center houses the offices of several major producers and the Tribeca Grill, a chic eatery usually filled with more celebrity-watchers than celebrities.

At Greenwich and Harrison Streets stand the Harrison Houses, a group of nine restored Federal-style homes. Several were designed by John McComb, Jr., New York's first architect. East of the houses, at the northwest corner of Harrison and Hudson Streets is the former New York Mercantile Exchange. In this five-story building, complete with gables and a tower, $15,000 worth of eggs would change hands in an hour around the turn-of-the-century. Today, Tribeca is still the city's distribution center for eggs, cheese, and butter. A few remaining wholesalers cluster around Duane Park, one block south of the former exchange, between Hudson and Greenwich streets.

SOHO

Short for *So*uth of *Ho*uston (HOW-stun), Soho is New York's trendiest neighborhood, filled with an impossible number of upscale eateries, fancy boutiques, of-the-moment bars and, most recently, a few astronomically expensive hotels. Contained in just 25 blocks bounded by Houston and Canal Streets, Lafayette and West Broadway, Soho attracts trend followers and tourists by the thousands, especially on weekend afternoons, when the place sometimes feels like one giant open-air bazaar.

From the late 1800s to the mid-1900s, Soho was primarily a light manufacturing district, but starting in the 1960s, most of the factories moved out and artists—attracted by the area's low rents and loft spaces—began moving in. Soon thereafter, the art galleries arrived, and then the shops and restaurants. Almost overnight, Soho became too expensive for the artists—and, more recently, the art galleries—who had originally settled the place, and transformed into a mecca for big-bucks shoppers from all over the world.

Nonetheless, Soho still has plenty to offer art lovers. Broadway is lined with one first-rate museum after another, while Mercer and Greene Streets in particular boast a large number of galleries. Some top spots on Broadway include the Museum for African Art (593 Broadway), presenting an excellent array of changing exhibits and the New Museum for Contemporary Art (583 Broadway), one of the oldest, best-known and most controversial art spaces in Soho. To find out who's exhibiting what and where in Soho, pick up a copy of the "Art Now Gallery Guide," available at many bookstores and galleries.

Soho is also home to an extraordinary number of cast-iron buildings. Originally meant to serve as a cheap substitute for stone buildings, the cast-iron façades were an American invention, prefabricated in a variety of styles—from Italian Renaissance to Classical Greek—and bolted onto the front of iron-frame structures. Most of Soho's best cast-iron gems can be found along Broadway. Keep an eye out for the Haughwout Building (488 Broadway), the Singer Building (561 Broadway) and the Guggenheim Museum Soho (575 Broadway).

Top thoroughfares for shopping include Prince and Spring Streets, Broadway and West Broadway. Numerous clothing and accessory boutiques are located along all these streets; West Broadway also offers several interesting bookstores. For antiques and furnishings, check out Lafayette Street; for craft and toy stores, try Greene and Mercer streets.

Restaurants and bars line almost every street in Soho, but one especially lively nexus is the intersection of Grand Street and West Broadway. West Broadway itself is also home to a large number of eateries, some of which offer outdoor dining in the summer.

EAST VILLAGE

Once considered part of the Lower East Side, the East Village is considerably scruffier and more rambunctious than its better-known sister to the West. For years, it was the refuge of immigrants and the working class, but in the 1950s, struggling writers, actors and artists—forced out of Greenwich Village by rising rents—began moving in. First came well-known names such as Willem de Kooning and W. H. Auden followed by the beatniks, the hippies, the yippies, the rock groups, the punk musicians and the fashion designers.

Only in the 1980s did the neighborhood start to gentrify, as young professionals moved in, bringing with them upscale restaurants and smart shops. Ever since, New York's continuously rising rents have forced out many of the younger, poorer and more creative types that the East Village was known for just two decades ago. Nonetheless, the neighborhood has not completely succumbed and offers an interesting mix between the cutting edge and the mainstream.

The heart of the East Village is St. Mark's Place, an always-packed thoroughfare where you'll find everything from punked-out musicians to well-heeled business types, leather shops to sleek bistros. Many of the street's noisiest addresses are between Third and Second Avenues; many of its most appealing, farther east. At the eastern end of St. Mark's Place stretches Tompkins Square Park, once known for its drug dealers, now known for its families and jungle gyms. Some of the best shops that fill the East Village can be found on Avenue A near the park; others line Seventh and Ninth Streets east of Second Avenue.

The neighborhood's second major thoroughfare, Second Avenue, was home to many lively Yiddish theaters early in the 20th century. At Second Avenue and East Tenth Street is St. Marks-in-the-Bowery, an historic church where Peter Stuyvesant—the last of the Dutch governors who ruled Manhattan in the 1600s—is buried. The church is also known for its poetry readings, performance art and leftist politics.

On the western edge of the East Village sprawls Astor Place, home to Cooper Union—the city's first free educational institution, now a design school—and a huge cube sculpture oddly balanced on one corner. On Lafayette Street at the southern end of Astor Place sits the Joseph Papp Public Theater, housed in an imposing columned building that was once the Astor Library. The theater is renowned for its first-run productions and for Shakespeare in the Park, a free festival that it produces every summer in Central Park.

GREENWICH VILLAGE

Although New York's fabled bohemian neighborhood has gone seriously upscale and more mainstream in recent decades, evidence of its iconoclastic past can still be found in its many narrow streets, off-Broadway theaters, cozy coffee shops, lively jazz clubs and tiny bars. Stretching from 14th Street south to Houston Street, and from Broadway west to the Hudson River, Greenwich Village remains one of the city's best places for idle wandering, people-watching, boutique browsing and conversing over glasses of cabernet or cups of cappuccino.

Washington Square Park anchors the neighborhood to the east and, though it's nothing special to look at, is still the heart of the Village. On a sunny afternoon, everyone comes here: kids hotdogging on skateboards, students strumming guitars, old men playing chess. Bordering the edges of the park are a mix of elegant townhouses and New York University buildings.

Just south and west of Washington Square are Bleecker and MacDougal Streets, home to coffee shops and bars once frequented by the likes of James Baldwin, Jack Kerouac, Allen Ginsberg and James Agee. Le Figaro (corner of Bleecker and Mac-Dougal) and the San Remo (93 MacDougal) were favorites back then and still attract crowds today, albeit mostly made up of tourists.

A bit farther west is Seventh Avenue South, where you'll find the Village Vanguard (178 Seventh Avenue S., at 11th Street), the oldest and most venerable jazz club in the city. Also nearby are the Blue Note (131 West Third Street, near Avenue of the Americas), New York's premier jazz supper club and Smalls (183 West 10th St. near Seventh Avenue S.), one of the best places to catch up-and-coming talent.

At the corner of Seventh Avenue South and Christopher Street stands Christopher Park, where a George Segal sculpture of two gay couples commemorates the Stonewall Riots, which marked the launch of the gay-rights movement. The Stonewall Inn, where the demonstration began in 1969, once stood directly across from the park at 51 Christopher, and Christopher Street itself is still lined with many gay establishments. At the corner of Sixth Avenue and West 10th Street reigns the gothic towers and turrets of Jefferson Market Library, a stunning brick building that dates to 1876.

CHELSEA

Primarily middle-class residential and still somewhat industrial, Chelsea—stretching between 14th and 30th Streets, from Sixth Avenue to the Hudson River—is not the most tourist-oriented neighborhood. However, the area does offer an exciting, avant-garde arts scene, as well as many lovely quiet blocks lined with attractive row houses. A gay community has moved in, bringing with it trendy cafes, shops and bars, while an enormous state-of-the-art sports complex, the Chelsea Piers, beckons from the river's edge (between 18th and 22nd Streets).

Most of Chelsea was once owned by Captain Thomas Clarke, whose grandson, Clement Charles Clarke, laid out the residential district in the early 1800s. Clement Charles was also a scholar and a poet who wrote the famous poem beginning with the line, "'Twas the night before Christmas..." Another of Clement Charles's legacies is the General Theological Seminary, a peaceful enclave of ivy-covered buildings bounded by the block between Ninth and Tenth Avenues and 20th and 21st Streets.

Also on the western edge of Chelsea are many of the city's foremost art galleries, which began moving here in the early 1990s as rents in Soho—their former home—began skyrocketing. An especially large number can be found on West 21st and 22nd Streets between Tenth and Eleventh Avenues; among them are the Paula Cooper Gallery (534 West 21st St.) and the Maximum Protech Gallery (511 West 22nd St.).

Most of Chelsea's thriving shops, restaurants and bars—many of which are predominantly gay—stand along Sixth and Eighth Avenues between 14th and 23rd Streets. Some of the neighborhood's prettiest blocks, lined with elegant row houses, are West 20th, 21st and 22nd Streets between Eighth and Tenth Avenues. Also, be sure to take a gander at the Chelsea Hotel (222 W. 23rd St., near Eighth Avenue), a brick landmark that has all-black gables, chimneys and balconies. Built in 1884, the Chelsea has housed dozens of artists, writers and musicians over the years, including Arthur Miller, Jackson Pollock, Bob Dylan and Sid Vicious.

Just north of Chelsea lies the underground Pennsylvania Station (Seventh Avenue at 32nd Street), topped with circular Madison Square Garden, as well as the General Post Office (Eighth Avenue between 31st and 33rd Streets), a gorgeous building designed by McKim, Mead & White in 1913. The Garment District, centering on Seventh Avenue in the 30s, also begins here.

GRAMERCY PARK AND UNION SQUARE

Largely residential, the East Side between 14th and 34th Streets is home to two inviting squares—Gramercy Park at Irving Place between 20th and 21st Streets, and Union Square at Broadway between 14th and 17th Streets. A long line of buzzing restaurants and bars beckon along Park Avenue between 17th and 23rd Streets, while a bit farther north is Little India, found on Lexington Avenue between 27th and 29th Streets. The neighborhood has a quiet charm of its own, with residents ranging from young professionals to middle-class families to the upper middle class.

One of the fashionable squares in the city, Gramercy Park comprises elegant brownstones and townhouses surrounding an enclosed green to which only residents have the key. At the southern edge of the park stand two especially impressive buildings—the National Arts Club (15 Gramercy Park South) and the Players Club (16 Gramercy Park South.) The National Arts Club was once home to New York Governor Samuel Tilden, whereas the Players Club once belonged to the great thespian Edwin Booth, the brother of the man who assassinated Abraham Lincoln. Just east of Gramercy Park stands Theodore Roosevelt's Birthplace (28 E. 20th St.), a museum filled with the world's largest collection of Roosevelt memorabilia.

Farther south is Union Square, a booming park surrounded by sleek megastores, upscale restaurants and fashionable bars. The popular Farmers' Greenmarket operates in the park on Monday, Wednesday, Friday and Saturday mornings, and free concerts and other events sometimes take place here during the summer. To the immediate east of the square are several excellent off-Broadway theaters.

Broadway between Union Square and Madison Square (between 23rd and 26th Streets, Fifth and Madison Avenues) was once known as the Ladies' Mile because of the many fashionable department stores located here. Many were housed in extravagant cast-iron buildings, which still stand, now holding more modern emporiums.

At the corner of Broadway and 23rd Street is the famous 1902 Flatiron building, built in the shape of a narrow triangle and only six feet wide at its northern end. Reigning over Madison Park to the east are the enormous Art Deco Metropolitan Life Insurance Building (Madison Avenue, between 23rd and 25th Streets) and the impossibly ornate Appellate Division of the New York State Supreme Court (Madison Avenue at 25th Street).

MIDTOWN

Stretching from 34th Street to 57th Street, the Harlem River to the East River, Midtown is the heart of Manhattan. Most of the city's skyscrapers are here, along with most of its offices, major hotels, famous shops, the Empire State Building, Times Square, the Broadway theaters, the Museum of Modern Art (MoMA), Rockefeller Center, Grand Central Station and the New York Public Library.

Fifth Avenue is the center of Midtown, dividing the city into east and west. Although nothing more than a line on a map as late as 1811, the thoroughfare had become New York's most fashionable address by the Civil War. It turned commercial in the early 1900s and is now lined with mostly shops and office buildings.

Towering over the southern end of Midtown is the Empire State Building (350 Fifth Ave. at 34th Street), one of the world's most famous skyscrapers. Built in the early 1930s, the building took just 14 months to erect and remains an Art Deco masterpiece.

On the corner of Third Avenue and 42nd Street soars the magnificent Chrysler Building, another Art Deco masterpiece. Grand Central Station, whose magnificent concourse was recently restored to the tune of $200 million, is at Lexington Avenue. At Fifth Avenue and 42nd Street find the New York Public Library, behind which spreads sublime Bryant Park, where many free events are held during the summer months.

West of Seventh Avenue along 42nd Street begins Times Square, which stretches north to 48th Street along the Seventh Avenue-Broadway nexus. The best time to come here is at night, when the huge state-of-the-art neon lights that line the square shine. Much cleaned up in recent years, Times Square is also a good place to catch street performers and, of course, Broadway theater. Many of the city's most famous theaters are located on the side streets around Times Square.

North and a little east of Times Square, Rockefeller Center reigns as an Art Deco complex stretching between 48th and 51st Streets, Sixth and Fifth Avenues. Built by John D. Rockefeller during the height of the Depression, Rockefeller Center is home to the landmark Radio City Music Hall, NBC Studios and a famed skating rink filled with outdoor enthusiasts during the winter months.

Along Fifth Avenue just south and north of Rockefeller Center are some of the city's most famous shops—Saks Fifth Avenue, Tiffany & Co., Gucci and Cartier, along with Trump Tower at 56th Street. Between 50th and 51st Streets soars the

Gothic Saint Patrick's Cathedral, the largest Roman Catholic cathedral in the United States. The Museum of Modern Art, a must-stop for any art lover, is on 53rd Street just west of Fifth Avenue.

UPPER EAST SIDE

Long associated with wealth, much of the Upper East Side—stretching from 57th Street north to 106th Street and Fifth Avenue east to the East River—is filled with elegant mansions and brownstones, clubs and museums. Many of the city's most famous museums—including the Metropolitan Museum of Art—are located here, along with several posh hotels and Gracie Mansion, home to New York City's mayor.

But the neighborhood is about more than just wealth. Remnants of what was once a thriving German community can be found along 86th Street and Second Avenue, while a Puerto Rican and Latin community begins in the upper 80s, east of Lexington Avenue. At the corner of 96th Street and Third Avenue is a surprising sight—the Islamic Cultural Center, a modern, gold-domed mosque flanked by a skinny minaret.

Many of the Upper East Side's cultural institutions are located on Fifth Avenue, facing Central Park along what is known as Museum Mile. The Frick Collection, housing the private art collection of the former 19th-century industrialist Henry Clay Frick, marks the mile's southernmost end, at 70th Street. El Museo del Barrio, dedicated to the art and culture of Latin America, marks the northernmost end, at 104th Street. In between stand the grand Metropolitan Museum of Art (at 82nd Street) and the circular, Frank Lloyd Wright-designed Guggenheim Museum (at 88th Street), to name just two.

The restored condo-hotel development The Plaza Hotel beckons from the southern end of the Upper East Side (Fifth Ave., between 58th and 59th Streets). This magnificent French Renaissance-style edifice was built in 1907. Directly across Fifth Avenue from the hotel, FAO Schwarz is an imaginative toy store that's as much fun for adults as it is for kids. Central Park is just across 59th Street. Horse-drawn hansoms and their drivers congregate along the streets here, waiting hopefully for tourists interested in taking a clip-clopping tour. The small but state-of-the-art Central Park Zoo can be found in the park near Fifth Avenue and 65th Street.

Shoppers will want to browse the many upscale boutiques lining Madison Avenue between 57th and 90th Streets or take a stroll over to Bloomingdale's (Lexington Avenue at 59th St.). Fifty-Seventh Street holds numerous world-famous galleries, including PaceWildenstein (32 E. 57th St.) and Andre Emmerich (41 E. 57th St.), as well as such popular tourist stops as Niketown (6 E. 57th St.). The infamous St. Patrick's Day Parade, attracting hordes of rowdy revelers, travels down Fifth Avenue from 86th Street to 44th Street every March 17th.

UPPER WEST SIDE

Primarily residential, the Upper West Side has traditionally been known as the liberal-leaning home of writers, intellectuals, musicians, dancers, doctors, lawyers and other upper-middle-class professionals. A mix of ornate 19th-century landmarks, pre-World War II apartment buildings and tenement houses, the Upper West Side stretches from 57th Street north to 110th Street and from Fifth Avenue west to the Hudson River. At its eastern border, between Fifth Avenue and Central Park West and 59th and 110th Streets, Central Park sprawls out in a vast and beautifully landscaped expanse of green.

Anchoring the neighborhood to the south is one of its best-known addresses—the Lincoln Center for the Performing Arts (Broadway, between 62nd and 66th Streets), which presents about 3,000 cultural events a year. Centering on a large, circular fountain, the 14-acre complex is home to renowned institutions such as the Metropolitan Opera House and Avery Fisher Hall. Many free outdoor concerts are presented on the plaza during the summer.

Directly across from Lincoln Center beckons a row of attractive restaurants and cafes, many with outdoor seating in summer. The Museum of American Folk Art (Broadway, between 65th and 66th Streets), one of the city's smaller and more unusual museums, is also here. Another dozen or so blocks farther north, the Museum of Natural History (Central Park West at 79th Street) is packed with everything from more than 100 dinosaur skeletons to artifacts from peoples around the world. Adjoining the museum on its north side is the state-of-the-art Rose Center for Earth and Space. Completed in 2000, the center is instantly recognizable for its unusual glass architecture revealing a globe within a triangle.

The Upper West Side didn't begin developing until the late 1800s, when a grand apartment building called the Dakota was built at what is now the corner of Central Park West and 72nd Street. At the time, the building was so far north of the rest of the city that New Yorkers said it was as remote as the state of Dakota—hence the name. Still standing today, the Dakota has been home to many celebrities, including Lauren Bacall, Gilda Radner, Boris Karloff and John Lennon, who was fatally shot outside the building on December 8, 1980. In Central Park, directly across the street from the Dakota, is Strawberry Fields, a teardrop-shaped acre of land that Yoko Ono had landscaped in her husband's memory.

Central Park can be entered at major intersections all along Central Park West. Near the park's southern end is Tavern on the Green (near Central Park West and 67th Street), a glittering extravaganza of a restaurant packed with mirrors and chandeliers. A bit farther north, find an odd-shaped body of water simply known as "the Lake" (between 72nd and 77th Streets); rowboats can be rented at the Loeb Boathouse at the lake's eastern edge.

★ HARLEM
★
★
★
★

Stretching from 110th to 168th Streets between the Harlem and Hudson rivers, Harlem is in the midst of a renaissance. After years of being known primarily for its grinding poverty, drugs and despair, the historic African-American neighborhood is sprucing itself up, attracting mainstream businesses such as Starbucks and Ben & Jerry's, and becoming home once again to the middle class—both African-American and other ethnicities.

Harlem can be divided in two: west-central Harlem, which is primarily African-American, and east (or Spanish) Harlem, home to many Latinos and a smaller number of Italians. Between 110th and 125th Streets west of Morningside Park is Morningside Heights, where Columbia University is located. Washington Heights, north of 155th Street, is home to Fort Tyron Park and the Cloisters, which houses the medieval collection of the Metropolitan Museum of Art.

First a farming community and then an affluent white suburb, Harlem began attracting African-American residents after the construction of the IRT subway in 1901, and soon became the nation's premier African-American neighborhood. The area boomed during Harlem Renaissance of the 1920s and 1930s, attracting writers and intellectuals such as Langston Hughes and W. E. B. DuBois, and the streets were packed with nightclubs, dance halls and jazz clubs. Everything changed, however, with the Depression, when poverty gained a stronghold that remains in many parts of the neighborhood today. When exploring Harlem, it's best to stick to the main thoroughfares.

The heart of Harlem is 125th Street, where you'll find a Magic Johnson Theater complex, several restaurants and sweet shops offering soul food and baked goods, and the famed Apollo Theater (253 W. 125th St.). Nearly every major jazz, blues, R&B and soul artist to come along performed here, and the theater still presents its famed Amateur Night every Wednesday. Just down the street from the Apollo is the Studio Museum of Harlem (144 W. 125th St.), a first-class fine arts institution spread over several floors of a turn-of-the-century building.

Another Harlem landmark is the Schomburg Center for Research in Black Culture (Lenox Avenue at 135th Street), founded by Arthur C. Schomburg, a Puerto Rican of African descent who was told as a child that his race had no history. Although primarily a library, the center also houses a large exhibit area where a wide array of changing exhibits is presented.

Not far from University, which is centered on Broadway and 116th Street, the Cathedral of St. John the Divine (Amsterdam Avenue at 112th Street) is the world's largest Gothic cathedral, said to be big enough to fit both Notre Dame and Chartres inside. Another major attraction nearby is Grant's Tomb (122nd St. at Riverside Dr.), an imposing mausoleum sitting high on a bluff overlooking the Hudson.

BROOKLYN

The largest borough in population and second largest in area, Brooklyn was a city in its own right—separate from New York—until 1898. Brooklyn had its own city hall, central park, downtown shops and cultural attractions, which helps account for the unusual amount the borough has to offer visitors today. Brooklyn is also home to multiple ethnic groups, socioeconomic groups and neighborhoods, one of which—Coney Island—is world famous.

Brooklyn Heights and Williamsburg are located at the northern end of Brooklyn, closest to Manhattan. Brooklyn Heights is a quiet, upper-middle-class and dignified, filled with lovely brownstones, historic buildings and the wide riverside Promenade, which offers magnificent views of the Manhattan skyline and New York Harbor. Williamsburg was once inhabited mostly by Jewish immigrants and is still home to the Satmarer Hasidim, a major orthodox sect. Today the area is better known for its large young, arts-oriented hipster population. Along Bedford Avenue are plethora of lively, inexpensive restaurants, bars, art galleries and shops.

Bordering Brooklyn Heights is downtown Brooklyn, home to a number of imposing government buildings that date back to the days when Brooklyn was a city in its own right. The Greek Revival Borough Hall, at the intersection of Joralemon, Fulton and Court Streets, was once Brooklyn's City Hall and is still filled with government offices. Not far away is the New York Transit Museum (Schermerhorn Street at Boerum Place), an excellent place to learn the story behind the New York subway.

Near the center of Brooklyn sprawls Prospect Park, one of the city's loveliest retreats. Spread out over 525 acres of forests and meadows, the park was designed by Frederick Law Olmsted and Calvert Vaux, the two men who also planned Central Park in Manhattan.

Brooklyn's foremost cultural attractions—the Brooklyn Museum of Art (200 Eastern Parkway at Washington Avenue) and the Brooklyn Botanic Gardens (1000 Washington Avenue, near Eastern Parkway)—are located on the eastern edge of the park. The northwestern edge is Park Slope, a genteel neighborhood filled with elegant Victorian brownstones, now mostly inhabited by urban professionals with young children.

At the far southern end of Brooklyn, you'll find three most unusual neighborhoods—Coney Island, Brighton Beach and Sheepshead Bay. Once home to a famed amusement park, Coney Island still beckons with an idiosyncratic collection of creaky historic rides, tawdry newer ones, the first-rate Aquarium for Wildlife Conservation (West Eighth Street, between the Boardwalk and Surf Avenue) and a wide, windswept boardwalk that stretches along a beach. The popular Mermaid Parade, featuring eye-popping costumes and bawdy revelry, takes place here every June. Next door to Coney Island is Brighton Beach, home to a thriving a Russian community, and Sheepshead Bay, a tiny port filled with fishing boats, retirees and seafood restaurants.

QUEENS

New York City's biggest borough, Queens is home to many large and vibrant ethnic neighborhoods as well as some important cultural and historic gems. It also holds John F. Kennedy International and La Guardia airports and Shea Stadium, the ballpark of the New York Mets. At the western end of Queens stretch Long Island City and Astoria, both just a stop or two away from Manhattan on the subway. Although largely an industrial area, Long Island City has recently gained favor for its burgeoning artistic community and holds a number of first-rate galleries and museums. Foremost among them are the Isamu Noguchi Garden Museum (32-37 Vernon Blvd., at 33rd Road), containing many works of the late great sculptor, and the P.S.1 Contemporary Art Center (22-25 Jackson Ave., at 46th Street), a premier showcase for art on the cutting edge.

Meanwhile, Astoria is home to a large Greek population, as well as to an increasing number of Pakistani, Italian and Latino residents. Along 30th Avenue and Broadway between 31st and Steinway Streets, you'll find many Greek restaurants, food shops and bakeries. The American Museum of the Moving Image (34-12 36th St.) is also nearby. Astoria was once the site of the Astoria Movie Studios, which produced legends such as Rudolf Valentino and Gloria Swanson; renovated and reopened in the late 1970s, the studios are now known as the Kaufman Astoria Studios. Travel a bit farther east on the No. 7 subway line—the borough's main transportation artery—to find Jackson Heights. Nicknamed the "cornfield of Queens" in the early 1900s, Jackson Heights now holds large Colombian and Indian populations, as well as smaller Peruvian, Uruguayan, Filipino and Thai populations. A number of excellent Colombian restaurants are located along Roosevelt Avenue near 82nd and 83rd Streets. Tasty Indian food can be sampled between 70th and 74th Streets near Roosevelt Avenue and Broadway.

East of Jackson Heights, Flushing Meadows-Corona Park is an enormous green oasis that housed both the 1939 and 1964 World's Fairs. The park's Unisphere—a shiny 140-foot-high hollow globe—dates back to the 1964 fair, as do the buildings that now contain the Queens Museum of Art and the New York Hall of Science. The Queens Wildlife Center and Shea Stadium are also in the park.

Beyond the park, find Flushing, home to a clutch of historic buildings and large Asian communities. The historic buildings include the Bowne House (37-01 Bowne

St.), used for illegal Quaker meetings in the 1660s, and the 1785 Kingsland House (143-35 37th Ave.), now the headquarters of the Queens Historical Society. The Asian community is centered on Main and Union Streets. Asian restaurants serving delicious, authentic food are everywhere here.

THE BRONX

New York City's second-smallest borough both in size and in population, the Bronx is also the only one attached to the mainland. In it you'll discover legendary New York institutions such as the Bronx Zoo, the New York Botanical Gardens, Yankee Stadium and some of the city's biggest parks.

However, in the 1970s and 1980s, the borough also garnered a reputation for urban decay, as headlining stories involving murder, drugs and arson seemed to come out of the neighborhood daily. In more recent years, more than $1 billion in public funds has been spent on the South Bronx—where most of the decay occurred—and the place is in better shape. Elsewhere in the borough, large residential neighborhoods, most working class and middle-class (City Island, Co-Op City), a few quite exclusive (Riverdale, Fieldston) have always flourished.

First settled in 1644 by a Scandinavian named Jonas Bronck, the area soon became known as "the Broncks," and remained a predominantly agricultural community up until the late 1800s. But then the Third Avenue Elevated Railway arrived, and by 1900, the borough's population had soared to 200,000. During the 1920s and 1930s, grand Art Deco apartment buildings sprang up along the wide thoroughfare called the Grand Concourse—a considerably more dilapidated version of which still exists today.

The New York Botanical Garden and Bronx Zoo sit adjacent to each other in the heart of the Bronx. Since they're both enormous, however, it's hard to visit them both in one day. Instead, opt for one of the two and then head to Belmont, an Italian community just west of the zoo. One of the city's older and more established ethnic neighborhoods, it is packed with Italian restaurants, pastry shops, bakeries, butcher shops and food markets.

Also in the Bronx is Van Cortlandt Park, which, at two square miles, is one of the city's largest parks. In its northernmost section sits the Van Cortlandt House Museum, a charming 18th-century mansion that once belonged to a wealthy landowner.

Across Jerome Avenue from the park stretches Woodlawn Cemetery, a lush 19th-century burial ground filled with rolling hills, meandering walkways, mausoleums and tombs. Author Herman Melville, financier Jay Gould, and musicians Duke Ellington and Miles Davis are all buried here.

At the northern end of the Bronx reigns City Island, one of New York City's more unusual communities. A sailor's haven that had once hoped to become an important port, City Island is still home to a small shipbuilding industry. The place had only one main street—City Island Avenue—which is lined with a number of fish restaurants ranging in style from simple to old-fashioned elaborate.

STATEN ISLAND

Significantly more rural and suburban than the four other New York City boroughs, Staten Island is also predominantly white, politically conservative and mostly working class and middle class. Many residents own their own homes here, complete with tidy front lawns and garages—something you don't see much in the rest of the city.

Unless you have access to a car, Staten Island is also quite difficult to explore. Buses run much less frequently and have more ground to cover than they do elsewhere in the city, making travel a time-consuming affair.

At 14 miles long by seven miles wide, Staten Island was originally settled by American Indians who successfully fought off the Dutch until 1661. Later it became a military camp for the British during the Revolutionary War and then remained predominantly rural throughout the 1800s and early 1900s. Even as late as 1964, when the Verrazano-Narrows Bridge was completed, connecting the borough to the rest of the city, Staten Island was largely undeveloped.

The Staten Island Ferry is the borough's biggest attraction, carrying about 3½ million visitors back and forth every year, with few actually disembarking to explore the Staten Island side. Rides on the ferry are free, and the views they offer of Manhattan and New York Harbor are spectacular, especially at night.

The ferry docks at St. George, a small and often empty town with many deserted storefronts. About a mile away is the Snug Harbor Cultural Center (1000 Richmond Terrace; take the S40 bus), an odd complex of buildings that was once a home for retired sailors. Today, the center holds several galleries, a botanical garden and a Chinese scholars' garden.

In the center of Staten Island stretches the Greenbelt, a 2,500-acre nature preserve made up of several tracts of woodlands, wetlands and open fields, interspersed with a golf course, a nature center, a considerable amount of human settlement and a few historic sites. A favorite stop for migrating birds, the Greenbelt also supports diverse flora, thanks to a wide variety of soils deposited here by glaciers about 10,000 years ago.

South of the Greenbelt, find the Jacques Marchais Museum of Tibetan Art (338 Lighthouse Ave.; take the S74 bus), housing what is said to be the largest collection of Tibetan art in the Western world. Within walking distance of the Museum of Tibetan Art is Historic Richmond Town (441 Clarke Ave.), a recreated historic village filled with 29 buildings, most moved here from elsewhere on the island.

Until recently, Staten Island was also the butt of many jokes, as the city's largest dump, the Fresh Kills landfill, was located here. However, Fresh Kills was closed in early 2001.

WHAT TO SEE AND DO

ADVENTURE ON A SHOESTRING
300 W. 53rd St., New York, 212-265-2663
Year-round walking tours of various neighborhoods, including Soho, Haunted Greenwich Village and Chinatown.

AMERICAN FOLK ART MUSEUM
45 W. 53rd St., New York, 212-265-1040; www.folkartmuseum.org
Folk arts of all types, including paintings, sculptures, quilts, needlework, toys, weather vanes and handmade furniture. Changing exhibits; lectures and demonstrations. Admission is free on Friday evenings. Tuesday-Thursday, Saturday-Sunday 10:30 a.m.-5:30 p.m., Friday to 7:30 p.m.; closed holidays.

AMERICAN MUSEUM OF NATURAL HISTORY
79th Street and Central Park West, New York, 212-769-5100; www.amnh.org
Kids love this behemoth of a museum recently featured in the film *Night at the Museum*. Among its 36 million specimens are at least 100 dinosaur skeletons, including a huge *Tyrannosaurus rex* whose serrated teeth alone measure six inches

long. You may prefer to stroll through a roomful of free-flying butterflies or examine the 563-carat Star of India sapphire. Expect to be blown away by the Rose Center for Earth and Space and the Hayden Planetarium. The Planetarium Space Show is only 30 minutes long, but it's dazzling. Narrated by the likes of Tom Hanks and Harrison Ford, it uses the world's largest, most powerful projector, the Zeiss Mark IX, which was built to the museum's specifications. Seating is limited, so choose a day for the museum and order tickets in advance. Daily 10 a.m.-5:45 p.m.; closed holidays.

ANGELIKA FILM CENTER

18 W. Houston St., New York, 212-995-2000; www.angelikafilmcenter.com

Get a taste of genuine Soho living at this cultural institution that has attracted lovers of artsy movies for years. And the Angelika Cafe in the lobby area is a great little place to grab a latte and a scone before the flick or a soda and a sandwich after the movie. On Sunday mornings, you'll find locals relaxing in the cafe, enjoying their coffee and *The New York Times*.

ASIA SOCIETY AND MUSEUM

725 Park Ave., New York, 212-288-6400; www.asiasociety.org

Masterpieces of Asian art, donated by founder John Rockefeller, make up most of this museum's permanent collection. Its works include sculptures, ceramics and paintings from places such as China, Korea, Japan and India. In addition, the museum offers a schedule of films, performances and lectures. The Asia Society also has a lovely indoor sculpture garden and cafe, which make for a nice stop on a hectic day of sightseeing. Tuesday-Thursday, Saturday-Sunday 11 a.m.-6 p.m., Friday to 9 p.m.; closed holidays.

BERGDORF GOODMAN

754 Fifth Ave., New York, 212-753-7300; www.bergdorfgoodman.com

With designer handbags that can set you back as much as $4,000, $700 swimsuits and nightgowns that cost $500, Bergdorf Goodman is one of the city's most posh department stores. Ladies who lunch, yuppie professionals and stylish hipsters with trust funds are equally at home in this shopping mecca. The store's windows are show-stoppers. Monday-Wednesday, Friday-Saturday 10 a.m.-7 p.m., Thursday to 8 p.m., Sunday noon-6 p.m.

BLOOMINGDALE'S

1000 Third Ave., 212-705-2000; www.bloomingdales.com

Everyone in New York knows the name Bloomingdale's and the sight of its famous brown shopping bags. This world-renowned department store loved by locals and tourists alike, sells a mix of merchandise in a modern setting. You can find designer clothing for men and women, high-quality housewares, jewelry, cosmetics and just about everything else. A newer Soho location (*504 Broadway*) focuses on contemporary collections. Daily, hours vary.

BLUE NOTE

131 W. Third St., New York, 212-475-8592; www.bluenote.net

For some of the world's best names in jazz, head downtown to Greenwich Village and the Blue Note. This nightclub has played host to many well-known jazz performers, as well as rising stars. Although the cover charge is higher here than at many other venues, the acts are worth it. Monday nights, when the record companies promote new releases, cost $10. The club also serves a variety of food and drinks. Daily 8 p.m. and 10:30 p.m.

BOWLING GREEN
Broadway and Whitehall Street, New York
Originally a Dutch market, this is the city's oldest park, and it's said to be the place where Peter Minuit purchased Manhattan for $24 worth of trinkets. The park fence dates from 1771. You'll also find *Charging Bull* here, a 7,000-pound bronze statue that stock market investors often rub for good luck.

BOWLMOR LANES
110 University Place, New York, 212-255-8188; www.bowlmor.com
A New York landmark since 1938, this 42-lane, two-level bowling alley features a retro bar and lounge. Richard Nixon, Cameron Diaz and the Rolling Stones have all bowled at these lanes, where a colorful Village crowd stays until all hours. Snack on anything from nachos and hamburgers to fried calamari and grilled filet mignon in the restaurant or have your meal brought straight to your lane. It's a funky, fun hangout, even if you don't bowl. Note that no one under 21 is admitted after 5 p.m. Monday-Saturday, 7 p.m. Sunday.

BROOKLYN BRIDGE
Park Row near Municipal Building, New York
For an awesome view of Lower Manhattan, Brooklyn and the New York Harbor, take a 40-minute stroll across downtown's historic Brooklyn Bridge, the first bridge to cross the East River (actually a tidal estuary between Long Island Sound and New York Harbor) to Brooklyn. Opened on May 24, 1883, the bridge was and still is seen as a monument to American engineering and creativity. Two massive stone pylons, each pierced with two soaring Gothic arches, rise 272 feet to support an intricate web of cables. At the Brooklyn end of the bridge is a half-mile promenade with equally grand views. The bridge is also near the South Street Seaport, at the foot of Fulton Street and the East River.

CARNEGIE HALL
57th Street and Broadway, 212-247-7800; www.carnegiehall.org
Completed in 1891, the celebrated auditorium has been home to the world's great musicians for more than a century. Guided one-hour tours: September-June, Monday-Friday 11:30 a.m., 2 p.m. and 3 p.m., performance schedule permitting.

CASTLE CLINTON NATIONAL MONUMENT
Battery Park, New York, 212-344-7220; www.nps.gov/cacl
Built as a fort in 1811, this later was a place of public entertainment called Castle Garden where Jenny Lind sang in 1850 under P. T. Barnum's management. In 1855, it was taken over by the state of New York for use as an immigrant receiving station. More than eight million people entered the United States here between 1855 and 1890; Ellis Island was opened in 1892. The castle became the New York City Aquarium in 1896, which closed in 1941 and reopened at Coney Island in Brooklyn. The site has undergone modifications to serve as the visitor orientation/ferry departure center for the Statue of Liberty and Ellis Island. Ferry ticket booth; exhibits on Castle Clinton, Statue of Liberty and Ellis Island; visitor center. Daily 9 a.m.-5 p.m.

CATHEDRAL CHURCH OF ST. JOHN THE DIVINE

1047 Amsterdam Ave., New York, 212-316-7540; www.stjohndivine.org

Under construction since 1892, when completed, this will be the largest Gothic cathedral in the world at 601 feet long and 124 feet high. Bronze doors of the central portal represent scenes from the Old and New Testaments. The great rose window, 40 feet in diameter, is made up of more than 10,000 pieces of glass. A tapestry, painting and sculpture collection is also housed here. The cathedral and five other buildings are on 13 acres with a park and garden areas, including the Biblical Garden. Daily 7:30 a.m.-6 p.m.

CENTRAL PARK

59th St. and Fifth Ave., New York, 212-360-3444; www.centralpark.org

Central Park was reclaimed in 1858 from 843 acres of swampland that was used as a garbage dump and occupied by squatters. Landscape designer Frederick Law Olmsted's dream was to bring city dwellers the kind of refreshment found only in nature. A century-and-a-half later, the park still does that; today, it's a source of varied outdoor entertainment. Stop at the visitors' center, called the Dairy—mid-park at 65th Street—for a map and a calendar of events. Jog around the Reservoir or rent ice skates at Wollman Rink or at Lasker Rink, which becomes a swimming pool in the summer. Rent a rowboat at Loeb Boathouse or a kite from Big City Kites at Lexington and 82nd Street and walk over to the park to catch the breeze on the Great Lawn. If you have kids, visit one of the 19 themed playgrounds, the zoo and petting zoo, the Carousel, the raucous storytelling hour at the Hans Christian Andersen statue and the Model Boat Pond, where serious modelers race their tiny remote-controlled boats on weekends. In summer, something's going on every night, and it's free! See Shakespeare in the Park at the Delacorte Theater. Get comfortable on the Great Lawn to hear the New York Philharmonic or the Metropolitan Opera under the stars. SummerStage brings well-known artists to Rumsey Playfield for jazz, dance, traditional and contemporary musical performances. The Band Shell is the venue for classical concerts. Amble through the forested Ramble. Stroll down the venerable, elm-lined Mall and past the bronze statues of Balto the dog, Alice in Wonderland and forgotten poets.

CENTURY 21

22 Cortlandt St., New York, 212-227-9092; www.c21stores.com

This is a can't-miss store if you want designer merchandise at rock-bottom prices and have time to look through aisles of items. The three-story department store sells men's, women's and children's clothing; cosmetics; housewares and electronics. The store's extended morning hours are a benefit for both New Yorkers who want to make purchases before work and tourists who are early birds. Daily, hours vary; closed holidays.

CHELSEA PIERS SPORTS AND ENTERTAINMENT COMPLEX

24th Street and West Side Highway, New York, 212-336-6666; www.chelseapiers.com

For the best in recreational activities all in one location, keep heading west until you hit Chelsea Piers. The 1.7-million-square-foot complex features an ice-skating rink, a bowling alley, climbing walls, a driving range, basketball, in-line skating and more. There also are pubs and restaurants where you can grab a meal. Stop in for a beer at the Chelsea Brewing Co., the state's largest microbrewery. Monday-Friday 6 a.m.-11 p.m., Saturday-Sunday 8 a.m.-9 p.m.

131

NEW YORK

★
★
★
★
★

CHILDREN'S MUSEUM OF MANHATTAN

The Tisch Building, 212 W. 83rd St., New York, 212-721-1234; www.cmom.org

Hands-on exhibits for children ages 2-10; kids can draw and paint, learn crafts, play at being newscasters, listen to stories or explore changing play areas. Late June-mid September, Tuesday-Sunday 10 a.m.-5 p.m.; rest of the year, Wednesday-Sunday 10 a.m.-5 p.m.; closed holidays.

CHRISTIE'S

20 Rockefeller Plaza, New York, 212-636-2000; www.christies.com

Get a taste of high society at a Christie's auction. Whether you're just a spectator or you have lots of spare cash to purchase something wonderful, attending an auction at this institution is a thrilling, fast-paced experience. Items sold at auction at Christie's have included the "Master of Your Domain" script from the television show *Seinfeld*, gowns worn by the late Princess Diana and a Honus Wagner baseball card (the most expensive card ever sold). Special departments are devoted to areas like wines, cameras and cars. Monday-Friday 9:30 a.m.-5:30 p.m.; closed holidays.

CHRYSLER BUILDING

405 Lexington Ave., New York, 212-682-3070

New York's most famous Art Deco skyscraper. The graceful pointed spire with triangular windows set in arches is lighted at night. The impressive lobby features beautiful jazz-age detailing.

CIRCLE LINE CRUISES

Pier 83, W. 42nd St. and 12th Ave., New York, 212-563-3200; www.circleline42.com

Grab a seat on the port (left) side for a spectacular view of the skyline. Narrated by knowledgeable, personable guides, these tours take you past the Statue of Liberty and under the Brooklyn Bridge; if you opt for the three-hour cruise, you'll also see the New Jersey Palisades, a glorious sight in autumn. Food and drinks are available on board. Closed Tuesday-Wednesday in January, Tuesday in March, holidays.

CITY CENTER

131 W. 55th St., New York, 212-581-1212, 877-581-1212; www.citycenter.org

This landmark theater hosts world-renowned dance companies, including the Alvin Ailey American Dance Theater, the Paul Taylor Dance Company and Merce Cunningham Dance Company. It also presents American music and theater events. Downstairs, City Center Stages I and II host the Manhattan Theatre Club.

CITY HALL PARK

Broadway and Chambers Street, New York, 212-788-3000

Architecturally, City Hall is a combination of American Federalist and English Georgian, with Louis XIV detailing, and is built of marble and brownstone.

THE CLOISTERS

99 Margaret Corbin Drive, Fort Tryon Park, New York, 212-923-3700;
www.metmuseum.org/cloisters

To escape the frantic pace of the city, take the A train to Fort Tryon Park in Upper Manhattan where the Cloisters, the medieval branch of the Metropolitan Museum, perches on a bluff overlooking the Hudson River. Funded in large part by John D. Rockefeller, Jr., the Cloisters houses an extraordinary collection of sculpture, illuminated manuscripts, stained glass, ivory and precious metalwork, as well as the famed Unicorn tapestries. The architectural setting is as remarkable as its contents. Five cloisters (quadrangles enclosed by a roofed arcade, a chapter house and chapels) were taken from monasteries in France and Spain and reassembled stone by stone. Rockefeller also purchased the land across the river along the Palisades and restricted development there. Tuesday-Sunday 9:30 a.m.-5:15 p.m.; until 4:45 p.m. November-February; closed holidays.

COLUMBIA UNIVERSITY
2960 Broadway, New York, 212-854-1754; www.columbia.edu
This Ivy League university was originally King's College; classes were conducted in the vestry room of Trinity Church. King's College still exists as Columbia College, with 3,000 students. The campus has more than 62 buildings, including the Low Memorial Library and the administration building (which has the Rotunda and the Sackler Collection of Chinese Ceramics and Butler Library, with more than five million volumes). The university numbers Alexander Hamilton, Gouverneur Morris and John Jay among its early graduates and Nicholas Murray Butler, Dwight D. Eisenhower and Andrew W. Cordier among its former presidents. Barnard College (1889), with 2,300 women, and the Teachers College (1887), with 5,000 students, are affiliated with Columbia.

COOPER UNION
Cooper Square, New York, 212-353-4100; www.cooper.edu
All-scholarship college for art, architecture and engineering. The Great Hall, where Lincoln spoke in 1861, is used as an auditorium for readings, films, lectures and performing arts.

THE DAKOTA
1 W. 72nd St., New York
The first and most famous of the lavish apartment houses on Central Park West, the Dakota got its name because it was considered so far north that New Yorkers joked that it might as well be in the Dakotas. Planned as a turreted, chateau-like structure, it was then embellished with Wild West ornamentation. It has been the home of many celebrities, including Judy Garland, Boris Karloff, John Lennon and Yoko Ono. On December 8, 1980, Lennon was shot and killed by a crazed fan at its gate. Five years later, Yoko Ono—who still resides here—had a section of Central Park visible from the Dakota landscaped with foliage and a mosaic with the title of Lennon's song *Imagine*. Today, that area is known as Strawberry Fields.

EL MUSEO DEL BARRIO
1230 Fifth Ave., New York, 212-831-7272; www.elmuseo.org
Dedicated to Puerto Rican, Caribbean and other Latin American art, this museum features changing exhibits on both contemporary and historic subjects and houses a superb permanent collection of *santos de palo* or carved wooden saints. The museum also hosts films, theater, concerts and educational programs. Wednesday-Sunday 11 a.m.-5 p.m.; closed holidays.

★
★
★
★
★

ELLIS ISLAND IMMIGRATION MUSEUM

Ellis Island, New York, 212-344-0996; www.ellisisland.com

This is the most famous port of immigration in the country. From 1892 to 1954, more than 12 million immigrants began their American dream here. The principle structure is the Main Building with its Great Hall, where the immigrants were processed. There is a fee for the round-trip ferry ride to the island. Daily 9:30 a.m.-5 p.m., extended hours in the summer.

EMPIRE STATE BUILDING

350 Fifth Ave., New York, 212-736-3100; www.esbnyc.com

A beloved city symbol since it opened in 1931, the Empire State Building is where King Kong perched in the movie classic and where visitors go for a panoramic view of Manhattan. The slender Art Deco skyscraper is exceptionally popular, so expect a long wait. Ordering tickets in advance from the Web site will save you time. Daily 8 a.m.-11:30 p.m.

EVA AND MORRIS FELD GALLERY

2 Lincoln Square, New York, 212-595-9533; www.folkartmuseum.org

The original site of the American Folk Art Museum is now a sister gallery, function space and museum shop. Tuesday-Saturday noon-7:30 p.m., Sunday noon-6:30 p.m.

FAO SCHWARZ

767 Fifth Ave., New York, 212-644-9400; www.fao.com

Children will instantly recognize the entrance to FAO Schwarz when they see the tall, brightly colored musical clock that guards the door. Inside, two floors are crowded with live clowns, chemistry sets, train sets, Madame Alexander dolls, giant stuffed animals, child-sized motorized cars and all the latest electronic baubles in incredible profusion and magical, mechanical display. During the holidays, shoppers often have to stand in line just to get in. Monday-Wednesday 10 a.m.-7 p.m., Thursday-Saturday 10 a.m.-8 p.m., Sunday 11 a.m.-6 p.m.

FEDERAL HALL NATIONAL MEMORIAL

26 Wall St., New York, 212-825-6888; www.nps.gov/feha

Greek Revival 1842 building on the site of the original Federal Hall, where the Stamp Act Congress met in 1765, George Washington was inaugurated April 30, 1789 and the first Congress met from 1789-1790. Originally a custom house, the building was for many years the sub-treasury of the United States. The John Quincy Adams Ward statue of Washington is on the Wall Street steps. Monday-Friday 9 a.m.-5 p.m.; closed holidays.

FEDERAL RESERVE BANK OF NEW YORK

33 Liberty St., New York, 212-720-6130; www.ny.frb.org

Approximately one-third of the world's supply of gold bullion is stored here in a vault 80 feet below ground level; cash handling operation and historical exhibit of bank notes and coins. Tours Monday-Friday at 9:30 a.m., 10:30 a.m., 11:30 a.m., 1:30 p.m., 2:30 p.m. and 3:30 p.m.; closed holidays. Tour reservations required at least one week in advance.

FRAUNCES TAVERN MUSEUM

54 Pearl St., New York, 212-425-1778; www.frauncestavernmuseum.org

The museum is housed in the historic Fraunces Tavern and four adjacent 19th-century buildings. It interprets the history and culture of early America through permanent collections of prints, paintings, decorative arts and artifacts, changing exhibitions and period rooms, one of which, the Long Room, is the site of George Washington's farewell to his officers at the end of the Revolutionary War. Monday-Saturday 12-5 p.m.; closed Sunday.

THE FRICK COLLECTION

1 E. 70th St., New York, 212-288-0700; www.frick.org

The mansion of Henry Clay Frick, wealthy tycoon, infamous strikebreaker and avid collector of art, contains a remarkably diverse assemblage of paintings. The walls of one room are covered with large, frothy Fragonard depicting the Progress of Love. In other rooms are masterworks by Bellini, Titian, Holbein, Rembrandt, El Greco, Turner, Degas and many others. Tuesday-Saturday 10 a.m.-6 p.m., Sunday 11 a.m.-5 p.m.; closed holidays. No children under 10; under 16 only with adult.

GENERAL GRANT NATIONAL MEMORIAL

122nd St., and Riverside Drive, New York, 212-666-1640; www.nps.gov/gegr

The largest mausoleum in North America, the General Grant National Monument is the home of Ulysses S. Grant's tomb, along with that of his wife. When Grant died in 1885, he had led the North to victory in the Civil War and served two consecutive terms as President of the United States before retiring to New York City. General Grant was so popular that upon his death, more than 90,000 private citizens donated a total of $600,000 (the equivalent of over $11.5 million in today's dollars) to help in the building of his tomb. The tomb was dedicated on April 27, 1897, on the 75th anniversary of Grant's birth. Located near picturesque Columbia University, the monument draws more than 75,000 visitors annually. Daily 9 a.m.-5 p.m.; closed holidays.

THE GEORGE GUSTAV HEYE CENTER OF THE NATIONAL MUSEUM OF THE AMERICAN INDIAN

1 Bowling Green St., New York, 212-514-3700; www.nmai.si.edu

World's largest collection of materials of the native people of North, Central and South America. Sunday-Wednesday, Friday-Saturday 10 a.m.-5 p.m., Thursday to 8 p.m.

GRAND CENTRAL TERMINAL

450 Lexington Ave., New York, 212-935-3960; www.grandcentralterminal.com

Built in the Beaux-Arts style and recently renovated for $200 million, this is one of New York's most glorious buildings (and often incorrectly called Grand Central Station). It has a vast 125-foot-high concourse, glassed-in catwalks, grand staircases, shops, restaurants and a star-studded aquamarine ceiling. Daily.

HAMILTON GRANGE NATIONAL MEMORIAL

287 Convent Ave., New York, 212-283-5154; www.nps.gov/hagr

Federal-style residence of Alexander Hamilton. Visitor information center and museum. Friday-Sunday 9 a.m.-5 p.m.

HENRI BENDEL

712 Fifth Ave., New York, 212-247-1100

The name Henri Bendel was synonymous with chic during the disco era. Today, the store still features trendy women's designer clothes, hats, fragrances, handbags and jewelry. Daily, Monday-Saturday 10 a.m.-8 p.m., Sunday noon-7 p.m.; closed holidays.

INTERNATIONAL CENTER OF PHOTOGRAPHY

1133 Avenue of the Americas, New York, 212-857-0000; www.icp.org

Photography buffs won't want to miss the International Center for Photography, recently relocated from the Upper East Side to Midtown. In these spacious galleries, you'll find changing exhibits featuring everyone from Weegee (Arthur Fellig) to Annie Leibovitz. Tuesday-Thursday 10 a.m.-6 p.m., Friday 10 a.m.-8 p.m., Saturday-Sunday 10 a.m.-6 p.m.; closed July 4.

JACOB K. JAVITS CONVENTION CENTER

655 W. 34th St., New York, 212-216-2000; www.javitscenter.com

This exposition hall has 900,000 square feet of exhibit space and more than 100 meeting rooms. Designed by I. M. Pei, the center is easily recognized by its thousands of glass cubes that reflect the skyline by day.

JEWISH MUSEUM

1109 Fifth Ave., New York, 212-423-3200; www.jewishmuseum.org

Devoted to Jewish art and culture, ancient and modern. Historical exhibits; contemporary painting and sculpture. Sunday-Wednesday 11 a.m.-5:45 p.m., Thursday 11 a.m.-8 p.m., Friday 11 a.m.-3 p.m.; closed holidays.

JOSEPH PAPP PUBLIC THEATER

425 Lafayette St., New York, 212-539-8500; www.publictheater.org

Complex of six theaters where Shakespeare, new American plays, new productions of classics, films, concerts and poetry readings are presented.

KITCHEN ARTS & LETTERS

1435 Lexington Ave., New York, 212-876-5550; www.kitchenartsandletters.com

Great cooks and novices alike can spend hours in this store, which features more than 10,000 cookbooks from all over the world. You can find the hottest new books by the most popular chefs, as well as those that have been out of print for years. Tuesday-Friday 10 a.m.-6:30 p.m., Monday 1-6 p.m., Saturday 11 a.m.-6:30 p.m.; closed holidays.

LIBERTY HELICOPTER TOURS

Downtown Manhattan Heliport, West 30th Street and 12th Avenue, New York, 212-967-6464, 800-542-9933; www.libertyhelicopters.com

See the grand sights of the city—from the Empire State Building to Yankee Stadium to the Chrysler Building—all from magnificent heights. Liberty offers six different tours on its seven-passenger helicopters, which last from five minutes to as long as 30 minutes. A photo ID is required, and your bags will be screened. No carry-ons are allowed, except for cameras and video equipment. Monday-Saturday 9 a.m.-6:30 p.m., call for Sunday tours.

LINCOLN CENTER FOR THE PERFORMING ARTS

70 Lincoln Center Plaza, New York, 212-875-5456; www.lincolncenter.org

The Metropolitan Opera House, at the heart of Lincoln Center, is home to one of the world's greatest opera companies and the renowned American Ballet. At the right side of the square is Avery Fisher Hall, where Lorin Maazel conducts the New York Philharmonic and an impressive roster of guest artists perform. The Philharmonic's Mostly Mozart Festival in August and frequent Young People's Concerts for children are perennial favorites. Opposite is the New York State Theater, shared by the New York City Opera and the New York City Ballet, especially famous for its beloved holiday classic, Balanchine's *The Nutcracker*. In addition to the three main buildings, the 14-acre campus contains a multitude of other venues, including the Vivian Beaumont Theater, which presents Broadway plays; Alice Tully Hall, home of the Chamber Music Society and the New York Film Festival; and the world-famous Juilliard School. Damrosch Park and its band shell offer many free summer programs, including folk, jazz and classical concerts. Daily; closed holidays.

THE LION KING

Minskoff Theater, 1515 Broadway, New York, 212-869-0550; www.minskofftheatre.com

Based on the Disney animated film of the same name, this wildly popular musical is a feast for the eyes, ears and soul. It has action, adventure, amazing costumes and inventive characters, and even though it's a kid's story, adults of all ages have come to see this musical since it opened in 1998. Daily.

LOWER EAST SIDE TENEMENT MUSEUM

108 Orchard St., New York, 212-431-0233; www.tenement.org

The highlight at this one-of-a-kind living history museum is the guided tour of an actual tenement once inhabited by Lower East Side immigrants from the late 19th and early 20th centuries. Three apartments have been restored to their original condition. (You will need reservations for any of the guided tours, of which several are offered.) The museum also offers walking tours around the Lower East Side itself. Monday 11 a.m.-5:30 p.m., Tuesday-Friday 11 a.m.-6 p.m., Saturday-Sunday 10:45 a.m.-6 p.m.

MACY'S HERALD SQUARE

151 W. 34th St., New York, 212-695-4400; www.macys.com

This massive department store has everything from international fashion collections for men and women to antiques galleries. Monday-Saturday 10 a.m.-9 p.m., Sunday 11 a.m.-8 p.m.; closed holidays.

MADISON SQUARE GARDEN

4 Pennsylvania Plaza, New York, 212-465-6741; www.thegarden.com

The Garden has been the site of major sporting events, concerts and other special events for more than a century. The present Garden, the fourth building bearing that name, opened in 1968. (The original Garden was actually on Madison Square.) It is the home of the New York Knicks and Liberty basketball teams, and New York Rangers hockey club. The Garden complex includes the 20,000-seat arena and the theater at Madison Square Garden, which features performances of the holiday classic *A Christmas Carol* every year as well as innumerable big-ticket concerts.

MERCHANT'S HOUSE MUSEUM

29 E. Fourth St., New York, 212-777-1089; www.merchantshouse.com

This East Village home, dating back to the 1830s, offers a look into family life in the mid-19th century. The house has been totally preserved inside and out. Original furnishings, architectural details and family memorabilia from retired merchant Seabury Tredwell and his descendants can be viewed here. The house was lived in until 1933, when it became a museum. Tours are available on weekends. Thursday-Monday noon-5 p.m.

METROPOLITAN MUSEUM OF ART

1000 Fifth Ave., New York, 212-535-7710; www.metmuseum.org

The Metropolitan Museum of Art contains more than two million objects spanning a period of more than 5,000 years. Even with a map and an audio guide (for which you pay extra), getting lost is not difficult—it is part of the experience. Finding the Rooftop Garden and its population of modern sculptures is easy. Stumbling across Michelangelo's sketch for the Sistine Chapel or the stunning state-of-the-art Costume Gallery may be a rewarding surprise. From the ancient Roman tomb, the Temple of Dendur, to a room designed by Frank Lloyd Wright in 1912, the Met presents both familiar masterpieces and intriguing hidden treasures. You could spend days here. Sunday, Tuesday-Thursday 9:30 a.m.-5:30 p.m.; Friday-Saturday 9:30 a.m.-9 p.m.; closed holidays.

METROPOLITAN OPERA COMPANY

Metropolitan Opera House, Lincoln Center, Broadway and 64th St., New York, 212-362-6000; www.metoperafamily.org

This is one of the world's leading opera company. Tickets go on sale in March for the upcoming season, so book in advance. While prices can be high, it is worth spending the money on the best seats you can get if you are a true opera aficionado. September-May.

MORRIS-JUMEL MANSION

Roger Morris Park, 65 Jumel Terrace, New York, 212-923-8008; www.morrisjumel.org

Built in 1765 by Colonel Roger and Mary Philipse Morris, this mansion was George Washington's headquarters in 1776 and later became a British command post and Hessian headquarters. Purchased by French merchant Stephen Jumel in 1810, the house was the scene of the marriage of his widow, Madame Eliza Jumel, to former Vice President Aaron Burr in 1833. The mansion is the only remaining colonial residence in Manhattan. Wednesday-Sunday 10 a.m.-4 p.m.; closed holidays.

MURRAY'S CHEESE

254 Bleecker St., New York, 212-243-3289, 888-692-4339; www.murrayscheese.com

For the best gourmet cheese selection in the city, pop into this 68-year-old New York institution in the Village. The shop will entice any discerning palate with its 250 varieties of domestic and imported cheeses, as well as a selection of breads, olives, antipasti and personalized gift baskets. Monday-Saturday 8 a.m-8 p.m.; Sunday 10 a.m-7 p.m. Murray's also has a second, newer location in Midtown at 73 Grand Central Terminal.

MUSEUM OF ARTS AND DESIGN

40 W. 53rd St., New York, 212-956-3535; www.madmuseum.org

Dedicated to the history of American crafts, including textiles, ceramics and glasswork. Changing exhibits. Wednesday-Sunday 11 a.m-6 p.m., Thursday 11 a.m-9 p.m.; closed holidays.

MUSEUM OF CHINESE IN THE AMERICAS (MOCA)

70 Mulberry St., New York, 212-619-4785; www.moca-nyc.org

This cultural and historical museum in Chinatown, also known as MoCA, is a small but fascinating place filled with photographs, mementos and poetry culled from nearly two decades of research in the community. Women's roles, religion and Chinese laundries are among the subjects covered in the exhibits. Tuesday-Thursday, Saturday-Sunday noon-6 p.m., Friday (free) noon-7 p.m.

MUSEUM OF JEWISH HERITAGE-A LIVING MEMORIAL TO THE HOLOCAUST

Battery Park City, 36 Battery Place, New York, 646-437-4200; www.mjhnyc.org

Opened in 1997, this museum features thousands of moving photographs, cultural artifacts and archival films documenting the Holocaust and the resilience of the Jewish community. It's housed in a building the shape of a hexagon, symbolic of the Star of David. The East Wing houses a theater, special-exhibit galleries, a memorial garden and a café. Sunday-Tuesday, Thursday 10 a.m.-5:45 p.m., Wednesday 10 a.m.-8 p.m., Friday and the eve of Jewish holidays 10 a.m.-3 p.m.; closed Saturday, Jewish holidays and Thanksgiving.

MUSEUM OF THE CITY OF NEW YORK

1220 Fifth Ave., New York, 212-534-1672; www.mcny.org

Explore unique aspects of the city in this Upper East Side mansion dating to 1930. Displays include a toy gallery; collections of decorative arts, prints and photographs; and an exhibit on Broadway, complete with costumes and set designs. Other exhibits feature slide shows, paintings, memorabilia and sculptures, all dedicated to the fascinating history of the city up to the present day. Tuesday-Sunday 10 a.m.-5 p.m.; closed holidays.

THE PALEY CENTER FOR MEDIA

25 W. 52nd St., New York, 212-621-6800; www.paleycenter.org

William Paley, the former head of CBS, founded this museum to collect, preserve and make available to the public the best of broadcasting. View special screenings or, at a private console, hear and see selections of your own choosing from the vast archive of more than 100,000 programs. From the comedy of Burns and Allen to the Beatles in America, and from a teary-eyed Walter Cronkite reporting on President Kennedy's assassination to a tireless Peter Jennings persevering through an endless 9/11, it's there for the asking. Tuesday-Sunday noon-6 p.m., Thursday to 8 p.m.; closed holidays.

NEW YORK CITY FIRE MUSEUM

278 Spring St., New York, 212-691-1303; www.nycfiremuseum.org

Although it isn't really a children's museum, the New York City Fire Museum has great appeal for kids. Housed in an actual firehouse that was used until 1959, the museum is filled with new and old fire engines, helmets and uniforms, hoses and lifesaving nets. Retired firefighters take visitors through the museum, reciting fascinating tidbits of firefighting history along the way. Tuesday-Saturday 10 a.m.-5 p.m., Sunday 10-a.m.-4 p.m.

139

NEW YORK

★
★
★
★
★

NEW YORK HISTORICAL SOCIETY

170 Central Park West, New York, 212-873-3400; www.nyhistory.org

This monument to the history of the city recently reawakened after years of inactivity due to financial troubles. Spread out over many high-ceilinged rooms, the society presents temporary exhibits on everything from the legendary Stork Club—frequented by everyone from Frank Sinatra to JFK—to the small African-American communities that once dotted Central Park. The Henry Luce III Center for the Study of American culture features 40,000 objects, including George Washington's camp bed at Valley Forge and the world's largest collection of Tiffany lamps, as well as a nice collection of paintings, sculpture, furniture and decorative objects. Tuesday-Saturday 10 a.m.-6 p.m, Sunday 11 a.m.-5:45 p.m.; free admission on Friday 6-8 p.m.

NEW YORK ISLANDERS (NHL)

Nassau Coliseum, 1255 Hempstead Turnpike, Uniondale, 516-542-9348, 800-882-4753; www.newyorkislanders.com

Pro hockey's Islanders were the dominant team of the early 1980s, winning three Stanley Cups in a row from 1980 to 1982.

NEW YORK KNICKS (NBA)

Madison Square Garden, 4 Pennsylvania Plaza, New York, 212-465-5867; www.nyknicks.com

Knicks tickets are sometimes difficult to get because corporations and season ticket-holders have snatched them up; call early to maximize your chances. Be on the lookout for celebrities—Woody Allen and Spike Lee often attend games.

NEW YORK LIBERTY (WNBA)

Madison Square Garden, 2 Pennsylvania Plaza, New York, 212-564-9622; www.nyliberty.com

Professional women's basketball games.

NEW YORK METS (MLB)

Shea Stadium, 123-01 Roosevelt Ave., 718-507-8499; www.mets.com

Although the Mets may not have as long and colorful history as the Yankees, they are a fun team to watch. Tickets are usually available for most games, except the annual matchup against the Bronx Bombers. Bring extra cash and do the game right by feasting on hot dogs and peanuts, loading up on souvenirs and cheering loudly for your favorite players. April-September.

NEW YORK PUBLIC LIBRARY

Fifth Avenue and 42nd Street, New York, 212-930-0501; www.nypl.org

One of the best research libraries in the world, with more than 10 million volumes. Exhibits of rare books, art materials; free programs at branches. One-hour tours of central building Tuesday-Saturday, library tours at 11 a.m. and 2 p.m. Many interesting collections on display at the Central Research Library and The New York Public Library for the Performing Arts (also tours).

NEW YORK UNIVERSITY

22 Washington Square N., New York, 212-998-4524; www.nyu.edu

One of the largest private universities in the country, NYU is known for its undergraduate and graduate business, medical and law schools, school of performing arts and fine arts programs. Most programs, including the Graduate Business Center, are located on the main campus surrounding Washington Square Park; the medical and dental schools are on the East Side.

THE PLAZA HOTEL

768 Fifth Ave., New York, 212-759-3000, 800-257-7544; www.fairmont.com

Considered by many to be the grande dame of New York City lodgings, this massive hotel has played host to dignitaries, celebrities and even the literary character *Eloise*, the precocious 6-year-old who lived in the hotel. The Plaza was sold in 2005 to a development group, which closed the building for renovations. It reopened in 2008, and now offers both luxe condos and hotel rooms.

POLICE MUSEUM

100 Old Slip, New York, 212-480-3100; www.nycpolicemuseum.org

Exhibits of police uniforms, badges and equipment. Tuesday-Saturday 10 a.m.-5 p.m., Sunday 11 a.m.-5 p.m.; closed holidays.

RIVERSIDE PARK

475 Riverside Drive, New York, 212-639-9675; www.nycgovparks.org

This city park on the Upper West Side offers a pleasant, bucolic setting that is even more laid back than Central Park. The long, narrow, breezy park has a promenade for bike riders between West 72nd and West 110th Streets. Bike rentals are available at the nearby Toga Bike Shop (110 West End Ave., 212-799-9625). The 79th Street Boat Basin (212-496-2105) provides a quiet respite for walking on the river's edge. There's also a cafe that's open in summer and serves knockout margaritas and hamburgers. The park offers some sightseeing in the way of Grant's Tomb, a towering granite tomb that is one of the world's largest mausoleums. It holds the remains of President Ulysses S. Grant and his wife, Julia—a must-see for Civil War history buffs.

ROCKEFELLER CENTER

30 Rockefeller Plaza, New York, 212-632-3975; www.rockefellercenter.com

Conceived by John D. Rockefeller during the 1930s, Rockefeller Center is the largest privately owned business and entertainment complex in the world. Enter through the Channel Gardens (Fifth Avenue between 49th and 50th Streets) and walk toward the central sunken plaza. Here, a golden statue of Prometheus sprawls benevolently beside a pool and an outdoor café that becomes an ice-skating rink in winter. (Yes, you can rent skates.) The center is magical at Christmastime, when a 78,000-light tree towers over Prometheus. The backdrop of the scene is the core skyscraper, the GE Building, home to NBC Studios. You can take a studio tour (no children under 6; 212-664-7174) or catch *The Today Show* being broadcast live through the street-level picture windows at West 49th Street and Rockefeller Plaza. The 21-acre complex contains 19 buildings, most built of limestone with aluminum streamlining. The Art Deco gem of the group is Radio City Music Hall, America's largest theater. Tour the theater or see a show especially if the high-kicking Rockettes are performing (*212-247-4777; www.radiocity.com*).

SMITHSONIAN COOPER-HEWITT, NATIONAL DESIGN MUSEUM

2 E. 91st St., New York, 212-849-8400; www.ndm.si.edu

Once home to 19th-century industrialist Andrew Carnegie, this 64-room 1901 Georgian mansion is now a branch of the Smithsonian Institution dedicated to design and the decorative arts. The exhibits are temporary and focus on mediums such as ceramics, furniture, textiles and metalwork. Out back is a romantic garden, where concerts are sometimes presented. Monday-Friday 10 a.m.-5 p.m., Saturday 10 a.m.-6 p.m., Sunday noon-6 p.m.; closed holidays.

SOLOMON R. GUGGENHEIM MUSEUM

1071 Fifth Ave., New York, 212-423-3500; www.guggenheim.org

Some say that the Guggenheim looks like a giant snail or an upside-down wedding cake. Few would deny that Frank Lloyd Wright's brilliant concept of ever-widening concrete circles around a central atrium provided an intriguing new way to display art—especially in 1959 when the museum opened. Take the elevator to the top and walk down the gently sloping spiral to view temporary exhibits that draw a diversity of viewers. A smaller adjoining rotunda and tower hold a stunning permanent collection heavy in works by Wassily Kandinsky, Paul Klee, Francois Leger and Marc Chagall, as well as by the French Impressionists. Pablo Picasso is well represented, especially in his early Blue Period, including *Woman Ironing*, the artist's well-known depiction of labor and fatigue. Free docent-led tours are scheduled daily at noon. Saturday-Wednesday 10 a.m.-5:45 p.m., Friday 10 a.m.-7:45 p.m.; closed holidays.

SOTHEBY'S

1334 York Ave., New York, 212-606-7000; www.sothebys.com

Attending an auction at this institution is a thrilling, fast-paced experience. Sotheby's has held auctions for items belonging to the Duke and Duchess of Windsor and innumerable other celebrities and jet-setters, and it has fashion, book and manuscript, and vintage car departments, just to name a few. Publications such as *New York* magazine and *The New York Times* contain listings of upcoming events. Closed holidays.

SOUTH STREET SEAPORT

19 Fulton St., New York, 212-732-7678; www.southstreetseaport.com

This 12-block area was restored to display the city's maritime history, with an emphasis on South Street in the days of sailing vessels. The South Street Museum piers at South and Fulton Streets now moor the *Ambrose*, a lightship (1908); the *Lettie G. Howard*, a Gloucester fishing schooner (1893); the fully-rigged *Wavertree* (1885); the *Peking*, a German four-masted barque (1911) and the *Pioneer*, a schooner (1885). Permanent and changing maritime exhibits include models, prints, photos and artifacts. If history isn't your thing, this festival marketplace has more than 100 souvenir and mall-type stores, as well as 35 mostly casual restaurants. Don't miss the three-story glass and steel Pier 17 Pavilion, which extends into the East River and offers great views of the Brooklyn Bridge and New York Harbor. Mall hours Monday-Saturday 10 a.m.-9 p.m., Sunday 11 a.m.-8 p.m.; Restaurants and bars have extended hours.

ST. PATRICK'S CATHEDRAL

460 Madison Ave., New York, 212-753-2261; www.saintpatrickscathedral.org

Irish immigrants and their descendents were largely responsible for the construction and dedication of St. Patrick's Cathedral, the largest Catholic cathedral in the United

States. A standout on Fifth Avenue since 1859, the white marble and stone structure dominates the surrounding skyscrapers. Twin Gothic spires reach heavenward, and some of the stained-glass windows were made in Chartres. This is the resting place of New York's deceased archbishops; they are buried in tombs under the high altar, and their hats hang from the ceiling above. Thursday-Tuesday.

ST. PAUL'S CHAPEL

209 Broadway, New York, 212-602-0874, 212-233-4164; www.saintpaulschapel.org
A chapel of Trinity Church, this example of Georgian architecture, finished in 1766, is the oldest public building in continuous use on Manhattan Island. George Washington's pew is in the north aisle; Waterford chandeliers. Daily.

STATUE OF LIBERTY NATIONAL MONUMENT

Liberty Island, New York, 212-363-3200; www.nps.gov/stli
This worldwide symbol of freedom is the first thing passengers see as their ships sail into New York Harbor. A gift from France in 1886 (her iron skeleton was designed by Gustave Eiffel, creator of Paris' Eiffel Tower), she stands 152 feet high on an 89-foot pedestal. Ellis Island, the most famous port of immigration in the United States, became part of the national monument in 1965. Between 1892 and 1954, 12 million immigrants first stepped on American soil at Ellis Island. When it closed in 1954, the center had processed 40 percent of living American families. You can look for your ancestor's names on the Wall of Honor or visit the dramatic Immigrants Living Theater and the cavernous Great Hall, where nervous immigrants awaited processing. Ferries for the trip leave from Battery Park. Daily 9:30 a.m.-5 p.m.

143

STUDIO MUSEUM IN HARLEM

144 W. 125th St., New York, 212-864-4500; www.studiomuseum.org
Founded in 1968, this museum is dedicated to black art in America and is spread out over several well-lit floors of a turn-of-the-century building. The permanent exhibit features works by masters such as Romare Bearden, James VanDerZee and Jacob Lawrence; temporary exhibits present a mixture of both world-renowned and emerging artists. The Studio is also known for its lively lecture and concert series, presented September through May. Wednesday-Friday, Sunday noon-6 p.m., Saturday 10 a.m.-6 p.m.; closed holidays.

THEODORE ROOSEVELT BIRTHPLACE NATIONAL HISTORIC SITE

28 E. 20th St., New York, 212-260-1616; www.nps.gov/thrb
The reconstructed birthplace of the 26th president, who lived here from 1858 to 1872. Guided tours (every hour with the last tour at 4 p.m.) of five rooms restored to their 1865 appearance. Tuesday-Saturday 9 a.m.-5 p.m.; closed holidays.

TKTS DISCOUNT THEATER TICKETS

Broadway at 47th St., New York; www.tkts.com
With the price of Broadway shows closing in at $100 for the best seats in the house, TKTS is a godsend to theater lovers. The more popular TKTS booth at Times Square (just look for lots of people standing in two lines) provides up to 50 percent discounted tickets on Broadway, off-Broadway, and some musical and dance events. Tickets are sold for the day of performance for matinees and evening shows. The downtown booth (199 Water St.) sells tickets for evening day of performance and for matinees one day

NEW YORK

★
★
★
★

in advance. Generally, you will not be able to get tickets for the hottest shows in town through TKTS, but usually for ones that have been playing for a while. Lines are long and you are guaranteed nothing by waiting on line. Have a first, second and third choice in mind. Only cash and travelers checks are accepted. Daily.

TRINITY CHURCH
Broadway at Wall St., New York, 212-602-0800; www.trinitywallstreet.org
This is the third building to occupy this site; the original was built in 1697. Its famous graveyard, favorite lunchtime spot of workers in the Financial District, contains the graves of Robert Fulton and Alexander Hamilton. The Gothic Revival brownstone church houses a museum. Parish center with dining room open to the public. Daily 7 a.m.-6 p.m., Saturday 8 a.m.-4 p.m., Sunday 7 a.m.-4 p.m.

UNION SQUARE GREENMARKET
17th St. E. and Broadway, New York, 212-788-7476; www.cenyc.org
This busy year-round farmers' market is located at Union Square between 14th and 17th Streets and Broadway and Park Avenue. It's a chance to experience a bit of the country in the Big Apple, as farmers and other vendors sell fresh fruits, vegetables, cheeses, homemade pies, herbs, cut flowers and potted plants. Arrive early for the best selection. Monday, Wednesday, Friday-Saturday 8 a.m.-6 p.m.; closed holidays.

UNITED NATIONS
First Avenue at 46th Street, New York, 212-963-8687; www.un.org
These four buildings, designed under the direction of Wallace K. Harrison, were completed between 1950 and 1952. Regular sessions of the General Assembly start on the third Tuesday in September. Tickets are occasionally available to certain official meetings on a first-come basis. The UN book and gift shops and the UN Post Office are in the basement, where visitors can mail letters bearing United Nations' stamps. The Conference Building is where the various UN Councils meet. The Secretariat Building is a 550-foot-high rectangular glass-and-steel building; here the day-to-day work of the UN staff is performed. The fourth building is the Dag Hammarskjöld Library, open only to UN staff and delegations or by special permission for serious research. Guided tours leave the public entrance lobby at frequent intervals. Daily; closed some holidays; also weekdays in January-February; no children under 5 years.

WALL STREET
New York
New York's Wall Street stands for much more than an address: it is the symbol of American capitalism, known around the world. The street begins at Broadway, where you'll find Trinity Church (built in 1846 and a symbol of the city's strength when it survived the nearby September 11, 2001 terrorist attacks), and stretches east to the East River. If you walk the street's six or so blocks, you'll pass the Federal Hall National Monument, the site where George Washington took the Oath of Office and became the first President of the United States in 1789. Step inside the building to view the impressive rotunda and check out an exhibit on the Constitution. Just half a block south of Wall Street, on Broad Street, is the New York Stock Exchange, where fortunes are made and lost with every clang of the opening bell.

WASHINGTON SQUARE PARK

West Fourth Street, and Waverly Place, New York

For the ultimate in people-watching, head downtown to the heart and soul of Green-wich Village. The nine-acre park, dating to 1827, serves up a cacophony of jugglers, street musicians, magicians and countless students from nearby New York University. The park hosts outdoor art fairs in spring and fall, as well as jazz performances in summer. The north end of the park features the historic Washington Memorial Arch (14 Washington Square North). This marble structure was modeled after Paris' Arc de Triomphe and was erected in 1889.

WHITNEY MUSEUM OF AMERICAN ART

945 Madison Ave., New York, 212-570-3600, 800-944-8639; www.whitney.org

Bauhaus-trained architect Marcel Breuer's museum is menacingly cantilevered toward Madison Avenue. Its bold, sculptural quality makes it a fitting home for modern and contemporary art. The impressive permanent collection takes American art from the early 20th century into the 21st century, showing works by Thomas Hart Benton, Edward Hopper and Georgia O'Keeffe, as well as those by later artists such as Alexander Calder, Louise Nevelson, Robert Rauschenberg and Jasper Johns. The controversial Whitney Biennial showcases the latest works of contemporary artists. Wednesday-Thursday, Saturday-Sunday 11 a.m.-6 p.m., Friday 1-9 p.m. (6-9 p.m. pay-what-you-wish admission); closed holidays.

WOOLWORTH BUILDING

233 Broadway, New York

This neo-Gothic skyscraper by Cass Gilbert was the tallest building in the world (792 feet, 58 stories) when it was built. Frank W. Woolworth, the dime-store king, paid $13.5 million cash for his "cathedral of commerce" when it was completed in 1913.

YESHIVA UNIVERSITY MUSEUM

15 W. 16th St., New York, 212-294-8330; www.yumuseum.org

This teaching museum devoted to Jewish art, architecture, history and culture has permanent exhibits, including scale models of synagogues from the third to 19th centuries; reproduction of frescoes from the Dura-Europos Synagogue; ceremonial objects, rare books; audiovisual presentations; theater; changing exhibits. Academic year, Tuesday-Thursday, Sunday 11 a.m.-5 p.m. Monday 3:30-7:30 p.m.; closed holidays, Jewish holidays.

ZABAR'S

2245 Broadway, New York, 212-787-2000; www.zabars.com

This second-generation gourmet food market has graced Manhattan's Upper West Side since 1934. Occupying close to one city block and employing 250 people, Zabar's sells wonderful breads and pastries, meats, cheeses, smoked fish, condiments and cookware. Monday-Friday 8 a.m.-7:30 p.m., Saturday 8 a.m.-8 p.m., Sunday 9 a.m.-6 p.m.

SPECIAL EVENTS

BRYANT PARK SUMMER FILM FESTIVAL

42nd St., New York, 212-768-4242; www.bryantpark.org

Park yourself on the lawn at Bryant Park for its weekly film showing on summer evenings. Hundreds come each Monday night to see a movie and hang out once the sun goes down. Check the local newspapers to find out what's playing each week. Monday, June-August.

CENTRAL PARK CONCERTS
72nd St., and Fifth Avenue, New York, 212-860-1370; www.centralparknyc.org
Free performances by the New York Philharmonic and the Metropolitan Opera Company on the Great Lawn, mid-Park at 81st Street. June-August.

CHINESE NEW YEAR
Mott and Pell Streets, New York, 212-226-1330
Parade with lions, dragons, costumes, firecrackers. Early-mid-February.

FLEET WEEK
Pier 88, New York, 212-245-0072; www.fleetweek.navy.mil
In a scene right out of the Gene Kelly Navy-themed musical, *On the Town*, Navy and Coast Guard ships gather for a parade up the Hudson River that is a true spectacle of springtime in New York. After the ships dock by the museum, they are open to the public for tours. Expect to find Navy men and women all over the city, looking for a good time. Late May.

GREENWICH VILLAGE HALLOWEEN PARADE
West Fourth Street, New York; www.halloween-nyc.com
Straights, gays, men, women, kids seniors and everyone in between dress in the wildest of costumes for this annual Halloween tradition in the West Village. Strangers become instant friends and everyone gets into the spirit of what has become the largest Halloween parade in the United States. Late October.

INDEPENDENCE DAY HARBOR FESTIVAL
East River and South Street, Seaport, New York
This is the nation's largest July 4 celebration; fireworks; food; music. Weekend of July 4.

JVC JAZZ FESTIVAL
Park Row between Beekman and Ann Streets, New York, 212-501-1390;
www.festivalproductions.net
World-famous musicians perform in Avery Fisher Hall, Carnegie Hall, Town Hall and other sites throughout the city. Last two weeks in June.

MACY'S THANKSGIVING DAY PARADE
Broadway between 34th and 72nd Streets, New York, 212-397-8222;
www.macysparade.com
Amazing floats, cheerful clowns (who are all volunteers and are either Macy's employees or friends and families of Macy's employees), and celebrities are all part of the parade, which starts at 9 a.m. and ends around noon (with Santa's arrival). One of the best viewing spots is on Herald Square in front of Macy's.

NATIONAL PUERTO RICAN DAY PARADE

Fifth Avenue between 45th and 86th Streets, New York, 718-401-0404;
www.nationalpuertoricandayparade.org

The National Puerto Rican Day Parade, Inc. was established to bring a national aware-ness to the Puerto Rican culture and its contribution to the culture and society of the United States. In addition, it promotes the study, improvement and/or advancement of Puerto Rican culture and the arts by encouraging, promoting, coordinating, develop-ing, managing and participating in various cultural events. Mid-June.

NEW YORK SHAKESPEARE FESTIVAL & SHAKESPEARE IN THE PARK

81st St., and Central Park West, New York, 212-260-2400; www.publictheater.org

At the 2,000-seat outdoor Delacorte Theater in Central Park, near West 81st Street. Tuesday-Sunday. Free tickets are distributed on the day of the performance at the Public Theater. June-September.

NEW YORK CITY MARATHON

New York; www.nycmarathon.org

Which event attracts more than two million spectators, 30,000 participants from every corner of the globe and 12,000 volunteers? The grueling 26.2-mile New York City Marathon. Whether you're an experienced runner or a couch potato, to stand on the sidelines and cheer on these amazing athletes during the world's largest mara-thon is a thrilling and rewarding experience. The event begins on the Staten Island side of the Verrazano-Narrows Bridge, goes through all five boroughs of the city and finishes up by Tavern on the Green restaurant in Central Park. First Sunday in November.

147

RINGLING BROS. AND BARNUM & BAILEY CIRCUS

Madison Square Garden, Seventh Ave. and 32nd St., New York, 212-465-6741;
www.ringling.com

The Greatest Show on Earth visits the city every spring. Expect the usual circus fare—elephants, trapeze artists, clowns and the like. For a special treat, view the parade of circus people and animals from 12th Avenue and 34th Street to the Garden on the morning before the show opens. March-April.

SAN GENNARO FESTIVAL

Little Italy, Mulberry Street between Canal and Houston Streets, New York;
www.sangennaro.org

More than 75 years old, this giant street festival in Little Italy salutes the patron saint of Naples with a celebratory Mass and a candlelit procession of the Statue of the Saint. More than a million people descend on Little Italy during these 11 days to feast on food from the old country, watch the parades, enjoy the live music and compete for the title of cannoli-eating champion. Mid-September.

ST. PATRICK'S DAY PARADE

Fifth Ave. between 44th and 86th Streets, New York; www.saintpatricksdayparade.com

New York's biggest annual parade; approximately 100,000 marchers.

WESTMINSTER KENNEL CLUB DOG SHOW

Madison Square Garden, 4 Pennsylvania Plaza, New York, 212-213-3165;
www.westminsterkennelclub.org

Nearly 3,000 top dogs and their owners take part in this two-day annual extravaganza leading up to the crowning of Best in Show on the second night of competition. Arrive two hours early each night, at about 6 p.m., and go to the huge backstage area. Here, you will be able to pet the dogs that vied for Best in Breed in competitions held earlier in the day. (Always ask the owner/handler for permission before petting an animal.) The owners and handlers welcome the public since they love showing off their pooches—they may even convince you to buy a future offspring of their show dogs. Best in Group competitions for the seven groups run from 8-11 p.m. each night. You can buy tickets for one or both nights. For the best deal, purchase a general admission, two-day pass. Mid-February.

WINTER AND SUMMER RESTAURANT WEEKS

New York; www.nycvisit.com

Many of the city's finest restaurants offer two- or three-course, fixed-price lunches at bargain prices during two weeks in summer. This is a wildly popular promotion that natives can't wait to experience. Check local newspapers at the beginning of your trip to see which restaurants are participating and make a reservation. Third and fourth weeks in June.

HOTELS

★★★6 COLUMBUS

6 Columbus Circle, New York, 212-204-3000; www.sixcolumbus.com

There's an über-chic aesthetic and chilly, too-cool-for-school vibe at this mod hotel which replaced the fleabag dive that long sat here before it. The lobby's slender leather couch, white shag rug and powder blue saucer chairs scream *I Dream of Jeannie*, and that '60s feel carries through to the blue-toned Steven Sclaroff-designed rooms, decked out with teak walls, Saarinen style side chairs and tables, and classic Guy Bourdin prints on the wall. The Euro crowd doesn't seem to mind unloading their Euros for more current amenities, like maki from the Blue Ribbon Sushi outpost off the lobby, or shelling out $2,500 a night for the privilege of staying in a two-story loft space with a terrace overlooking Central Park and Columbus Circle. 88 rooms. Restaurant, bar.

★★★60 THOMPSON

60 Thompson St., New York, 212-431-0400, 877-431-0400; www.60thompson.com

This Soho boutique hotel features contemporary rooms decorated in brown and gray tones with full-wall leather headboards swathed in Frette linens. Other amenities include in-room spa products by Philosophy and oversized showers in the marble bathrooms (along with the requisite high-speed Internet connections, DVD players and CD stereo systems). The hotel's Thai restaurant, Kittichai, is popular with the hipster crowd who also frequent Thom Bar, a clubby, intimate setting off the lobby in which to relax and enjoy a drink. See if you can wangle an invite to the members-only, rooftop lounge, A-60, with its stellar views.

★AFFINIA GARDENS

215 E. 64th St., New York, 212-355-1230, 866-246-2203; www.affinia.com

130 rooms, all suites. Wireless Internet access. Airport transportation available. $$$

★★★THE ALEX HOTEL

205 E. 45th St. New York, 212-867-5100; www.thealexhotel.com

A new luxury hotel located near the United Nations and Midtown's east side, the Alex is popular with the diplomats and media types who live and work in the neighborhood (in fact, some choose to live at the hotel, which is loaded with amenities for long-term stays). Rooms include luxe touches such as Frederic Fekkai bath products and the Dean & Deluca snack trays. Suites have Poggenpohl kitchens stocked with Sub-Zero fridges. Star chef Marcus Samuelsson's Riingo (which means "apple" in Swedish, a nod to the city's nickname) is a stylish spot for sampling his take on Japanese-influenced dishes such as seared striped bass with rice noodles and spicy bean sauce. 203 rooms. Wireless Internet access. Restaurant, bar. Business center. Fitness center. Spa. Valet parking. $$$$

★★ALGONQUIN HOTEL

59 W. 44th St., New York, 212-840-6800; www.algonquinhotel.com

174 rooms. Wireless Internet access. Two restaurants, bar. Airport transportation available. Fitness center. $$$

★★AMERITANIA HOTEL

230 W. 54th St., New York, 212-247-5000; 800-555-7555;
www.ameritaniahotelnewyork.com

219 rooms. Restaurant, bar. Fitness center. $

★★★THE AVALON

16 E. 32nd St., New York, 212-299-7000, 888-442-8256; www.avalonhotelnyc.com

Stately black marble columns and a mosaic floor make an elegant first impression at this Murray Hill boutique hotel. Rooms feature desk chairs designed for comfort and functionality, as well as Irish cotton linens and velour bathrobes. 100 rooms. High-speed Internet access. Restaurant, bar. Fitness center. Airport transportation available. $$

★★★THE BENJAMIN

125 E. 50th St., New York, 212-715-2500, 800-637-8483; www.thebenjamin.com

Set in a classic 1927 building, this hotel has all the high-tech amenities a business traveler could want. It also offers comfortable accommodations in a sophisticated setting with earth tones and contemporary furnishings. A standout amenity is the pillow menu, which offers a choice of 10 different kinds of bed pillows and a guarantee of a refund if you do not wake well rested. The Benjamin's Wellness Spa offers body treatments with a holistic approach. 209 rooms. High-speed Internet access. Restaurant. Spa. $$$$

★★BENTLEY HOTEL

500 E. 62nd St., New York, 800-555-7555; www.bentleyhotelnewyork.com

196 rooms. Restaurant, bar. Valet parking. $

★★★BOWERY HOTEL

335 Bowery, New York, 212-505-9100; www.theboweryhotel.com

This boutique spot in the Bowery—an area once home to legendary punk bar CBGB and long known as gritty rather than pretty—represents the area's continuing

★
★
★
★

gentrification but still manages to maintain its street cred. A short walk from Nolita, the East Village, Lower East Side and Soho, the redesigned SRO from hoteliers Eric Goode and Sean MacPherson (Waverly Inn, Maritime Hotel), has a dimly lit lobby with leather- and velvet-upholstered furniture that feels old and cozy, minus any mustiness. The lounge, with its velvet banquettes, dark wood walls and fireplace draws a cocktail-seeking crowd as do the outdoor patio and small back bar known for its Absinthe concoctions. Guest suites have wood-slatted floors, marble bathrooms and floor-to-ceiling paned factory windows that overlook the neighboring tenements, just to remind you that–despite that HD TV, iPod stereo system and docking station, this still ain't the Upper West Side, honey. 135 rooms. Restaurant, bar. $$$$

★★★BRYANT PARK HOTEL
40 W. 40th St., New York, 212-869-0100, 877-640-9300; www.bryantparkhotel.com

It's no surprise that this hip hotel hosts a who's who list of designers, media big wigs and celebs during New York's Fall and Spring Fashion Weeks thanks to its proximity to the tents erected to host the runway shows across the street. But many of these fashionistas frequent this boutique property the rest of the year, too. They enjoy the amenities in the mod rooms (think leather chairs, Tibetan rugs and Travertine marble bathrooms) like hi-def flat screen televisions, Bose Wave music systems and Obusforme Sound Therapy Machines that can lull them to sleep with gentle waterfall sounds and awake them to chirping birds. There's also a loft meeting space that's popular for sample sales, a 70-seat theater-style screening room and "entertainment planner" (really just a snooty title for the concierge) at guests' disposal. Japanese restaurant Koi and the large underground Cellar Bar are always packed with the young and pretty whether they stay at the hotel or not. Book one of the 20 rooms that face the park where you can take in all the action from a high vantage point. 127 rooms. High-speed Internet access. Restaurant, bar. Fitness center. Airport transportation available. $$$

★★★★THE CARLYLE, A ROSEWOOD HOTEL
35 E. 76th St., New York, 212-744-1600, 888-767-3966; www.thecarlyle.com

Discreetly tucked away on Manhattan's Upper East Side, the Carlyle has maintained the allure of being one of New York's best-kept secrets for more than 70 years. A favorite of movie stars, presidents and royals, the Carlyle feels like an exclusive private club. Its art collection is extraordinary, from Audubon prints and Piranesi architectural drawings to English country scenes by Kips. Frequented by power brokers and socialites, the Carlyle Restaurant defines elegance. Bemelmans Bar proudly shows off its murals by *Madeline* creator Ludwig Bemelmans, while Café Carlyle is one of the city's most beloved piano bars. 179 rooms. Wireless Internet access. Two restaurants, bar. Fitness room. Spa. Airport transportation available. Business center. Pets accepted. $$$$

★★★CHAMBERS
15 W. 56th St., New York, 212-974-5656, 866-204-5656; www.chambershotel.com

Located steps from Fifth Avenue's retail glitz, this boutique hotel has a modern, open quality thanks to the soaring lobby and its double-sided fireplace. The spacious, high-tech rooms feature amenities like slippers you can actually keep, umbrellas, Frette bathrobes, flat-screen TVs and baths stocked with products from Bumble + Bumble. Just off the lobby, Town restaurant serves highly regarded American cuisine accented with French and Asian influences in an elegant setting. Guests of the hotel receive complimentary passes to the New York Sports Club. 100 rooms. Complimentary continental breakfast. Restaurant, bar. $$$$

★★★CITY CLUB HOTEL
55 W. 44th St., New York, 212-921-5500; www.cityclubhotel.com
The City Club Hotel is all about contemporary style and elegance. From the Frette bed linens to the luxury bath products, this intimate boutique hotel spoils its guests with luxurious amenities, not to mention attentive service and stunning appointments. Acclaimed chef Daniel Boulud's DB Bistro Moderne is adjacent to the hotel lobby. 65 rooms. High-speed Internet access. Restaurant, bar. $$

★★COURTYARD BY MARRIOTT TIMES SQUARE SOUTH
114 W. 40th St., New York, 212-391-0088, 800-321-2211; www.courtyard.com
244 rooms. Wireless Internet access. Restaurant. Fitness center. $$$

★★★CROWNE PLAZA HOTEL TIMES SQUARE MANHATTAN
1605 Broadway, New York, 212-977-4000; www.manhattan.crowneplaza.com
With a prominent location on Broadway in the center of Times Square, this contemporary hotel sits steps from the Great White Way's attractions. Guest rooms provide comfortable, high-quality bedding, relaxation CDs, eye masks and earplugs and lavender aromatherapy spray. Guests can even request a quiet-zone floor. 770 rooms. High-speed Internet access. Restaurant, two bars, Children's activity center. Business center. Indoor pool. Airport transportation available. $$$

★★★DOUBLETREE GUEST SUITES TIMES SQUARE-NEW YORK CITY
1568 Broadway, New York, 212-719-1600, 800-222-8733; www.doubletree.com
If you're looking for an all-suite hotel in Times Square, the Doubletree sits in the center of the action. The spacious, two-room suites feature a bedroom and a separate living/dining/work area with a pullout sofa bed, microwave and refrigerator. The Center Stage Cafe in the atrium offers breakfast, lunch and dinner, and the Cabaret Lounge is perfect for an end-of-day, cocktail. 460 rooms, all suites. Wireless Internet access. Restaurant, bar. Fitness center. Valet parking. Airport transportation available. $$$$

★★★DOUBLETREE METROPOLITAN HOTEL NEW YORK CITY
569 Lexington Ave., New York, 212-752-7000, 800-222-8733; www.doubletree.com
This Midtown hotel caters primarily to business travelers. The hotel's premium business-class program includes a separate check-in and check-out area, private lounge with wine and cheese, continental breakfast and snacks and special in-room amenities. 755 rooms. Wireless Internet access. Restaurant, bar. Airport transportation available. Fitness center. $$

★★★DREAM HOTEL NEW YORK
210 W. 55th St., New York, 212-247-2000, 866-437-3266; www.dreamny.com
Vikram Chatwal, the brains behind Time Hotel, turned the former Majestic Hotel into this slumber-themed luxe property in 2004. You'll feel like you walked into a trippy dream the moment you hit the lobby, where a giant two-story aquarium and bronze Catherine the Great statue are part of the eclectic design mix. The restaurant here is an outpost of the Serafina chain of northern Italian spots known all over town for their specialty pizzas. An ayurvedic spa was designed by Deepak Chopra to allow guests to

massage and meditate their way to peacefulness before turning in for the night in the minimalist rooms, outfitted with feather beds and 300 thread-count Egyptian sheets, and awash in blue lights that give them a twilight feel. If a nightcap is more your style, head to the penthouse Ava Lounge, with a seasonal rooftop garden that sits between neighboring skyscrapers. 220 rooms. Restaurant, bar. Fitness center. Spa. $$$

★★★DYLAN HOTEL
52 E. 41st St., New York, 212-338-0500, 866-553-9526; www.dylanhotel.com
The former Chemist's Club, this 1903 Beaux Arts-style building features an ornate façade and spiraling marble staircase as well as bright and airy guest rooms with 11-foot ceilings and elegant marble baths. The hotel houses the wonderful Benjamin Steakhouse with its well-spaced tables and prime chops. 107 rooms. Wireless Internet access. Restaurant, bar. Fitness center. Airport transportation available. Business center. $$$

★★★EASTGATE TOWER HOTEL
222 E. 39th St., New York, 212-687-8000, 866-233-4642; www.affinia.com
Located on the east side of Midtown, this all-suite hotel is a convenient choice for both business and leisure travelers. Grand Central Station, the United Nations and terrific shopping are all nearby, and the guest suites are large and feature fully equipped kitchens—a plus for guests with long-term business assignments or families. 187 rooms, all suites. Wireless Internet access. Restaurant, bar. Fitness center. Pets accepted. $$$

★★★★★FOUR SEASONS HOTEL NEW YORK
57 E. 57th St., New York, 212-758-5700, 800-545-4000; www.fourseasons.com
Designed by legendary architect I. M. Pei, the Four Seasons is the tallest hotel in New York, and the rooms and suites are testaments to chic simplicity with neutral tones, English sycamore furnishings and state-of-the-art technology. But it's the service that defines the Four Seasons experience: the staff is wonderfully helpful, courteous and terrifically discreet. The views are terrific, too: floor-to-ceiling windows showcase the dazzling city skyline or the verdant swath of Central Park. Some rooms offer furnished terraces so that guests can further admire the vistas. 368 rooms. Wireless Internet access. Restaurant, bar. Fitness center. Spa. Airport transportation available. Business center. Pets accepted. $$$$

★★★THE GRAMERCY PARK HOTEL
2 Lexington Ave., New York, 212-920-3300; www.gramercyparkhotel.com
A legendary hotel that's hosted the likes of Babe Ruth, Madonna and David Bowie, this long-neglected hostelry was reborn in 2006 under the direction of famed hotelier Ian Schrager and the design of artist Julian Schnabel. With the hefty price tag of a room comes access to keys to the adjacent, very exclusive and very private Gramercy Park. Rooms can be petite, but details like iPod players, plush beds and plasma TVs make up for any shortcomings. The Rose Bar, with its Andy Warhol and Damien Hirst paintings, fireplaces and cozy chairs is a prime spot for a cocktail, though the newly opened private roof club and garden is the toughest velvet rope to cross in town. 185 rooms. Wireless Internet access. Restaurant, two bars. Fitness room. Spa. Business center. Pets accepted. $$$$

★HAMPTON INN MANHATTAN CHELSEA

108 W. 24th St., New York, 212-414-1000; www.hamptoninn.com
144 rooms. High-speed Internet access. Complimentary full breakfast. Fitness center. Business center. **$$**

★★HILTON GARDEN INN TIMES SQUARE

790 Eighth Ave., New York, 212-581-7000, 800-544-8313; www.hilton.com
367 rooms. High-speed Internet access. Restaurant, bar. Fitness center. Business center. **$**

★★★HILTON NEW YORK

1335 Avenue of the Americas, New York, 212-586-7000, 800-445-8667;
www.hilton.com
This large convention hotel—the largest in Manhattan—has a prime Midtown setting. The spacious, contemporary rooms offer work desks, on-demand entertainment systems, marble bathrooms and Internet access. There are several in-house restaurants, bars and shops as well as a fitness center and full-service spa. 2,058 rooms. Wireless Internet access. Two restaurants, two bars. Spa. Airport transportation available. **$$$**

★HOLIDAY INN EXPRESS NEW YORK CITY FIFTH AVENUE

15 W. 45th St., New York, 212-302-9088; www.ichotelsgroup.com
124 rooms. Complimentary continental breakfast. Wireless Internet access. Airport transportation available. **$$$**

★★HOLIDAY INN MANHATTAN-DOWNTOWN SOHO

138 Lafayette St., New York, 212-966-8898, 800-465-4329; www.holiday-inn.com
227 rooms. Wireless Internet access. Restaurant, bar. Airport transportation available. **$$**

★★HOLIDAY INN NEW YORK CITY-MIDTOWN-57TH STREET

440 W. 57th St., New York, 212-581-8100; www.holiday-inn.com
597 rooms. Two restaurants, bar. **$$**

★★HOTEL BEACON

2130 Broadway, New York, 212-787-1100, 800-572-4969; www.beaconhotel.com
255 rooms. Wireless Internet access. Restaurant. Airport transportation available. **$$**

★★★HOTEL ELYSEE

60 E. 54th St., New York, 212-753-1066, 800-535-9733; www.elyseehotel.com
Celebrities such as Tennessee Williams, Joe DiMaggio, Ava Gardner and Marlon Brando have called this historic hotel home over the years since it opened in the 1920s. The guest rooms have marble baths; some have terraces, solariums or kitchenettes. The hotel's restaurant, the Monkey Bar and Grill, remains a New York hot spot, serving Asian-inspired cooking by acclaimed chef Patricia Yeo. 103 rooms. Complimentary continental breakfast. Restaurant, bar. **$$$$**

★★★HOTEL GANSEVOORT

18 Ninth Ave., New York, 212-206-6700, 877-426-7386; www.hotelgansevoort.com
The first full-service hotel to open in New York's rejuvenated (but still rough around the edges) Meatpacking District, this boutique property offers stylish rooms and an

even more glamorous scene that centers around its rooftop pool and its onsite Japanese restaurant and bar, Ono. Contemporary creature comforts include a full-service spa, free Wi-Fi, concierge service, a fitness center, business center and more. 187 rooms. Wireless Internet access. Restaurant, bar. Fitness center. Spa. Pool. Valet parking. Pets accepted. $$$

★★★HOTEL ON RIVINGTON

107 Rivington St., New York, 212-475-2600, 800-915-1537; www.hotelonrivington.com
New York's Lower East Side is the last place you'd expect to find a luxury boutique hotel. (And the hipsters who haunt this grungy, no-frills 'hood are probably less than thrilled about one opening here.) But this hotel blends in to the landscape quietly, offering a contemporary space with respect for good design and an appreciation for creature comforts. Rooms are streamlined, with minimalist furnishings, sleek flatscreen TVs, Japanese soaking tubs and floor-to-ceiling windows with views of Manhattan's skyline. Thor restaurant serves breakfast, lunch and dinner while the onsite Annie O. boutique stocks everything from toothbrushes to Lucite jewelry. 101 rooms. Wireless Internet access. Complimentary breakfast. Restaurant, bar. Airport transportation available. Fitness center. Business center. Pets accepted. $$$

★★★HOTEL PLAZA ATHENEE

37 E. 64th St., New York, 212-734-9100, 800-447-8800; www.plaza-athenee.com
This elegant hotel is a deluxe hideaway thanks to its decidedly residential feel, yet the hotel is perfectly placed among the boutiques of Madison Avenue, the townhouses and apartment buildings of Park Avenue and the greenery of Central Park. Some suites have dining rooms while others have indoor terraces or outdoor balconies. Arabelle Restaurant combines gracious French style with smart continental cuisine. Arabelle also offers high tea and a traditional Sunday brunch. 149 rooms. Wireless Internet access. Restaurant, bar. Airport transportation available. $$$$

★★HOTEL WALES

1295 Madison Ave., New York, 212-876-6000, 866-925-3746; www.waleshotel.com
87 rooms. Wireless Internet access. Restaurant. Airport transportation available. $$$

★★★INN AT IRVING PLACE

56 Irving Place, New York, 212-533-4600, 800-685-1447; www.innatirving.com
Step back in time to 19th-century New York at this intimate, romantic brownstone hideaway located in a row of 1830s townhouses just south of Gramercy Park. The high-ceilinged guest rooms feature antiques, four-poster beds and couches without sacrificing modern amenities like remote climate control and Internet access. Enjoy breakfast in bed or take it in the elegant guest parlor. Afternoon tea at Lady Mendl's Tea Salon is a special treat. The staff can arrange special services including an in-room massage or the booking of theater tickets. 12 rooms. Children over 12 years only. Complimentary continental breakfast. Bar. $$$$

★★★INTERCONTINENTAL THE BARCLAY NEW YORK

111 E. 48th St., New York, 212-755-5900, 800-782-8021; www.intercontinental.com
This hotel boasts an opulent lobby with marble floors and fine furnishings. It's a hint of what guests will find in their rooms. An array of hotel services provides convenience:

babysitting services, laundry and dry-cleaning service, a concierge and a 24-hour business center. The clubby Barclay Bar and Grille offers a comfortable setting and a creative menu of American and Continental cuisine. 600 rooms. High-speed Internet access. Restaurant, bar. Airport transportation available. $$$

★★★THE IROQUOIS

49 W. 44th St., New York, 212-840-3080, 800-332-7220; www.iroquoisny.com

The Iroquois underwent a $10 million renovation a few years back that restored this landmark property to its original 1923 elegance. Guest rooms are individually decorated with works of art reflecting New York themes and feature luxe Frette linens and Italian marble baths. Triomphe restaurant features French cuisine, and the Burgundy Room offers breakfast and cocktails. 114 rooms. Wireless Internet access. Restaurant, bar. Airport transportation available. $$$$

★★★JUMEIRAH ESSEX HOUSE ON CENTRAL PARK

160 Central Park S., New York, 212-247-0300, 888-645-5697; www.jumeirahessexhouse.com

An elegant hotel on Central Park South, the Jumeirah Essex House has a vaunted history. Recently revamped, this Art Deco gem boasts many luxurious touches including large rooms with dramatic lighting displays and touch pad controls as well as spectacular views of Central Park. 583 rooms. High-speed Internet access. Two restaurants, bar. Spa. Airport transportation available. $$$$

★★★THE KIMBERLY HOTEL

145 E. 50th St., New York, 212-702-1600, 800-683-0400; www.kimberlyhotel.com

The Kimberly's one- and two-bedroom suites feature living rooms, dining areas and fully equipped separate kitchens. Many have private terraces with city views. Guests receive free use of the nearby New York Health and Racquet Club and can take a complimentary cruise on the hotel's 75-foot yacht on weekends from May through October. 193 rooms, all suites. Wireless Internet access. Restaurant, bar. Airport transportation available. $$$$

★★★THE KITANO NEW YORK

66 Park Ave., New York, 212-885-7000, 800-548-2666; www.kitano.com

This Japanese import just south of Grand Central features modern guest rooms with soft tones of beige and tan and soundproof windows that ensure peace and quiet. The rooms also feature duvets, large desks and samplings of green tea. The Nadaman Hakubai restaurant specializes in gourmet Japanese cuisine, and the sun-drenched Garden Cafe features contemporary European and Asian cuisines. 149 rooms. High-speed Internet access. Two restaurants, bar. $$$$

★★★LIBRARY HOTEL

299 Madison Ave., New York, 212-983-4500, 877-793-7323; www.libraryhotel.com

As the name suggests, this unique Midtown hotel was inspired by the New York City Public Library, which sits one block away. Each of the 10 floors is dedicated to one of the 10 categories of the Dewey Decimal System, which include languages, literature, history, the arts and religion. Guest rooms are stocked with books and art relevant to the floor's particular topic. In keeping with this theme, the hotel houses a

★
★
★
★
★

reading room and a poetry garden with a terrace for relaxing and reading. 60 rooms. High-speed Internet access. Complimentary continental breakfast. Restaurant, bar. Airport transportation available. $$$

★★★THE LOMBARDY HOTEL

111 E. 56th St., New York, 212-753-8600, 800-223-5254; www.lombardyhotel.com

An elegant Midtown hotel, the somewhat sleepy Lombardy was built in the 1920s by William Randolph Hearst and features oversized rooms decorated in a classic, old-world style. The marble baths have oversized showers and an array of upscale toiletries. Above-and-beyond personal services include a seamstress and white-glove attendant service in the elevators. 167 rooms. High-speed Internet access. Restaurant, bar. Airport transportation available. $$$

★★★LONDON NYC

151 W. 54th St., New York, 866-690-2029; www.thelondonnyc.com

This recently opened boutique hotel is luxurious, sophisticated and chic. With interiors by famed designer David Collins, the space has been updated with quietly contemporary and glamorous furnishings, artwork and luxury touches like Waterworks bathrooms, Egyptian cotton linens, iPod docking stations and flatscreen TVs. The hotel is the location of British star chef Gordon Ramsay's first U.S. restaurant, which serves outrageously delicious takes on French-influenced contemporary cuisine (think lobster ravioli with celery root cream and shellfish vinaigrette.) The property also boasts a concierge desk manned by Quintessentially, the renowned international service that can handle requests for anything from a private jet to tickets to the city's hottest show. 561 rooms. Wireless Internet access. Bar, restaurant. Valet parking. $$$$

★★★★THE LOWELL

28 E. 63rd St., New York, 212-838-1400, 800-221-4444; www.lowellhotel.com

Located in a landmark 1920s building on the Upper East Side, the Lowell captures the essence of an elegant country house with a delightful blend of English prints, floral fabrics and Chinese porcelains. Many suites boast wood-burning fireplaces—a rarity in Manhattan. All rooms are individually decorated, and the Lowell's specialty suites are a unique treat. The glamour of the 1930s silver screen is recalled in the Hollywood Suite while the Gym Suite, originally created for Madonna, is perfect for exercise buffs. The English influences extend to the Pembroke Room, where a proper tea is served, as are breakfast and brunch. The clubby Post House, a well-respected New York steakhouse, serves terrific chops. 70 rooms. Wireless Internet access. Complimentary continental breakfast. Two restaurants, bar. Airport transportation available. $$$$

★★★★★MANDARIN ORIENTAL, NEW YORK

80 Columbus Circle, New York, 212-805-8800, 866-801-8880;
www.mandarinoriental.com/newyork

Located in the Time Warner Center, the first floor of this luxury hotel's 54 floors sits high atop the city and offers views of Central Park, the Hudson River and the city skyline. Though serene guest rooms make it tempting to laze about for hours, slip out to explore all that the hotel has to offer. Take a swim in the 36th-floor pool or indulge in a Balinese body massage at the spa. The hotel's Asian theme carries over into Asiate, which serves French and Japanese fusion cuisine, and MObar, which features drinks like the East Meets West, a combination of pear and cinnamon-infused brandy, chilled champagne and a sugar cube. Want to be dazzled by one of the world's best chefs? Make reservations at one of the much talked-about restaurants in the Time Warner Center, including Thomas Keller's Per Se and Masa Takayama's Masa. 248 rooms. Wireless Internet access. Two restaurants, bar. Fitness center. Pool. Spa. Business center. Pets accepted. $$$$

★★THE MANSFIELD
12 W. 44th St., New York, 212-277-8700, 800-255-5167; www.mansfieldhotel.com
126 rooms. Wireless Internet access. Complimentary continental breakfast. Restaurant, bar. Airport transportation available. $$

★★★THE MERCER
147 Mercer St., New York, 212-966-6060; www.mercerhotel.com
Catering to a fashion-forward crowd and situated in Soho, the Mercer Hotel epitomizes relaxed chic with its exposed brick, steel beams and hardwood floors. French designer Christian Liaigre, darling of the minimalist décor movement, crafted a sophisticated look for the hotel with simple furnishings and serene neutral colors. The lobby also serves as a lending library stocked with favorite books and videos, and the nearby Crunch Gym is available for guests' use. Mercer Kitchen and Bar reign serve comfort food under the direction of Jean-Georges Vongerichten. 75 rooms. Wireless Internet access. Restaurant, bar. $$$$

★★★THE MICHELANGELO
152 W. 51st St., New York, 212-765-0505, 800-237-0990; www.michelangelohotel.com
If you are aficionado of all things Italian, book a room at the Michelangelo. Opera music plays in the public spaces, frothy cappuccino and Italian pastries are breakfast standouts and Baci chocolates appear at turndown. The extra-large rooms are decorated in Art Deco, country French or neoclassical style and feature woven fabrics from Italy. 178 rooms. High-speed Internet access. Complimentary continental breakfast. Restaurant, bar. Fitness center. Airport transporation available. $$$$

★★★MILLENIUM HILTON
55 Church St., New York, 212-693-2001, 800-445-8667; www.hilton.com
This tall, sleek Financial District hotel was built to match the skyscrapers around it and features slick, contemporary rooms catering to a Wall Street-focused crowd. The hotel's restaurant, Church & Dey, serves a casual, bistro-style menu heavy on seafood. 569 rooms. Wireless Internet access. Restaurant, two bars. Fitness center. Pool. Spa. Airport transportation available. Business center. Pets accepted. $$$

★★★MILLENNIUM BROADWAY HOTEL NEW YORK
145 W. 44th St., New York, 212-768-4400, 866-866-8086; www.millenniumhotels.com
Colorful murals that evoke the 1930s adorn the lobby of this contemporary Midtown hotel, located near Times Square, the Theater District, shopping and Grand Central. Spacious guest rooms are tastefully appointed with a satellite TV, minibar, high-speed Internet access, iron and ironing board, hairdryer and views of Manhattan. 750 rooms. Wireless Internet access. Restaurant, bar. Airport transportation available. $$

★★★MILLENNIUM UN PLAZA HOTEL

One United Nations Plaza, New York, 212-758-1234, 877-866-7529;
www.millennium-hotels.com

Situated just across from the United Nations, the Millennium has a slick, contemporary design and views of the East River. Bright lights and big mirrors add glamour to the lobby while rooms are modern and contemporary and feature amenities such as satellite television, high-speed Internet access and minibars. 427 rooms. High-speed Internet access. Restaurant, bar. Spa. Airport transportation available. **$$$**

★★★MORGANS

237 Madison Ave., New York, 212-686-0300; www.morganshotel.com

Guest rooms at this Midtown hotel are decorated in soft, muted tones. Asia de Cuba restaurant offers an inventive Asian-Latin menu courtesy of restaurateur Jeffrey Chodorow. And Morgans' Bar is the perfect place for a late-night elixir. Complimentary breakfast and afternoon tea add to the value. 113 rooms. Wireless Internet access. Complimentary continental breakfast. Restaurant, two bars. Airport transportation available. **$$$**

★★★THE MUSE

130 W. 46th St., New York, 212-485-2400, 877-692-6873; www.themusehotel.com

Style abounds at this theater district hotel with a triple-arched, limestone-and-brick façade and lobby that has a 15-foot vaulted ceiling with a mural depicting the nine muses. Original artwork celebrating the theater and the performing arts hangs in each room, decorated in a warm colors and cherry wood furniture. Custom linens and duvet-covered feather beds further enliven the spaces. Pets are given special beds and snacks, and the hotel will arrange sitting services if needed. 200 rooms. High-speed Internet access. Restaurant, bar. Airport transportation available. **$$$**

★★★NEW YORK MARRIOTT FINANCIAL CENTER

85 West St., New York, 212-385-4900, 800-228-9290; www.marriott.com

Walking distance to Wall Street and the ferry to the Statue of Liberty, the Marriott caters to business travelers and visitors wishing to explore downtown attractions. 497 rooms. Wireless Internet access. Restaurant, bar. Airport transportation available. **$$$$**

★★★NEW YORK MARRIOTT MARQUIS

1535 Broadway, New York, 212-398-1900, 800-843-4898; www.marriott.com

Located in Times Square, this mammoth, family-friendly hotel is a city in itself—filled with shops, restaurants and theaters, all built around the towering atrium where glass elevators zip up and down at vertiginous speeds. The spacious rooms feature the 300-thread count linens, fluffy pillows, down comforters and thick mattresses. 1,950 rooms. Wireless Internet access. Three restaurants, three bars. Airport transportation available. **$$$**

★★★★THE NEW YORK PALACE

455 Madison Ave., New York, 212-888-7000, 800-804-7035; www.newyorkpalace.com

Return to the Gilded Age at the New York Palace. Marrying the historic 1882 Villard Houses with a 55-story contemporary tower, this hotel brings the two worlds together under one roof. The glorious public rooms are masterfully restored and recall their former incarnations as fin de siècle ballrooms and sitting areas. The Palace's rooms and suites are a blend of contemporary flair and period décor. The hotel's restaurant, Gilt, serves exceptional food in a dramatic, modern-yet-classic setting. 893 rooms. Wireless Internet access. Restaurant, bar. Fitness center. Spa. Airport transportation available. Business center. Pets accepted. $$$$

★★★OMNI BERKSHIRE PLACE

21 E. 52nd St., New York, 212-753-5800, 888-444-6664; www.omnihotels.com

A soaring atrium with a wood-burning fireplace sets an elegant focal point for this Midtown hotel. The rooms feature luxurious linens, pillow top mattresses, plush robes and marble bathrooms. Business travelers are provided in-room wireless Internet access, in-room fax machines, two dual-lines and dataports. 396 rooms. Wireless Internet access. Restaurant, bar. Airport transportation available. $$$$

★★★LE PARKER MERIDIEN

118 W. 57th St., New York, 212-245-5000, 800-543-4300; www.parkermeridien.com

This chic hotel has contemporary décor and rooms that feature city views, DVD/CD players and 32-inch televisions. There's also a rooftop pool with impressive views. The hotel's restaurant, Norma's, is a prime spot for people-watching and is considered one of the city's premier power-breakfast hot spots. 731 rooms. Wireless Internet access. Three restaurants, bar. Spa. Airport transportation available. $$$$

★★★★THE PENINSULA NEW YORK

700 Fifth Ave., New York, 212-956-2888, 800-262-9467; www.peninsula.com

The lobby of this Midtown hotel is magnificent with a sweeping staircase and elegant bar. Bellhops in crisp white uniforms escort guests to rooms and suites, where lush fabrics and warm tones create a soothing ambience. The fitness center, overlooking the city, is a favorite among those in the know. With its views above the city, the Pen-Top Terrace and Bar is a prime spot for a drink. 239 rooms. Wireless Internet access. Two restaurants, three bars. Spa. Airport transportation available. $$$$

THE PIERRE NEW YORK, A TAJ HOTEL

2 E. 61 St., New York, 212-940-8111, 866-969-1825; www.tajhotels.com/pierre

Regal and luxurious, this is the definition of a grand old hotel. The Pierre has been a city landmark since its construction in 1930. Following a lengthy close for renovations, rooms now include contemporary touches such as wireless Internet and flat-screen TVs. However, the hotel's 1930s detailing and Trompe l'oeil artwork by Edward Melcarth remain intact. 200 rooms. Wireless Internet access. Two restaurants, bar. Fitness center. Airport transportation available. Business center. Pets accepted. $$$$

★★RADISSON LEXINGTON HOTEL NEW YORK

511 Lexington Ave., New York, 212-755-4400, 800-448-4471;
www.lexingtonhotelnyc.com

705 rooms. Wireless Internet access. Four restaurants, bar. Airport transportation available. $$

★★★THE REGENCY HOTEL

540 Park Ave., New York, 212-759-4100, 800-233-2356;
www.loewshotels.com/hotels/newyork

Home of the original power breakfast where deals are sealed and fortunes made, the Regency consistently ranks as one of New York's top hotels. Combining the appearance of a library and a private club, this hotel provides attentive service that extends beyond the ordinary. Pets are even welcomed in grand style with room service, dog-walking services and listings of pet-friendly establishments. Unwind at Feinstein's, where Grammy-nominated Michael Feinstein entertains nightly or savor a meal at 540 Park or the Library. 351 rooms. High-speed Internet access. Three restaurants, bar. Spa. Airport transportation available. $$$$

★★★RENAISSANCE NEW YORK HOTEL TIMES SQUARE

714 Seventh Ave., New York, 212-765-7676; www.renaissancehotels.com

Business guests will appreciate the hotel's Midtown location and services such as meeting rooms, business center and in-room Internet access. The lobby, located on the second floor, has an Art Deco theme that carries into the comfortable guest rooms. 310 rooms. High-speed Internet access. Restaurant, two bars. Airport transportation available. $$$

★★★★THE RITZ-CARLTON NEW YORK, BATTERY PARK

2 West St., New York, 212-344-0800, 800-542-8680; www.ritzcarlton.com

Watch the world from the Ritz-Carlton New York, Battery Park. While only a five-minute walk from Wall Street and the Financial District, the Ritz-Carlton seems removed from the fray, thanks to its staggering views of the Hudson River, the Statue of Liberty and Ellis Island from its location on the southern tip of Manhattan. This 38-story glass and brick tower is a departure from the traditional Ritz-Carlton European style, from the contemporary glass artwork to the modern furnishings. The service is distinctly Ritz-Carlton, however, with exceptional concierge service and amenities like Bath Butlers who create special concoctions for bath time. The view takes center stage throughout the hotel, whether you're gazing through a telescope in a harbor view room, enjoying a cocktail at Rise (the 14th-floor bar with outdoor space) or savoring a meal at 2 West Street. 298 rooms. Wireless Internet access. Restaurant, two bars. Fitness center. Spa. Business center. Pets accepted. $$$$

★★★★★THE RITZ-CARLTON NEW YORK, CENTRAL PARK

50 Central Park S., New York, 212-308-9100, 800-542-8680; www.ritzcarlton.com

Rising above Central Park and flanked by prestigious Fifth Avenue and fashionable Central Park West, this hotel has one of the most coveted locations in town. This genteel property is exquisite down to every last detail, from the priceless antiques and artwork in the glamorous lobby to the floral displays. The rooms and suites have sumptuous fabrics and plush furnishings. No detail is overlooked; rooms facing the park include telescopes for closer viewing. The white-glove service makes this a top choice of well-heeled travelers. The hotel includes an outpost of the renowned European La Prairie Spa and star chef Laurent Tourondel's BLT Market. 259 rooms. Wireless Internet access. Restaurant, bar. Fitness center. Spa. Airport transportation available. Business center. Pets accepted. $$$$

★★THE ROGER WILLIAMS

131 Madison Ave., New York, 212-448-7000, 888-448-7788;
www.hotelrogerwilliams.com
193 rooms. Wireless Internet access. Restaurant, bar. Airport transportation available. $$$

★★ROOSEVELT HOTEL

45 E. 45th St., New York, 212-661-9600, 888-833-3969; www.theroosevelthotel.com
1015 rooms. High-speed Internet access. Restaurant, bar. Fitness center. $$

★★★ROYALTON HOTEL

44 W. 44th St., New York, 212-869-4400, 800-697-1791; www.royalton.com
Many consider the Royalton to be the original boutique hotel: the one that set the standard for hipness with its famously intense Philippe Starck design and a fashion mag crowd that frequented the lobby bar in the 1990s. A recent renovation upped the sophistication level in a quiet, clubby way. The dark lobby with a mix of icy glass, varnished wood, steel and brass, is softened by a giant fireplace, warm leather-covered walls and furniture upholstered in suede and hide. The large guest rooms designed by Charlotte Macaux have also been updated, and use soft colors like light blues, grays and whites as backdrop for the built-in banquettes that run from one end of the room to the other. Flowing curtains, down comforters and chic Philippe Starck bathrooms with five-foot circular tubs and steel sinks continue the cozy-meets-mod aesthetic. Back downstairs, restaurateur John McDonald (Lure Fishbar, Lever House), has overhauled Bar 44 and the cozy 100-seat Brasserie 44 with honey teak walls, rope arches and white glass globe lighting. 168 rooms. Restaurant, two bars. Fitness center. Pets accepted. $$$$

★★★SAN CARLOS HOTEL

150 E. 50th St., New York, 212-755-1800, 800-722-2012; www.sancarloshotel.com
The San Carlos is an elegant, low-key hotel located in the center of Midtown. Rooms are spacious and comfortable with clean, contemporary décor. Amenities such as wet bars, fluffy robes and bath towels, Aveda bath products and flatscreen televisions set the stage for a luxurious experience while the well-equipped Wi-Fi business center and large in-room desks appeal to the business-minded. 147 rooms. Wireless Internet access. Complimentary continental breakfast. Restaurant, bar. Airport transportation available. $$$

★★★SHERATON NEW YORK HOTEL AND TOWERS

811 Seventh Ave., New York, 212-581-1000; www.sheraton.com
This large, comfortable hotel is one of Sheraton's flagships—good for business or pleasure. Close to the theater district, the rooms are large by New York standards, and the service is crisp and professional. 1,748 rooms. High-speed Internet access. Two restaurants, bar. Spa. Airport transportation available. $$$

★★★THE SHERRY NETHERLAND

781 Fifth Ave., New York, 212-355-2800, 877-743-7710; www.sherrynetherland.com
If your style is more classic than contemporary, this landmark 1927 hotel and apartment tower on Fifth Avenue across from Central Park is the address for you. Suites are spacious and decorated with antiques (some even have crystal chandeliers in the

bathrooms) and feature fully-stocked kitchens and pantries. To keep the property up-to-date, a fitness center and high-speed Internet access have been added. 50 rooms, all suites. High-speed Internet access. Fitness center. Valet parking. $$$$

★★★THE SHOREHAM HOTEL

33 W. 55th St., New York, 212-247-6700, 800-553-3347; www.shorehamhotel.com

Terrifically situated just off Fifth Avenue, the Shoreham mixes contemporary elegance with smart attention to detail. The rooms are comfortable and spacious with modern furnishings, high-definition television sets, Bose Wave Radios, 300-thread count linens and multijet showers. Begin your day with the complimentary coffee and cappuccino service in the spacious, lounge-like lobby and wind down at the spiffy Shoreham Bar with a signature Shoreham Happy Martini and plate of chickpea hummus fries. 177 rooms. Wireless Internet access. Restaurant, bar. Fitness center. Business center. Pets accepted. $$$

★★★SOFITEL NEW YORK

45 W. 44th St., New York, 212-354-8844; www.sofitel.com

After a busy day of sightseeing, this hotel provides a serene and comfortable retreat. With the Sofitel's signature and super-luxurious beds along with soundproof windows, it's easy to get a good night's sleep. 398 rooms, Wireless Internet access. Restaurant, bar. Fitness center. Airport transportation available. Business center. Pets accepted. $$$$

★★★SOHO GRAND HOTEL

310 West Broadway, New York, 212-965-3000, 800-965-3000; www.grandhospitality.com

Calculated cool defines this downtown hotel, perched at the base of Broadway and just north of Tribeca. Public spaces are airy and industrial chic: the lobby provides a comfortable gathering place, with high ceilings, couches and exotic, sculptural plants. Rooms are simple in design and have stereos. Each floor also features a pantry with complimentary coffee, tea and espresso. 363 rooms. Wireless Internet access. Restaurant, two bars. Fitness center. Business center. Pets accepted. $$$$

★★★★★THE ST. REGIS

2 E. 55th St., New York, 212-753-4500, 888-625-4988; www.stregis.com/newyork

Located just off Fifth Avenue, the St. Regis reigns as New York's Grande Dame. Opened in 1904, this Beaux Arts landmark defines elegance with its gleaming marble, glittering gold leafing and sparkling chandeliers. The guest rooms are elegantly decorated in soft pastel colors with Louis XVI-style furnishings. The Astor Court is the perfect place to enjoy traditional afternoon tea. Renowned for its famous Red Snapper cocktail and bewitching Maxfield Parrish mural, the King Cole Bar is a favorite of hotel guests and locals alike. Be sure to ask the bartender why crafty Old King Cole is smirking. 256 rooms. Wireless Internet access. Restaurant, bar. Fitness center. Spa. Airport transportation available. Business center. $$$$

★★★SURREY HOTEL

20 E. 76th St., New York, 212-288-3700; www.affinia.com

Understated elegance takes center stage at this Upper East Side sleeper positioned off Madison Ave. You'll see the old-world charm upon entering the lobby, with its 18th-century English décor, wood-paneled elevators and leather sofas. The studio, one-bedroom and two-bedroom suites have a similar look. Some have kitchenettes, and others have full kitchens. World-renowned chef Daniel Boulud's Cafe Boulud serves relaxed-chic French cooking in a refined setting. 132 rooms, all suites. Restaurant. Fitness center. Airport transportation available. Business center. Pets accepted. $$$$

★★★TRIBECA GRAND HOTEL

2 Avenue of the Americas, New York, 212-519-6600, 800-965-3000; www.tribecagrand.com

A contemporary vibe pervades this Tribeca retreat, from the spacious lobby with its hopping Church Lounge, to the ultramodern guest rooms with digital cable, iPods and DVD/CD players. This is a perfect spot from which to explore Tribeca, its terrific shopping and restaurants such as Odeon and Bouley. 203 rooms. Wireless Internet access. Restaurant, bar. Airport transportation available. $$$

★★★★★TRUMP INTERNATIONAL HOTEL & TOWER

1 Central Park W., New York, 212-299-1000, 888-448-7867; www.trumpintl.com

Occupying an enviable site across from Central Park and the Time Warner Center on Manhattan's Upper West Side, the 52-story Trump International Hotel and Tower delivers glitz and glam. The guest rooms and suites reflect a contemporary European flavor while the floor-to-ceiling windows focus attention on the views of Central Park and Columbus Circle. All suites and most rooms feature kitchens, and in-room chefs are available to craft memorable meals. Room service comes courtesy of top chef Jean-Georges Vongerichten, whose restaurant, Jean Georges, sits just off the lobby. The Personal Attaché service ensures that all guests are properly coddled. 167 rooms. Wireless Internet access. Restaurant, bar. Fitness center. Spa. Pool. Airport transportation available. Business center. Pets accepted. $$$$

★★★W NEW YORK

541 Lexington Ave., New York, 212-755-1200; www.whotels.com

The buzzing lobby of the W has the air of an urban ski lodge, complete with a sunken lobby bar that has tree trunk end tables and colorful rugs. The guest rooms have an organic feel with natural cotton linens and neutral tones. The W is a perfect location for exploring Midtown's museums. 688 rooms. Wireless Internet access. Two restaurants, bar. Fitness center. Spa. Airport transportation available. Business center. Pets accepted. $$$$

★★★W NEW YORK - TIMES SQUARE

1567 Broadway, New York, 212-930-7400; www.whotels.com

Located in Times Square, this hotel is just as exciting as its surroundings. The ultra contemporary lobby, located on the seventh floor, has off-white walls, tile floors and leather benches and houses the always-hopping Living Room bar. Guest rooms are spare and stylish with contemporary furnishings, and the views can't be beat. There are plenty of amenities and services to keep guests busy here, from the full-service spa and Blue Fin restaurant to the Whiskey bar and well-equipped fitness center. 507 rooms. Wireless Internet access. Restaurant, four bars. Fitness center Spa. Airport transportation available. $$$$

★★★W NEW YORK-UNION SQUARE

201 Park Ave. S., New York, 212-253-9119; www.whotels.com

The Union Square outpost of this contemporary hotel chain caters to both business and leisure travelers (and their pets, too). Located within the 1911 Guardian Life

Building, a landmark Beaux Arts-style structure, the W is one of the few hotels on happening Union Square, which offers shops, restaurants, bars, theaters and the famous vegetable-and-flower-packed Greenmarket. The hotel houses such buzzworthy spots as Olives, chef Todd English's Mediterranean restaurant, and Underbar, owned by Rande Gerber. Guest rooms, done in shades of purple, feature the W's signature feather beds with pillow top mattresses, large work desks and Aveda bath products. 270 rooms. Wireless Internet access. Restaurant, two bars. Airport transportation available. $$$$

★★★THE WALDORF-ASTORIA
301 Park Ave., New York, 212-355-3000, 800-925-3673; www.waldorfastoria.com
Enjoy a taste of old New York at this landmark, 1931 Art Deco hotel which has played host to countless U.S. presidents and international luminaries. The lobby features murals, mosaics and a piano that once belonged to Cole Porter. The rooms are individually decorated, elegant and traditional in style. The Bull & Bear steakhouse has a 1940s feel and attracts a sophisticated, steak-loving crowd. The ultra exclusive Waldorf Towers, from floor 28 and above, is even more upscale and private with its own entrance. 1,416 rooms. Wireless Internet access. Two restaurants, two bars. Spa. Airport transportation available. Business center. $$$$

★★★WARWICK HOTEL
65 W. 54th St., New York, 212-247-2700; www.warwickhotelny.com
Originally opened as a residential hotel in 1928, this Midtown Manhattan property has retained its sense of history while remaining current, thanks to its modern amenities and services. The public spaces feature traditional chandeliers, potted flowers, contemporary furnishings and a small library in the lobby while guest rooms have a European-style décor and marble-clad bathrooms. Murals on 54, the in-house, Continental cuisine restaurant, is a great choice for dinner, followed by a nightcap at Randolph's Bar, named for the hotel's builder, William Randolph Hearst. 426 rooms. Wireless Internet access. Two restaurants, bar. Airport transportation available. $$$

★★★WESTIN TIMES SQUARE
270 W. 43rd St., New York, 212-201-2700, 866-837-4183; www.westinny.com
Located at New York's epicenter, the Westin Times Square keeps guests in the center of it all—theaters, shops and entertainment. Sleek and simple rooms include soundproof windows and the Westin's signature Heavenly Bed as well as deluxe bathrobes and bath amenities. Guests can also indulge in a spa-inspired room, which features amenities such as an electric massage chair, minibar stocked with healthy snacks and an aromatherapy air diffuser. 863 rooms. Wireless Internet access. Restaurant, two bars. Spa. $$$$

RESTAURANTS
★★★'21' CLUB
21 W. 52nd St., New York, 212-582-7200; www.21club.com
This one-time speakeasy is one of New York City's most celebrated spots for lunch, dinner and lots of drinks for the Wall Street crowd, media and regulars who frequent its tables. The chef turns out stellar, seasonal American fare. The restaurant has a

distinguished air to it, with a clubby, brass-railed bar, luxurious linen-topped tables and old photos hung on wood-paneled walls. The Upstairs at '21' is a restaurant within a restaurant and provides a more intimate dining experience. Dress sharp: It's coat and tie at dinner and no jeans. American menu. Lunch, dinner. Closed Sunday; three weeks in August; holidays. Bar. Jacket required in Upstairs at 21. Reservations recommended. $$$

★88 PALACE
88 E. Broadway, New York, 212-941-8886
Chinese menu. Lunch, dinner. Casual attire. $$

★A SALT & BATTERY
112 Greenwich Ave., New York, 212-691-2713; www.asaltandbattery.com
British/Continental menu. Lunch, dinner. Casual attire. $$

★★★★ADOUR
The St. Regis New York, 2 E. 55th St., New York, 212-710-2277;
www.adour-stregis.com
Another New York foodie goes wino, as celebrated chef Alain Ducasse joins the ranks with his vino-inspired venture, Adour. Claiming to have drastically rewritten the formula by designing the menu "with wine in mind," Adour's menu looks pretty similar to its peers' from our point of view. But no matter, offering the usual suspects—Maine lobster and Colorado lamb—Ducasse also procures inimitable ingredients like wild Oregon mushrooms, Canadian foie gras, California citrus, French mustard and cucumber vinegar. And the effort is evident in such dishes as the Australian barramundi. Of course, it better be at these prices. French menu. Dinner. Bar. Business attire. Reservations recommended. Valet parking. $$$

★★★AL BUSTAN
827 Third Ave., New York, 212-759-8439; www.albustanny.com
Head to Al Bustan and discover the aromatic and exquisite world of Lebanese cooking. Al Bustan is very popular, especially at lunch, as its Midtown location makes it a nice choice for dealmakers. When the sun sets, this restaurant becomes an elegant respite for dinner, offering guests a luxurious dining experience that includes some of the best bread in the city, served with a magnificent array of mezze, not to mention a full menu of authentic Lebanese dishes. Middle Eastern menu. Lunch, dinner. Bar. Casual attire. Reservations recommended. $$$

★★ALFAMA
551 Hudson St., New York, 212-645-2500; www.alfamarestaurant.com
Portuguese menu. Lunch, dinner, Sunday brunch. Bar. Casual attire. Reservations recommended. $$$

★★★ALLEN & DELANCEY
115 Allen St., New York, 212-253-5400; www.allenanddelancey.net
An upscale island on the Lower East Side, somehow Allen & Delancey makes it work. Because if hipsters feel betrayed by this Upper East Side invasion, they don't show it once they've tasted the food. Maybe the low-lit, windowless dining room with

exposed brick helps them feel at home, but it has to be the caramelized bone marrow, caviar and shallot puree that wins them over. If you don't believe us, try it. At Allen & Delancey, airs of British and French cuisine like those in the rabbit terrine with chickpeas, tarragon and anchovy overwhelm even those of the LES clientele. A decidedly suitable destination for special occasions, the kitchen graciously takes custom cake orders up to four days in advance. Contemporary American menu. Dinner, Saturday-Sunday brunch. Bar. Casual attire. Reservations recommended. $$$

★★AMMA
246 E. 51st St., New York, 212-644-8330; www.ammanyc.com
Indian menu. Lunch, dinner. Jacket required. Reservations recommended. $$$

★★AMY RUTH'S
113 W. 116th St., New York, 212-280-8779; www.amyruthsharlem.com
Southern menu. Breakfast, lunch, dinner. Casual attire. $$

★★★ANNISA
13 Barrow St., New York, 212-741-6699; www.annisarestaurant.com
At Annisa, a cozy, off-the-beaten-path gem in Greenwich Village, chef/partner Anita Lo and partner Jennifer Scism (who runs the front of the house) bring a bit of Asia and a lot of flavor and savvy style to the contemporary American table. The restaurant's golden glow and elegant, sheer-white curtains draped along the tall walls create a stylish backdrop for the simple, approachable menu. An array of wines by the glass and a strong sommelier make pairing wine with dinner a breeze. American menu. Dinner. Bar. Business casual attire. Reservations recommended. $$$

★★AOC BEDFORD
14 Bedford St., New York, 212-414-4764; www.aocbedford.com
French, Italian, Spanish menu. Dinner. Bar. Casual attire. Reservations recommended. $$$

★★★AQUAGRILL
210 Spring St., New York, 212-274-0505; www.aquagrill.com
A perennial favorite for swimmingly fresh seafood (and great dry-aged steak), Aquagrill has a terrific location at the edge of Soho. Take advantage of the stellar outdoor seating in warm months. With its tall French doors flung open to the street, Aquagrill has a European elegance that makes it an irresistible spot to settle in, even if only for a glass of sparkling wine and a dozen (or two) shimmering oysters. Seafood menu. Lunch, dinner, brunch. Closed Monday; holidays. Bar. Casual attire. Reservations recommended. Outdoor seating. $$$

★★★AQUAVIT
65 E. 55th St., New York, 212-307-7311; www.aquavit.org
Chef/partner Marcus Samuelsson introduced New York to his splashy brand of modern Scandinavian cuisine a decade ago at Aquavit. After 10 years and a move to the ultramodern Park Avenue Tower, the restaurant has a sleek, sophisticated vibe, and the cuisine is even more spectacular. While ingredients like herring, lamb, salmon, caviar and dill show up with regularity, the food is more uniquely Samuelsson than anything else. A shot of smooth, yet decidedly potent aquavit complements dinner

nicely, as does a selection from the impressive wine list Scandinavian menu. Lunch, dinner, Sunday brunch. Closed holidays. Bar. Business casual attire. Reservations recommended. $$$$

★★★ARABELLE

37 E. 64th St., New York, 212-606-4647; www.arabellerestaurant.com

From the dramatic gold dome and brass chandeliers of the main dining area to the exotic atmosphere of the Bar Seine, Arabelle offers a romantic dining experience. The restaurant is situated in the elegant Hotel Plaza Athénée. Several intimate dining alcoves, which serve as extensions of both the Bar Seine and the main dining room, are offered to guests during hours when the main dining is closed. Specialty dishes on the classic American menu include coffee-rubbed New York strip steak and grilled diver sea scallops. There's also a traditional Sunday brunch and afternoon high tea. American menu. Lunch, dinner, brunch. Closed three weeks in summer. Bar. Children's menu. Business casual attire. Reservations recommended. Valet parking. $$$

★★ARTISANAL

2 Park Ave., New York, 212-725-8585; www.artisanalbistro.com

French bistro menu. Lunch, dinner, brunch. Bar. Casual attire. Reservations recommended. $$$

★★★★ASIATE

80 Columbus Circle, New York, 212-805-8800; www.mandarinoriental.com

Asiate offers a spectacular view of Central Park and a modern Franco-Asian menu on the 35th floor of the Mandarin Oriental Hotel. World-renowned restaurant designer Tony Chi was the creative force behind this stunning space, which features a jeweled tree branch sculpture that hangs from the cathedral-styled ceiling. Chef Noriyuki Sugies' inspired menu, like the ambience, impresses even the most sophisticated traveler, borrowing from both Old Europe and New Asia. Highlights include the seafood yuzu ceviche, surf clam salad and pickled vegetables; grilled Maine lobster with cuttlefish noodles and goji berries; and chocolate fondant cake with raspberry compote. Asian, French menu. Breakfast, lunch, dinner, brunch. Business casual attire. Reservations recommended. Valet parking. $$$$

★★★★AUREOLE

34 E. 61st St., New York, 212-319-1660; www.charliepalmer.com/aureole_ny

Hidden inside an elegant brownstone on Manhattan's Upper East Side, Aureole is a luxurious space bathed in cream tones and warm lighting and furnished with overstuffed wine-colored banquettes. (An enclosed courtyard garden opens for warmweather dining.) The restaurant is friendly and cozy and well suited for just about any occasion, from couples looking for romance to colleagues looking to have a luxe business dinner. Owner and celebrity chef Charlie Palmer offers his guests a wonderfully prepared menu of what he calls "Progressive American" fare. There are always two tasting menus—one vegetarian and another inspired from the market in addition to a parade of terrific à la carte selections. The extensive and celebrated wine program includes bold wines from California, Spain and Italy. Aureole is expected to move sometime in 2009 into the Bank of America Tower at 1 Bryant

Park; but until it's settled into its new digs, enjoy what is Aureole now. American menu. Lunch, dinner. Closed Sunday; holidays. Bar. Jacket required. Reservations recommended. $$$$

★★AVRA

141 E. 48th St., New York, 212-759-8550; www.avrany.com

Mediterranean menu. Lunch, dinner, brunch. Closed holidays. Bar. Business casual attire. Reservations recommended. Outdoor seating. $$$

★★AZUL BISTRO

152 Stanton St., New York, 646-602-2004

Latin American menu. Dinner. Casual attire. Reservations recommended. Outdoor seating. $$$

★★★BABBO

110 Waverly Place, New York, 212-777-0303; www.babbonyc.com

Dressed in his signature orange clogs and shorts, Mario Batali is the king of rustic, authentic Italian cuisine on television's Food Network. Before he was a star of the small screen, he was a cook—and he is one celebrity chef who still actually cooks. Find him at Babbo, a charming West Village carriage house-turned-stylish hot spot where a glam crowd fills tables to feast on Batali's unique brand of robust Italian fare. The man is known for serving braised pigs' feet, warm lamb tongue and testa (head cheese). Cult status signature pastas like beef cheek ravioli and mint love letters—spicy lamb sausage ragu with mint wrapped in envelopes of fresh pasta—demonstrate that some culinary risks are worth taking. Italian menu. Dinner. Bar. Casual attire. Reservations recommended. $$$

★★★BALTHAZAR

80 Spring St., New York, 212-965-1414; www.balthazarny.com

From the attractive crowds at the bar to the attractive folks who squeeze into the restaurant's tiny tables—you'll be seated as close to a stranger as is possible without becoming intimate—Balthazar is a dazzling, wonderfully chaotic destination. It sports a menu of brasserie standards like frisée aux lardons, pan bagnat, steak frites and a glistening raw bar platter, not to mention fresh-baked bread from the Balthazar bakery next door. Pick up a bag of croissants, a couple of baguettes and a dozen tarts on your way out for breakfast or lunch the next day. French menu. Breakfast, lunch, dinner, late-night, brunch. Bar. Casual attire. Reservations recommended. $$$

★★BAO 111

111 Ave. C, New York, 212-254-7773; www.bao111.com

Vietnamese menu. Dinner. Bar. Casual attire. Reservations recommended. $$$

★★★BAR BLANC

142 W. 10th St., New York, 212-255-2330; www.barblanc.com

You know what they say about size. Well, lucky for Bar Blanc, which epitomizes it, New Yorkers live by that maxim. The compact joint clothed completely in white (which makes everything appear larger, right?) is refreshingly simple with a casual-chic vibe accompanying a short seasonal menu. Start with the crispy sweetbread salad with sherry-poached cherries, watercress and lemon vinaigrette, move on to the seared black cod with wilted Arrowleaf spinach, celery root, fennel saffron sauce and salt cod brandade. And thus arrives the evolution of the bar. Contemporary American menu. Dinner. Bar. Casual attire. Reservations recommended. $$$

★★★BAR BOULUD
1900 Broadway, New York, 212-595-0303; www.danielnyc.com/barboulud
Conveniently situated across the street from Lincoln Center, Daniel Boulud's most laidback foray into the New York dining scene takes aim at hurried opera- and ballet-goers, offering his world-class cuisine sans frills and fuss. That's not to say, however, that you won't pay a pretty penny for this French pub fare. You stand forewarned on both the early evening crowds and the price of your steak-frites and roasted chicken. But Boulud executes the wine bar concept fittingly. The design pays homage to the winemaking industry with a long vaulted ceiling reminiscent of a wine cellar, a gravel wall conjuring images of vineyard terroir, furnishings made from wine barrel oak. Of course chef Boulud's menu doesn't disappoint. The highlight here, besides the wine, are the over 18 varieties of house-made charcuterie. Best bet is to sip Burgundy wine while sharing some patés and the aioli appetizer, an olive oil-poached cod and Louisiana shrimp garlic dip with quail eggs, veg etables and mussels. French menu. Lunch (Monday-Friday), dinner (Monday-Friday), Saturday-Sunday brunch. Bar. Casual attire. Reservations recommended. Outdoor seating. $$$

★★BAR JAMON
125 E. 17th St., New York, 212-253-2773; www.barjamonnyc.com
Spanish menu. Lunch, dinner, late-night. Casual attire. Reservations recommended. $

★★★BAR MASA
10 Columbus Circle, New York, 212-823-9800; www.masanyc.com
If Masa, chef Masa Takayama's celebrated (and incredibly expensive) Japanese and sushi restaurant, is too hard on your wallet, try going next door to Bar Masa. Both restaurants are located in the Time Warner Center and have some identical items on their menus, but Bar Masa is more affordable and has a casual ambience. The attractive space is narrow, with the bar (topped with an African plank) on one side of the room and long, ultrasuede banquettes and tables on the other. Lunch, dinner and á la carte sushi menus are available, and the restaurant offers a cocktail menu as well as wine and sake lists. Japanese menu. Lunch, dinner. Bar. Business casual attire. $$$

★★★BARBETTA
321 W. 46th St., New York, 212-246-9171; www.barbettarestaurant.com
This classic Italian restaurant opened its doors in 1906 and is still owned by the same family, the Maioglios. Located in a pair of historic early 19th-century townhouses, this restaurant is a classic charmer that's all about elegant, old-world dining. The menu doesn't aim anywhere other than where its heart is—Italy—but don't expect just pasta. The kitchen offers a great selection of seafood, poultry and beef prepared with seasonal ingredients and lively flavors. Italian menu. Lunch, dinner. Closed Monday. Bar. Business casual attire. Reservations recommended. Outdoor seating. $$$

★
★
★
★
★

THE BIG APPLE'S BEST CHEFS

Manhattan is home to extraordinary restaurants—from tiny neighborhood places with cult followings (like **Lupa** and **Five Points**) to upscale dens of haute cuisine (like **Daniel, Aquavit** and **Craft**) to sultry hotspots (like **Spice Market** and **Pastis** in the Meatpacking District). Dining out in New York is, more than ever, exhaustingly fabulous. Every day, chefs fill the city with miraculous food, blazing a mouthwatering path into the future of American cuisine.

When the Time Warner Center opened, New Yorkers were officially in a culinary frenzy. **Café Gray**, a luxurious shrine to seafood, features dishes that incorporate his travels across Southeast Asia with his impeccable classical French training. Joining him in the Time Warner Center is West Coast culinary master **Thomas Keller** of the **French Laundry**, whose restaurant, **per se**, is on the short list of every gourmand in the city.

These patriarchs of modern American cuisine are joined by pioneers like **Mario Batali**, who started out on his mission of bringing simple, seasonal Italian cuisine to the masses with **Po** and grew his empire to include glorious Italian eateries like **Babbo, Lupa** and **Esca**. With **Casa Mono** and **Bar Jamon**, he brings the same sense of adventure and passion to Spanish cuisine. The spotlight also shines on **Bobby Flay** of Mesa Grill and **Charlie Palmer**, whose restaurant Aureole remains one of the city's most elegant places to dine. And we can't leave out Daniel Boulud (Daniel, DB Bistro), **David Bouley** (Bouley), **Jonathan Waxman** (still going strong after Jams and Washington Park with Barbuto) and **Alfred Portale** (who has manned the stoves for more than 20 years at Gotham Bar and Grill).

But these old-timers have some serious competition. A groundswell of youthful energy and creativity is bubbling up downtown, where baby-faced chefs (many age 30 and under) are turning up the heat.

The rising star spotlight shines on **Galen Zamarra**, a protege of David Bouley. Zamarra is the chef/partner of **Mas**, where he showcases locally farmed seasonal ingredients in exquisite dishes like medallions of Cooperstown lamb wrapped in ramps with eggplant moussaka and a vibrant swoosh of tomato harissa.

Women are also getting in the game. **Sue Torres** owns the deliciously authentic regional Mexican restaurant **Suenos**. At the **Spotted Pig**, a West Village gastro-pub with a cult following, chef/partner **April Bloomfield**—plucked from London's lauded **River Café** by Spotted Pig owners Mario Batali and Ken Friedman—has crowds lining the sidewalks for her ricotta gnudi with brown butter and sage and beautifully blistered pork sausages with arugula and lentils.

The list of talent, young and old, is always growing. The best way to keep track of the culinary gods is to get out there and dine.

★★BARBUTO

775 Washington St., New York, 212-924-9700; www.barbutonyc.com

Occupying a trendy space in one of city's hippest locations, chef and owner Jonathan Waxman, who was seasoned by Alice Waters, developed a successful recipe for a New

York City restaurant: a dash of contemporary design combined with a hefty dose of casual yet happening ambience finished with helping of fabulous food. Funky yet functional garage doors act as the restaurant walls and in warm weather transform Barbuto into an indoor-outdoor dining room, which runs right into the open kitchen. The downside: the modern industrial design doesn't do much to dampen noise. (Read: It can get loud.) But who needs conversation when you have pan-fried monk fish, with farroto and butternut squash puree in front of you and beautiful people surrounding you? Italian menu. Lunch, dinner. Bar. Casual attire. Reservations recommended. Outdoor seating. $$$

★BARNEY GREENGRASS

541 Amsterdam Ave., New York, 212-724-4707; www.barneygreengrass.com
Deli menu. Breakfast, lunch. Closed Monday; Jewish holidays. Bar. Casual attire. $$

★★★BAYARD'S

1 Hanover Square, New York, 212-514-9454; www.bayards.com
Fresh flowers, a rare Buddha collection, crafted ship models, stately antiques, fine china, mahogany double staircases and hand-carved working fireplaces are just some of the charming details you will encounter at Bayard's—an exquisite French-American restaurant located in the India House, a historic landmark building near Wall Street. American, French menu. Dinner. Closed Sunday. Bar. Casual attire. Reservations recommended. $$$

★★BECCO

355 W. 46th St., New York, 212-397-7597; www.becconyc.com
Italian menu. Lunch, dinner. Closed holidays. Casual attire. Reservations recommended. $$$

★★★BEN BENSON'S STEAKHOUSE

123 W. 52nd St., New York, 212-581-8888; www.benbensons.com
At this popular steakhouse, you'll find yourself elbow to elbow with celebrities, politicians, sports stars and the city's financial elite. As you might expect from a power steak spot, the menu is as big as the egos in the room and includes solid standards like salads, poultry and seafood that are simply and impeccably prepared. The signature selection of USDA dry-aged prime beef is served in the form of about a dozen cuts and portion sizes. The huge steaks are matched in size by lobsters the size of small pets. Don't miss the house's signature crispy hashed browns. Steak menu. Lunch, dinner. Closed holidays. Bar. Business casual attire. Reservations recommended. Outdoor seating. $$$

★★★BENOIT

60 W. 55th St., New York, 646-943-7373; www.benoitny.com
This former home of La Côte Basque brasserie got a new resident when Alain Ducasse brought the century-old Parisian brasserie Benoit stateside. Attempting to bring the old French favorites to the Big Apple, the menu doesn't deviate from the 50- to 100-year-old recipes for the classics—onion soup gratinée, marinated salmon with warm potato salad and foie gras confit. The paté en croute recipe dates back to 1892. If the new-fangled French that you'll get at Ducasse's higher-end Adour is more your thing, go there or be disappointed. French menu. Lunch, dinner. Bar. Casual attire. $$$

★★BEPPE

45 E. 22nd St., New York, 212-982-8422; www.beppenyc.com

Italian menu. Lunch, dinner. Closed Sunday. Bar. Casual attire. Reservations recommended. $$$

★★BEYOGLU

1431 Third Ave., New York, 212-650-0850

Middle Eastern menu. Lunch, dinner. Bar. Casual attire. Reservations recommended. Outdoor seating. $$

★★BICE

7 E. 54th St., New York, 212-688-1999; www.bicenewyork.com

Italian menu. Lunch, dinner. Bar. Children's menu. Business casual attire. Reservations recommended. Outdoor seating. $$$

★★★BLUE FIN

1567 Broadway, New York, 212-918-1400; www.brguestrestaurants.com

Located in the W Times Square Hotel, Blue Fin is restaurateur Steve Hanson's (Blue Water Grill, Dos Caminos) elaborate seafood palace. Blue Fin features high-end fish dishes and a stunning array of sushi, sashimi and maki. The bar on the ground floor is always packed with bright young things sipping tall, cool cocktails, while the upstairs bar is mellower. American, seafood, sushi menu. Breakfast, lunch, dinner, late-night. Bar. Children's menu. Casual attire. Outdoor seating. $$$

★★★BLUE HILL

75 Washington Place, New York, 212-539-1776; www.bluehillnyc.com

Blue Hill is a gem that offers extraordinary seasonal American fare such as veal with English peas and pistachios and a stellar wine list in a warm, cozy, contemporary space in the West Village. Chocolate tones, soft lighting and superlative service make this restaurant a luxurious experience perfect for special occasions, and the distinctive menu ensures a delicious evening. American menu. Dinner. Bar. Business casual attire. Reservations recommended. Outdoor seating. $$$

★★BLUE RIBBON

97 Sullivan St., New York, 212-274-0404; www.blueribbonrestaurants.com

International menu. Lunch, dinner. Closed holidays. Bar. Casual attire. $$$

★★BLUE RIBBON BAKERY

35 Downing St., New York, 212-337-0404; www.blueribbonrestaurants.com

American, French menu. Lunch, dinner, brunch. Bar. Casual attire. $$$

★★BLUE SMOKE

116 E. 27th St., New York, 212-447-7733; www.bluesmoke.com

American menu. Lunch, dinner, late-night. Bar. Children's menu. Casual attire. $$

★★BLUE WATER GRILL

31 Union Square W., New York, 212-675-9500; www.brguestrestaurants.com

Seafood menu. Lunch, dinner. Bar. Children's menu. Business casual attire. Reservations recommended. Outdoor seating. $$$

★★BOATHOUSE RESTAURANT

72nd Street and Park Drive N., New York, 212-517-2233;www.thecentralparkboathouse.com

American menu. Breakfast, lunch, dinner, brunch. Bar. Children's menu. Casual attire. Reservations recommended. Outdoor seating. **$$$**

★★★BOND STREET

6 Bond St., New York, 212-777-2500; www.bondstrestaurant.com

High-art sushi and sashimi are the calling cards of Bond Street, a hipster hangout disguised as a modern Japanese restaurant. The whitewashed, airy restaurant has a dark and sexy lower-level bar. Japanese menu. Dinner. Bar. Business casual attire. Reservations recommended. **$$$**

BOULEY

161 Duane St., Tribeca, 212-964-2525; www.davidbouley.com

When a restaurant has seen a bevy of Hollywood A-listers and its namesake chef was named one of *People* magazine's "50 Most Beautiful People," you know you're in for an over-the-top treat. David Bouley doesn't hold back—the dining room's vaulted gold-leafed ceiling is bold, his determination to serve high-end ingredients is fierce, and freebies like a lemon tea cake for ladies to take home for the next morning's breakfast are a godsend. You won't be able to restrain your glee at Bouley's classic-yet-unconventional French fare, like seared foie gras served in a pool of apple-rosemary purée, and seafood dishes adorned with fennel and ginger sauce or coconut and tamarind dressing. Bouley will be re-rated in the near future. Contemporary French menu. Lunch, dinner. **$$$$**

★★★BRASSERIE

100 E. 53rd St., New York, 212-751-4840; www.rapatina.com

As you step inside sleek Brasserie, you may feel all eyes upon you, which is probably because they are. The dining room is set down a level, and when you enter, you must walk down a futuristic glass staircase, a dramatic walkway that turns heads. The menu mixes classics and contemporary dishes, from duck cassoulet and frisee aux lardons to onion soup, escargots and goujonettes of sole. Contemporary French menu. Breakfast, lunch, dinner, late-night, brunch. Bar. Business casual attire. Reservations recommended. **$$$**

★★★BRASSERIE 8 1/2

9 W. 57th St., New York, 212-829-0812; www.rapatina.com

Located in the sleek, Gordon Bunshaft-designed 9 building on West 57th Street, Brasserie 8½ is the perfect spot for a power lunch, post-work cocktails or a pre-theater meal. A chic, curved staircase is backed by bright, salmon-hued walls and leads down to the long, backlit bar and dramatic, modern art-filled dining room. The kitchen incorporates accents from Asia and the Mediterranean into updated bistro classics. American, French menu. Lunch, dinner, Sunday brunch. Bar. Business casual attire. Reservations recommended. **$$$**

★★BRICK LANE CURRY HOUSE

306-308 E. 6th St., New York, 212-979-8787; www.bricklanecurryhouse.com

Indian menu. Lunch, dinner, late-night. Bar. Casual attire. Reservations recommended. **$$**

★BROOKLYN DINER USA

212 W. 57th St., New York, 212-977-1957; www.brooklyndiner.com

American menu. Breakfast, lunch, dinner, late-night. Children's menu. Casual attire. $$

★★BRYANT PARK GRILL

25 W. 40th St., New York, 212-840-6500; www.arkrestaurants.com

American menu. Lunch, dinner, brunch. Bar. Children's menu. Casual attire. Reservations recommended. Outdoor seating. $$

★★★BULL AND BEAR STEAKHOUSE

301 Park Ave., New York, 212-872-4900; www.waldorfastoria.com

Located in the stately Waldorf-Astoria Hotel, the Bull and Bear Steakhouse is a meat-eater's haven. The street-level dining room is elegant in a clubby, macho sort of way, and the steaks, all cut from certified aged Black Angus, are fat, juicy and the way to go, even though the menu does offer a wide variety of other choices, including chicken, lamb, potpie and assorted seafood. Classic steakhouse sides like creamed spinach, garlic mashed potatoes and buttermilk fried onion rings are sinful accompaniments. American, Steak menu. Lunch, dinner. Bar. $$$

★★★CAFÉ BOULUD

20 E. 76th St., New York, 212-772-2600; www.danielnyc.com

Daniel Boulud is the renowned star of a small empire of French restaurants extending from Manhattan to Las Vegas. Café Boulud is a less formal version of his haute temple of French gastronomy, Daniel. But "less formal" is a relative term. Café Boulud is a majestic space, perfect for quiet conversation and intimate dining. The service is helpful and unobtrusive. The chef is a whiz at pleasing the palate and offers a choice of four á la carte menus: La Tradition (French Classics and Country Cooking), La Saison (The Rhythm of the Seasons), Le Potager (Vegetarian Selections from the Farmers' Market) and Le Voyage (a menu inspired from a changing international destination—Mexico, Morocco, etc). The wine program is ambitious, and the staff is eager to assist with pairings, making the experience a small slice of Parisian perfection. American, French menu. Lunch, dinner. Business casual attire. Reservations recommended. Outdoor seating. $$$

★★CAFÉ DE BRUXELLES

118 Greenwich Ave., New York, 212-206-1830

Belgian menu. Lunch, dinner, brunch. Closed holidays. Bar. Casual attire. Reservations recommended. $$

★★★CAFÉ DES ARTISTES

1 W. 67th St., New York, 212-877-3500; www.cafenyc.com

Café des Artistes is a timeless New York City classic, boasting incredible floral displays and murals of cavorting nymphs. The restaurant remains an old-guard favorite for its luxurious, sophisticated setting, impeccable service and menu of up-to-the-minute (yet approachable) seasonal French fare. French bistro menu. Lunch, dinner, brunch. Bar. Business casual attire. Reservations recommended. $$$

★★CAFÉ FIORELLO

1900 Broadway, New York, 212-595-5330; www.cafefiorello.com

Northern Italian menu. Lunch, dinner, brunch. Bar. Casual attire. Reservations recommended. $$$

★CAFÉ HABANA

17 Prince St., New York, 212-625-2001; www.ecoeatery.com

Cuban menu, Mexican menu. Breakfast, lunch, dinner, late-night, brunch. Casual attire. $

★★CAFÉ LOUP

105 W. 13th St., New York, 212-255-4746; www.cafeloupnyc.com

French menu. Lunch, dinner. Bar. Casual attire. Reservations recommended. $$

★★CAFÉ LUXEMBOURG

200 W. 70th St., New York, 212-873-7411; www.cafeluxembourg.com

American, French menu. Breakfast, lunch, dinner, brunch. Bar. Casual attire. Reservations recommended. $$$

★★CAFÉ SABARSKY

1048 Fifth Ave., New York, 212-288-0665; www.wallserestaurant.com

Continental menu. Breakfast, lunch, dinner. Closed Tuesday. Casual attire. Reservations recommended. $$$

★★CAFETERIA

119 Seventh Ave., New York, 212-414-1717

American menu. Breakfast, lunch, dinner, late-night, brunch. Bar. Children's menu. Casual attire. Outdoor seating. $$

★★★CAPSOUTO FRERES

451 Washington St., New York, 212-966-4900; www.capsoutofreres.com

As its name suggests, Capsouto Freres is owned by the Capsouto brothers who watch over this romantic retreat. Set in a restored 1891 factory in Tribeca, the restaurant has an understated elegance, with original beam floors and exposed brick walls. The eclectic menu features an impressive variety of choices, from calf's liver in sherry vinegar sauce to cassoulet, salmon with green herb sauce and wild Scottish venison. If you are wandering around downtown on a Sunday, the brunch is a great choice, with omelets and excellent French toast at reasonable prices. French menu. Lunch, dinner, brunch. Bar. Casual attire. Reservations recommended. Outdoor seating. $$$

★★★CARLYLE RESTAURANT

35 E. 76th St., New York, 212-744-1600; www.thecarlyle.com

This lavishly decorated restaurant is housed in the elegant Carlyle Hotel. From the plush velvet walls covered with rare 19th-century prints to the crystal chandeliers and unique floral arrangements, guests will delight in the atmosphere. Meticulous attention is paid to the visual presentation of the gourmet dishes served by a wonderfully attentive staff. Live entertainment includes a pianist and jazz trio. French menu. Breakfast, lunch, dinner. Brunch bar. Children's menu. Business casual attire. Reservations recommended. Valet parking. $$$

★
★
★
★
★

★CARMINE'S

2450 Broadway, New York, 212-362-2200; www.carminesnyc.com
Italian menu. Lunch, dinner. Bar. Casual attire. Reservations recommended. Outdoor seating. $$$

★CARNEGIE DELI

854 Seventh Ave., New York, 212-757-2245, 800-334-5606; www.carnegiedeli.com
Deli menu. Breakfast, lunch, dinner, late-night. Casual attire. No credit cards accepted. $$

★CARRY ON TEA & SYMPATHY

108 Greenwich Ave., New York, 212-807-8329; www.teaandsympathynewyork.com
English menu. Breakfast, lunch, dinner. Casual attire. $$

★★CASA MONO

52 Irving Place, New York, 212-253-2773; www.casamononyc.com
Spanish menu. Lunch, dinner, late-night. Bar. Children's menu. Business casual attire. Reservations recommended. $$

★★CENTOLIRE

1167 Madison Ave., New York, 212-734-7711; www.pinoluongo.com/Centolire.html
Italian menu. Lunch, dinner, Sunday brunch. Bar. Casual attire. $$$

★★★'CESCA

164 W. 75th St., New York, 212-787-6300; www.cescanyc.com
'Cesca is an earthy and lively restaurant specializing in rustic, authentic and often slow-cooked Italian fare like the whole wheat orecchiette with housemade pork sausage. And should you forget to reserve, head for the warm, chocolate-toned bar, decked out in dark wood with amber lighting, the perfect place to sit and sup. Southern Italian menu. Lunch, dinner. Bar. Business casual attire. Reservations recommended. $$$

★★★CHANTERELLE

2 Harrison St., New York, 212-966-6960; www.chanterellenyc.com
Long hailed as one of the city's most romantic restaurants, Chanterelle has been the scene of many bent-knee, velvet-box-in-hand proposals. Indeed, this restaurant is a New York dining icon. But Chanterelle, located on a sleepy corner in Tribeca, offers much more than romance. Husband-and-wife owners David and Karen Waltuck (he is the chef, she works the room) have served brilliant, unfussy, modern French fare for more than 20 years. The menu, handwritten each week, reflects the best products available from regional farmers, and the award-winning wine list makes meals here near perfect. French menu. Lunch, dinner. Closed Sunday; holidays; also the first week of July. Business casual attire. Reservations recommended. $$$$

★★CHAT 'N' CHEW

10 E. 16th St., New York, 212-243-1616; www.chatnchew.ypguides.net
American menu. Lunch, dinner, brunch. Bar. Casual attire. Outdoor seating. $

★★CHIKALICIOUS

203 E. 10th St., New York, 212-475-0929; www.chikalicious.com

Dessert, American menu. Dinner, late-night. Closed Monday-Tuesday. Bar. Casual attire. $$

★★CHOW BAR

230 W. Fourth St., New York, 212-633-2212

Asian fusion menu. Dinner, late-night, Sunday brunch. Bar. Casual attire. Reservations recommended. $$

★★CHURRASCARIA PLATAFORMA

316 W. 49th St., New York, 212-245-0505; www.churrascariaplataforma.com

Brazilian menu. Lunch, dinner. Bar. Casual attire. Reservations recommended. $$$

★CITY BAKERY

3 W. 18th St., New York, 212-366-1414; www.citybakerycatering.com

American menu. Breakfast, lunch, brunch. Casual attire. $

★★★CONVIVIO

45 Tudor City Place, New York, 212-599-5045; www.limpero.com

This high-style Italian eatery is tucked away in Tudor City. There are simple plates of pasta, such as a wonderful bowl of perfect handmade spaghetti with tiny clams and more intricate plates like roast guinea hen with dandelion greens. The service is flawless, the wine list is an Italian encyclopedia and the décor is serene and civilized. On summer evenings, sit outside in the tiny front courtyard. Italian menu. Lunch, dinner. Closed Sunday. Bar. Business casual attire. Reservations recommended. Outdoor seating. $$$

★CORNER BISTRO

331 W. Fourth St., New York, 212-242-9502

American menu. Lunch, dinner, late-night. Bar. Casual attire. No credit cards accepted. $

★★★★COUNTRY

90 Madison Ave., New York, 212-889-7100; www.countryinnewyork.com

Housed in a Beaux Arts building that includes the Carlton Hotel, this creation of chef Geoffrey Zakarian (with designs by David Rockwell) combines classic Manhattan elegance with contemporary flair in both décor and cuisine. The seasonal, French-influenced menu comes in three-course pre-theater, four-course or six-course chef's tasting versions. Entrées change daily and might include everything from Berkshire pork with apple jam, chestnut and polenta to snapper with clams and lemon. The space also includes a more casual café, which serves breakfast, lunch and dinner, as well as a champagne lounge. French, American menu. Breakfast, lunch, dinner. $$$

★★★CRAFT

43 E. 19th St., New York, 212-780-0880; www.craftrestaurant.com

Craft attracts inventive, adventurous diners who like to "craft" their own meals and gourmets who appreciate perfectly executed portions of meat, fish, fowl and vegetables. Why these two sorts of folks? Because at Craft, diners create dinner from the list-like menu of meat, fish, vegetables, mushrooms and condiments: You choose what two foods should come together on your plate. (Those who prefer to defer to the chef may opt for a pre-planned menu.) American menu. Lunch, Dinner. Bar. Business casual attire. Reservations recommended. $$$

★★CRAFTBAR

900 Broadway, New York, 212-461-4300; www.craftrestaurant.com
American, Mediterranean menu. Lunch, dinner. Bar. Casual attire. $$$

★★CRISPO

240 W. 14th St., New York, 212-229-1818; www.crisporestaurant.com
Italian menu. Dinner. Bar. Casual attire. Reservations recommended. Outdoor seating. $$$

★★★CRU

24 Fifth Ave. (near Ninth St.), New York, 212-529-1700; www.cru-nyc.com
If *Sex and the City's* Charlotte York owned a restaurant, it might be Cru. The elegantly restrained décor oozes wealth in that subtly showy old-money kind of way, and service is warm and proper. And like Charlotte's multi-cultural uptown family, chef Shea Gallante draws upon global influences in his creative cooking but keeps the dishes high-end. The seasonal menu changes often, but you can expect dishes like Gallante's riff on Latin mole lightly dusts duck tortellini with cocoa, and Japanese hon-shimeji mushrooms in pumpkin-and-kale soup (which brings together the unlikely pairing of East Asia and the Italian countryside). The award-winning wine list—it's the size of a phone book—will make you gasp out loud. Cru boasts an astounding 150,000 bottles in the private cellar of its owner, Roy Welland, and sways toward French wines from Burgundy. New American. Dinner. Closed Sunday. $$$$

★★CUB ROOM CAFÉ

131 Sullivan St., New York, 212-677-4100; www.cubroom.com
American menu. Lunch, dinner, late-night, brunch. Bar. Children's menu. Casual attire. $$$

★★★DA SILVANO

260 Sixth Ave., New York, 212-982-2343; www.dasilvano.com
Da Silvano is a scene and a great one at that. With such a loyal and fabulous following, the food could be mediocre, but the kitchen does not rest on its starry laurels. This kitchen offers wonderful, robust, regional Italian fare. The sliver of a wine bar next door, Da Silvano Cantinetta serves Italian-style tapas paired with a wide selection of wines by the glass. But perhaps the best way to experience Da Silvano is on a warm day, where a seat at the wide, European-style sidewalk cafe offers prime people-watching. Italian menu. Lunch, dinner. Bar. Casual attire. Reservations recommended. Outdoor seating. $$$

★★DA UMBERTO

107 W. 17th St., New York, 212-989-0303
Italian menu. Lunch, dinner. Closed Sunday. Bar. Business casual attire. Reservations recommended. $$$

★★★★★DANIEL

60 E. 65th St., New York, 212-288-0033; www.danielnyc.com

Daniel is not just dinner, it's a dining experience that begins when you enter the palatial front room and continues as you sip an old-fashioned cocktail in the romantic, low-lit lounge. From there, it's on to the formal dining room, where superstar chef Daniel Boulud serves sublime cooking in the most gracious of settings overflowing with flowers. Potato-crusted sea bass is a signature dish: a crisp, golden coat, fashioned from whisper-thin slices of potatoes, wraps the fish while it cooks and seals in the flavor. After dessert, there are petit fours, of course, and then the pièce de résistance: warm madeleines. French menu. Dinner. Closed Sunday. Bar. Children's menu. Jacket required. Reservations recommended. **$$$$**

★★★DAWAT

210 E. 58th St., New York, 212-355-7555; www.restaurant.com/dawat

Serving elegant haute cuisine in a posh, hushed townhouse setting, Dawat is one of the most popular destinations for seekers of upscale, authentic Indian cuisine, including curries, rice dishes, poori, naan and chutneys. The interior is decorated with simple wall groupings of surreal nomadic sculptures, and tables are elegantly set with gleaming copper plates. Indian menu. Lunch, dinner. Bar. Business casual attire. Reservations recommended. **$$$**

★★★DB BISTRO MODERNE

55 W. 44th St., New York, 212-391-2400; www.danielnyc.com

This cool, sexy, ultrastylish Midtown bistro is Daniel Boulud's most casual outpost. His signature DB Burger is an excellent example of creative interpretation. Boulud builds a juicy round of beef and stuffs it with short ribs and sinful amounts of foie gras and truffles. He serves it on a homemade Parmesan brioche bun, with house-stewed tomato confit (instead of ketchup) and a big vat of fries, perfect for sharing. American, French menu. Lunch, dinner. Business casual attire. Reservations recommended. **$$$$**

★★★★DEL POSTO

85 Tenth Ave., New York, 212-497-8090; www.delposto.com

A dream team of star chefs—Joe Bastianich, Lidia Bastianich and Mario Batali—is behind this Italian restaurant, which has a menu that spans the many regions of the country and features dishes that range from classic to contemporary. The garganelli is topped with a ragu Bolognese any Nonna would be proud of while the rare tuna with bresaola is a more modern offering. The grand tasting menu (the whole table must participate in order to try it) offers seven courses and is a great way to sample the varied dishes the kitchen prepares. Service is polished and polite, and the presentation is pleasing. The enoteca serves reasonably priced portions of the menu's more simple dishes from humble spaghetti to housemade gelati. Be sure to reserve a table well in advance—Del Posto requests a one-month notice. Italian menu. Lunch, dinner. Bar. Business casual attire. Reservations recommended. **$$$$**

★DIM SUM GO GO

5 E. Broadway, New York, 212-732-0797

Chinese menu. Breakfast, lunch, dinner. Casual attire. **$$**

★★DINOSAUR BBQ

646 W. 131st St., New York, 212-694-1777; www.dinosaurbarbque.com
American, Barbecue menu. Lunch, dinner. Closed Monday. Bar. Casual attire. Outdoor seating. $$

★★★DISTRICT

130 W. 46th St., New York, 212-485-2999; www.districtnyc.com
Located within the Muse Hotel in Times Square, District is surrounded by Broadway theaters, making it a great spot for pre- and post-theater dining. In keeping with the neighborhood, the restaurant features theatrical décor, including spotlights designed by renowned set designer David Rockwell. Signature dishes on the New American menu include citrus-roasted chicken, grilled Atlantic salmon and diver scallop ceviche. New American menu. Lunch, dinner, brunch. Bar. Casual attire. Reservations recommended. Valet parking. $$$

★★DIWAN

148 E. 48th St., New York, 212-593-5425
Indian menu. Lunch, dinner. Bar. Casual attire. Reservations recommended. Valet parking. $$$

★★DO HWA

55 Carmine St., New York, 212-414-1224; www.dohwanyc.com
Korean menu. Lunch, dinner, late-night. Bar. Casual attire. Reservations recommended. $$

★★DOS CAMINOS

373 Park Ave. S., New York, 212-294-1000; www.brguestrestaurants.com
Mexican menu. Lunch, dinner, brunch. Bar. Casual attire. Reservations recommended. $$$

★
★
★
★
★

★★★DOVETAIL

103 W. 77th St., New York, 212-362-3800; www.dovetailnyc.com
Widely touted as one of just a handful of young chefs to watch, John Fraser has already acquired quite a resume with heavy hitters like Thomas Keller's French Laundry and Paris's Maison Blanche before opening Snack Taverna in New York's West Village. For his first venture at both the helm of business and kitchen, Fraser wanted to create a neighborhood restaurant, a genre poorly represented on Manhattan's Upper West Side. He describes the menu as "seasonal American," highlighting simple and profound flavors. He sources most of his ingredients from the Northeast. The products speak for themselves: dungeness crab ravioli with snow peas and chorizo, roasted sirloin with King Trumpet mushrooms, basil and beef cheek lasagna, buffalo with baby romaine, sunchokes, and ginger béarnaise. That supplemented by superior service and thoughtful touches, like the breakfast granola they give you as you're leaving, has earned Dovetail accolades as one of the top establishments in the neighborhood. But Fraser hasn't let it go to his head, substantiating his original aim, he offers a $38 three-course Sunday Suppa, encouraging neighbors and families to come together for a casual weekly meal. Contemporary American menu. Dinner. Bar. Business casual attire. Reservations recommended. $$$

★★★EIGHTY-ONE
45 W. 81st St., New York, 212-873-8181; www.81nyc.com

In February 2008, chef Ed Brown (most recently of NYC's The Sea Grill) realized a decades-old dream and opened his own restaurant. He chose Manhattan's Upper West Side, where his family resides, in hopes of raising its—traditionally mediocre—dining bar. It seems he may have succeeded as *The New York Post*'s Page Six reported that Mayor Bloomberg makes the trek from the Upper East Side to dine here. From elegant artisanal ingredients, such as custom-grown lettuces, heirloom legumes, exotic white soy sauce and hand-selected peppercorns, he offers an array of appetizers from baby Montauk calamari a la plancha stuffed with chorizo, fennel, boullabaise sauce and an herb salad to an heirloom tomato salad with ricotta cheese, fino basil and tomato sorbet to a duck pate of pickled onion, whole grain mustard, tomato confit and tarragon. Your main course could be organic Scottish salmon with cranberry beans, preserved tomatoes and titan parsley. The backdrop is red velvet and a creative wine cooler built into the restaurant's south wall with four temperature zones to keep all bottles in their ideal climate and provide some supplementary reading material for you. Contemporary American menu. Dinner, Sunday brunch. Bar. Business casual attire. Reservations recommended. **$$$**

★THE ELEPHANT
58 E. First St., New York, 212-505-7739; www.elephantrestaurant.com

French, Thai menu. Lunch, dinner. Bar. Casual attire. Reservations recommended. **$$**

★ELEPHANT AND CASTLE
68 Greenwich Ave., New York, 212-243-1400; www.elephantandcastle.com

Continental menu. Breakfast, lunch, dinner, brunch. Casual attire. **$$**

★★★★ELEVEN MADISON PARK
11 Madison Ave., New York, 212-889-0905; www.elevenmadisonpark.com

Located across from the leafy, historic Madison Square Park, Danny Meyer's grand New American restaurant is a wonderful, soothing spot. The magnificent dining room boasts old-world charm with vaulted ceilings, clubby banquettes, giant floor-to-ceiling windows and warm, golden lighting. The crowd is equally stunning: a savvy blend of sexy, suited power types and chic, fashion-forward New Yorkers. The contemporary seasonal menu, created by chef Daniel Humm, features updated American classics as well as a smart selection of dishes that borrow accents from Spain, France and Asia. American menu. Lunch, dinner, brunch. Closed holidays. Bar. Business casual attire. Reservations recommended. **$$$**

★★ELMO
156 Seventh Ave., New York, 212-337-8000; www.elmorestaurant.com

American menu. Lunch, dinner, brunch. Bar. Casual attire. Outdoor seating. **$$**

★★ESSEX RESTAURANT
120 Essex St., New York, 212-533-9616; www.essexnyc.com

International menu. Dinner, late-night, brunch. Closed Monday. Bar. Casual attire. Reservations recommended. **$$**

★★★ESTIATORIO MILOS

125 W. 55th St., New York, 212-245-7400; www.milos.ca

Milos, as it's called for short, is a luxurious, cavernous, whitewashed eatery decorated with umbrella-topped tables and seafood market-style fish displays. Showcasing simple, rustic Greek cooking, this restaurant serves seafood priced by the pound and prepared either perfectly grilled over charcoal or in the Greek style called *spetsiota* filleted and baked with tomatoes, onions, herbs and olive oil. Greek, Mediterranean, seafood menu. Lunch, dinner. Bar. Business casual attire. Reservations recommended. Outdoor seating. $$$

★★FANELLI'S CAFÉ

94 Prince St., New York, 212-226-9412

American menu. Lunch, dinner. Bar. Children's menu. Casual attire. $$

★★★FELIDIA

243 E. 58th St., New York, 212-758-1479; www.lidiasitaly.com

Celebrated chef and TV personality Lidia Bastianich is the unofficial matriarch of Italian-American cuisine. Her restaurant, Felidia (she and son Joe are partners in Becco), is warm and elegant and draws an elite New York crowd. Diners are expected to eat as they do in Italy, so you'll start with a plate of antipasti or a bowl of zuppe (soup), move on to a fragrant bowl of fresh pasta and then to a grilled whole fish, and finally dessert. The Italian wine list is extra special, so be sure to pair your meal with a few glasses. Italian menu. Lunch, dinner. Bar. Business casual attire. Reservations recommended. $$$

★★★FIAMMA OSTERIA

206 Spring St., New York, 212-653-0100; www.brguestrestaurants.com

This upscale, multi-level spot for refined Italian fare in Soho is the first chef-driven restaurant from Steve Hanson, the owner of hip, casual eateries like Blue Water Grill and Dos Caminos. For this project, Hanson pulled out all the stops, creating an elegant Italian dining experience. From homemade pastas to tender fish and grilled meats to the all-Italian cheese course to the massive wine list, Fiamma is a standout. Italian menu. Lunch, dinner. Bar. Business casual attire. Reservations recommended. $$$

★★★FIREBIRD

365 W. 46th St., New York, 212-586-0244; www.firebirdrestaurant.com

Set in a lavish double townhouse, this restaurant and cabaret is furnished like a majestic Russian palace, with ornate antique furniture, intricate china and etched glass, old-world oil paintings and 19th-century photographs. The extravagance extends to the food, with Russian classics like blinis with sour cream and caviar, *zakuska* (the Russian equivalent of tapas), borscht made with pork and dill and sturgeon baked in puff pastry. Eastern European menu. Lunch, dinner. Closed Monday; holidays. Bar. Business casual attire. Reservations recommended. Outdoor seating. $$$

★★★FLEUR DE SEL

5 E. 20th St., New York, 212-460-9100; www.fleurdeselnyc.com

Located on a sleepy Gramercy side street, Fleur de Sel is a lovely buttercup-colored cottage-like restaurant, one of the most enchanted hideaways in the city. Fleur serves sophisticated French-American fare in a serene dining room decorated with sheer curtains and bouquets of fresh flowers. It's a lovely setting to enjoy a dinner of stunningly presented, delicate and deliciously prepared food. French, American menu. Lunch, dinner. Closed Sunday in August. Business casual attire. Reservations recommended. $$$$

★★★FOUR SEASONS RESTAURANT

99 E. 52nd St., New York, 212-754-9494; www.fourseasonsrestaurant.com

The Four Seasons is a true New York classic. Since 1959, this Philip Johnson and Mies van der Rohe-designed room has been the de facto dining room of media power-houses, financial movers and shakers, legal dealmakers and the generally fabulous crowd that follows them. Lunch can be an exercise in connect-the-famous-faces. The food at the Four Seasons is simple but well prepared and takes its cues from around the world. You'll find classic French entrées as well as more contemporary American fare accented with flavors borrowed from Asia, Morocco and Latin America. Expect a high tariff to match the high-octane people-watching. American menu. Lunch, dinner. Closed Sunday; holidays. Bar. Jacket required. Reservations recommended. $$$$

★FRANK

88 Second Ave., New York, 212-420-0202; www.frankrestaurant.com

Italian menu. Breakfast, lunch, dinner, brunch. Bar. Casual attire. Reservations recommended. Outdoor seating. No credit cards accepted. $$

★★★GABRIEL'S

11 W. 60th St., New York, 212-956-4600; www.gabrielsbarandrest.com

Gabriel's is the creation of owner Gabriel Aiello, a charming host who knows how to make guests feel at home in this elegant Lincoln Center spot for sumptuous Tuscan fare. (Think gorgonzola tortellini with a shiitake mushroom tomato sauce, lasagna Bolognese and a daily house-made risotto.) The restaurant is elegantly dressed with contemporary art cloaking the warm saffron-toned walls. While Gabriel's may look like a see-and-be-seen hot spot, the restaurant is refreshingly warm and welcoming. Northern Italian menu. Lunch, dinner. Closed Sunday; holidays. Bar. Business casual attire. Reservations recommended. $$$

★★★GALLAGHER'S

228 W. 52nd St., New York, 212-245-5336; www.gallaghersnysteakhouse.com

This steakhouse is a New York City landmark and former speakeasy and remains decorated as it was the day it opened in November 1927, with plain-planked floors, red-checked tablecloths and dark wood-paneled walls covered in old photos. Specializing in dry-aged beef, the kitchen stays true to simple American fare. American, steak menu. Lunch, dinner. Bar. Casual attire. Reservations recommended. $$$

★★GASCOGNE

158 Eighth Ave., New York, 212-675-6564; www.gascognenyc.com

French menu. Lunch, dinner, brunch. Closed holidays. Bar. Casual attire. Reservations recommended. Outdoor seating. $$$

NEW YORK

★
★
★
★
★

★★★GEISHA

33 E. 61st St., New York, 212-813-1113; www.geisharestaurant.com

Set in a modern townhouse on the Upper East Side, Geisha is seafood whiz kid Eric Ripert's inspired translation of Japanese cuisine. While he is still manning the stoves at Le Bernardin, here at Geisha, his love affair with seafood is in full bloom. Dishes include coconut-marinated fluke with coconut ponzu, lime vinaigrette and orange essence, bowls of tiger shrimp dumplings with toasted pumpkin in a green curry broth and dishes of day boat cod with warm pepper and snow pea salad in soy ginger butter—not to mention chic platters of sushi, sashimi and signature rolls prepared by a pair of seriously skilled sushi chefs. Japanese menu. Lunch, dinner. Closed Sunday. Bar. Business casual attire. Reservations recommended. Outdoor seating. **$$$**

★★ GHENET ETHIOPIAN RESTAURANT

284 Mulberry St., New York, 212-343-1888; www.ghenet.com

Middle Eastern menu. Lunch Tuesday-Sunday, dinner. Bar. Casual attire. **$$**

★★GIGINO TRATTORIA

323 Greenwich St., New York, 212-431-1112; www.gigino-trattoria.com

Italian menu. Lunch, dinner. Children's menu. Closed holidays. Bar. Casual attire. Outdoor seating. **$$$**

★★★★GILT

455 Madison Ave., New York, 212-891-8100; www.giltnewyork.com

When the staff at New York's celebrated Le Cirque 2000 packed up their knives in 2004, foodies everywhere wondered what would take the restaurant's place in the New York Palace Hotel's historic Villard Mansion. The answer: the opulent Gilt, whose name pays homage to the late 19th-century's Gilded Age, when the mansion was created. The 55-seat space, with carved-wood and gilded walls, cathedral ceilings and marble fireplaces, features contemporary elements that give the dining room a modern twist while retaining its historic beauty. The menu features New American options like crispy sea bass with chorizo, red bliss potatoes, garlic aioli and saffron mussel broth. Wine is a large part of the experience, and Gilt offers an expansive and expensive selection to complement each dish on the modern American menu. Continental menu. Dinner. Closed Sunday-Monday. Bar. Jacket required. Reservations recommended. Valet parking. **$$$$**

★★GINGER

1400 Fifth Ave., New York, 212-423-1111; www.gingerexpress.com

Pacific-Rim/Pan-Asian menu. Dinner. Bar. Children's menu. Casual attire. **$$**

★★★★GORDON RAMSAY AT THE LONDON

151 W. 54th St., New York, 212-468-8888; www.thelondonnyc.com/gordon_ramsay

The culinary world's mad genius now has a stateside playground in which to romp at the recently opened London NYC hotel. The menu is French influenced and sophisticated, and the room, designed by David Collins, matches that aesthetic. Chef de cuisine Josh Emmett interprets Ramsay's recipes when the star chef is away—they include everything from fillet of beef with braised oxtail, baby onions and creamed mushrooms to pan-fried John Dory with eggplant, tomato and zucchini. Service is crisp and polished, and the wine list compliments the cuisine perfectly. French/Continental. Lunch, dinner. Reservations recommended. $$$$

★★★★GOTHAM BAR & GRILL
12 E. 12th St., New York, 212-620-4020; www.gothambarandgrill.com
Alfred Portale, the chef and owner of Gotham Bar and Grill, is an icon in New York's culinary circles. The leader of the "tall food" movement and a passionate advocate of seasonal Greenmarket ingredients, he has been a gastronomic force from behind the stoves at his swanky, vaulted-ceilinged Gotham Bar and Grill for more than a decade. The room is loud, energetic and packed with a very stylish crowd at both lunch and dinner. The menu offers something for everyone—salad, fish, pasta, poultry, beef and game—and each dish is prepared with a bold dose of sophistication and plenty of architectural plating for extra drama. American menu. Lunch, dinner. Bar. Casual attire. Reservations recommended. $$$

★★★★GRAMERCY TAVERN
42 E. 20th St., New York, 212-477-0777; www.gramercytavern.com
Owner Danny Meyer's perpetually bustling New York eatery is warm and charming without a smidge of pretension. In the glorious main room, you can choose from a pair of seasonal tasting menus or a wide array of equally tempting á la carte selections. If you don't have a reservation, stroll in, put your name on the list and you'll have the chance to sample some spectacular food in the bar. There's a terrific house cocktail list, too. American menu. Lunch, dinner. Bar. Business casual attire. Reservations recommended. $$$

★GREAT NY NOODLETOWN
28 Bowery, New York, 212-349-0923
Chinese menu. Breakfast, lunch, dinner, late-night. Bar. Casual attire. No credit cards accepted. $

★★★HAKUBAI
66 Park Ave., New York, 212-885-7111; www.kitano.com
Located in the Kitano hotel, Hakubai offers authentic Japanese fare in a tranquil space. The menu features a myriad of traditionally prepared seafood dishes like chopped salted squid, vinegar-marinated jellyfish and fried, grilled or simmered flounder. For a special treat, call ahead and reserve a private room for the multi-course chef's choice menu ($150 to $170), or to savor a simpler meal, choose from the restaurant's selection of sushi, sashimi and maki rolls, as well as udon and soba noodle dishes. Japanese menu. Lunch, dinner. Casual attire. Reservations recommended. $$$

★★★THE HARRISON
355 Greenwich St., New York, 212-274-9310; www.theharrison.com
With its amber lighting, hardwood floors and inviting bar, the Harrison personifies comfortable chic. Owned by Jimmy Bradley and Danny Abrams, the savvy team behind the Red Cat and the Mermaid Inn, this Mediterranean-accented restaurant is a charming neighborhood hot spot with a stylish clientele. Sample the signature

fried clams with fried slivered rounds of lemon at the happening bar or at one of the well-spaced, linen-topped tables. American menu. Dinner. Bar. Business casual attire. Reservations recommended. Outdoor seating. $$$

★★★HARRY CIPRIANI

781 Fifth Ave., New York, 212-753-5566; www.cipriani.com
If you are searching for a place to see and be seen by New York's most moneyed crowds, Harry's is your spot. Located across the street from Central Park, this posh restaurant features Italian cuisine and clipped service at an astronomical price point. American, Italian menu. Lunch, dinner. Bar. Business casual attire. Reservations recommended. $$$

★★★HEARTH

403 E. 12th St., New York, 646-602-1300; www.restauranthearth.com
White walls, recessed lighting and red ceilings add to the warm setting at Hearth. Guests can dine in the main area, fronting the street, the four-seat bar/chef's table, facing the kitchen or the intimate, cozy back room, which is ideal for groups ordering the five-course tasting menu. Specialties include ricotta tortelli with spring vegetables, roasted monkfish and braised veal breast with sweetbreads, onions and morels. For dessert, try the carrot cake with candied pecans and cinnamon raisin ice cream. American menu. Dinner. Bar. Casual attire. Reservations recommended. $$$

★HEARTLAND BREWERY

35 Union Square West, New York, 212-645-3400; www.heartlandbrewery.com
American menu. Lunch, dinner. Bar. Children's menu. Casual attire. Outdoor seating. $$

★HOG PIT

22 Ninth Ave., New York, 212-604-0092; www.hogpit.com
American menu. Lunch, dinner. Bar. Casual attire. $$

★★HOME

20 Cornelia St., New York, 212-243-9579; www.homerestaurantnyc.com
American menu. Lunch, dinner, brunch. Casual attire. Outdoor seating. $$

★★★I TRULLI

122 E. 27th St., New York, 212-481-7372; www.itrulli.com
This restaurant envelops you with warmth, whether in the winter with its hearth-style, wood-burning fireplace or in the summer when the lovely outdoor courtyard garden opens up for dining under the stars. This is a true neighborhood place, with charming service that features the rustic Italian cuisine of the Apulia region. Favorites include ricotta-stuffed cannelloni, orecchiette with veal ragu and fantastic calzones made by hand and baked to a golden brown in the wood-burning oven. Italian menu. Lunch, dinner. Bar. Casual attire. Reservations recommended. Outdoor seating. $$$

★★IL BUCO

47 Bond St., New York, 212-533-1932; www.ilbuco.com
Italian, Mediterranean menu. Lunch Tuesday-Saturday, dinner. Bar. Casual attire. $$$

★★IL CORTILE

125 Mulberry St., New York, 212-226-6060; www.ilcortile.com

Italian menu. Lunch, dinner. Casual attire. Reservations recommended. Outdoor seating. $$$

★★★IL MULINO

86 W. Third St., New York, 212-673-3783; www.ilmulinonewyork.com

Il Mulino is the kind of Italian spot where the service is excellent and the rich, heavy food is read from long lists of specials and served in huge portions (the herb-crusted lamb chops are massive). Tableside theatrics like making a Caesar salad and filleting a whole fish give guests even more of a show. Il Mulino is a boy's club with lots of loud, brash eaters who don't mind the stellar tabs. Italian menu. Lunch, dinner. Closed Sunday. Bar. Reservations recommended. $$$$

★★★IL NIDO

251 E. 53rd St., New York, 212-753-8450; www.ilnidonyc.com

A bit more rustic than its Il Monello sister, this eatery offers a plethora of antipasti and pastas to begin its northern Italian menu, including rigatoni Toscana with tomatoes, white beans and sage. For added entertainment, many entrées are prepared tableside. Italian menu. Lunch, dinner. Closed Sunday; holidays. Bar. Business casual attire. Reservations recommended. $$$

★INO

21 Bedford St., New York, 212-989-5769; www.cafeino.com

Italian menu. Breakfast, lunch, dinner, brunch. Bar. Casual attire. $

★★'INOTECA

98 Rivington St., New York, 212-614-0473; www.inotecanyc.com

Italian menu. Lunch, dinner, late-night, brunch. Bar. Casual attire. Reservations recommended. Outdoor seating. $$

★★★INSIEME

777 Seventh Ave., New York, The Michelangelo Hotel, 212-582-1310;
www.restaurantinsieme.com

From the owners of downtown darling Hearth comes Insieme and its as different from its sister restaurant as Times Square is from the East Village. This separate take on Italian cuisine was, however, inspired by unity, bringing "together," as the name says, traditional and contemporary Italian cuisine on one menu. For example the insalata di misticanza of lettuce, vegetables, three-year-old parmesan and balsamic vinegar is countered by an octopus carpaccio with soffritto crudo, fennel, sweet potato and red wine vinaigrette; the clam linguine by mushroom risotto; the roasted pork loin with beans, sage and garlic by lamb accented by squash, tomato confit, green olive and mint. Couples with differing tastes will likely leave pleased, others possibly on the fence as to whether they chalk the experience up to identity crisis or creative genius. Italian menu. Breakfast (Monday-Friday), lunch (Monday-Saturday), dinner, brunch Saturday-Sunday. Bar. Business casual attire. Reservations recommended. Valet parking. $$$

★JACKSON HOLE

1611 Second Ave., New York, 212-737-8788; www.jacksonholeburgers.com

American, Mexican menu. Breakfast, lunch, dinner, late-night, brunch Saturday-Sunday. Closed holidays. Bar. Outdoor seating. $$

★★★★★JEAN GEORGES

1 Central Park West, New York, 212-299-3900; www.jean-georges.com

Perfection is a word that comes to mind when speaking of meals at Jean-Georges. Located in the Trump International Hotel and Tower, Jean-Georges is a shrine to haute cuisine. Drawing influences from around the world, the menu is conceived and impeccably executed by celebrity chef/owner Jean-Georges Vongerichten. If you can't secure a table at Jean-Georges, try your luck at Nougatine, the popular onsite cafe. It has a more simple menu but will give you a taste of Vongerichten's cuisine. The bar is also a lovely place to meet for an aperitif or a cocktail before dinner or a walk through the park. Continental, French menu. Lunch, dinner, brunch. Bar. Business casual attire. Reservations recommended. Valet parking. Outdoor seating. $$$$

★★★JEWEL BAKO

239 E. Fifth St., New York, 212-979-1012

This shoebox-sized jewel of a place serves precious, glorious sushi and sashimi, as well as more traditional Japanese meals. Jewel Bako is owned by a husband-wife team who place a premium on gracious hospitality. The dining areas are calming and elegant, with diffused lighting peeking through the wooden ceiling slats. The restaurant's small size and popular following make reserving a table ahead of time a must. Japanese, sushi menu. Dinner. Closed Sunday. Casual attire. Reservations recommended. $$$

★JING FONG

20 Elizabeth St., New York, 212-964-5256

Chinese menu. Lunch, dinner. Casual attire. $$

★JOHN'S PIZZERIA

278 Bleecker St., New York, 212-243-1680; www.johnsbrickovenpizza.com

Italian menu. Lunch, dinner. Casual attire. No credit cards accepted. $$

★★★JOJO

160 E. 64th St., New York, 212-223-5656; www.jean-georges.com

Located in a charming old townhouse, JoJo was one of the first restaurants from acclaimed star-chef and restaurateur Jean-Georges Vongerichten and features a turn-of-the-century feel, with deep jewel tones, velvet and silk fabrics, and 17th-century terra-cotta tiles. The dishes highlight Vongerichten's French-Asian style, such as goat cheese and potato terrine with chive oil, roast chicken with chickpea fries and tuna spring rolls with a soybean coulis. French menu. Lunch, dinner, brunch. Closed holidays. Bar. Business casual attire. Reservations recommended. $$$

★★★★KAI

822 Madison Ave., New York, 212-988-7277; www.itoen.com

Retreat to this restaurant and teahouse on the second floor of renowned tea merchant Ito En. Along with an afternoon tea featuring many of Ito En's premium teas and sweets like black sesame and green tea layer cake, the restaurant is open for lunch and dinner. At lunch, diners delight in flavors and textures of soups and dishes made with noodles, tea-scented rice, vegetables, seafood or beef. Bento boxes or sashimi lunches are also popular choices. At dinner, order à la carte or a tasting menu such as the nine-course Iron Goddess, which features dishes like chilled purée of lily bulb soup and "live" unagi with seasonal vegetables and spicy miso. Japanese menu. Lunch, dinner. Closed Sunday and Monday; holidays. Business casual attire. Reservations recommended. $$$

★KELLEY & PING
127 Greene St., New York, 212-228-1212; www.eatrice.com
Pacific-Rim/Pan-Asian menu. Lunch, dinner. Children's menu. Casual attire. Reservations recommended. $$

★★KINGS' CARRIAGE HOUSE
251 E. 82nd St., New York, 212-734-5490; www.kingscarriagehouse.com
Continental menu. Lunch, dinner. Closed holidays; also two weeks in late August. Bar. Business casual attire. Reservations recommended. $$$$

★★★KURUMA ZUSHI
7 E. 47th St., New York, 212-317-2802
Kuruma Zushi is an understated, small Japanese spot located on the second floor of a less-than-impressive Midtown building, with only a tiny sign to alert you to its presence. Impossibly fresh fish is served with freshly grated wasabi and bright, fiery shavings of ginger. And while many consider this the pinnacle of sushi, it does come with quite a sky-high price tag. Japanese menu. Lunch, dinner. Closed Sunday. Bar. Casual attire. Reservations recommended. $$$$

★★★★L'ATELIER DE JOËL ROBUCHON
57 E. 57th St., New York, 212-758-5700; www.fourseasons.com/newyork
Housed in the Four Seasons Hotel, this offering from star French chef Joël Robuchon—his first in New York—delivers an intimate, sophisticated and unique dining experience. The name means "artist's workshop," and this concept, with outposts in Las Vegas, Paris and Tokyo, is a space for Robuchon and his well-trained staff to churn out small plates of perfectly executed culinary art. Diners sit at a 20-seat bar or at one of the 26 seats arranged around the dining room's tables and sample creations like truffled mashed potatoes or sea urchin in lobster gelee with cauliflower cream. Service is precise and professional, which allows the food in all its glory to take center stage. French. Dinner. Reservations recommended. Upscale attire. $$$$

★★L'EXPRESS
249 Park Ave. South, New York, 212-254-5858; www.lexpressnyc.com
French menu. Breakfast, lunch, dinner, late-night, brunch. Bar. Casual attire. $$

★★LA BONNE SOUPE
48 W. 55th St., New York, 212-586-7650; www.labonnesoupe.com
French bistro menu. Lunch, dinner, Sunday brunch. Bar. Children's menu. Casual attire. Outdoor seating. $$

★★★★LA GRENOUILLE

3 E. 52nd St., New York, 212-752-1495; www.la-grenouille.com

Housed in a former carriage house in Midtown, La Grenouille is an elegant New York classic overflowing with gorgeous flowers that mixes wildly attentive service and beautifully prepared French fare. Sample the signature frog legs served sautéed Provencal style or savor less adventurous but wonderful choices such as the grilled Dover sole with a mustard sauce. French menu. Lunch, dinner. Closed Sunday; also three weeks in August. Bar. Jacket required. Reservations recommended. $$$$

★★★LA MANGEOIRE

1008 Second Ave., New York, 212-759-7086; www.lamangeoire.com

This charming restaurant serves up hearty Mediterranean-influenced food in a rustic setting. Star dishes include sautéed monkfish medallions with lobster sauce and duck breast with fig, chestnut and cranberry sauce. French menu. Lunch, dinner, Sunday brunch. Closed holidays. Bar. Casual attire. Reservations recommended. Outdoor seating. $$$

★★LA PAELLA

214 E. Ninth St., New York, 212-598-4321; www.lapaellanyc.com

Spanish menu. Lunch, dinner. Bar. Casual attire. Reservations recommended. Outdoor seating. $$$

★★LA PALAPA

77 St. Marks Place, New York, 212-777-2537; www.lapalapa.com

Mexican menu. Lunch, dinner, brunch. Bar. Casual attire. Reservations recommended. Outdoor seating. $$

★★LAFAYETTE GRILL & BAR

54 Franklin St., New York, 212-732-5600; www.lafgrill.com

Mediterranean menu. Lunch, dinner. Closed Sunday. Bar. Casual attire. Reservations recommended. $$

★★★★★LE BERNARDIN

155 W. 51st St., New York, 212-554-1515; www.le-bernardin.com

This fabled restaurant has impressed foodies and novices alike since it moved from Paris to Manhattan in 1986. Le Bernardin is very civilized and sophisticated, and it's certainly not the place for a quick bite. The sauces star chef Eric Ripert creates are light, aromatic and perfectly balanced, the ingredients are seasonal and stunning and the presentations are museum-worthy. Seafood is the star, and the menu features such knockout dishes as poached halibut with marinated grapes and cherry tomatoes and organic Chilean turbot in a lemon-miso broth. The wine list is equally exquisite. French, Seafood menu. Lunch, dinner. Closed Sunday; holidays. Bar. Jacket required. Reservations recommended. $$$$

★★★★LE CIRQUE

151 E. 58th St., Midtown, 212-644-0202; www.lecirque.com

This venerable New York City mainstay of haute cuisine reincarnated itself in 2006 when it moved from its old digs at the New York Palace Hotel to the Bloomberg

★
★
★
★

Tower in Midtown. The move proved to be a good one—the old mainstay now boasts a creative menu of classics prepared with contemporary flourishes. Plump foie gras ravioli is a standout appetizer, followed by a main lamb dish that includes lamb flank and braised shoulder with gremolata crust, mint jus and mini ravioli stuffed with pecorino. The new Le Cirque also boasts a subdued dining room that has an Upper East Side party atmosphere. Wrap it up with a towering napoleon dessert. Contemporary French-Italian menu. Lunch (Monday-Friday), dinner (Monday-Saturday). Closed Sunday. **$$$$**

★★LE COLONIAL
149 E. 57th St., New York, 212-752-0808; www.lecolonialnyc.com
Vietnamese, French menu. Lunch, dinner. Closed holidays. Bar. Casual attire. Reservations recommended. **$$$**

★★★LE PERIGORD
405 E. 52nd St., New York, 212-755-6244; www.leperigord.com
Le Perigord is one of New York's old-time favorites for sophisticated French dining. The menu of classic dishes, including the restaurant's signature game selection (in season), is geared for diners who define luxury in terms of impeccable, attentive service, elegant furnishings, inspired haute cuisine of the nouvelle French variety and the quiet of a dining room filled with an older, sophisticated crowd. French menu. Lunch, dinner. Bar. Jacket required. Reservations recommended. **$$$$**

★★★LE REFUGE
166 E. 82nd St., New York, 212-861-4505; www.lerefugenyc.com
Located within walking distance of the Metropolitan Museum of Art and the lush greenery of Central Park, Le Refuge is a classically charming French restaurant offering a small slice of Paris in New York. A sophisticated crowd gathers at Le Refuge for its Parisian elegance and its impressive wine list that pairs up perfectly with the selection of simple, bistro-style fare, such as farm-raised duck with fresh fruit and filet mignon with peppercorn sauce. Continental, French menu. Lunch, dinner. Closed holidays. Bar. Children's menu. Casual attire. Reservations recommended. Outdoor seating. **$$$**

★★LE SOUK
47 Ave. B, New York, 212-777-5454; www.lesoukny.com
Middle Eastern menu. Dinner. Bar. Casual attire. Outdoor seating. **$$**

★★LES HALLES
411 Park Ave. S, New York, 212-679-4111; www.leshalles.net
French menu. Breakfast, lunch, dinner, brunch. Bar. Casual attire. **$$$**

★★LES HALLES DOWNTOWN
15 John St., New York, 212-285-8585; www.leshalles.net
French, steak menu. Lunch, dinner, brunch. Bar. Children's menu. Casual attire. **$$**

★★★LEVER HOUSE
390 Park Ave., New York, 212-888-2700; www.leverhouse.com
Designed by superstar Marc Newson, Lever House is a postmodern dining room packed with whiplash-worthy celebrities. The kitchen sends out small plates of fluke

tartare, heated up with chiles and orange zest or heartier fare like the juicy Lever House burger. American menu. Lunch, dinner. Bar. Business casual attire. Reservations recommended. $$$

★LOMBARDI'S
32 Spring St., New York, 212-941-7994; www.firstpizza.com
Pizza. Lunch, dinner. Casual attire. Outdoor seating. No credit cards accepted. $

★★LONDEL'S SUPPER CLUB
2620 Frederick Douglas Blvd., New York, 212-234-6114; www.londelsrestaurant.com
American menu. Lunch, dinner, brunch. Closed Monday. Bar. Casual attire. Reservations recommended. $$

★★LUCKY STRIKE
59 Grand St., New York, 212-941-0772; www.luckystrikeny.com
American, French menu. Lunch, dinner, late-night, brunch. Bar. Casual attire. $$

★★LUPA OSTERIA ROMANA
170 Thompson St., New York, 212-982-5089; www.luparestaurant.com
Italian menu. Lunch, dinner. Bar. Casual attire. Outdoor seating. $$

★★LUSARDI'S
1494 Second Ave., New York, 212-249-2020; www.lusardis.com
Italian menu. Lunch, dinner. Closed holidays. Bar. Casual attire. Reservations recommended. $$$

★★★MALONEY & PORCELLI
37 E. 50th St., New York, 212-750-2233; www.maloneyandporcelli.com
Named for the restaurant owner's attorneys, Maloney & Porcelli prepares simple, well-executed cuisine served in a classic, clubby environment. The New American menu offers straightforward choices like a raw bar, thin-crust pizza and filet mignon. The wine list contains some real gems as well, making Maloney & Porcelli a favorite for Midtown dining. American, steak menu. Lunch, dinner. Bar. Casual attire. Reservations recommended. Outdoor seating. $$$

★★★MAMLOUK
211 E. Fourth St., New York, 212-529-3477
This cozy Middle Eastern spot in the East Village will carry you to an Arabic land filled with sitar music and warm, fragrant spiced meals. Dinner is a six-course affair, with dishes such as zatter, a flatbread topped with a paste of sesame seeds, olive oil and thyme, vegetarian moussaka, and mujadarra, a sweet spice-flecked lentil purée served with tender grilled chicken. Middle Eastern menu. Dinner. Casual attire. Reservations recommended. Outdoor seating. $$$

★★MARY'S FISH CAMP
64 Charles St., New York, 646-486-2185; www.marysfishcamp.com
Seafood menu. Lunch, dinner. Closed Sunday. Bar. Casual attire. $$

★★★★★MASA

10 Columbus Circle, New York, 212-823-9800; www.masanyc.com

You need deep pockets to indulge at Masa. This is the high roller's table for gourmands, given that you've already committed to spending $400 just by walking through the 2,500-year-old Japanese cedar door—before you've had a drink, tacked on tax or paid the gratuity. Chef/owner Masa Takayama creates a different dining experience each day based on market offerings. A mere shiitake mushroom, for example, is raised to shrine-worthy status. Every detail at Masa is aesthetically exquisite, from the amazing cuisine to the top-flight service. Japanese, sushi menu. Lunch, dinner. Closed Sunday. Bar. Business casual attire. Reservations recommended. $$$$

★★★MATSURI

369 W. 16th St., New York, 212-242-4300; www.themaritimehotel.com

Located in the Meatpacking District's Maritime Hotel, Matsuri is an Asian wonderland. From the bamboo and paper-lanterned movie set décor to the shimmering sushi, sashimi and expertly plated haute Japanese stylings, this restaurant is an ode to the exotic senses of the Far East, attracting glamorous crowds seeking high-style fare and flair. Japanese menu. Dinner. Bar. Casual attire. Reservations recommended. $$$

★★MAX

51 Ave. B, New York, 212-539-0111; www.max-ny.com

Italian menu. Lunch, dinner. Bar. Casual attire. Outdoor seating. No credit cards accepted. $$

★★★MAYA

1191 First Ave., New York, 212-585-1818; www.modernmexican.com/mayany

A native of Mexico City, Maya's talented chef/owner Richard Sandoval knows authentic Mexican cuisine. His popular Upper East Side restaurant is perpetually packed with neighborhood locals who love the hacienda-style room—wood-paneled walls accented with native art and terra-cotta tiled floors—and such dishes as cordero en mole verde, a lamb shank braised in a chocolate sauce with pan-roasted potatoes, chayote squash and baby carrots. The house mariscada—a mammoth bowl bobbing with sea scallops, shrimp, mussels and clams, served with black rice and a coriander seed-red pepper emulsion—is superb. Mexican menu. Dinner. Closed holidays. Bar. Business casual attire. Reservations recommended. $$$

★★MELBA'S

300 W. 114th St., New York, 212-864-7777; www.melbasrestaurant.com

American menu. Dinner, brunch. Closed Mon. Bar. Casual attire. Reservations recommended. $$

★★★MERCER KITCHEN

99 Prince St., New York, 212-966-5454; www.jean-georges.com

This sleek, sexy room inside the Mercer Hotel is the brainchild of star chef Jean-Georges Vongerichten. Here he practices his talent for comfort food, albeit the most luxe, delectable, gourmet kind you'll ever taste. The menu includes several kinds of pizzas topped with ingredients like black truffle and fontina cheese, and every entrée can be accompanied by sides like unctuous macaroni or corn pudding. American,

Continental menu. Breakfast, lunch, dinner, brunch. Closed holidays. Bar. Business casual attire. Reservations recommended. $$$

★★MERMAID INN

96 Second Ave., New York, 212-674-5870; www.themermaidnyc.com

American, seafood menu. Dinner. Closed Thanksgiving. Bar. Casual attire. Reservations recommended. Outdoor seating. $$

★★MESA GRILL

102 Fifth Ave., New York, 212-807-7400; www.mesagrill.com

Southwestern menu. Lunch, dinner, brunch. Closed holidays. Bar. Casual attire. $$$

★★MI COCINA

57 Jane St., New York, 212-627-8273; www.micocinany.com

Mexican menu. Dinner, brunch. Closed holidays. Children's menu. Casual attire. Reservations recommended. Outdoor seating. $$

★★★MIA DONA

206 E. 58th St., New York, 212-750-8170; www.miadona.com

With several slam dunks in just a few years, Donatella Arpaia took another shot, opening Mia Dona with partner Michael Psilakis. And they made it—garnering points for everything except the décor, which aimed at homey, and hit humdrum. Still, Arpaia's vision of a Sunday-supper-inspired menu saves the game. Excelling at affordable, comfortable classics from minestrone to lamb fettuccine to poached halibut, you can't really go wrong here. But should you be disappointed with your entrée, simply order the cannoli to set things right. Italian menu. Lunch (Monday-Friday), dinner, Sunday brunch. Bar. Casual attire. Reservations recommended. $$$

★MICKEY MANTLE'S

42 Central Park S., New York, 212-688-7777; www.mickeymantles.com

American menu. Lunch, dinner, late-night, brunch. Bar. Children's menu. Casual attire. Reservations recommended. Outdoor seating. $$

★★MOBAY UPTOWN

17 W. 125th St., New York, 212-876-9300; www.mobayrestaurant.com

Caribbean menu. Lunch, dinner, brunch. Bar. Casual attire. Reservations recommended. $$$

★★★★THE MODERN

9 W. 53rd St., Midtown, 212-333-1220; www.themodernnyc.com

This elegant sun-lit Midtown spot is relly two restaurants in one—the sophisticated Dining Room and a less-formal Bar Room. Split up in two rooms separated by frosted glass, both restaurants reside in The Modern Museum of Art, and most seats afford great views of the MoMA sculpture garden next door. Chef Gabriel Kreuther creates bold, flavorful dishes, such as chorizo-crusted codfish with white cocoa bean purée and harissa oil; roasted lobster with salsify and apple; and a Pennsylvania duck breast with a black trumpet marmalade, fleischschneke and banyuls jus. In the less-formal Bar Room, you can find an earthy menu emphasizing small plates with big tastes, such as a pasta dish elevated by chewy, salty escargots and fragrant wild mushrooms. French, Contemporary American menu. Lunch (Monday-Friday), dinner. Closed Sunday. $$$

★★★MOLYVOS
871 Seventh Ave., New York, 212-582-7500; www.molyvos.com
Located near Carnegie Hall and City Center, Molyvos is a great choice before or after a dance or concert, with a wonderful menu of modern Greek specialties such as assorted mezze served with warm pita, grilled whole fish, stunning takes on lamb and an impressive international wine list. The restaurant feels like it fell from the shores of Mykonos, thanks to its blue-and-white tiles and sturdy wooden tables. Greek menu. Lunch, dinner. Bar. Casual attire. Reservations recommended. $$$

★★MOMOFUKU NOODLE BAR
171 First Ave., New York, 212-475-7889; www.momofuku.com
Japanese, Korean menu. Lunch, dinner. Bar. Casual attire. $$

★★MOMOFUKU SSÄM BAR
207 Second Ave. (at 13th St.), New York, 212-254-3500; www.momofuku.com
Asian menu. Lunch, dinner. $$$

★★★MORTON'S, THE STEAKHOUSE
551 Fifth Ave., New York, 212-972-3315; www.mortons.com
This steakhouse chain, which originated in Chicago in 1978, serves such specialties as a 24-ounce porterhouse, as well as fresh fish, lobster and chicken. Steak menu. Lunch, dinner. Closed holidays. Bar. Business casual attire. Reservations recommended. $$$$

★★★MR. K'S
570 Lexington Ave., New York, 212-583-1668; www.mrks.com
Forget any thoughts you may have had about Chinese food because Mr. K's breaks all the rules, bringing New Yorkers wonderful, upscale, exotic dishes from the various regions of China and serving them in an ultraelegant, posh setting filled with fresh flowers, plush banquettes and, most notably, waiters who know the meaning of service. Chinese menu. Lunch, dinner. Bar. Business casual attire. Reservations recommended. $$$

★★NAM
110 Reade St., New York, 212-267-1777; www.namnyc.com
Vietnamese menu. Lunch, dinner. Bar. Casual attire. $$

★NEW YORK KOM TANG
32 W. 32nd St., New York, 212-947-8482
Korean menu. Breakfast, lunch, dinner, late-night. Casual attire. $$

★NHA TRANG CENTRE
148 Centre St., New York, 212-941-9292
Vietnamese menu. Lunch, dinner. Casual attire. $

★
★
★
★
★

★★★NOBU

105 Hudson St., New York, 212-219-0500; www.myriadrestaurantgroup.com

Nobu's lively dining room on an otherwise quiet corner of Tribeca has a serene vibe despite the high-energy, high-fashion crowd that packs in nightly for famed chef Nobu Matsuhisa's spectacular sushi and unique brand of Asian-Latin-inspired seafood. Lime, soy, chiles, miso, cilantro and ginger are flavors frequently employed to accent many of the chef's succulent creations. A signature dish is the almost-melting black cod with miso. The omakase (chef's choice) menu is an option for those with an adventurous palate. If you can't get a reservation (call well in advance and be prepared for a busy signal), you can always try for a seat at the sushi bar. Japanese menu. Lunch, dinner. Closed holidays. Casual attire. Reservations recommended. **$$$**

★NYONYA

194 Grand St., New York, 212-334-3669; www.penangusa.com

Malaysian, Pacific-Rim/Pan-Asian menu. Lunch, dinner. Casual attire. Reservations recommended. **$$**

★★★OCEANA

55 E. 54th St., New York, 212-759-5941; www.oceanarestaurant.com

Highly regarded Oceana serves practically every fish in the sea, from halibut to tuna, dorade to turbot. Scallops, lobster and glistening oysters are also on the menu. The service is warm and efficient, and the cream-colored, nautical-themed room (portholes dot the walls) is peaceful and comfortable, making Oceana a perennial favorite for power lunchers and pre-theater diners. The wine list is impressive, with a good number of seafood-friendly options at a variety of price points. Seafood menu. Lunch, dinner. Closed Sunday; holidays. Bar. Jacket required. Reservations recommended. Outdoor seating. **$$$$**

★★THE ODEON

145 W. Broadway, New York, 212-233-0507; www.theodeonrestaurant.com

American, French menu. Lunch, dinner, late-night, brunch. Bar. Children's menu. Casual attire. Outdoor seating. **$$**

★★★OLIVES

201 Park Ave. S., New York, 212-353-8345; www.toddenglish.com

Celebrity chef Todd English's eclectic restaurant in the W Union Square Hotel has an open kitchen, an open-hearth fireplace and deep, oval banquettes. The menu stars English's standard, but well-presented, Mediterranean formula: boldly flavored dishes that are impeccably prepared and artfully presented on the plate. His signature tart filled with olives, goat cheese and sweet caramelized onions is a winner, but the menu also offers lamb, fish, homemade pastas and pizzas from the wood oven. Sadly, the service is decidedly lackluster. Mediterranean menu. Breakfast, lunch, dinner, late-night, brunch. Bar. Casual attire. Reservations recommended. **$$$**

★★★ONE IF BY LAND, TWO IF BY SEA

17 Barrow St., New York, 212-255-8649; www.oneifbyland.com

This classic French restaurant, set in a restored, turn-of-the-century carriage house in Greenwich Village that was once owned by Aaron Burr, is one of New York's most romantic eateries (and the setting for many marriage proposals). Dark and elegant, the hushed, candlelit, two-story dining room is richly appointed with antique sconces, oriental carpets and blazing fireplaces. The menu here is straight-ahead French, with seasonal accompaniments and modern flourishes that add sparkle to the plate. American, French menu. Dinner. Closed holidays. Bar. Business casual attire. Reservations recommended. $$$

★★★ONO

18 Ninth Ave., New York, 212-660-6766; www.hotelgansevoort.com
Japanese cuisine is the star at this stunningly designed multi-level restaurant inside the chic Meatpacking District Hotel Gansevoort. The extensive sushi menu is creative and contemporary (a humble tuna roll comes with sesame mustard and crispy tempura flakes) while the small dishes that make up the rest of the menu include sake steamed manilla clams and udon noodles with shrimp, clams and mussels. A vast selection of ingredients is available to be grilled over an open flame in a Japanese method called robatayaki. Japanese. Dinner. Reservations recommended. $$$

★★OSTERIA AL DOGE

142 W. 44th St., New York, 212-944-3643; www.osteria-doge.com
Italian menu. Lunch, dinner. Bar. Business casual attire. Reservations recommended. $$$

★★★OSTERIA DEL CIRCO

120 W. 55th St., New York, 212-265-3636; www.osteriadelcirco.com
Owned by Sirio Maccioni of Le Cirque fame, Osteria del Circo carries on his signature brand of homespun hospitality in a more casual, yet no less spirited, atmosphere. The rustic menu of Italian fare includes delicious homemade pastas as well as thin Tuscan-style pizzas, classic antipasti and signature main courses such as salt-baked Mediterranean sea bass and brick-pressed chicken. Entrées are available in both large and small portions, and meals can be eaten in either the dining room, ablaze with banquettes in dazzling colors, in the lounge or on the street-side patio. Italian menu. Lunch, dinner. Closed holidays; also Sunday in summer. Bar. Business casual attire. Reservations recommended. Outdoor seating. $$$

★★OTTO

1 Fifth Ave., New York, 212-995-9559; www.ottopizzeria.com
Italian menu. Breakfast, lunch, dinner. Bar. Casual attire. $$

★OUR PLACE

1444 Third Ave., New York, 212-288-4888; www.ourplaceuptown.com
Chinese menu. Lunch, dinner, brunch. Casual attire. Reservations recommended. $$

★★OYSTER BAR

Grand Central Terminal, Lower Level, New York, 212-490-6650; www.oysterbarny.com
Seafood menu. Lunch, dinner. Closed Sunday; holidays. Bar. Casual attire. $$

★★★PARK AVENUE CAFÉ

100 E. 63rd St., New York, 212-644-1900; www.parkavenyc.com
A sophisticated, savvy crowd heads to the slick, high-design Park Avenue Café for

★
★
★
★
★

dishes such as the fire-roasted lamb chops and John Dory with summer truffles. American menu. Lunch, dinner, brunch. Closed holidays. Bar. Business casual attire. Reservations recommended. $$$

★★★PATROON

160 E. 46th St., New York, 212-883-7373; www.patroonrestaurant.com
Owner Ken Aretsky's popular, clubby, low-lit Patroon is a chic steakhouse, but the terrific kitchen turns out wonderful seafood and poultry dishes, too. Steak Diana (named for Aretsky's wife) is prepared tableside with brown butter, shallots and wine. A rooftop deck makes summertime fun with great grilled fare and chilled cocktails. American menu. Lunch, dinner. Closed Saturday-Sunday; holidays; also week of December 25. Bar. Business casual attire. Reservations recommended. $$$

★PATSY'S PIZZERIA

509 Third Ave., New York, 212-689-7500; www.patsyspizzeriany.com
Italian menu, pizza. Lunch, dinner. Bar. Casual attire. No credit cards accepted. $$

★★★PAYARD PATISSERIE AND BISTRO

1032 Lexington Ave., New York, 212-717-5252; www.payard.com
Aside from the great selection of sandwiches, salads and Parisian bistro staples served in this lovely, butter-yellow French pastry shop, this Upper East Side staple serves wildly tempting desserts crafted by renowned pastry chef François Payard. French menu. Breakfast, lunch, dinner. Closed Sunday; holidays. Bar. Business casual attire. $$$

★
★
★
★
★

★★PEARL OYSTER BAR

18 Cornelia St., New York, 212-691-8211; www.pearloysterbar.com
Seafood menu. Lunch, dinner. Closed Sunday. Bar. Desserts. Casual attire. $$$

★★★★★PER SE

10 Columbus Circle, New York, 212-823-9335; www.perseny.com
Thomas Keller, the chef at the fabled French Laundry, calls his restaurant in the Time Warner Center "per se" because its not exactly the French Laundry, per se. What's missing is the bucolic setting of the Napa Valley, but in its place are eye-popping views and equally incredible cooking. The best way to experience per se is to order a tasting menu and enjoy three hours of culinary epiphanies exemplified by small dishes such as truffles and custard in an eggshell and foie gras accompanied by various salts. American, French menu. Lunch, dinner. Bar. Closed two weeks in late July-early August. Business casual attire. Reservations recommended. Valet parking. $$$$

★★★PERIYALI

35 W. 20th St., New York, 212-463-7890; www.periyali.com
Offering authentic Greek fare in a soothing Mediterranean-accented setting, elegant, recently revamped Periyali serves octopus marinated in red wine, sautéed sweetbreads with white beans, grilled whole fish and mezze such as taramosalata (caviar mousse), melitzanosalata (grilled-eggplant mousse) and spanakopita (spinach and cheese pie). Greek menu. Lunch, dinner. Closed Sunday. Bar. Reservations recommended. $$$

★★★PETROSSIAN RESTAURANT

182 W. 58th St., New York, 212-245-2214; www.petrossian.com

Caviar, caviar and caviar is the reason for visiting this elegant, old-fashioned eatery with its mirrors and sculptures. In addition to the great salty roe, you'll find an ultra-luxurious brand of Franco-Russian cuisine that includes classics such as borscht, assorted Russian *zazuska* (tapas) such as smoked salmon (served with cold shots of vodka—ask for Zyr, one of the best from Russia), and other glamorous plates, including foie gras prepared several different ways and, of course, beef Stroganoff. Continental, French menu. Lunch, dinner. Bar. Business casual attire. Reservations recommended. $$$

★★★★PICHOLINE

35 W. 64th St., New York, 212-724-8585; www.picholinenyc.com

Located on Manhattan's Upper West Side, Picholine is a great choice for dinner if you are attending an opera, ballet or play at the Lincoln Center. But chef/owner Terrance Brennan's lovely, serene restaurant is also wonderful for any special occasion. The menu changes with the seasons, and the chef uses organic and local ingredients to create such dishes as the olive oil-poached halibut and morel and rabbit risotto. French, Mediterranean menu. Lunch, dinner. Closed holidays. Bar. Jacket required. Reservations recommended. $$$

★PIE BY THE POUND

124 Fourth Ave., New York, 212-475-4977; www.piebythepound.com

Pizza. Lunch, dinner, late-night, brunch. Children's menu. Casual attire. $

★PIG HEAVEN

1540 Second Ave., New York, 212-744-4887; www.pigheaven.biz

Chinese menu. Lunch, dinner. Bar. Casual attire. Outdoor seating. $$

★★PING'S

22 Mott St., New York, 212-602-9988

Chinese, seafood menu. Lunch, dinner. Casual attire. $$

★★PIPA

38 E. 19th St., New York, 212-677-2233

Spanish menu. Lunch, dinner. Bar. Casual attire. Reservations recommended. $$$

★★★POST HOUSE

28 E. 63rd St., New York, 212-935-2888; www.theposthouse.com

The Post House elevates the typical steakhouse with polished parquet floors, wainscoting and leather armchair seating. The menu includes wonderful salads, signature appetizers such as cornmeal-fried oysters and a shimmering raw bar as well as such entrées as grilled chicken, rack of lamb, prime rib, filet mignon and the signature stolen Cajun rib steak. Steak menu. Lunch, dinner. Closed holidays. Bar. Business casual attire. Reservations recommended. $$$

★★PRAVDA

281 Lafayette St., New York, 212-226-4944; www.pravdany.com

Eastern European menu. Dinner, late-night. Closed Sunday. Bar. Casual attire. Reservations recommended. $$

★★PRUNE

54 E. First St., New York, 212-677-6221; www.prunerestaurant.com

American menu. Lunch. Dinner, brunch. Bar. Casual attire. Reservations recommended. Outdoor seating. **$$**

★★RAOUL'S

180 Prince St., New York, 212-966-3518; www.raouls.com

French menu. Dinner, late-night. Bar. Casual attire. Reservations recommended. Outdoor seating. **$$$**

★★THE RED CAT

227 Tenth Ave., New York, 212-242-1122; www.theredcat.com

American menu. Dinner. Closed holidays. Bar. Casual attire. Reservations recommended. **$$**

★★REDEYE GRILL

890 Seventh Ave., New York, 212-541-9000; www.redeyegrill.com

American, Seafood menu. Lunch, dinner, late-night, brunch. Bar. Casual attire. Outdoor seating. **$$$**

★★★REMI

145 W. 53rd St., New York, 212-581-4242; www.remi-ny.com

The cuisine of Venice is the focus of the menu at Remi, an airy, lofty restaurant in Midtown decorated with ornate Venetian blown-glass lights, hand-painted murals of the Italian city's romantic canals and teak flooring. Remi has long been a favorite for local business people who want to dish over lunch but also makes a terrific choice for drinks, dinner or a visit before or after the theater. The kitchen's specialty is handmade pastas, but the menu also features contemporary Mediterranean takes on fish, beef, poultry and game. A "cicchetti" menu of Venetian tapas is also available at the bar for a lighter meal. Italian menu. Lunch, dinner. Bar. Business casual attire. Reservations recommended. Outdoor seating. **$$$**

★REPUBLIC

37 Union Square West, New York, 212-627-7172; www.thinknoodles.com

Pacific-Rim/Asian menu. Lunch, dinner. Bar. Children's menu. Casual attire. Outdoor seating. **$$**

★★★RIINGO

205 E. 45th St., New York, 212-867-4200; www.riingo.com

Marcus Samuelsson, the heartthrob, boy-wonder chef behind the very popular contemporary Scandinavian spot Aquavit, is the man behind Riingo, his Asian outpost in Midtown's Alex Hotel. Japanese for "apple," Riingo is a sleek and sexy bi-level space featuring dark ebony woodwork, bamboo floors and luxurious banquettes that offer a sublime setting for supping on Samuelsson's inventive brand of Japanese-American fare. American, Japanese, sushi menu. Breakfast, lunch, dinner, brunch. Bar. Business casual attire. Reservations recommended. Valet parking. Outdoor seating. **$$$**

★★ROCK CENTER CAFÉ

20 W. 50th St., New York, 212-332-7620; www.rockcentercafeny.com

American, Italian menu. Breakfast, lunch, dinner, brunch. Bar. Children's menu. Reservations recommended. Outdoor seating. $$$

★★★ROSA MEXICANO

61 Columbus Ave., New York, 212-977-7700; www.rosamexicano.com

One of the first restaurants to introduce New Yorkers to authentic Mexican cuisine, Rosa Mexicano was founded by chef Josefina Howard in the early 1980s. It remains an essential stop for anyone who craves strong, chilly margaritas and knockout bowls of guacamole mixed tableside to your desired level of heat (mild to scorching). The menu is a tribute to the regional home cooking of Mexico—steamy pork tamales, chicken in a rich, savory blanket of mole, terra-cotta cazuelas brimming with shrimp, tomatoes, garlic and chiles and a longtime entrée signature, budin Azteca, a wonderful tortilla casserole with layers of shredded chicken and cheese. Mexican menu. Lunch, dinner, brunch, late-night. Bar. Casual attire. Reservations recommended. Outdoor seating. $$

★★★RUTH'S CHRIS STEAK HOUSE

148 W. 51st St., New York, 212-245-9600; www.ruthschris.com

At this steakhouse chain, aged prime Midwestern beef is broiled to your liking and served on a heated plate, sizzling in butter, a staple ingredient used generously in most entrées. Sides like creamed spinach and fresh asparagus with hollandaise are the perfect companion to any dish. Steak menu. Lunch, dinner. Bar. Business casual attire. Reservations recommended. $$$

★★★SAKAGURA

211 E. 43rd St., New York, 212-953-7253; www.sakagura.com

At this subterranean hideaway in Midtown, you'll find one of the most extensive sake collections in the city, as well as a talented knife-wielding team of sushi chefs turning out delicious sashimi. (There is no sushi here, though, as it is forbidden to serve rice with sake.) Sakagura is tough to find; you enter through the lobby of an office building and follow a small gold sign that points you toward this buried basement space. The hunt is worth it. Japanese menu. Lunch, dinner. Business casual attire. Reservations recommended. $$$

★★★SAN DOMENICO

240 Central Park S., New York, 212-265-5959; www.sandomeniconewyork.com

Located on Central Park South, San Domenico is one of city's most well-regarded restaurants for sophisticated, contemporary Italian cuisine. Pasta, fish and meat dishes manage to feel rustic yet updated, as the chef teams new-world ingredients and twists with authentic old-world recipes and style. An impressive, Italian wine list enriches every bite. Italian menu. Lunch, dinner, brunch (fall-spring). Bar. Jacket required. Reservations recommended. $$$

★★★SAN PIETRO

18 E. 54th St., New York, 212-753-9015; www.sanpietro.net

Located on a busy Midtown street, glitzy San Pietro is owned and run by the three Bruno brothers, who grew up on a family farm along the Amalfi Coast in the southern

Italian region of Campagna. They pay homage to their homeland by serving traditional dishes—antipasti, pasta, poultry, fish, veal and beef—accented with seasonal ingredients. The wine list contains a knockout selection of southern Italian wines to complete the experience. Southern Italian menu. Lunch, dinner. Closed Sunday; holidays. Bar. Business casual attire. Reservations recommended. $$$

★★SARABETH'S WEST
423 Amsterdam Ave., New York, 212-496-6280; www.sarabethswest.com
American menu. Breakfast, lunch, dinner, brunch. Casual attire. Reservations recommended. Outdoor seating. $$$

★★SARDI'S
234 W. 44th St., New York, 212-221-8440; www.sardis.com
Continental menu. Lunch, dinner, late-night. Closed Monday. Bar. Business casual attire. Reservations recommended. $$$

★★SAVORE
200 Spring St., New York, 212-431-1212; www.savoreny.com
Italian menu. Lunch, dinner, brunch. Bar. Casual attire. Reservations recommended. Outdoor seating. $$$

★★★SAVOY
70 Prince St., New York, 212-219-8570; www.savoynyc.com
Peter Hoffman, the chef and an owner of Soho's comfortable Savoy, has been a proponent of the Greenmarket cooking style for more than 10 years. You'll find him with his tricycle-pulled wagon at the local farmers' markets several times a week, picking produce for his inspired menu of global fare—dishes taken from Spain, Latin America, France, Morocco and Greece, as well as America's various regions— brought to life with simple, brilliant ingredients. The intimate dining room features an open fireplace where many of Hoffman's rustic dishes are cooked in the blazing hearth. American, Mediterranean menu. Lunch, dinner. Closed holidays. Bar. Casual attire. Reservations recommended. $$$

★★SCHILLER'S LIQUOR BAR
131 Rivington St., New York, 212-260-4555; www.schillersny.com
American menu. Breakfast, lunch, dinner, brunch. Bar. Casual attire. Reservations recommended. $$

★★★SEA GRILL
19 W. 49th St., New York, 212-332-7610; www.rapatina.com/seagrill
The Sea Grill is home to some of the most delicious seafood in the city, paired with a magical setting. This lavish, ocean-blue restaurant houses a slick bar and offers prime wintertime views of ice skaters twirling on the rink under the twinkling Christmas tree at Rockefeller Plaza. Summertime brings alfresco dining and lots of icy cocktails to pair up with the fantastic contemporary seafood menu. Crab cakes are its signature, and other dishes—salmon, cod, halibut and skate—are just as special, as the kitchen infuses dishes with techniques and flavors from Asia and the world at large. Seafood, Japanese sushi menu. Lunch, dinner. Closed Sunday; holidays. Bar. Business casual attire. Reservations recommended. Outdoor seating. $$$

★★SERAFINA FABULOUS PIZZA

1022 Madison Ave., New York, 212-734-2676; www.serafinarestaurant.com

Italian menu. Lunch, dinner. Casual attire. **$$$**

★SETTEPANI BAKERY & CAFÉ

196 Lenox Ave., New York, 917-492-4806; www.settepani.com

American, bakery menu. Breakfast, lunch, dinner, brunch. Children's menu. Casual attire. Outdoor seating. **$**

★★★SHUN LEE PALACE

155 E. 55th St., New York, 212-371-8844; www.shunleepalace.com

The lovely, swirling décor of the Adam Tihany-designed dining room sets the scene for restaurateur Michael Tong's haute Chinese cantina where diners sup on sliced duckling with young ginger root and ostrich steak, Hunan style. (This spot is such a New York favorite that a second location has opened on the West Side.) Guest chefs visit frequently from Hong Kong, and the special prix fixe lunch is a deal. Chinese menu. Lunch, dinner. Closed Thanksgiving. Bar. Business casual attire. Reservations recommended. **$$$**

★SIAM GRILL

592 Ninth Ave., New York, 212-307-1363; www.siamgrillnyc.com

Thai menu. Lunch, dinner. Casual attire. **$**

★★★SMITH & WOLLENSKY

49th Street and Third Avenue, New York, 212-753-1530; www.smithandwollensky.com

The original steakhouse for which the national chain was modeled, this 390-seat, wood-paneled dining room is renowned for sirloin steaks and filet mignon but also offers lamb and veal chops. Sides are huge and straightforward, with the likes of creamed spinach and hash browns. Good wines and personable service complete the experience. Steak menu. Lunch, dinner. Closed holidays. Bar. Casual attire. Reservations recommended. Outdoor seating. **$$$**

★★SOBA-YA

229 E. Ninth St., New York, 212-533-6966; www.sobaya-nyc.com

Japanese menu. Lunch, dinner. Casual attire. **$$**

★★★SOUTH GATE

Jumeira Essex House, 154 Central Park South, New York, 212-484-5120; www.jumeirahessexhouse.com

Alain Ducasse moved out and Eleven Madison Park's Kerry Heffernan moved in—after the place got a no-holds-barred facelift that transformed the space into a gleaming, imposing, high-ceilinged dining room focused on floor-to-ceiling windows looking out on the park. The menu hosts satisfactory seafood and experimental plates like seared foie gras with tarragon and muscat and pear wafers. The crowd is what you'd expect at a high-end Midtown hotel restaurant—local expense-account opportunists and well-heeled international guests. Contemporary American menu. Lunch (Monday-Saturday), dinner, Sunday brunch. Bar. Business casual attire. Reservations recommended. **$$$**

★★★SPARKS STEAK HOUSE
210 E. 46th St., New York, 212-687-4855; www.sparkssteakhouse.com

This cavernous steakhouse has a classic old-world charm to it, with oil paintings, etched glass, dark wood paneling and a large bar that is refreshingly homey and welcoming. Portions are huge, so come ready to feast on thick, juicy steaks, burgers, roasts, racks and fish. Steak menu. Lunch, dinner. Closed Sunday; holidays. Bar. Business casual attire. Reservations recommended. $$

★★SPICE MARKET
403 W. 13th St., New York, 212-675-2322; www.jean-georges.com

Pacific-Rim/Pan-Asian menu. Lunch, dinner. Bar. Casual attire. Reservations recommended. Outdoor seating. $$$

★STAGE DELI
834 Seventh Ave., New York, 212-245-7850; www.stagedeli.com

Deli menu. Breakfast, lunch, dinner, late-night. Children's menu. Casual attire. $$

★★STEAK FRITES
225 Varick St., New York, 212-463-7101; www.steakfritesnyc.com

French menu. Lunch, dinner, brunch. Closed holidays. Bar. Casual attire. Outdoor seating. $$

★★★STRIP HOUSE
13 E. 12th St., New York, 212-328-0000; www.striphouse.com

This low-lit restaurant, swathed in deep red fabric and decorated with old black-and white photos of burlesque stars, has a sexy, not tawdry, vibe. The kitchen does a great job with its selection of steakhouse favorites (a half-dozen steaks and chops cooked to perfection) and adds some inspired sides, like truffle-scented creamed spinach, goose fat potatoes and mixed heirloom tomatoes in season. Steak menu. Dinner. Bar. Business casual attire. Reservations recommended. $$$

★★SUEÑOS
311 W. 17th St., New York, 212-243-1333; www.suenosnyc.com

Mexican menu. Dinner, brunch. Bar. Casual attire. Reservations recommended. $$$

★★★★SUGIYAMA
251 W. 55th St., New York, 212-956-0670; www.sugiyama-nyc.com

Zen-like, spare Sugiyama is well known for its prix fixe kaiseki-style meals (multi-course offerings that were originally part of elaborate, traditional Japanese tea ceremonies). At Sugiyama, the kaiseki dishes have evolved into a procession of precious little plates, holding small, beautifully presented portions. Meals are tailored to suit your appetite and preferences and start with sakizuke (an amuse bouche) followed by a seasonal special (zensai), soup, sashimi, sushi, salad and beef or seafood cooked over a hot stone (ishiyaki), among other sumptuous Japanese delicacies. Japanese menu. Dinner. Closed Sunday-Monday. Casual attire. Reservations recommended. $$$

★★★SUMILE

154 W. 13th St., New York, 212-989-7699; www.sumile.com

Sumile, a windowless and soothing Zen space, feels like a movie set with star-quality guests to match. The menu is a celebration of Japanese ingredients and contrasting textures, temperatures and flavors. Innovative plates include striped bass in a nori sauce or roasted miso cod. This is not a place for timid eaters—bring your sense of adventure. Japanese menu. Dinner. Bar. Casual attire. Reservations recommended. Outdoor seating. $$$

★★SURYA

302 Bleecker St., New York, 212-807-7770; www.suryany.com

Indian menu. Lunch, dinner. Bar. Casual attire. Reservations recommended. Outdoor seating. $$

★★★SUSHI OF GARI

402 E. 78th St., New York, 212-517-5340; www.sushiofgari.com

Sushi of Gari is one of those spots frequented by New Yorkers in the know. This restaurant is always packed to capacity with sushi-loving trendsetters, and at times, it's hard to hear yourself order, let alone have a conversation. If you're sticking to the basics, the kanpachi (Japanese yellowtail) and the toro (fatty tuna) are silky and luscious. Japanese, sushi menu. Dinner. Closed Monday. Casual attire. Reservations recommended. $$$

★★★SYLVIA'S

328 Lenox Ave., New York, 212-996-0660; www.sylviassoulfood.com

Simple décor balances with the rich quality of the cuisine at Sylvia's, the self-proclaimed "Queen of Soul Food." Celebrity photos line the walls, and separate dining areas offer various experiences, from relaxed formal to casual breakfast. Menu items include barbecue ribs (served with Sylvia's original Sassy Sauce), Southern-fried chicken and collard greens and farm-raised fried catfish, and desserts like Southern-style banana pudding, peach cobbler and sweet potato pie. Southern, soul food menu. Breakfast, lunch, dinner, brunch. Bar. Children's menu. Casual attire. $$

★★★TABLA

11 Madison Ave., New York, 212-889-0667; www.tablany.com

Tabla is the Indian-inspired concept from restaurant tour-de-force Danny Meyer (Gramercy Tavern, Union Square Café). Chef/partner Floyd Cardoz cleverly peppers his menu with the intoxicating flavors of India—sweet and savory spices, chutneys, meats from a tandoor oven and soft rounds of pillowy, handmade breads. And the result is a delicious introduction to the sumptuous flavors of India. The stunning, bi-level dining room mixes muted jewel-toned accents, rich redwood floors and soaring windows that face Madison Square Park. American, Indian menu. Lunch, dinner. Bar. Reservations recommended. Outdoor seating. $$$

★★★TAMARIND

41-43 E. 22nd St., New York, 212-674-7400; www.tamarinde22.com

The fragrant cuisine of India is served at Tamarind, an elegant restaurant in the Flat-iron District with a lively bar and a serene and beautiful dining room. The attraction

NEW YORK

★
★
★
★
★

here is a menu of dishes showcasing perfect-pitch flavors—spicy, sweet, sour and hot play together wonderfully on the plate. The kitchen serves stunning samosas, naan, poori, chutneys and traditional curries, alongside more contemporary dishes that play to the sophisticated crowd. Indian menu. Lunch, dinner. Bar. Jacket required. Reservations recommended. **$$$**

★★TASTING ROOM
264 Elizabeth St., New York, 212-358-7831; www.thetastingroomnyc.com
American menu. Dinner. Bar. Closed Monday; also one week in summer and one week in winter. Casual attire. Reservations recommended. **$$$**

★★TAVERN ON THE GREEN
Central Park at W. 67th St., New York, 212-873-3200; www.tavernonthegreen.com
American menu. Lunch, dinner, brunch. Bar. Valet parking. **$$$**

★★★TERRACE IN THE SKY
400 W. 119th St., New York, 212-666-9490; www.terraceinthesky.com
Set high in the sky on the top floor of a pre-war Columbia University-area building, this restaurant offers panoramic views of the city and a rich selection of eclectic fare to match. The haute menu of seared sweetbreads, foie gras torchon, smoked salmon, lobster and caviar make dining a luxe event. And Terrace in the Sky is ideal for romance with its elegant linen-topped tables, soft candlelit ambience and views that are truly beyond compare. French, Mediterranean menu. Lunch, dinner, brunch Sunday. Closed Monday. Business casual attire. Reservations recommended. Valet parking. Outdoor seating. **$$$**

★★★THOR
107 Rivington St., New York, 212-475-2600, 800-915-1537; www.hotelonrivington.com
Though its name conjures images of the Norse god of thunder, Thor (an acronym for its location inside the Hotel on Rivington) is a subdued and stylish spot for contemporary takes on American comfort food classics. A sampling from the large selection of small plates could make a meal in itself, from the red beet terrine with horseradish and fresh goat cheese to the crispy cod sticks with malt vinegar foam and tartar sauce. Entrées include butter poached whole lobster with creamed cauliflower and truffles. Late-night the restaurant offers abbreviated versions of the dinner menu along with live music spun by a DJ. Modern American menu. Breakfast, lunch, dinner, late-night, brunch. Bar. Casual attire. Reservations recommended. Valet parking. **$$$**

★★★TOCQUEVILLE
1 E. 15th St., New York, 212-647-1515; www.tocquevillerestaurant.com
Owned by husband Marco Moreira (chef) and wife Jo-Ann Makovitzky (front-of-house manager), Tocqueville will calm you the moment you walk through the tall, blond doors into the small, elegant room warmed with butter-yellow walls. Chef Moreira offers impeccably prepared, inventive New American fare crafted with care from seasonal ingredients handpicked from local farmers and the nearby Greenmarket. American, French menu. Closed Sundays. Lunch, dinner. Bar. Business casual attire. **$$$**

★★★TOWN

15 W. 56th St., New York, 212-582-4445; www.townnyc.com

Located in the Chambers hotel, Town is an oasis of hip and hot, featuring a white-hot, low-lit lounge and bar with zippy, well-made cocktails. Downstairs, the sexy, David Rockwell-designed dining room attracts high-powered media and fashion folks digging into chef/owner Geoffrey Zakarian's modern American fare. American menu. Lunch, dinner, Sunday brunch. Bar. Casual attire. Reservations recommended. **$$$**

★★★TRATTORIA DELL'ARTE

900 Seventh Ave., New York, 212-245-9800; www.trattoriadellarte.com

Trattoria dell'Arte is the perfect choice if Carnegie Hall or a performance at City Center is on your list. This lively and popular restaurant offers easy, approachable Italian cuisine in a comfortable, neighborly setting. The scene here is festive, so expect it to be loud with diners enjoying the generous plates of homemade pastas, selections from the colorful antipasti bar, seafood and meats, all prepared in simple Mediterranean style. Italian menu. Lunch, dinner, brunch. Closed holidays. Bar. Business casual attire. Reservations recommended. **$$$**

★★★TRIBECA GRILL

375 Greenwich St., New York, 212-941-3900; www.tribecagrill.com

This New York icon from Drew Nieporent (Nobu, Montrachet) and partner Robert De Niro is a shining example of how a restaurant should be run. First, hospitality—the service is warm, attentive and knowledgeable without pretension. Second, atmosphere—the Grill is a comfortable, urban dining room with exposed brick walls, oil paintings by Robert De Niro, Sr., and a magnificent cherry wood. Third, food—the kitchen features an approachable, seasonal American menu with dishes from the simple to the ornate. Finally, wine—Tribeca Grill offers an impressive wine program. American menu. Lunch, dinner, late-night, Sunday brunch. Closed holidays. Bar. Children's menu. Casual attire. Reservations recommended. Outdoor seating. **$$$**

★★TURKISH KITCHEN

386 Third Ave., New York, 212-679-6633; www.turkishkitchen.com

Mediterranean, Turkish menu. Lunch, dinner, Sunday brunch. Casual attire. Reservations recommended. **$$$**

★★★UNCLE JACK'S STEAKHOUSE

440 Ninth Ave., New York, 212-244-0005; www.unclejacks.com

This classic steakhouse (which has a new Midtown location as well as a Queens outpost) sticks to well-prepared cuts of beef, from Kobe to USDA prime cuts like the porterhouse or T-bone. Traditional sides such as creamed spinach or garlic mashed potatoes complete every meal, as does the extensive wine selection, which is peppered with bottles from just about every corner of the world. Steak menu. Lunch, dinner. Upscale dress. **$$$**

★★★UNION SQUARE CAFÉ

21 E. 16th St., New York, 212-243-4020; www.unionsquarecafe.com

Union Square Café was the first restaurant from the man who brought New York Gramercy Tavern, Eleven Madison Park, Tabla and Blue Smoke: Danny Meyer. This warm, cheery, bi-level restaurant and bar is still packing in locals and wooing tourists

★
★
★
★
★

with Meyer's signature hospitality, chef Michael Romano's inspired New American fare and an award-winning wine list. While the menu changes with the seasons and often features produce from the Greenmarket across the way, the chef's signature grilled tuna burger deserves special mention. American menu. Lunch, dinner. Closed holidays. Bar. Casual attire. Reservations recommended. $$$

★★★VERITAS

43 E. 20th St., New York, 212-353-3700; www.veritas-nyc.com

At this stylish Gramercy Park gem, you'll find a magnificent wine list that features some 192,000 bottles. Whether you're seated at the bar or tucked into a snug and intimate booth, the restaurant's contemporary American menu is easy to love. Robust flavors and seasonal ingredients make for magical meals. American menu. Dinner. Bar. Business casual attire. Reservations recommended. $$$$

★★VESPA RESTAURANT

1625 Second Ave., New York, 212-472-2050; www.barvespa.com

Italian menu. Lunch, dinner, late-night. Closed holidays. Bar. Casual attire. Outdoor seating. Reservations recommended. $$

★★VICTOR'S CAFÉ

236 W. 52nd St., New York, 212-586-7714; www.victorscafe.com

Cuban menu. Lunch, dinner. Bar. Casual attire. Reservations recommended. $$$

★VIRGIL'S REAL BARBECUE

152 W. 44th St., New York, 212-921-9494; www.virgilsbbq.com

American menu. Lunch, dinner, late-night. Bar. Children's menu. Casual attire. $$$

★★★VONG

200 E. 54th St., New York, 212-486-9592; www.jean-georges.com

At Vong, Jean-Georges Vongerichten, the sensational Alsatian-born chef, creates French riffs on fiery Thai classics, incorporating spices and flavors of the East with a New York sensibility. The restaurant feels like a wild night in the Orient: it's decorated with long, deep banquettes covered with silk pillows in brilliant jewel tones, walls painted crimson red and accented with gold leaf, and a long table showcasing a Buddhist altar. Thai, French menu. Lunch, dinner. Closed holidays. Bar. Casual attire. Reservations recommended. Outdoor seating. $$$

★★★WALLSE

344 W. 11th St., New York, 212-352-2300; www.wallserestaurant.com

Enter this charming restaurant and you are instantly transported to Vienna. Decorated with contemporary art and filled with antique furnishings, deep blue banquettes and a long, romantic stretch of rich mahogany bar (where the cocktails are stellar), chef Kurt -Gutenbrunner's eatery is a personal and delicious ode to the hearty yet delicate cuisine of his native Austria. The thin, golden-crusted Wiener schnitzel should not be missed. A terrific selection of Austrian wines complements the meal, and a nice slice of strudel is the perfect finish. Continental menu. Dinner, brunch. Bar. Casual attire. Reservations recommended. $$$

★★★WATER CLUB

East 30th Street and East River, New York, 212-683-3333; www.thewaterclub.com

Special occasions were made for the Water Club, a lovely restaurant with romantic views of the East River. While poultry and beef are on the menu, the Water Club is known for its seafood. In addition to a gigantic raw bar, you'll find an impressive selection of lobster, scallops, cod, tuna, salmon and other ever-changing selections. On a sunny day, settle in on the deck with a fiery Bloody Mary in hand and watch the ships sail by. American, seafood menu. Lunch, dinner, brunch. Bar. Business casual attire. Reservations recommended. Valet parking. Outdoor seating. **$$$$**

★★★WD-50

50 Clinton St., New York, 212-477-2900; www.wd-50.com

Using his kitchen as a laboratory, chef Wylie Dufresne is intent on creating his own category of American cuisine. The result of a multitude of ingredients and culinary techniques, nothing is as it seems at wd-50, but most everything is delicious. Sup on lamb loin with potato noodles and mustard crumbs or ocean trout with fava beans and lovage. The cocktail and wine list are as equally impressive and adventurous—expect to sample lots of lesser-known grape varietals from all over the globe. American menu. Dinner. Bar. Casual attire. Reservations recommended. **$$$**

★★★WOO LAE OAK

148 Mercer St., New York, 212-925-8200; www.woolaeoaksoho.com

This sleek, cavernous multiplex-style space offers some of the best Korean barbecue in the city. Guests grill marinated meats and seafood to a savory char on cool smokeless grill tables. Melt-in-your-mouth creamy black cod simmered in a sweet-hot, garlicky soy sauce is a one of the restaurant's most famous plates, but there isn't a bad choice on the menu. Korean menu. Lunch, dinner. Bar. Casual attire. Reservations recommended. **$$$**

★★ZARELA

953 Second Ave., New York, 212-644-6740; www.zarela.com

Mexican menu. Lunch, dinner. Bar. Casual attire. Reservations recommended. **$$**

★★★ZOE

90 Prince St., New York, 212-966-6722; www.zoerest.com

Thalia and Stephen Loffredo opened Zoe in the heart of Soho more than 15 years ago, and they have managed to maintain its chic yet comfortable American bistro vibe and inspired cooking. The focal point of the restaurant is the open kitchen with its imported Italian wood-burning oven, which, along with original tile work and pastel walls, creates a rustic-chic atmosphere. The menu offers creative, sophisticated American standards painted with global accents and seasonal flourishes and an extensive, heavily American wine list. There is also a terrific cocktail list and a tempting menu of bar snacks. Contemporary American menu. Lunch, dinner, brunch. Bar. Children's menu. Business casual attire. Reservations recommended. **$$$**

SPAS

★★★★FOUR SEASONS HOTEL NEW YORK SPA

57 E. 57th St., New York, 212-758-5700; www.fourseasons.com

Elegant, yet far from fussy, the spa at the Four Seasons mirrors the hotel's contemporary style. Try the signature Four Seasons in One treatment, which celebrates the seasons with a cooling scrub symbolizing winter, a floral body wrap for spring, a medley of massages for summer and a soothing scalp treatment for fall. In addition to shiatsu, aromatherapy and reflexology, this spa offers a full range of unique massage therapies. Facials harness the power of modern technology with microcurrent lifting, oxygen cellular renewal and DNA molecular regeneration.

★★★★THE PENINSULA SPA BY ESPA NEW YORK

700 Fifth Ave., New York, 212-903-3910, 800-262-9467; www.peninsulaspa.com

The Peninsula Spa is the embodiment of an urban oasis. The facial menu includes deep-cleansing, aromatherapy and sensitive skin treatments, while the specialty facials include signature therapies using June Jacobs or Valmont products. Microdermabrasion targets dull skin, while the body treatments include a papaya hydrating body mask or chai soy mud mask. Stressed-out executives head straight for the massage table to enjoy a Swedish, shiatsu, sports, deep-tissue or aromatherapy massage. Couples and pregnancy massages are also featured here.

★★★★★SPA AT MANDARIN ORIENTAL NEW YORK

80 Columbus Circle, New York, 212-805-8880; www.mandarinoriental.com/newyork

This sleek hotel marries Asian sensibilities with New York panache, and its 14,500-square-foot spa is its showcase. Bamboo and natural stone are used throughout, while Chinese, Ayurvedic, Balinese and Thai healing therapies are the highlight of a visit to this facility. Signature therapies celebrate the spa's Eastern heritage with Lomi Lomi massage, Chakra balancing and Ama releasing Abhyanga. This spa is capped off by a state-of-the-art fitness center, complete with a magnificent pool where swimmers can lap up the city skyline views.

★
★
★
★
☆

NEWBURGH

This manufacturing city was General George Washington's headquarters from April 1, 1782, until August 18, 1783. He announced the end of the Revolutionary War here and officially disbanded the army.

Newburgh is the small urban center of eastern Orange County. West Point, the U.S. Military Academy, lies 12 miles south of town.

Information: Chamber of Commerce of Orange County, 11 Racket Road, Newburgh, 845-567-6229; www.orangeny.org

WHAT TO SEE AND DO

NEW WINDSOR CANTONMENT STATE HISTORIC SITE

374 Temple Hill Road, Vails Gate, 845-561-1765; www.nysparks.state.ny.us

The Cantonment was the last winter encampment (1782-1783) of the Continental Army. Featured are demonstrations of 18th-century military life, including muskets and artillery, woodworking, blacksmithing and camp life activities. Exhibit buildings and picnic area. Monday-Saturday 10 a.m.-5 p.m., Sunday 1-5 p.m.; closed Tuesday

STORM KING ART CENTER

Old Pleasant Hill Road, Mountainville, 845-534-3115; www.stormking.org
This 500-acre sculpture park contains a museum with a permanent collection of 20th-century sculpture. Guided tours. April-mid-November, daily.

WASHINGTON'S HEADQUARTERS STATE HISTORIC SITE

84 Liberty St., Newburgh, 845-562-1195; www.nysparks.state.ny.us
The Jonathan Hasbrouck house (1750) was General George Washington's headquarters for 16½ months at the close of the Revolutionary War (April 1782-August 1783). The adjacent museum has permanent and changing exhibits, audiovisual program, tours and special events. Mid-April-October, Monday-Saturday 10 a.m.-5 p.m. Sunday 1-5 p.m; closed Tuesday; inquire for winter schedule.

HOTELS

★HOWARD JOHNSON INN

95 Route 17K, Newburgh, 845-564-4000, 800-446-4656; www.hojo.com
74 rooms. Complimentary continental breakfast. Wireless Internet access. Pool. Tennis. $

★★QUALITY INN

90 Route 17K, Newburgh, 845-564-9020; www.qualityinn.com
120 rooms. Wireless Internet access. Airport transportation available. Pets accepted. Pool. $

★★RAMADA INN

1289 Route 300, Newburgh, 845-564-4500, 800-272-6232; www.ramada.com
164 rooms. High-speed Internet access. Complimentary continental breakfast. Restaurant, bar. Airport transportation available. Pool. $

RESTAURANTS

★★BEEBS

30 Plank Road, Newburgh, 845-568-6102; www.beebsbistro.net
American menu. Lunch, dinner, brunch. Bar. Casual attire. Reservations recommended. $$

★CAFÉ PITTI

40 Front St., Newburgh, 845-565-1444
Italian menu. Lunch, dinner. Bar. Casual attire. Reservations recommended. Outdoor seating. $

★★COSIMO'S ON UNION

1217 Route 300 Union Ave., Newburgh, 845-567-1556; www.cosimosunion.com
Italian menu. Lunch, dinner. Closed holidays. Bar. Children's menu. Casual attire. Outdoor seating. $$

★★IL CENA'COLO

228 S. Plank Road, Newburgh, 845-564-4494
Italian menu. Lunch. Bar. Business casual attire. Reservations recommended. $$$

NIAGARA FALLS

Higher falls exist, but Niagara puts on a first-class performance. On the border with Canada, the American Falls are 184 feet high, the Canadian Horseshoe, 176 feet. The two are separated by Goat Island. For several hours in the evening, the beauty of the falls continues in a display of colored lights playing over the water.

Originally, after the glacial period, the falls were seven miles downstream at the Niagara escarpment. Rocks have crashed from top to bottom, causing the falls to retreat at a rate averaging about one foot per year. With a flow of more than 200,000 cubic feet of water per second, Niagara has a power potential of about four million horsepower. Electrical production is controlled by agreements between the United States and Canada so that each receives a full share while the beauty of the cataracts is preserved.

Information: Convention and Visitors Bureau, 310 Fourth St., Niagara Falls,
716-285-2400, 800-421-5223; www.niagrafalls-ua.com

WHAT TO SEE AND DO

AQUARIUM OF NIAGARA

701 Whirlpool St., Niagara Falls, 716-285-3575, 800-500-4609;
www.aquariumofniagara.org

See more than 1,500 aquatic animals from around the world here, including sharks, otters, piranha, endangered Peruvian penguins and exotic fish. There is a free outdoor sea lion pool with sessions every 90 minutes and shark feedings on alternate days. Admission: adult $9.50, senior $7.50, children 4-12 $6, children under 3 free. Daily 9 a.m.-5 p.m.; closed holidays.

★
★★
★★
★★
★

ARTPARK

450 S. Fourth St., Lewiston, 716-754-4375, 800-659-7275; www.artpark.net

This 150-acre state park and summer theater is devoted to the visual and performing arts. Events at the 2,300-seat theater with lawn seating include musicals, classical concerts by the Buffalo Philharmonic Orchestra, dance programs and jazz and pop music concerts.

CASTELLANI ART MUSEUM

Niagara University, 5795 Lewiston Road, Niagara Falls,
716-286-8200; www.niagara.edu/cam

The more than 3,700 artworks at this museum range from the Hudson River School to contemporary sculpture. It boasts a first-rate Folk Arts Program, including exhibits, artist demonstrations and performances. Tuesday-Saturday 11 a.m.-5 p.m.; Sunday 1-5 p.m.; closed holidays.

CAVE OF THE WINDS

2153 Juron Drive, Niagara Falls, 716-278-1770; www.niagarafallslive.com

Elevators from Goat Island take you 175 feet deep into the Niagara Gorge. From the elevator, walk over a series of wooden walkways to Hurricane Bridge, where you'll feel the spray at the base of the American Falls. Waterproof garments (including shoes) are supplied. Admission: adults $10, children 6-12 $7, children under 6 free. Daily 9 a.m.-7:30 p.m.

DEVIL'S HOLE STATE PARK

Robert Moses Parkway N., Niagara Falls, 716-284-4691; www.nysparks.state.ny.us

Enjoy views of the lower Whirlpool rapids and Power Authority generating plant, with a walkway leading along the Niagara River. There is also fishing, nature trails and picnicking. Household pets only.

FORT NIAGARA STATE PARK

Route 18F, Youngstown, 716-745-7273; www.nysparks.state.ny.us

Fishing, boating (two launches) hiking trails, playing fields, tennis, cross-country skiing, sledding and a awimming pool with water slide are available. Household pets only. Daily; closed holidays.

FOUR MILE CREEK STATE PARK

1055 Lake Road, Youngstown, 716-745-3802, 800-456-2267; nysparks.state.ny.us

Enjoy fishing, hiking and an available playground, Household pets only; 266 tent and trailer sites. Mid-April-October.

GOAT ISLAND

Niagara Falls, 716-278-1762; www.niagarafallslive.com

Goat Island separates the Canadian Horseshoe and American Falls. Drives and walks in a 70-acre park offer the closest possible views of the falls and upper rapids. Smaller Luna Island and Three Sister Islands can be reached by footbridge. Daily.

MAID OF THE MIST

Prospect Point Niagara Falls, 716-284-4233; www.maidofthemist.com

Maid of the Mist debarks from the base of the Observation Tower at Prospect Point and takes passengers close to the base of the American Falls, then to Horseshoe Falls. Fee includes the use of waterproof clothing. Admission: adults $12.50, children 6-12 $7.50, children under 6 free. June-early September: daily, approximately every 30 minutes.

MARTIN'S FANTASY ISLAND

2400 Grand Island Blvd., Grand Island, 716-773-7591; www.martinsfantasyisland.com

An 80-acre family theme park with more than 100 attractions, including a water park, thrill rides, children's rides, a western town and live shows. Mid-June-early September, daily; also weekends mid-May-mid-June.

NIAGARA FALLS STATE PARK

Robert Moses Parkway, Niagara Falls, 716-278-1770; www.nysparks.state.ny.us

This park, the oldest state park in the nation, provides many views of Niagara Falls and the rapids above and below the cataract from Prospect and Terrapin points, Luna Island and many other locations. It was designed by Frederick Law Olmsted, who also laid out New York's Central Park.

NIAGARA GORGE DISCOVERY CENTER

Robert Moses Parkway, Niagara Falls

Showcases geological formation and history of the falls. Audiovisual presentation. Rock garden, gorge overlook. Memorial Day-October: daily; rest of year: Thursday-Sunday; closed holidays.

★
★
★
★
★

NIAGARA FALLS STATE PARK

Niagara Falls is almost an American tourist cliché. But it's still one of the most spectacular natural sites in the country, and **Niagara Falls State Park** (established in 1885 as Niagara Reservation State Park)—the oldest state park in the United States—offers a wonderful opportunity for a walk. In warmer months, tickets can be purchased for a ride on the Viewmobile, which tours the entire park, so that if you get tired at any point, you can hop on for a ride.

Whether you're up for a stroll or just want to cruise along, start at the **Visitor Center** to obtain maps of the park, watch a wide-screen film about the falls and purchase a Niagara Master Pass. The Pass allows savings on all the major attractions in the park, including the **Observation Tower**, the geological museum, a guided walking tour, the boat tour and more. From the Visitor Center, walk toward the river to the Observation Tower (closed in winter). The Tower rises some 200 feet above the base of the gorge and presents terrific views of all three falls—Horseshoe, American and Bridal Veil. The glass elevator ride is fun, too. The elevator goes down to the dock from which the *Maid of the Mist* boat tour departs. This narrated 30-minute boat ride, in operation since 1846, goes to the base of American Falls and into the ring of Horseshoe Falls.

From the Tower, turn right and follow the pedestrian walkway to the edge of **American Falls**. Follow the walkway upriver and cross the **Goat Island Pedestrian Bridge**. On **Goat Island** are picnic grounds, a restaurant, a gift shop and snack bars. Follow the path to the **Bridal Veil Falls overlook**. Here, too, is the **Cave of the Winds** attraction, a boardwalk that leads right into the Bridal Veil Falls themselves. Continue around the downriver point of the island to **Terrapin Point**. This overlook sits just a few yards from the top of Horseshoe Falls and reveals the full power of the rushing water. From there, walk up the side of the island and follow the pedestrian bridge onto **Three Sisters Island**. This trio of small islands yields an excellent view of the river's upper rapids.

Coming off Three Sisters, either turn right and continue the **Goat Island** loop or turn left and follow the mid-island pathways back to the pedestrian bridge. Continue back past the Visitor Center and onto Main Street. A short way up Main stands the **Aquarium of Niagara** (*701 Whirlpool Street*). The aquarium houses an international collection of fish, a unique colony of endangered Peruvian penguins and California sea lions that perform every 90 minutes. Leaving the aquarium, cross the highway via the pedestrian bridge, and visit the **Schoellkopf Geological Museum** (Robert Moses Parkway at Main Street), which offers a multi-faceted look at the Niagara Gorge and its 12,000-year-old waterfalls. To reap the fullest experience, leave the museum along the riverside walkway and stroll across Rainbow Bridge, which leads to Canada. The bridge yields another spectacular view of all the falls. *Information: www.niagarafallsstatepark.com*

NEW YORK

★
★ ★
★ ★
★

NIAGARA POWER PROJECT VISITOR CENTER

5777 Lewiston Road, Lewiston, 866-697-2386; www.nypa.gov/vc/niagara.htm

Tour the glass-enclosed observation building with outdoor balcony, view the Niagara River Gorge, see the Father Louis Hennepin mural and hydroelectric projects on both sides of river and check out the displays explaining. power generation.Museum traces the development of power and industry at Niagara Falls with hands-on displays. Daily 9 a.m.-5 p.m.; closed holidays.

NIAGARA SCENIC TROLLEY

139 Niagara St., Niagara Falls, 716-278-1796; www.niagarafallsstatepark.com

This three-hour guided train ride travels from Prospect Point to Goat Island and back. It has seven stopovers, including the Cave of the Winds, the *Maid of the Mist*, Terrapin Point and Three Sister Islands. Ride all day for one price. Admission: adults $2, children 6-12 $1, children under 6 free. April-October: daily.

OLD FORT NIAGARA STATE HISTORIC SITE

Robert Moses Parkway, Youngstown, 716-745-7611; www.nysparks.state.ny.us

This restored fort, which dates to 1679 and has been held by France, Great Britain and the United States, played an important role in the French and Indian War and in the War of 1812. The buildings on the site are the oldest in the Great Lakes region and include the "French Castle," constructed by the French in 1726. Exhibits, living history programs, re-enactments; picnicking. Daily from 9 a.m.; closing time varies by season.

PROSPECT PARK VISITOR CENTER

Easter Parkway and Flatbush Ave., Niagara Falls, 716-278-1796;
www.niagarafallsstatepark.com

Tour the Great Lakes Garden, watch video displays and visit the wide-screen theater featuring the movie *Niagara Wonders*. Summer: daily 8 a.m.-10:15 p.m.; winter: daily 8 a.m.-6:15 p.m.

PROSPECT POINT OBSERVATION TOWER

Prospect Park, Robert Moses Parkway, Niagara Falls,
716-278-1770; www.niagarafallsstatepark.com

The 282-foot tower rises adjacent to the American Falls and has an elevator the to gorge below and *Maid of the Mist.* Daily.

RESERVOIR STATE PARK

Routes 31 and 265 and Military Road, Ogdensburg, 716-278-1762;
www.nysparks.state.ny.us

An overlook at the Robert Moses Power Plant Reservoir, tennis, picnicking, playground, ball field, cross-country skiing, biking and snowmobiling are available. Household pets only. Two basketball courts. Daily.

WHIRLPOOL STATE PARK

Robert Moses Parkway and Niagara Rapids Boulevard, Niagara Falls, 716-284-4691;
www.nysparks.state.ny.us/parks/info.asp?parkId=29

Take in splendid views of the famous Niagara River Gorge whirlpool and rapids. Ongiara Trail, nature and hiking trails, picnicking, playground. Daily.

★
★
★
★
★

WINTERGARDEN

Rainbow Blvd., Niagara Falls, 716-286-4940

This seven-story indoor tropical park has more than 7,000 trees, shrubs and flowers, a glass elevators and elevated walkways. It's adjacent to the falls and Convention Center. Daily 9 a.m.-5 p.m.; closed holidays.

HOTELS

★★BEST WESTERN SUMMIT INN

9500 Niagara Falls Blvd., Niagara Falls, 716-297-5050, 800-404-8217;
www.bestwestern.com

88 rooms. Complimentary continental breakfast. Wireless Internet access. Pets accepted. Fitness center. Pool. $

★COMFORT INN THE POINTE

One Prospect Pointe, Niagara Falls,716-284-6835, 800-284-6835;
www.choicehotels.com

118 rooms. Complimentary continental breakfast. Wireless Internet access. Restaurant. Exercise Room. $

★★★CROWNE PLAZA NIAGARA FALLS

300 Third St., Niagara Falls, 716-285-3361, 877-227-6963; www.ichotelsgroup.com

This recently renovated property is a refreshing change from the more touristy hotels (think heart-shaped beds) that pervade Niagara Falls. Rooms are cheerfully decorated with duvet-topped beds. The new, well-equipped fitness center is open 24 hours while the Old Falls Sports Bar & Grille is a prime spot for a burger or a brew while catching a sports game. 391 rooms. Restaurant, bar. Fitness center. Pool. Casino. High-speed Internet access. $$$

★★HOLIDAY INN NIAGARA FALLS

114 Buffalo Ave., Niagara Falls, 716-285-2521, 800-325-3535;
www.holidayinn.com

189 rooms. Restaurant, bar. Children's activity center. $

★★HOLIDAY INN GRAND ISLAND

100 Whitehaven Road, Grand Island, 716-773-1111; www.holidayinn.com

263 rooms. High-speed Internet access. Pets accepted. Center, indoor and outdoor pools. Restaurant, bar. Children's activity center. Whirlpool. $

★★QUALITY INN

7708 Niagara Falls Blvd., Niagara Falls, 716-283-0621, 800-508-8981;
www.qualityinnfalls.com

100 rooms. Wireless Internet access. Restaurant, bar. $

★★★THE RED COACH INN

2 Buffalo Ave., Niagara Falls, 716-282-1459, 866-719-2070; www.redcoach.com

Modeled after the Old Bell Inn in England, the Red Coach Inn has welcomed guests since 1923. Situated just 1,500 feet from the falls and near many other attractions, the English Tudor house has antique furniture, floral curtains and linens, whirlpool tubs and amazing views in its guest accommodations. Most suites have kitchens and fireplaces. Continental breakfast is included and champagne, fruit and cheese await you upon arrival. 19 rooms. Complimentary continental breakfast. Wireless Internet access. Restaurant, bar. $$

RESTAURANTS
★COMO RESTAURANT
2220 Pine Ave., Niagara Falls, 716-285-9341; www.comorestaurant.com
Italian menu. Lunch, dinner. Closed holidays. Bar. Children's menu. Casual attire. Reservations recommended. $$

★HONEY'S NIAGARA FALLS
2002 Military Road, Niagara Falls, 716-297-7900; www.honeysniagara.com
American menu. Lunch, dinner, late-night. Bar. Children's menu. Casual attire. Outdoor seating. $

★★THE RED COACH INN
2 Buffalo Ave., Niagara Falls, 716-282-1459; www.redcoachinn.com
Continental menu. Lunch, dinner. Children's menu. Casual attire. Reservations recommended. Outdoor seating. $$

NORTHPORT
An early English Puritan settlement, the land in and around Northport was purchased from the Matinecock.
Information: www.northportny.com

WHAT TO SEE AND DO
EATON'S NECK LIGHTHOUSE
Lighthouse Road and Huntington Bay, Northport
The second lighthouse built in the United States (1798), this 73-foot-high beacon warns ships more than 17 miles out at sea.

NORTHPORT HISTORICAL SOCIETY AND MUSEUM
215 Main St., Northport, 631-757-9859; www.northporthistorical.org
Changing exhibits of local history include photographs, artifacts, costumes and shipbuilding memorabilia. Tuesday-Sunday 1-4:30 p.m.; closed holidays. Walking tours of village on some Sunday afternoons in spring and summer.

SUFFOLK COUNTY VANDERBILT MUSEUM
180 Little Neck Road, Centerport, 631-854-5555; www.vanderbiltmuseum.org
If you want to see how the other half lived, come visit this grand 24-room mansion that was used as a summer getaway for William K. Vanderbilt II. The furnishings are elegant and the grounds are masterfully maintained. The planetarium is a favorite of visitors and offers an array of special shows. There are special children's performances held at the mansion; check out the Web site for these events.

VANDERBILT MUSEUM PLANETARIUM
180 Little Neck Road, Centerport, 631-854-5555; www.vanderbiltmuseum.org
Watch the Sky shows in the 60-foot, domed Sky Theater and view space-related exhibits in the lobby, including a meteorite and moon globe. Tuesday-Sunday.

NEW YORK

★
★
★
★
★

NORWICH

In central upstate New York, Norwich is a small town surrounded by forests, farms and the bucolic beauty for which this area is famous.

Information: City of Norwich, 607-334-1123; www.norwichnewyork.net

WHAT TO SEE AND DO
BOWMAN LAKE STATE PARK

745 Bliven Sherman Road, Oxford, 607-334-2718;
www.nysparks.state.ny.us/parks/info.asp?parkID=16

This 660-acre park borders on 11,000 acres of state forest land and offers a swimming beach, fishing, paddleboats, rowboats rentals, nature and hiking trails, cross-country skiing, snowmobiling and picnicking.

NORTHEAST CLASSIC CAR MUSEUM

24 Rexford St., Norwich, 607-334-2886; www.classiccarmuseum.org

View the largest collection of Franklin autos in the world, along with Duesenbergs, Cords, Auburns, Packards and more. All are restored, preserved and fully operational. Daily 9 a.m.-5 p.m.; closed holidays.

SPECIAL EVENT
GENERAL CLINTON CANOE REGATTA

168 E. Main St., Norwich, 607-334-9198; chenangocountyfair.homestead.com

The start of this 70-mile flatwater endurance race is at the source of the Susquehanna River on Otsego Lake in Cooperstown. It ends at General Clinton Park in Bainbridge. Memorial Day weekend.

HOTEL
★★HOWARD JOHNSON

75 N. Broad St., Norwich, 607-334-2200; www.hojo.com

86 rooms. Wireless Internet access. Pets Allowed. Fitness center. Restaurant, bar. Pool. $

NYACK

Many outstanding Victorian-style homes and an Edward Hopper art gallery grace this village.

Information: Chamber of Commerce, Nyack, 845-353-2221; www.nyack-ny.com

WHAT TO SEE AND DO
ANTIQUES ON THE HUDSON

366 Highway 9 West, Nyack, 845-358-3751

This collection of more than 75 art, craft and antique shops is located in upper Nyack on the Hudson. Tuesday-Sunday.

RESTAURANTS
★★KING & I

93 Main St., Nyack, 845-358-8588; www.kingandinyack.com

Thai menu. Lunch, dinner. Closed holidays. Bar. Casual attire. $$

★★RIVER CLUB
11 Burd St., Nyack, 845-358-0220; www.nyackriverclub.net
American, seafood menu. Lunch, dinner, brunch. Closed Monday; holidays. Bar. Children's menu. Casual attire. Reservations recommended. Outdoor seating. **$$**

★★WASABI
110 Main St., Nyack, 845-358-7977; www.wasabichi.com
Japanese menu. Lunch, dinner. Closed Monday. Bar. Casual attire. **$$**

OAKDALE
This affluent community on Long Island offers high-style suburban living.
Information: www.islipchamberofcommerce.com

RESTAURANTS
★★★RIVERVIEW
3 Consuelo Place, Oakdale, 631-589-2694
Overlooking the Great South Bay, this elegant waterfront restaurant is a respite for weary sailors. Docks are available for any size boat, and cocktails and appetizers are served on the covered deck. The facilities are reserved on Saturday afternoons. Lunch, dinner, Sunday brunch. Bar. Children's menu. Outdoor seating. **$$**

★★SNAPPER INN
500 Shore Drive, Oakdale, 631-589-0248; www.thesnapperinn.com
Seafood menu. Lunch, dinner, Sunday brunch. Closed Monday; holidays. Bar. Children's menu. Outdoor seating. **$$$**

OGDENSBURG
On the St. Lawrence Seaway, at the mouth of the Oswegatchie River, this busy port and industrial town had its beginnings as an outpost of New France, where the Iroquois were converted to Christianity. In 1837, it was the base from which American sympathizers worked "to free Canada from the yoke of England" in the abortive Patriots' War.
Information: Greater Ogdensburg Chamber of Commerce, 1020 Park St., Ogdensburg, 315-393-3620

WHAT TO SEE AND DO
FREDERIC REMINGTON ART MUSEUM
303 Washington St., Ogdensburg, 315-393-2425; www.fredericremington.org
This is the largest single collection of paintings, sculptures and drawings by Frederic Remington, foremost artist of the Old West. A re-created studio, Belter furniture, glass, china and silver are inside. May-October: daily; rest of year: Wednesday-Sunday; closed legal holidays.

GREENBELT RIVERFRONT PARK
State St. and Riverside Ave., Ogdensburg, 315-393-1980
Deep-water marina and launching ramp, picnicking, barbecue pits and lighted tennis courts. Daily.

JACQUES CARTIER STATE PARK

Route 12, Morristown, 315-375-6371, 800-456-2267; www.nysparks.com/parks

Swimming beach, bathhouse, fishing, boating (launch, anchorage); picnicking, playground, tent and trailer sites. Late May-early October.

OGDENSBURG, NY-JOHNSTOWN, ONTARIO INTERNATIONAL BRIDGE

One Bridge Plaza, Ogdensburg, 315-393-4080; www.ogdensport.com

This 13,510 feet long was opened September 1960 and boasts clear views of the St. Lawrence Valley and Seaway marine terminal. Duty-free shop.

SPECIAL EVENT
INTERNATIONAL SEAWAY FESTIVAL

330 Ford St., Ogdensburg, 315-393-3620; www.ogdensburgny.com

Summer festival includes concerts, fireworks, parade and canoe race. Last full week in July.

HOTELS
★★QUALITY INN GRAN-VIEW

6765 State Highway 37, Ogdensburg, 315-393-4550, 877-424-6423; www.qualityinn.com

46 rooms. Complimentary continental breakfast. Wireless Internet access. Exercise room. Pets accepted. Restaurant, bar. No Handicapped. $

★★STONE FENCE LODGING

7191 State Highway, 37 River Drive, Ogdensburg, 315-393-1545, 800-253-1545; www.stonefenceresort.com

31 rooms. Wireless Internet access. Boating. Fitness Center. Restaurant. Whirlpool. Pets accepted. Pool. Tennis. $

RESTAURANT
★SHOLETTE'S STEAK & ALE

1000 Linden St., Ogdensburg, 315-393-5172

Italian, American menu. Lunch, dinner. Closed holidays. Bar. Children's menu. $$

OLD FORGE

In almost any season, there is fun in this Adirondack resort town, located in the Fulton Chain of Lakes region—everything from hunting, fishing, snowmobiling and skiing to basking on a sunny beach.

Information: Visitor Information Center, Highway 28, Old Forge, 315-369-6983; www.oldforgeny.com

WHAT TO SEE AND DO
FERN PARK

South Shore Road, Old Forge, 315-357-5501; www.inletny.com

Hiking, cross-country skiing, snowshoeing, biking, ice skating, baseball, volleyball, basketball; special events.

MCCAULEY MOUNTAIN

3140 State Route 28, Old Forge, 315-369-3225; www.mccauleyny.com

Double chairlift, two T-bars, two rope tows, pony lift; patrol, school, rentals; snow-making; cafeteria. Longest run ¾ miles; vertical drop 633 feet. Thanksgiving-April, Monday and Wednesday-Sunday. Half-day rates. Chairlift to top of McCauley Mountain also operates June-October daily. Picnic area.

OLD FORGE LAKE CRUISE

Route 28, Main St., Old Forge, 315-369-6473; www.oldforgecruises.com

Cruises on the Fulton Chain of Lakes (28 miles). Pets not allowed. Memorial Day-Columbus Day. Also showboat and dinner cruises.

HOTEL
★ADIRONDACK LODGE OLD FORGE

2752 State Route 28, Old Forge, 315-369-6836; www.adirondacklodgeoldforge.com

52 rooms. Complimentary continental breakfast. Pets accepted. Pool. Tennis. **$**

RESTAURANT
★★OLD MILL

Highway 28, Old Forge, 315-369-3662; www.oldmilloldforge.com

American menu. Dinner. Closed November-December. Bar. Children's menu. **$$**

OLEAN

Only seven years after the landing of the Pilgrims, a Franciscan father was led by Native Americans to a mystical spring near the present city of Olean. There he found what he called "thick water which ignited like brandy." It was petroleum. Olean (from the Latin *oleum*, meaning "oil") was once an oil-boom town; now it is a manufacturing and retail center.

Information: Greater Olean Chamber of Commerce, 120 N. Union St., Olean, 716-372-4433; www.oleanny.com

WHAT TO SEE AND DO
FRIEDSAM MEMORIAL LIBRARY

Olean and Allegany, St. Bonaventure, 716-375-2323; www.sbu.edu/library

The wide-ranging collection includes: paintings by Rembrandt, Rubens and Bellini; works by 19th-century and contemporary artists; American Southwest and pre-Columbian pottery and porcelain collections; and rare books. September-mid-June: Monday-Thursday 8 a.m.-midnight, Friday to 8 p.m., Saturday 10 a.m.-6 p.m., Sunday noon-midnight; rest of year: Monday-Friday; closed school holidays.

RESTAURANTS
★★BEEF 'N' BARREL

146 N. Union St., Olean, 716-372-2985; www.beefnbarrel.com

American menu. Lunch, dinner. Closed Sunday; holidays. Bar. Children's menu. Casual attire. **$$**

★★OLD LIBRARY

116 S. Union St., Olean, 716-372-2226, 877-241-4348;
www.oldlibraryrestaurant.com

American menu. Lunch, dinner, late-night, Sunday brunch. Closed holidays. Bar. Children's menu. Casual attire. **$$**

ONEIDA

Perhaps the best known of the 19th-century American "Utopias" was established at Oneida in 1848 by John Humphrey Noyes, leader of the "Perfectionists." The group held all property in common, practiced complex marriage and undertook other social experiments. Faced with hostile attacks by the local population, the community was dissolved in 1880. In 1881, the Oneida Community became a stock corporation, and the silverware factory it built remains a major industry, making Community Plate and William A. Rogers silver.

Information: The Greater Oneida Chamber of Commerce, 136 Lenox Ave.,
Oneida, 315-363-4300

WHAT TO SEE AND DO

MADISON COUNTY HISTORICAL SOCIETY, COTTAGE LAWN MUSEUM

435 Main St., Oneida, 315-363-4136; www.mchs1900.org

An 1849 Gothic Revival cottage designed by Alexander Jackson Davis includes a Victorian period rooms, historical and traditional craft archives, 1862 stagecoach, 1853 gym and adjacent agricultural museum and changing exhibits. Monday-Friday, 10 a.m.-4 p.m.

THE MANSION HOUSE

170 Kenwood Ave., Oneida, 315-361-3671; www.oneidacommunity.org

The communal home built in the 1860s. Tours Wednesday-Saturday, morning and afternoon tours, also Sunday afternoon tours.

VERONA BEACH STATE PARK

Route 13 and Oneida Lake, Oneida, 315-762-4463, 800-456-2267;
www.nysparks.com/parks/info.asp?parkID=26

Located on the shores of Lake Oneida, this park offers a swimming beach, bathhouse, fishing, hiking (all year), cross-country skiing, snowmobiling, picnicking, baseball, basketball, fishing, horse trails, a playground, concessions and tent and trailer sites.

SPECIAL EVENTS

CRAFT DAYS

Madison County Historical Society Museum, 435 Main St., Oneida, 315-363-4136;
www.mchs1900.org

Traditional craftsmen demonstrate their skills; food, entertainment. First weekend after Labor Day weekend.

MADISON COUNTY HOP FEST

Madison County Historical Society Museum, 435 Main St., Oneida, 315-363-4136;
www.mchs1900.org

Celebrates historic buildings. Mid-September.

HOTELS

★SUPER 8

215 Genesee St., Oneida, 315-363-5168; www.super8.com

39 rooms. Complimentary continental breakfast. Business center. High-speed Internet access. $

★★TURNING STONE CASINO RESORT

5218 Patrick Road, Verona, 315-361-7711, 800-771-7711; www.turning-stone.com

281 rooms. Restaurant. Casino. Golf. $$

ONEONTA

Oneonta lies deep in the hills at the western edge of the Catskills, and it was here in 1883 that the Brotherhood of Railroad Trainmen had its beginnings. A branch of the State University College of New York is located here.

Information: City Hall, 258 Main St., Oneonta, 607-432-6450; www.oenonta.ny.us

WHAT TO SEE AND DO

GILBERT LAKE STATE PARK

Route 12, Laurens, 607-432-2114, 800-456-2267;
www.nysparks.state.ny.us/parks/info.asp?parkID=19

Swimming, fishing, boating, picnicking, hiking and snowmobiling are offered at this park, which sits at the foothill of the Catskills. Playground, concession, tent and trailer sites, cabins. Mid-May-mid-October, daily.

HANFORD MILLS MUSEUM

County Routes 10 and 12, East Meredith, 607-278-5744, 800-295-4992;
www.hanfordmills.org

The water-powered sawmill, gristmill and woodworking complex were built in 1840. Ten-foot diameter by 12-foot width overshot waterwheel drives machinery. Demonstrations of antique machine collection, tours. Special events. Picnicking. May-October, daily.

HARTWICK COLLEGE

5200 South Park Ave., Hamburg, 607-431-4200; www.hartwick.edu

Library and archives house collections of works by Willard Yager, Judge William Cooper and John Christopher Hartwick papers. Hall of Science displays fresh and saltwater shells and the Hoysradt Herbarium. Anderson Center for the Arts. Yager Museum contains more than 10,000 American Indian artifacts and the Van Ess Collection of Renaissance and Baroque Art. September-May: daily; rest of year: by appointment only.

NATIONAL SOCCER HALL OF FAME

Wright National Soccer Campus, 18 Stadium Circle, Oneonta, 607-432-3351;
www.soccerhall.org

Displays and exhibits on "the beautiful game" range from youth, amateur and collegiate to professional soccer; trophies, mementos, historical items, uniforms. Interactive games. Video theater with soccer films dating from 1930s. Labor Day-Memorial Day: daily 10 a.m.-5 p.m.; rest of year: daily 9 a.m.-6 p.m.; closed holidays.

HOTELS

★★★CATHEDRAL FARMS COUNTRY INN
4158 Highway 23, Oneonta, 607-432-7483, 800-327-6790
This country inn—a servants' house built in the 1930s—is located 20 minutes from Cooperstown and the Baseball Hall of Fame. The property offers rooms and suites, an outdoor heated pool and Jacuzzi and an onsite restaurant. 19 rooms. Restaurant. Whirlpool. **$$**

★★HOLIDAY INN
5206 State Highway 23, Oneonta, 607-433-2250; www.holiday-inn.com
120 rooms. Restaurant, bar. Pets accepted. Pool. **$**

RESTAURANTS

★CHRISTOPHER'S
Route 23, Southside Oneonta, 607-432-2444; www.christopherslodging.com
American menu. Lunch, dinner. Bar. Children's menu. Guest rooms available. **$$**

★★FARMHOUSE
5649 State Highway 7, Oneonta, 607-432-7374; www.farmhouserestaurant.com
American, seafood menu. Dinner, Sunday brunch. Bar. Children's menu. **$$**

★★SABATINI'S LITTLE ITALY
Route 23 Southside, Oneonta, 607-432-3000; www.sabatinislittleitaly.com
Italian, American menu. Dinner, lunch. Closed holidays. Bar. **$$**

OSWEGO

Oswego's location on Lake Ontario, at the mouth of the Oswego River, made it an important trading post and a strategic fort as early as 1722. Today, as a seaway port and northern terminus of the State Barge Canal, Oswego carries on its industrial and shipping tradition. The town has the largest U.S. port of entry on Lake Ontario.
Information: Chamber of Commerce, 44 E. Bridge St., 315-343-7681; www.oswegochamber.com

WHAT TO SEE AND DO

FAIR HAVEN BEACH STATE PARK
Route 104A, Oswego, 315-947-5205, 800-456-2267; wwww.nysparks.state.ny.us
Swimming beach, bathhouse, fishing, boating (rentals, launch, anchorage); hiking trails, cross-country skiing, picnicking, playground, concession, camping, tent and trailer sites, cabins. Late April-early November.

FORT ONTARIO STATE HISTORIC SITE
1 E. Fourth St., Oswego, 315-343-4711; www.nysparks.state.ny.us
The original fort was built by the British in 1755, taken by the French, and eventually used as a U.S. Army installation (1840-1946). Strategic fort commanded the route from the Hudson and Mohawk valleys to the Great Lakes. Restored site re-creates life at a military installation during the 1860s. Exhibits; guided and self-guided tours. Tuesday-Sunday 10 a.m.-4:30 p.m. Open from 1 May-31 October.

H. LEE WHITE MARINE MUSEUM

W. First Street Pier, Oswego, 315-342-0480; www.hleewhitemarinemuseum.com
Museum features 12 rooms of artifacts, models, documents and paintings relating to 300 years of Oswego Harbor and Lake Ontario history. Admission: adults $5, children 5-12 $3, children under 5 free. Daily 1-5 p.m.; July-August daily 10 a.m.-5 p.m.

OSWEGO COUNTY HISTORICAL SOCIETY

135 E. Third St., Oswego, 315-343-1342
Richardson-Bates House Museum includes local historical material, period furnishings and changing exhibits. Tuesday-Friday; Saturday, Sunday afternoons.

SELKIRK SHORES STATE PARK

7101 State Route 3, Pulaski, 315-298-5737, 800-456-2267;
www.nysparks.state.ny.us
Fishing, canoeing, hiking, cross-country skiing and picnicking available at park and campsite overlooking Lake Ontario. Beach, playground, concession, tent and trailer sites.

HOTELS

★BEST WESTERN CAPTAIN'S QUARTERS

26 E. First St., Oswego, 315-342-4040; www.bestwestern.com
93 rooms. Complimentary continental breakfast. Fitness center. Pool. High-speed Internet access. $

★DAYS INN

101 State Route 104, Oswego, 315-343-3136; www.daysinn.com
44 rooms. Complimentary continental breakfast. High-speed Internet access. Pets accepted. $

★OSWEGO

180 E. 10th St., Oswego, 315-342-6200; www.oswegoinn.com
13 rooms. Complimentary continental breakfast. $

OWEGO

In the southeast corner of the Finger Lakes Region, Owego sits on the Susquehanna River, which offers some of the state's best walleye fishing. Not an angler? Owego has historic homes to tour, farms to visit and plenty of charm to soak up.
Information: Tioga County Chamber of Commerce, 80 North Ave., Owego,
607-687-2020; www.visittioga.com

WHAT TO SEE AND DO

TIOGA COUNTY HISTORICAL SOCIETY MUSEUM

110 Front St., Owego, 607-687-2460; www.tiogahistory.org
American Indian artifacts, folk art; pioneer crafts; exhibits on early county commerce, industry and military history. Tuesday-Friday 1-4 p.m., Saturday 10 a.m.-4 p.m.; closed holidays.

TIOGA GARDENS

2217 State Route 17C, Owego, 607-687-2940; www.tiogagardens.com

Garden center features tropical plant conservatory with solar dome, greenhouses, a two-acre water garden with water lilies and a Japanese garden. Daily.

TIOGA SCENIC RAILROAD

25 Delphine St., Owego, 607-687-6786

Scenic rail excursions available. Early May-late October.

HOTEL

★★OWEGO TREADWAY INN

1100 State Route 17C, Owego, 607-687-4500; www.owegotreadway.com

92 rooms. Restaurant, bar. Fitness center. Pool. $

OYSTER BAY

On the North Shore of Long Island, this town gets its name from the oysters that have made Long Island famous with seafood-lovers. History buffs love Oyster Bay, too: President Teddy Roosevelt's summer residence, Sagamore Hill, is here.

Information: Chamber of Commerce, 120 South St., Oyster Bay, 516-922-6464; www.visitoysterbay.com

WHAT TO SEE AND DO

PLANTING FIELDS ARBORETUM AND COE HALL

1395 Planting Fields Road, Oyster Bay, 516-922-9201; www.plantingfields.org

The 409-acre estate of the late William Robertson Coe has, landscaped gardens (150 acres), large collections of azaleas and rhododendrons and a self-guided tour. Guided tours available; nature trails; greenhouses. Daily 9 a.m.-5 p.m.; closed holidays.

RAYNHAM HALL MUSEUM

20 W. Main St., Oyster Bay, 516-922-6808; www.raynhamhallmuseum.org

This historic colonial house museum with a Victorian wing was the home of Samuel Townsend, a prosperous merchant, and the headquarters for the Queen's Rangers during the Revolutionary War. Victorian garden. July-Labor Day: Tuesday-Sunday noon-5 p.m.; rest of year: 1-5 p.m.

SAGAMORE HILL NATIONAL HISTORIC SITE

20 Sagamore Hill Road, Oyster Bay, 516-922-4788; www.nps.gov/sahi

The former home of President Theodore Roosevelt, this 23-room mansion has been painstakingly preserved and shows off many animal trophies that Roosevelt caught during his legendary hunting trips. The house also features exotic gifts that Roosevelt received from his overseas trips, as well as original furnishings and paintings. Nearby is the Theodore Roosevelt Sanctuary, which cares for injured birds and offers nature walks. The whole experience is a must for history buffs and fans of this colorful, larger-than-life president. Daily 9:30 a.m.-4 p.m.; closed Monday and Tuesday, October-May.

THEODORE ROOSEVELT SANCTUARY & AUDUBON CENTER

134 Cove Road, Oyster Bay, 516-922-3200

Owned by the National Audubon Society, the memorial contains 12 acres of forest and nature trails. The sanctuary serves as a memorial to Theodore Roosevelt's pioneering conservation achievements. Museum contains displays on Roosevelt and the conservation movement; bird exhibits. Adjacent in Young's Cemetery is Theodore Roosevelt's grave. Trails, bird-watching, library. Daily.

SPECIAL EVENTS

FRIENDS OF THE ARTS LONG ISLAND SUMMER FESTIVAL

Planting Fields Arboretum, 1395 Planting Fields Road, Oyster Bay, 516-922-0061; www.fotapresents.org/summerfest.asp

For the ultimate evening in great music and relaxation, venture out to this beautiful 409-acre Gold Coast estate. The annual festival specializes in blues, jazz and easy listening concerts and has offered up such artists as Michael Feinstein, David Sanborn, David Benoit and Natalie Cole. Forget the more expensive pavilion seats and buy lawn seats. This way you can bring a picnic with your favorite wines and cheeses. Arrive at least 1½ hours before the concert starts to scope out your spot on the lawn and to spend some time admiring the flower gardens. One negative: the concerts go on rain or shine. Evenings in June-September.

OYSTER FESTIVAL

120 South St., Oyster Bay, 516-922-6464; www.visitoysterbay.com

Street festival with arts and crafts usually occurs the weekend after Columbus Day.

HOTEL

★EAST NORWICH INN

6321 Northern Blvd., East Norwich, 516-922-1500, 800-334-4798; www.eastnorwichinn.com

65 rooms. Complimentary continental breakfast. Fitness center. Business center. Pool. $

RESTAURANTS

★CANTERBURY ALES OYSTER BAR & GRILL

46 Audrey Ave., Oyster Bay, 516-922-3614; www.canterburyalesrestaurant.com

Seafood menu. Lunch, dinner, Sunday. brunch. Closed holidays. Bar. Children's menu. $$

★★★MILL RIVER INN

160 Mill River Road, Oyster Bay, 516-922-7768; www.millriverinn.com

The menu at this creative American restaurant changes weekly. Sample such favorites as Australian rack of lamb with a fig and almond couscous or the pan-seared diver scallops with toasted pine nuts. Dinner. Closed holidays. Bar. Reservations recommended. $$$

PALMYRA

In 1820, in the frontier town of Palmyra, 15-year-old Joseph Smith had a vision that led to the founding of a new religious group—the Church of Jesus Christ of Latter-Day Saints, better known as the Mormon Church. Members of the LDS church believe the Angel Moroni led Smith to Palmyra's Hill Cumorah, where he unearthed golden tablets he translated into the Book of Mormon.

Information: www.palmyrany.com

WHAT TO SEE AND DO
ALLING COVERLET MUSEUM
122 William St., Palmyra, 315-597-6737; www.historicpalmyrany.com/allingintro.htm
Largest collection of American Jacquard and hand-woven coverlets in the country. June-September, daily 1-4 p.m. or by appointment.

BOOK OF MORMON HISTORIC PUBLICATION SITE
217 E. Main St., Palmyra, 315-597-5982; www.hillcumorah.org
Between June 1829 and March 1830, the first edition of 5,000 copies of the Book of Mormon was printed here at a cost of $3,000. Daily; also summer evenings.

HILL CUMORAH
603 State Route 21, Palmyra, 315-597-5851; www.hillcumorah.org
This is the site where the golden plates from which Joseph Smith translated the Book of Mormon were delivered to him. A monument to the Angel Moroni now stands on the hill. The visitors center has religious exhibits and films. Daily; also summer evenings.

JOSEPH SMITH HOME
29 Stafford Road, Palmyra, 315-597-4383; www.hillcumorah.org
Mormon leader Joseph Smith lived in this house as a young man; period décor (1820-1830). Nearby is the Sacred Grove where he had his first vision.

PALMYRA HISTORICAL MUSEUM
132 Market St., Palmyra, 315-597-6981; www.historicpalmyrany.com
Displays feature 19th-century items including furniture, toys and household items. June-September, Saturday and Sunday afternoons or by appointment.

PHELPS GENERAL STORE MUSEUM
140 Market St., Palmyra, 315-597-6981; www.historicpalmyrany.com
Contains displays of turn-of-the-century merchandise and household furnishings. June-September, Saturday and Sunday afternoons or by appointment.

SPECIAL EVENT
THE HILL CUMORAH PAGEANT
603 State Route 21, Palmyra, 315-597-5851; www.hillcumorah.org
More than 600 cast members re-enact scenes from the Book of Mormon at Hill Cumorah. The Sacred Grove is open for self-guided tours all year-round. Seating for 6,500. Early-mid-July.

HOTEL
★★QUALITY INN
125 N. Main St., Newark, 315-331-9500; www.qualityinn.com
107 rooms. Restaurant, bar. Pets accepted. High-speed Internet access. Pool. **$**

PEEKSKILL
This city is named for Jan Peek, a Dutchman who set up a trading post on the creek that runs along the northern edge of town.
Information: Peekskill/Cortlandt Chamber of Commerce, 1 S. Division St., Peekskill, 914-737-3600; www.ci.peekskill.ny.us

HOTELS

★★BEAR MOUNTAIN INN

Bear Mountain Complex, Bear Mountain, 845-786-2731; www.bearmountaininn.com
60 rooms. Complimentary continental breakfast. Restaurant, bar. Pool. $

★★PEEKSKILL INN

634 Main St., Peekskill, 914-739-1500, 800-526-9466; www.peekskillinn.com
53 rooms. Complimentary continental breakfast. Restaurant, bar. Pool. $

RESTAURANTS

★★CRYSTAL BAY

5 John Walsh Blvd., Peekskill, 914-737-8332; www.crystal-bay.com
International menu. Lunch, dinner, Sunday brunch. Closed holidays. Bar. Children's menu. Casual attire. Reservations recommended. Outdoor seating. $$

★★MONTEVERDE RESTAURANT AT OLDSTONE

28 Bear Mountain Bridge Road, Cortlandt Manor, 914-739-5000;
www.monteverderestaurant.com
Continental menu. Lunch, dinner. Closed Tuesday. Bar. Casual attire. Reservations recommended. Outdoor seating. $$

★★SUSAN'S

12 N. Division St., Peekskill, 914-737-6624; www.susansinpeekskill.com
American menu. Lunch, dinner. Bar. Casual attire. Reservations recommended. $$

229

PENN YAN

Legend has it that the first settlers here, Pennsylvanians and Yankees, could not agree on a name for their town and finally compromised on Penn Yan. The town lies at the north end of Y-shaped Keuka Lake in resort country. Nearby is Keuka College.
Information: Yates County Chamber of Commerce, 2375 Highway 14A, Penn Yan, 315-536-3111, 800-868-9283; www.yatesny.com

WHAT TO SEE AND DO

KEUKA LAKE STATE PARK

3370 Pepper Road, Bluff Point, 315-536-3666; www.nysparks.state.ny.us
Swimming beach, bathhouse, fishing, boating (launch); hiking, cross-country skiing, playground, tent and trailer sites. May-October.

OLIVER HOUSE MUSEUM

200 Main St., Penn Yan, 315-536-7318; www.yatespast.com
Brick house built in 1852 that originally belonged to the Oliver family, distinguished by three generations of physicians. Now headquarters for the Yates County Genealogical and Historical Society operated as a local history museum. Includes period rooms, changing local history exhibits, research room. Tuesday-Friday. 9 a.m.-4 p.m.; Saturday by appointment.

THE OUTLET TRAIL

Keuka Street, Penn Yan to Seneca Street, Dresden

Six-mile trail that follows an abandoned railroad path built in 1884. The Outlet drops almost 300 feet between Keuka and Seneca Lakes, with waterfalls, wildlife and remains of early settlements and mills along the way.

SPECIALTY LODGING

FOX INN

158 Main St., Penn Yan, 315-536-3101, 800-901-7997; www.foxinnbandb.com

This Greek Revival inn, located in the winery-dotted countryside of the Finger Lakes region, has a stately white-pillared entrance and brick façade and formal, luxurious rooms outfitted with rich antiques. At breakfast, try the Fox Inn green flannel hash, poached eggs served on a bed of sautéed spinach with corned beef hash. Five rooms. Complimentary full breakfast. $

PIERMONT

In the last few years, Piermont has gotten a makeover. The town is now home to boutiques, art galleries, restaurants dishing up delicious meals and swanky condos.
Information: www.nyack-ny.com

RESTAURANT

★★★XAVIAR'S AT PIERMONT

506 Piermont Ave., Piermont, 845-359-7007, 845-424-3124; www.xaviars.com

This eccentric restaurant is located in a country club, and although the sparse room and banquet hall feel are odd, there is something appealing about its quirkiness. Luckily, the contemporary American food, the likes of a warm salad of sweetbreads and morels and Alaskan halibut served in a kale net, holds its own. American menu. Lunch, dinner. Closed Monday-Tuesday; holidays. Bar. Business casual attire. Reservations recommended. $$$

PITTSFORD

This darling town about eight miles from Rochester has a downtown district that is the definition of quaint. Shops, cafes and restaurants line the sidewalks. Stop for a pleasant afternoon in rural New York.
Information: www.townofpittsford.com

RESTAURANTS

★★★RICHARDSON'S CANAL HOUSE

1474 Marsh Road, Pittsford, 585-248-5000; www.richardsonscanalhouse.net

This is the oldest working tavern on the Erie Canal and is on the National Register of Historic Buildings. The bright-yellow structure, dating back to the early 1800s, houses a New American dining room and a pub for more casual fare. Start your meal with the house-smoked apple sausage with grainy mustard and black lentils before moving on to the perfectly prepared steak frites or grilled Block Island swordfish. American menu. Dinner. Closed Sunday; holidays. Bar. Historic inn. Outdoor seating. $$$

★VILLAGE COAL TOWER

9 Schoen Place, Pittsford, 585-381-7866; www.villagecoaltower.com

Breakfast, lunch, dinner. Closed holidays. Children's menu. Outdoor seating. $

HOTEL

★★BROOKWOOD INN

800 Pittsford-Victor Road, Pittsford, 585-248-9000, 800-396-1194;
www.thebrookwoodinn.com

108 rooms. Restaurant, bar. Airport transportation available. High-speed Internet access. Fitness center. Pool. **$**

PLATTSBURGH

The Cumberland Bay area of Lake Champlain has been a military base since colonial days. Plattsburgh, at the mouth of the Saranac River, has a dramatic history in the struggle for U.S. independence. The British won the Battle of Lake Champlain off these shores in 1776. Here, in 1814, Commodore Thomas Macdonough defeated a British fleet from Canada by an arrangement of anchors and winches that enabled him to swivel his vessels completely around, thus giving the enemy both broadsides. While this was going on, U.S. General Alexander Macomb polished off the Redcoats on shore with the help of school boys and the local militia. Today, Plattsburgh accommodates both industry and resort trade.

Information: Plattsburgh-North Country Chamber of Commerce, 7601 Highway 9,
Plattsburgh, 518-563-1000; www.northcountrychamber.com

WHAT TO SEE AND DO

ALICE T. MINER COLONIAL COLLECTION

9618 Main St., Chazy, 518-846-7336; www.minermuseum.org

Antiques, colonial household items and appliances are inside this 1824 house, along with a sandwich glass collection. Gardens. February-late December, Tuesday-Saturday 10 a.m.-4 p.m.; closed January.

KENT-DELORD HOUSE MUSEUM

17 Cumberland Ave., Plattsburgh, 518-561-1035; www.kentdelordhouse.org

Historic 1797 house served as British officers' quarters during the Battle of Plattsburgh (War of 1812) and has period furnishings. Tours March-December: Tuesday-Saturday afternoons; rest of year: by appointment only; closed holidays.

HOTELS

★★BEST WESTERN THE INN AT SMITHFIELD

446 Route 3, Plattsburgh, 518-561-7750, 800-243-4656; www.bestwestern.com

120 rooms. Complimentary breakfast. Pets accepted. Pool. Fitness center. High-speed Internet access. **$**

★DAYS INN & SUITES

8 Everleth Drive, Plattsburgh, 518-561-0403; www.daysinn.com

112 rooms. Complimentary continental breakfast. High-speed Internet access. Fitness center. Business center. Pool. **$**

★★HOLIDAY INN

412 Route 3, Plattsburgh, 518-561-5000; www.holiday-inn.com

102 rooms. Restaurant, bar. Whirlpool. Fitness center. High-speed Internet access. Pool. **$**

RESTAURANT

★★★ANTHONY'S

538 Route 3, Plattsburgh, 518-561-6420; www.anthonysrestaurantandbistro.com

An elegant, candlelit setting and unobtrusive, crisp service round out the dining experience at Anthony's where the menu includes such continental-American fare as grilled lamb sausage with an apple-mango chutney and broiled sea scallops with an herb butter. American menu. Lunch, dinner. Closed holidays. Bar. Children's menu. Casual attire. **$$**

PORT JEFFERSON

On a harbor that leads to the Long Island Sound, Port Jefferson is all about water. Swim, boat, fish, sail—you get the picture. Port Jefferson also has art galleries, restaurants and cafes, and shops worth a peek.

Information: Greater Port Jefferson Chamber of Commerce, 118 W. Broadway, Port Jefferson, 631-473-1414; www.portjeffchamber.com

WHAT TO SEE AND DO

FERRY TO BRIDGEPORT, CONNECTICUT

102 W. Broadway, Port Jefferson, 631-473-0286, 888-443-3779; www.bpjferry.com

Car and passenger service offered. Daily.

THOMPSON HOUSE

93 N. Country Road, Setauket, 631-692-4664

Historian Benjamin F. Thompson was born in 1784 in this 1704 saltbox house, which is now authentically furnished to depict 18th-century life on rural Long Island. Herb garden. Memorial Day-Columbus Day, Saturday-Sunday 1-5 p.m.; also Friday in July-August.

HOTELS

★★DANFORD'S ON THE SOUND

25 E. Broadway, Port Jefferson, 631-928-5200, 800-332-6367; www.danfords.com

86 rooms. High-speed Internet access. Restaurant, bar. Spa. Fitness center. **$$$**

★★★THE INN AND SPA AT EAST WIND

5720 Route 25A, Wading River, 631-929-3500; www.eastwindlongisland.com

This Long Island resort is set on 25 acres of landscaped grounds. Rooms and suites are traditionally decorated but feature modern amenities like free wireless Internet access and CD players. The new Spa at East Wind is a sprawling, soothing space with plenty of treatment rooms for hot stone massages, body wraps and facials. The onsite Desmond's restaurant is the perfect spot for romantic dinner. 50 rooms. Wireless Internet access. Spa. Pool. Business center. Fitness center. Restaurant, bar. **$$$**

RESTAURANTS

★★25 EAST AMERICAN BISTRO

25 E. Broadway, Port Jefferson, 631-928-5200; www.danfords.com

American menu. Breakfast, lunch, dinner, Sunday brunch. Bar. **$$**

★★★DESMOND'S

5720 Route 25A, Wading River, 631-846-2335; www.eastwindlongisland.com

This classic restaurant located inside the Inn at East Wind serves everything from sea scallops wrapped in bacon to porterhouse steak with truffle bordelaise. Tables are topped with white linens and the service is precise and professional. The pub offers more casual fare for lunch and dinner, with favorites such as a roasted turkey club and chopped salad with gorgonzola and raspberry vinaigrette on the menu. American menu. Dinner, Sunday brunch. **$$**

★PAPA JOE'S SHRIMP & CRAB FACTORY

111 W. Broadway, Port Jefferson, 631-473-5656; www.papajoesshrimpfactory.com

American, seafood menu. Lunch, dinner. Bar. Children's menu. Outdoor seating. **$$**

★VILLAGE WAY

106 Main St., Port Jefferson, 631-928-3395; www.villagewayrestaurant.com

Lunch, dinner, Sunday brunch. Closed holidays. Bar. Children's menu. Outdoor seating. **$$**

PORT JERVIS

Port Jervis is a popular area for whitewater canoeing and rafting. Fishing, nature trails and hot-air ballooning are highlights of the area.

Information: Tri-State Chamber of Commerce, 5 S. Broome St.,
Port Jervis, 845-856-6694; www.tristatechamber.org

WHAT TO SEE AND DO

GILLANDER GLASS FACTORY TOURS AND STORE

Erie and Liberty Streets, Port Jervis, 845-856-5375; www.gillinderglassstore.com

Observe skilled craftsmen at work as they transform molten glass into beautiful glass objects. Tours, museum, store. Monday-Friday; weekends seasonal; closed holidays.

RESTAURANT

★★CORNUCOPIA

176 Highway 209, Port Jervis, 845-856-5361

American, Continental menu. Lunch, dinner. Closed Monday. Bar. Children's menu. Casual attire. **$$**

POTSDAM

This Victorian village sits on a wide band of reddish-orange sandstone near the Adirondacks.

Information: Chamber of Commerce, Potsdam, 315-274-9000;
www.potsdam.ny.us/chamber

WHAT TO SEE AND DO

POTSDAM PUBLIC MUSEUM

Civic Center, Park and Elm streets, Potsdam, 315-265-6910; www.vi.potsdam.ny.us

Collection of English pottery augments local history and decorative arts displays. Changing exhibits. Walking tour brochures available. Memorial Day-Labor Day: Tuesday-Friday afternoons, rest of year: Tuesday-Saturday afternoons; closed holidays.

NEW YORK

★
★
★
★
★

HOTEL
★★THE CLARKSON INN
1 Main St., Potsdam, 315-265-3050, 800-790-6970; www.clarksoninn.com
40 rooms. Restaurant. High-speed Internet access. Business center. $

RESTAURANT
★TARDELLI'S
141 Market St., Potsdam, 315-265-8446
Italian menu. Dinner. Closed Sunday; holidays. Bar. Children's menu. $$

POUGHKEEPSIE

Many people know this Hudson River town as the site of Vassar College, founded in 1861 by a brewer named Matthew Vassar. The Smith Brothers also helped put Poughkeepsie (p'KIP-see) on the map with their cough drops, once made here. For a brief time during the Revolutionary War, this town was the state capital. It was here in 1788 that New York ratified the Constitution.

Information: Poughkeepsie Area Chamber of Commerce, 1 Civic Center Plaza, Poughkeepsie, 845-454-1700; www.pokchamb.org

WHAT TO SEE AND DO
BARDAVON OPERA HOUSE
35 Market St., Poughkeepsie, 845-473-5288; www.bardavon.org
This 1869 building is the oldest operating theater in the state. It presents various dance, theatrical and musical performances; also Hudson Valley Philharmonic concerts. September-June.

JAMES BAIRD STATE PARK
14 Maintenance Lane, Pleasant Valley, 845-452-1489; www.nysparks.state.ny.us
Extensive complex includes an 18-hole golf course and driving range, tennis, hiking trails, cross-country skiing, picnicking, playground, restaurant and nature center.

LOCUST GROVE
2683 South Road, Poughkeepsie, 845-454-4500; www.morsehistoricsite.org
Former house of Samuel F. B. Morse, inventor of the telegraph, it was remodeled by him into a Tuscan villa in 1847. Antiques; Morse Room, telegraph equipment and memorabilia; alternating exhibits of dolls, fans, costumes, books and souvenirs acquired by Young family (owners following Morse); paintings, art objects and American furnishings. Wildlife sanctuary and park (180 acres) with hiking trails, picnic area. Tours May-November: daily 10 a.m.-3 p.m., Visitor center May-November: daily 10 a.m.-5 p.m.; closed holidays. Gardens and grounds daily 8 a.m. to dusk; closed holidays.

MID-HUDSON CHILDREN'S MUSEUM
75 N. Water St., Poughkeepsie, 845-471-0589; www.mhcm.org
Interactive children's museum featuring more than 50 exhibits including gravity roll, Da Vinci inventions, virtual reality and climb-through-the-heart exhibit. Tuesday-Sunday 11 a.m.-5 p.m.; closed holidays.

VASSAR COLLEGE

124 Raymond Ave., Poughkeepsie, 845-437-7000; www.vassar.edu

A 1,000-acre campus; coeducational (since 1969) liberal arts college. Art gallery.

HOTELS

★★COURTYARD BY MARRIOTT

2641 South Road/Route 9, Poughkeepsie, 845-485-6336; www.marriott.com

149 rooms. Breakfast buffet. High-speed Internet access. Restaurant, bar. Pool. $

★HOLIDAY INN EXPRESS

2750 South Road, Poughkeepsie, 845-473-1151; www.holiday-inn.com

121 rooms. Complimentary continental breakfast. High-speed Internet access. Airport transportation available. Pool. Fitness center. $

★★★OLD DROVERS INN

196 E. Duncan Hill Road, Dover Plains, 845-832-9311; www.olddroversinn.com

This historic inn was built in 1750 and is arguably the oldest continuously operated inn in the United States. Each room is decorated with fine antiques. The service is top-notch, too, and the setting is truly sublime. The inn's restaurant, the Tap Room, is a must-visit for a memorable meal. Four rooms. Complimentary continental breakfast. Restaurant. $$

★★★POUGHKEEPSIE GRAND HOTEL

40 Civic Center Plaza, Poughkeepsie, 845-485-5300, 800-216-1034; www.pokgrand.com

Located adjacent to the Civic Center in the heart of the Hudson Valley, this hotel boasts plenty of meeting space and caters largely to a business traveler crowd and wedding parties. Rooms feature contemporary furnishings. 195 rooms. Complimentary full breakfast. Fitness center. High-speed Internet access. Restaurant, bar. $

★★★TROUTBECK INN

515 Leedsville Road, Amenia, 845-373-9681, 800-978-7688; www.troutbeck.com

This English country-style inn and conference center sits on 600 acres near the Berkshire foothills and features rooms beautifully appointed with overstuffed furnishings and elegant fabrics. Try for a room with a fireplace and whirlpool bath in the wonderful Garden House, which overlooks the formal walled English garden. 42 rooms. Complimentary continental breakfast. Restaurant, bar. Pool. Fitness center. Spa. $$

SPECIALTY LODGING

INN AT THE FALLS

50 Red Oaks Mill Road, Poughkeepsie, 845-462-5770, 800-344-1466; www.innatthefalls.com

Romance and relaxation are imparted by the charm of this intimate and stylish inn where period furnishings grace every room. 36 rooms. Complimentary continental breakfast. $$

RESTAURANTS
★★AROMA OSTERIA
114 Old Post Road, Wappingers, 845-298-6790; www.aromaosteriarestaurant.com
American, Italian menu. Lunch, dinner. Closed Monday; holidays. Bar. Casual attire. Reservations recommended. Outdoor seating. $$

★★BEECH TREE GRILL
1 Collegeview Ave., Poughkeepsie, 845-471-7279; www.beechtreegrill.com
American menu. Lunch, dinner. Bar. Casual attire. Reservations recommended. $$

★★★CHRISTOS
155 Wilbur Blvd., Poughkeepsie, 845-471-3400; www.christoscatering.com
Internationally influenced American cuisine is served in this elegant, wood-paneled dining room lit by sparkling chandeliers where smooth service from tuxedo-clad waiters and a golf course view combine for a relaxing ambience. The wine list includes excellent selections for all price ranges. American menu. Lunch, dinner. Closed Sunday-Monday; also January and August. Bar. Casual attire. Reservations recommended. $$

★★COSIMO'S TRATTORIA & BAR
120 Delafield St., Poughkeepsie, 845-485-7172; www.cosimospoughkeepsie.com
American, Italian menu. Lunch, dinner. Bar. Children's menu. Casual attire. Reservations recommended. Outdoor seating. $$

★COYOTE GRILL
2629 South Road, Poughkeepsie, 845-471-0600; www.coyotegrillny.com
Mexican menu. Lunch, dinner. Bar. Children's menu. Casual attire. Reservations recommended. $$

★★LE PAVILLON
230 Salt Point Turnpike, Poughkeepsie, 845-473-2525
American, French menu. Dinner. Closed Sunday-Monday; holidays. Bar. Casual attire. Reservations recommended. Outdoor seating. $$

POUND RIDGE
This community on the Connecticut border is home to many big-wigs in the worlds of music, entertainment and media.
Information: www.townofpoundridge.com

WHAT TO SEE AND DO
MUSCOOT FARM
51 Route 100, Somers, 914-864-7282; www.muscootfarm.org
This 777-acre park is a turn-of-the-century farm that includes farm animals, buildings and a 28-room main house. Demonstrations of sheep shearing, blacksmithing, beekeeping, harvesting and bread baking daily.

WARD POUND RIDGE RESERVATION
Highway 121 South, Cross River, 914-864-7317
In this 4,700-acre park is the Trailside Nature Museum Wednesday-Sunday. Cross-country ski trails, picnicking, playground, camping in lean-tos. Reservation daily; closed holidays.

RESTAURANT
★★★L'EUROPE
407 Smithridge Road, South Salem, 914-533-2570
Continental, French menu. Lunch, dinner, brunch. Closed Monday-Tuesday. Bar. Casual attire. Reservations recommended. Outdoor seating. **$$$**

QUEENS (NEW YORK CITY)
By far the largest borough of New York City geographically, Queens occupies 121 square miles of Long Island. Like Brooklyn, it was assembled from a number of small towns, and each of these neighborhoods has retained a strong sense of identity. Parts of the borough are less densely settled than Brooklyn, and the majority of Queens's population are homeowners. Many manufacturing plants, warehouses and shipping facilities are in the portion called Long Island City, near the East River. Forest Hills, with its West Side Tennis Club, at Tennis Place and Burns Street, is a world-famous center for tennis. Flushing Meadows-Corona Park has been the site of two World's Fairs, and many of the fairs' facilities still stand.
Information: www.queenschamber.org

WHAT TO SEE AND DO
AMERICAN MUSEUM OF THE MOVING IMAGE
35th Avenie at 36th Street, Astoria, 718-784-0077; www.ammi.org
On the site of historic Astoria Studios, where many classic early movies were filmed, this museum is devoted to the art and history of film, television and video and their effects on American culture. Permanent and changing exhibitions; two theaters with film and video series, screenings weekends. Wednesday-Thursday noon-5 p.m., Friday to 8 p.m., Saturday-Sunday 11 a.m.-6:30 p.m.; closed holidays.

ASTORIA
At the northwest end of Queens, 718-286-2667; nycvisit.com
This Hellenic community, just 15 minutes from Midtown Manhattan, offers the best Greek food this side of Athens. Astoria has an estimated Greek population of 70,000—the largest community outside of Greece—which means that the area is alive with music, culture, saganaki and baklava. Food markets, gift shops, bakeries, restaurants and intimate cafes await. Finish an excursion by relaxing on a nice, sunny day with a cup of Greek coffee in nearby Astoria Park and take in a great view of upper Manhattan. If you want to combine this experience with other area attractions, the American Museum of the Moving Image and the historic Kaufman Astoria Motion Picture Studios are located in Astoria.

BOWNE HOUSE
37-01 Bowne St., Flushing, 718-359-0528; www.bownehouse.org
One of the oldest houses in New York City was built in 1661 by John Bowne, a Quaker who led a historic struggle for religious freedom under Dutch rule. It's decorated in 17th- to 19th-century furnishings. Tuesday, Saturday and Sunday afternoons; closed Easter and mid-December-mid-January. Under 12 admitted only with adult.

CLEARVIEW PARK GOLF COURSE
202-12 Willets Point Blvd., Flushing, 718-229-2570; www.clearview.americangolf.com
Clearview is recognized as a good course for beginners in the New York area, so it's very popular. You can expect your round to take a little longer than normal, but the

237

★
★
★
★
★

price won't break the bank. The rough is deep, but if you can keep your shots straight, you can avoid it. A par-70 course, Clearview plays just over 6,200 yards from the back tees but that belies the challenge of the narrow fairways.

FLUSHING MEADOWS-CORONA PARK
Flushing and Metropolitan Aves., Flushing, 718-217-6034; www.nycgovparks.org
Originally a marsh, this 1,255-acre area became the site of two World's Fairs (1939-1940 and 1964-1965). It is now the home of the United States Tennis Association National Tennis Center, where the U.S. Open is held annually (718-760-6200). The park is also the site of some of the largest cultural and ethnic festivals in the city. Facilities include an indoor ice rink, carousel, 87-acre Meadow Lake and the playground for all children. Park rangers conduct occasional weekend tours.

ISAMU NOGUCHI GARDEN MUSEUM
32-37 Vernon Blvd, Long Island City, 718-204-7088; www.noguchi.org
Sculpture fans will want to visit the Isamu Noguchi Museum, just a short trip from Manhattan. Housed in the sculptor's former studio, complete with an outdoor sculpture garden, the museum is filled with Noguchi stone, metal and woodwork. April-November; Monday, Thursday, Friday 10 a.m.-5 p.m.; Saturday-Sunday 10 a.m.-6 p.m.; closed Tuesday, Wednesday.

NEW YORK HALL OF SCIENCE
47-01 111th St., Flushing, 718-699-0005; www.nyhallsci.org
Exhibition hall with hands-on science and technology exhibits. September-June: Tuesday-Thursday 9:30 a.m.-2 p.m., Friday to 5 p.m., Saturday-Sunday noon-5 p.m.; July-August: Monday 9:30 a.m.-2 p.m., Tuesday-Friday to 5 p.m., Saturday-Sunday 10:30 a.m.-6 p.m.; closed holidays. Free admission Thursday and Friday afternoons.

P. S. 1 CONTEMPORARY ART CENTER
22-25 Jackson Ave., Long Island City, 718-784-2084; www.ps1.org/warmup
A premier center for art on the cutting edge; specializes in the avant-garde, conceptual and experimental; housed in a newly renovated, four-story building that was once a public school; changing exhibits. The venue also features the Warm Up Music Series, which attracts the hippest of DJs and crowds to its Saturday afternoon/evening outdoor dance parties in its courtyard. All ages are welcome. July-August; Saturday evenings. Monday, Thursday-Sunday; closed holidays.

QUEENS BOTANICAL GARDEN
43-50 Main St., Flushing, 718-886-3800; www.queensbotanical.org
Plants and amenities showcased at this diverse garden include large roses, herbs, woodland and bird gardens and an arboretum. Tuesday-Sunday.

THE QUEENS MUSEUM OF ART
New York Building, 25th Avenue and 76th Street, Flushing, 718-592-9700; www.queensmuseum.org
Interdisciplinary fine arts presentations and major traveling exhibitions are displayed here. The permanent collection includes a 9,000-square-foot panorama of New York City, the world's largest three-dimensional architectural model. September-June:

Wednesday-Friday 10 a.m.-5 p.m., Saturday-Sunday noon-5 p.m., July-August: Wednesday-Sunday 1-8 p.m.; closed holidays.

SHEA STADIUM

126th Street and Roosevelt Avenue, Flushing, 718-507-6387; www.mets.com

This is the home of the New York Mets Major League Baseball team; the Mets are scheduled to move to their new home at Citi Field (126th Street and Roosevelt Avenue, Flushing, New York) for the 2009 season.

UNION STREET

Union and Main streets, Flushing

This section of Flushing, located one long block past Main Street, is home to a large, culturally-rich Korean community. Tiny shops feature American and Korean clothing and wedding gowns from both cultures. Gift shops sell miniature collectibles, and food markets offer exotic foods and spices. Korean restaurants serve traditional barbecue dishes and other items. In addition to being inexpensive, many eateries are open 24 hours a day to satisfy late-night cravings.

SPECIAL EVENTS

AQUEDUCT

11000 Rockaway Blvd., South Ozone Park, 718-641-4700

Hop on the subway for a short ride out to Queens for an afternoon of thoroughbred races, held from late October through early May. Races take place Wednesday through Sunday and begin at 1 p.m. The track also has pretty lawns and gardens that come alive in spring. Gates open at 11 a.m.

BELMONT PARK

2150 Hempstead Turnpike, Elmont, 516-488-6000; www.nyra.com

This 430-acre racetrack is the home of the third jewel in horse racing's Triple Crown, the Belmont Stakes. This major spectacle is held in June and attracts gamblers, horse lovers and spectators from all walks of life. It's one of the oldest annual sporting events in the nation, so make your plans in advance and reserve seats early. With any luck, you will get a good-weather day on which to enjoy this event. The regular season racing at Belmont Park is from May through July and from September through October. Sundays are Family Fun Days; kids can play in the playground in the backyard area. Wednesday-Sunday, May-July and September-October.

U.S. OPEN TENNIS

Flushing Meadows-Corona Park, USTA National Tennis Center, Flushing, 718-760-6200; www.usopen.org

Tennis fans swarm to the U.S. Open tennis tournament each September. You can see your favorite players, the stars of tomorrow and a host of celebrities in the audience at this upper-crust sporting event. Tickets go on sale in late May or by the beginning of June, and those matches held closer to the finals sell out first. Buying a ticket to the Arthur Ashe Stadium, the main court, gives you admission to all the other courts on the grounds. Late August-early September.

HOTELS

★★★CROWNE PLAZA HOTEL NEW YORK-LAGUARDIA AIRPORT

104-04 Ditmars Blvd., East Elmhurst, 718-457-6300, 800-227-6963;www.crowneplaza.com

The Crowne Plaza LaGuardia boasts a location and accommodations that are perfectly suited for both business and leisure travelers. Rooms feature VCRs, CD players and refrigerators. A state-of-the-art fitness center with cardio and weight equipment, an indoor pool, sauna and sundeck provide guests with ways to unwind while a business center with printing, fax, copying and secretarial services takes the stress out of working. LaGuardia airport is located across the street, and JFK is eight miles away. Other nearby attractions include Shea Stadium and the National Tennis Center. 358 rooms. Restaurant, bar. Busines center. Pool. **$$**

★★HOLIDAY INN

144-02 135th Ave., Jamaica, 718-659-0200, 800-972-3160; www.holiday-inn.com

360 rooms. Restaurant, bar. High-speed Internet access. Pets accepted. Pool. Airport transportation available. Pool. **$$**

RESTAURANTS

★★CAVO

4218 31st Ave., Astoria, 718-721-1001; www.cavocafelounge.com

Mediterranean menu. Dinner, late-night. Bar. Casual attire. Reservations recommended. Outdoor seating. **$$**

★★CHRISTOS HASAPO-TAVERNA

41-08 23rd Ave., Astoria, 718-726-5195; www.christossteakhouse.com

Greek menu. Lunch, dinner. Bar. Casual attire. Outdoor seating. **$$$**

★EL GAUCHITO

9460 Corona Ave., Flushing, 718-271-8198

Argentinean menu. Lunch, dinner. Closed Wednesday. Casual attire. **$$**

★ELIAS CORNER

24-02 31st St., Astoria, 718-932-1510

Greek menu. Dinner. Casual attire. Outdoor seating. No credit cards accepted. **$$**

★★IL TOSCANO

42-05 235th St., Douglaston, 718-631-0300; www.iltoscanony.com

Italian menu. Dinner. Closed Monday, holidays. Bar. Casual attire. Reservations recommended. **$$**

★JACKSON DINER

3747 74th St., Jackson Heights, 718-672-1232; www.jacksondiner.com

Indian menu. Lunch, dinner. Casual attire. **$**

★KABAB CAFÉ

25-12 Steinway St., Astoria, 718-728-9858

Middle Eastern menu. Lunch, dinner. Closed Monday. Casual attire. No credit cards accepted. **$**

★★MOMBAR

2522 Steinway St., Astoria, 718-726-2356

Middle Eastern menu. Dinner. Closed Monday. Children's menu. Casual attire. **$$**

★★★PICCOLA VENEZIA

42-01 28th Ave., Astoria, 718-721-8470; www.piccola-venezia.com

Piccola Venezia, an old-world trattoria offering authentic northern Italian fare, features delicious homemade pastas and a generous menu of salads, antipasti, seafood, meat and game prepared with imported ingredients and a strong nod to the wonderful culinary traditions of northern Italy. Italian menu. Lunch, dinner. Closed Tuesday; holidays; also late July-late August. Valet parking. **$$$**

★★PING'S SEAFOOD

83-02 Queens Blvd., Elmhurst, 718-396-1238

Chinese menu. Lunch, dinner. Closed Sunday. **$$**

★★RESTAURANT 718

35-01 Ditmars Blvd., Astoria, 718-204-5553

French menu. Dinner, brunch. Bar. Casual attire. Reservations recommended. **$$**

★S'AGAPO TAVERNA

34-21 34th Ave., Astoria, 718-626-0303

Greek menu. Lunch, dinner. Casual attire. **$$**

★SWEET BASIL

39-28 61st St., Woodside, 718-205-0080

Thai menu. Lunch, dinner. Casual attire. **$**

★SRIPRAPHAI

64-13 39th Ave., Woodside, 718-899-9599; www.sripraphairestaurant.com

Thai menu. Lunch, dinner. Closed Wednesday. Casual attire. Outdoor seating. No credit cards accepted. **$**

★UBOL'S KITCHEN

24-42 Steinway St., Astoria, 718-545-2874

Thai menu. Lunch, dinner. Casual attire. Closed on Monday; dinner only Tuesday-Wednesday. **$**

★★★UNCLE JACK'S STEAKHOUSE

39-40 Bell Blvd., Bayside, 718-229-1100; www.unclejacks.com

This classic steakhouse (which also has two Manhattan locations) sticks to well-prepared cuts beef, from Kobe to USDA prime cuts like the porterhouse or T-bone. Traditional sides such as creamed spinach or garlic mashed potatoes complete every meal, as does the extensive wine selection, which is peppered with bottles from just about every corner of the world. Steak menu. Lunch, dinner. Upscale dress. **$$$**

RHINEBECK

Rhinebeck was once known as "violet town" because it claimed to produce more hot-house violets than any other town in the United States. Today the town features numerous charming stores and restaurants as well as beautifully restored historic homes.

Information: Chamber of Commerce, 23F E. Market St., 845-876-4778;
www.rhinebeckchamber.com

WHAT TO SEE AND DO
HUDSON RIVER NATIONAL ESTUARINE RESEARCH RESERVE
Highway 9G, Annandale, 845-889-4745; www.dec.ny.gov/lands/4915.html
The Hudson River is an estuary, running from Manhattan to Troy, N.Y. More than 5,000 acres of this estuarine land have been reserved for the study of its life and eco-systems. The Reserve includes Piermont Marsh and Iona Island in Rockland County, Tivoli Bays in Dutchess County and Stockport Flats in Columbia County. The reserve's headquarters has lectures, workshops, special exhibits and public field programs.

MONTGOMERY PLACE
55 Montgomery place, Annandale, 845-758-5461;
www.hudsonvalley.org/content
This 1805 mansion estate along Hudson River was remodeled in the mid-1800s in the Classical-revival style. Grounds contain a coach house, visitor center, greenhouse with rose, herb, perennial and woodland gardens, a museum and a garden shop. Scenic trails and view of cataracts meeting the Hudson. April-October: Monday, Wednesday-Sunday; March and November-December: weekends. May-October Saturday and Sunday only 10 a.m.-5 p.m.

OLD RHINEBECK AERODROME
42 Stone Church Road, Rhinebeck, 845-752-3500; www.oldrhinebeck.org
Museum showcases antique airplanes (1900-1937). Planes from World War I and earlier are flown in air shows. 14 June-19 October with gates opening at 10 a.m. and Air Shows at 2 p.m. Saturday-Sunday.

SPECIAL EVENT
DUTCHESS COUNTY FAIR
Dutchess County Fairgrounds, Highway 9, Rhinebeck, 845-876-4001;
www.dutchessfair.com
Harness racing, livestock shows, farm machinery exhibits. Late August.

HOTEL
★★★BEEKMAN ARMS
6387 Mill St., Rhinebeck, 845-876-7077, 800-361-6517;
www.beekmandelamarterinn.com
This historic inn (America's oldest continually run inn) is the perfect weekend escape. Savor fine cuisine or visit many local attractions including the Roosevelt and Vanderbilt estates, the Culinary Institute of America (with its numerous restaurants) and the Rhinebeck Aerodrome's World War I Air Show. Many of the rooms feature fireplaces. 73 rooms. Restaurant, bar. $$

★AGRA TANDOOR

5856 Highway 9, Rhinebeck, 845-876-7510; www.tanjoreindiancuisine.com

Indian menu. Lunch, dinner. Casual attire. Reservations recommended. Outdoor seating. $$

★★CALICO CALICO RESTAURANT AND PATISSERIE

6384 Mills St., Rhinebeck, 845-876-2749; www.calicorhinebeck.com

American, French menu. Lunch, dinner, Sunday brunch. Bar. Casual attire. Reservations recommended. $$$

★★DIASPORA

1094 Route 308, Rhinebeck, 845-758-9601; www.diasporacuisine.com

Mediterranean and Greek menu. Dinner. Closed Monday-Wednesday Bar. Reservations recommended. Outdoor seating. $$

★★GIGI TRATTORIA

6422 Montgomery St., Rhinebeck, 845-876-1007; www.gigitrattoria.com

Italian, Mediterranean menu. Lunch, dinner. Bar. Business casual attire. Reservations recommended. Outdoor seating. $$

★★OSAKA

22 Garden St., Rhinebeck, 845-876-7338; www.osakasushi.net

Japanese, sushi menu. Lunch, dinner. Closed Tuesday. Casual attire. $$

RIVERHEAD

Suffolk County's thousands of acres of rich farmland, first cultivated in 1690, have made it one of the leading agricultural counties in the United States. Potatoes, corn and cauliflower are abundant here. Once in serious decline, Riverhead is perking up thanks to entrepreneurs who have made the most of its prime location between Long Island's North and South Forks.

Information: Chamber of Commerce, 542 E. Main St., Riverhead, 631-727-7600; www.riverheadchamber.com

WHAT TO SEE AND DO

ATLANTIS MARINE WORLD

431 E. Main St., Riverhead, 631-208-9200; www.atlantismarineworld.com

A themed aquatic park meant to recall the lost Greek isle, Marine World also houses the Riverhead Foundation for Marine Research and Preservation, where you can witness marine animals being nursed back to health. Daily 10 a.m.-5 p.m.; closed holidays.

BRIERMERE FARMS

4414 Sound Ave., Riverhead, 631-722-3931; www.briermere.com

Forget the calorie count when you walk into this small roadside farmstand and bakery. The many varieties of homemade fruit and cream pies are worth every delectable bite. From traditional flavors like cherry and peach to more exotic tastes such as blackberry apple and blueberry cream, the pies are so chock full of fresh fruit that they are actually heavy to carry. Also indulge in Briermere's home-baked breads, muffins and cookies. For healthier interests, they also sell fresh fruits and vegetables. Go early in the day for the best selection and be ready to wait in line on just about any day in the summer. Daily 9 a.m.-5 p.m.

BROOKHAVEN NATIONAL LABORATORY

William Floyd Parkway, Upton, 631-344-2345
The Exhibit Center Science Museum is housed in the world's first nuclear reactor built to carry out research on the peaceful aspects of nuclear science. Participatory exhibits, audiovisual presentations and historic collections are inside. Tours mid-July-August, Sunday; closed holiday weekends.

PALMER VINEYARDS

108 Sound Ave., Riverhead, 631-722-9463; www.palmervineyards.com
Opened in 1986, this 55-acre winery is one of the most acclaimed on the North Fork, with an interesting, eclectic variety of wines. Palmer offers everything from Cabernet Franc to Chardonnay to special reserve wines that have a unique, rich flavor. Pack a picnic, enjoy a tasting and a tour and buy some wine to enjoy with lunch. June-October: daily 11 a.m.-6 p.m.; November-May: daily 11 a.m.-5 p.m.

PINDAR VINEYARDS

37645 Main Road, Peconic, 631-734-6200; www.pindar.net
Even though Long Island's wine country does not have the reputation of Napa Valley, this well-known winery and its smaller counterparts in this lovely agricultural area are making a name for themselves. On 550 lush acres, Pindar is the North Fork's largest winery and one of the most established. Founded in 1979, it offers free tastings of the 16 varieties of wine it produces. They include Merlot, Chardonnay and Cabernet Sauvignon. The winery is airy and comfortable and provides daily guided tours.

SUFFOLK COUNTY HISTORICAL SOCIETY

300 W. Main St., Riverhead, 631-727-2881; www.suffolkcountyhistoricalsociety.org
Dating back to 1886, this museum chronicles Suffolk County's colorful history and rich traditions in farming, whaling and American Indian culture. Displays include furniture, tools, antique bicycles and carriages and a library containing newspapers, books and photographs relating to Suffolk and its people. Tuesday-Saturday 12:30-4:30 p.m.

TANGER OUTLET CENTER

1770 W. Main St., Riverhead, 631-369-2732; www.tangeroutlet.com
This outdoor outlet mall is a great place to pick up almost any kind of merchandise—clothes, china, jewelry—at below retail prices. The mall has nearly 200 stores, most of them name brands such as Banana Republic and J. Crew. Monday-Saturday 9 a.m.-9 p.m., Sunday 10 a.m.-8 p.m.

VINTAGE TOURS

Peconic, 631-765-4689; www.vintagetour1.com
Vintage Tours will pick you up at your hotel in a comfortable 15-passenger van and take you to at least three wineries in a four- to five-hour jaunt. Also included

are wine tastings, behind-the-scene winery tours, a gourmet picnic lunch suited to your tastes and stops at the North Fork's wonderful farm stands for the best in fresh vegetables and fruit. The company operates Friday-Sunday, but weekday trips can be arranged.

SPECIAL EVENT
RIVERHEAD COUNTRY FAIR
200 Howell Ave., Riverhead, 631-727-1215; www.riverheadcountryfair.com
Annual celebration includes agricultural and needlecraft exhibits and competitions, farm animal exhibits entertainment, a midway and music. Mid-October.

HOTEL
★★BEST WESTERN EAST END
1830 Route 25, Riverhead, 631-369-2200, 800-528-1234;
www.bestwesterneastend.com
100 rooms. Complimentary continental breakfast. High-speed Internet access. Restaurant, bar. Swimming pool. Pets accepted. Fitness center. Business center. **$$**

ROCHESTER
Rochester is a high-tech industrial and cultural center and the third-largest city in the state. Its educational institutions include the University of Rochester with its Eastman School of Music and Rochester Institute of Technology with its National Technical Institute for the Deaf. The Vacuum Oil Company, a predecessor of Mobil Oil Corporation, was founded here in 1866. The city also has a symphony orchestra and professional theatre.

Rochester has had its share of famous citizens, too: Susan B. Anthony, champion of women's rights; Frederick Douglass, black abolitionist and statesman; George Eastman, inventor of flexible film and founder of Kodak; Hiram Sibley, founder of Western Union; and musicians Mitch Miller, Cab Calloway and Chuck Mangione.

Information: Greater Rochester Visitors Association, 45 East Ave.,
Rochester, 800-677-7282; www.visitrochester.com

WHAT TO SEE AND DO
GENESEE COUNTRY VILLAGE & MUSEUM
1410 Flint Hill Road, Mumford, 585-538-6822; www.gcv.org
This 19th-century working village has 68 restored and furnished buildings, where locals in period costumes teach visitors about what life in this part of the country was like more than 150 years ago. The village also boasts an art gallery, base ball (two words in the 19th century) park, nature center and heirloom gardens. July-Labor Day, Tuesday-Sunday 10 a.m.-4 p.m., closed Monday; June and September, Tuesday-Friday 10 a.m.-4 p.m., Saturday, Sunday 10 a.m.-5 p.m.; May and October, Saturday, Sunday 10 a.m.-5 p.m., closed weekdays.

GEORGE EASTMAN HOUSE
900 East Ave., Rochester, 585-271-3361; www.eastmanhouse.org
Kodak founder George Eastman's 50-room mansion and gardens contain restored rooms with their original 1920s furnishings and décor. Adjacent to the house

is the archive building; eight exhibit spaces display an extensive collection of 19th- and 20th-century photography representing major photographers of the past 150 years. Chronological display presents evolution of photographic and imaging industries. Interactive displays present history of imaging with touch screens, video stations and programmed audiovisual shows. Admission: adults $8.00, seniors $6.00, students $5.00, children 5-12 $3.00. Tuesday-Wednesday and Friday-Saturday 10 a.m.-5 p.m., Thursday 10 a.m.-8 p.m., Sunday 1-5 pm.; closed Monday.

HAMLIN BEACH STATE PARK
1 Camp Road, Hamlin, 585-964-2462; www.nysparks.state.ny.us/parks
Park contains swimming beach, open mid-June-Labor Day, and offers fishing, hiking and biking trails, cross-country skiing, snowmobiling, picnicking and playground. Daily 6 a.m.-10 p.m.

HIGH FALLS IN THE BROWN'S RACE HISTORIC DISTRICT
60 Brown's Race, Rochester, 585-325-2030; www.ci.rochester.ny.us
This is the area between Inner Loop and Platt and State Streets, along the Genesee River Gorge. One of Rochester's earliest industrial districts has been renovated to preserve the area where flour mills and manufacturers once operated and Eastman Kodak and Gleason Works originated. Today, the district still houses businesses in renovated historic buildings such as the Eastman Technologies Building. Center at High Falls, on Brown's Race Street, is an interpretive museum with hands-on interactive exhibits on the history of the area, as well as information on other attractions to visit in Rochester. Brown's Race Market has been transformed from a maintenance facility of the Rochester Gas and Electric Corporation into three levels of attractions including a nightclub, a jazz club and a restaurant. A laser light show can be viewed from the pedestrian bridge that crosses the Genesee River.

THE LANDMARK CENTER (CAMPBELL-WHITTLESEY HOUSE MUSEUM)
123 S. Fitzhugh St., Rochester, 585-546-7029
Greek Revival home boasts Empire furniture. Adjacent Hoyt-Potter House has gift shop and exhibit area. March-December, Thursday-Friday noon-3 p.m.

MEMORIAL ART GALLERY (UNIVERSITY OF ROCHESTER)
500 University Ave., Rochester, 585-276-8900; www.mag.rochester.edu
The permanent collection spans 50 centuries of art and includes masterworks by Monet, Matisse and Homer; changing exhibitions. The Gallery's permanent collection of more than 12,000 objects has been called the best balanced in the state outside of metropolitan New York City. In addition to its collection, the Gallery offers a year-round schedule of temporary exhibitions, lectures, concerts, tours and family activities. Tuesday-Saturday 10 a.m.-5 p.m., Tuesday-Saturday 10 a.m.-5 pm, Sunday 11 a.m.-5 p.m. Closed Monday.

ROCHESTER HISTORICAL SOCIETY
485 East Ave., Rochester, 585-271-2705; www.rochesterhistory.org
The Rochester Historical Society, the brainchild of anthropologist Louis Henry Morgan, was established in 1860 only to languish as the Civil War loomed over

Rochester and the nation. In 1887, Mrs. Caroline Perkins, philanthropist and wife of businessman Gilman H. Perkins, revived the Society and led it to local prominence. For decades the Society has collected and preserved what today amounts to over 200,000 objects and documents. The headquarters for the society is "Woodside," a Greek Revival mansion (1839), which contains a collection of portraits and memorabilia, costumes, a reference library and a manuscript collection. Garden. Monday-Friday 10 a.m.-3 p.m., also by appointment; closed holidays.

ROCHESTER INSTITUTE OF TECHNOLOGY

1 Lomb Memorial Drive, Rochester, 585-475-2411; www.rit.edu
Seven college and the National Technical Institute for the Deaf are on campus. Also on campus are the Bevier Gallery and Frank Ritter Memorial Ice Arena.

ROCHESTER MUSEUM & SCIENCE CENTER

657 East Ave., Rochester, 585-271-4320; www.rmsc.org
Complex features a regional museum of natural science, anthropology, history and technology. Changing and permanent exhibits. Monday-Saturday 9 a.m.-5 p.m., Sunday noon-5 p.m.; closed holidays.

SENECA PARK ZOO

2222 St. Paul St., Rochester, 585-336-7200; www.senecazoo.org
Animals from all over the world; free-flight bird room, reptiles, Children's Discovery Center. Rocky Coasts features underwater viewing of polar bears and seals. April 1 to October 31: 10 a.m.-5 p.m., November 1-December 31: 10 a.m.-4 p.m., January 1-March 31: 10 a.m.-4 p.m. Adults (ages 12-62) $8, seniors (ages 63 and older) $7, youth (ages 3-11) $5, children (ages 2 and younger) free, members are always free.

STONE-TOLAN HOUSE

2370 East Ave., Rochester, 585-546-7029
Restored pioneer homestead and tavern from 1790 have four acres of gardens and orchards. March-December: Friday-Saturday, noon-3 p.m.; closed holidays

STRASENBURGH PLANETARIUM OF THE ROCHESTER MUSEUM AND SCIENCE CENTER

657 East Ave., Rochester, 585-271-1880; www.rmsc.org/StrasenburghPlanetarium
Star Theatre shows thousands of stars and planets on a massive, high-tech screen (call for times), educational exhibits. Daily; hours vary.

STRONG MUSEUM

1 Manhattan Square, Rochester, 585-263-2700; www.strongmuseum.org
This children's learning center features hands-on exhibits, 25,000 toys, dolls, miniatures and more. There is also an interactive 3-D exhibit based on the Children's Television Workshop program *Sesame Street*. The glass atrium features a historic street scene with an operating 1956 diner and 1918 carousel. Daily; closed holidays.

SUSAN B. ANTHONY HOUSE

17 Madison St., Rochester, 585-235-6124; www.susanbanthonyhouse.org
Susan B. Anthony lived here for 40 years and was arrested at her house in 1872 for voting illegally in the presidential election. Contains mementos of the women's suffrage

movement; furnishings. Labor Day-Memorial Day: Wednesday-Sunday 11 a.m.-4 p.m.; Memorial Day-Labor Day: Tuesday-Sunday 11 a.m.-5 p.m.; closed holidays.

SPECIAL EVENTS

CLOTHESLINE FESTIVAL

Memorial Art Gallery, 500 University Ave., Rochester, 585-473-8900; www.mag.rochester.edu/clothesline

Outdoor art show features live entertainment, from gospel to hula music, along with food and children's activities. Mid-September.

LILAC FESTIVAL

Highland Park, Rochester, 585-256-4960; www.lilacfestival.com

This 10-day festival features more than 500 varieties of lilacs. Parade, art show, entertainment and tours. Mid-May.

ROCHESTER PHILHARMONIC ORCHESTRA

108 East Ave., Rochester, 585-454-2100; www.rpo.org

Symphonic concerts presented by this ensemble founded by George Eastman in 1922. October-May.

SUMMER MUSIC

108 East Ave., Rochester, 585-454-7311

Rochester Philharmonic Orchestra, Finger Lakes Performing Arts Center. Symphonic, classical and pops concerts. Indoor/outdoor seating. Picnic sites. July.

★
★
★
★
★

HOTELS

★★CLARION HOTEL

120 E. Main St., Rochester, 585-546-6400, 877-424-6423; www.clarionriversidehotel.com

465 rooms. Restaurant, bar. Pool. Fitness center. **$**

★COMFORT INN

1501 Ridge Road West, Rochester, 585-621-5700, 877-424-6423;www.comfortinn.com

82 rooms. Complimentary continental breakfast. Exercise room. Wireless Internet access. Pets accepted. Whirlpool. **$**

★★★CROWNE PLAZA

70 State St., Rochester, 585-546-3450, 866-826-2831; www.rcpny.com

This Crowne Plaza offers a convenient location in the center of downtown Rochester. Airport shuttle service, a concierge, same-day laundry service and a business center with an array of offerings provide convenience, while a well-equipped fitness facility and an outdoor heated pool offer onsite recreation. 362 rooms. Wireless Internet access. Restaurant, bar. Airport transportation available. Pool. Fitness center. Pets accepted. **$**

★HAMPTON INN

717 E. Henrietta Road, Rochester, 585-272-7800, 800-426-7866;www.hamptoninn.com

112 rooms. Complimentary continental breakfast. Business center. Fitness room. Airport transportation available. **$**

★★HOLIDAY INN

911 Brooks Ave., Rochester, 585-328-6000, 888-465-4329; www.holiday-inn.com

279 rooms. Wireless Internet access. Restaurant, bar. Pool. Business center. Fitness center. Indoor pool. Whirlpool. Sauna. Pets accepted. **$**

★★HOLIDAY INN HOTEL & SUITES MARKETPLACE

800 Jefferson Road, Rochester, 585-475-9190, 888-465-4329; www.holiday-inn.com

120 rooms. Complimentary full breakfast. Restaurant, bar. Fitness center. Wireless Internet access. Pool. **$**

★★★HYATT REGENCY ROCHESTER

125 E. Main St., Rochester, 585-546-1234, 800-492-8804; www.hyatt.com

A skywalk connects the hotel to the convention center, which is located near shopping, entertainment, wineries and the airport. Guests will find well-appointed rooms and a health club, extraordinary meeting space and nice service. 338 rooms. Restaurant, bar. Fitness center. Pool. Gym and whirlpool. Business center. Complimentary airport transportation. **$$**

★★★STRATHALLAN HOTEL

550 East Ave., Rochester, 585-461-5010, 800-678-7284; www.strathallan.com

This European-style hotel offers warm and spacious studios and one-bedroom suites. Located in a stately residential neighborhood, the property is convenient to area attractions. The restaurant offers dishes such as sweet potato-crusted Hawaiian snapper in a country club setting, and the bar is a quiet place to relax. 156 rooms, all suites. Restaurant, bar. Wireless Internet access. Complimentary airport transportation available. Fitness center. Business center. Valet parking. **$$**

SPECIALTY LODGING

DARTMOUTH HOUSE BED AND BREAKFAST INN

215 Dartmouth St., Rochester, 585-271-7872, 800.724.6298;
www.dartmouthhouse.com

This bed-and-breakfast, a 1905 English Tudor, is situated in a quiet residential neighborhood near Rochester's main sights. Guests awake to a six-course breakfast by candlelight, featuring such goodies as baked blueberry blintz soufflé and raspberry fudge truffle bars. The guest rooms are spacious, with antiques and comfortable chairs and couches. Four rooms. Closed late December-early Mar. Children over 12 years only. Wireless Internet access. Complimentary continental breakfast. **$$**

RESTAURANTS

★DINOSAUR BAR-B-QUE

99 Court St., Rochester, 585-325-7090; www.dinosaurbarbque.com

American menu. Lunch, dinner. Closed Sunday. Bar. **$$$**

★★★THE GRILL AT STRATHALLAN

550 East Ave., Rochester, 585-461-5010; www.strathallan.com

This sophisticated yet casual Mediterranean dining room serves fresh, creative and elegantly prepared food paired with selections from an extensive wine cellar. Steak menu. Lunch, dinner. Closed Sunday. Jacket required. **$$$**

★★★MARIO'S ITALIAN STEAKHOUSE
2740 Monroe Ave., Rochester, 585-271-1111; www.mariosviaabruzzi.com

This charming villa is built and decorated in authentic central Italian style. Mario's unique Italian cuisine includes signatures like steak Diane and pork loin and fig chutney. The Sunday brunch has won many accolades. Italian menu. Dinner, Sunday brunch. Closed holidays. Bar. Children's menu. Casual attire. Outdoor seating. **$$**

★★★ROONEYS
90 Henrietta St., Rochester, 585-442-0444; www.rooneysrestaurant.com

This atmospheric downtown spot, with its intimate mood lighting and white silk tablecloths, is housed in an 1860 tavern, and the original bar is still in use. Many of the meat dishes are wood grilled; there's even venison. European Menu. Dinner. Closed holidays, Sunday in summer. Bar. **$$**

★★SCOTCH 'N SIRLOIN
3450 Winton Place, Rochester, 585-427-0808; www.scotchnsirloin.com

Seafood, steak menu. Dinner. Closed Monday; holidays. Bar. Children's menu. **$$$**

ROCKVILLE CENTRE

Incorporated in 1893, Rockville Centre boasts 200 acres of parkland and is a short ride from several fine beach areas.

Information: Chamber of Commerce, Rockville Centre, 516-766-0666;
www.rvcchamber.com

WHAT TO SEE AND DO
ROCK HALL MUSEUM
199 Broadway, Lawrence, 516-239-1157

Historic house built in 1767 with period furnishings and exhibits. Saturday-Sunday afternoons.

RESTAURANT
★★GEORGE MARTIN
65 N. Park Ave., Rockville Centre, 516-678-7272; www.georgemartingroup.com

American menu. Lunch, dinner. Closed holidays. **$$**

ROME

Originally the site of Fort Stanwix, where, during the Revolutionary War, tradition says the Stars and Stripes were first flown in battle. The author of the "Pledge of Allegiance," Francis Bellamy, is buried in Rome. Griffiss Air Force Base is located here.

Information: Rome Area Chamber of Commerce, 139 W. Dominick St., Rome,
315-337-1700; www.romechamber.com

WHAT TO SEE AND DO
DELTA LAKE STATE PARK
8797 Highway 46, Rome, 315-337-4670; www.nysparks.state.ny.us/parks

.Swimming beach Memorial Day weekend-mid-June, limited days; mid-June-Labor Day, full-time; bathhouse, fishing, boating, tent and trailer sites, hiking, biking, cross-country skiing, picnicking, playground.

ERIE CANAL VILLAGE

5789 New London Rd., Rome, 315-337-3999, 888-374-3226; www.eriecanalvillage.net

Take trips on restored section of the Erie Canal aboard mule-drawn 1840 canal packet boat, The Chief Engineer. Buildings of 1840s canal village include church, blacksmith shop, train station, museums, schoolhouse, Victorian home, stable, Settlers house; hotel; orientation center; picnic area and restaurant. Adult $10.00, seniors (ages 62 and up) $7.00, children (ages 5-17) $5.00, children (ages 4 and under) free. Wednesday-Saturday 10 a.m.-5 p.m., Sunday 12 noon-5 p.m. Memorial Day and Labor Day 12 noon-5 p.m.

FORT RICKEY CHILDREN'S DISCOVERY ZOO

5135 Rome-New London Road, Rome, 315-336-1930; www.fortrickey.com

Restoration of 1700s British fort is site of a zoo that emphasizes animal contact. Wide variety of wildlife. Mid-May-mid-June: Monday-Friday 10 a.m.-2 p.m., Saturday-Sunday 10 a.m.-4 p.m.; late June-Labor Day: daily 10 a.m.-5:30 p.m.

FORT STANWIX NATIONAL MONUMENT

112 E. Park St., Rome, 315-338-7300; www.nps.gov/fost

Reconstructed earth-and-log fort on location of 1758 fort. The Iroquois signed a treaty here opening territory east of the Ohio River to colonial expansion. In 1777, the fort was besieged by the British; General Benedict Arnold forced their retreat. Costumed guides; film; museum. April-December, daily; closed holidays.

TOMB OF THE UNKNOWN SOLDIER OF THE AMERICAN REVOLUTION

201 N. James St., Rome

Designed by Lorimar Rich, who also designed the tomb at Arlington National Cemetery.

WOODS VALLEY SKI AREA

Dopp Hill Road, Westernville, 315-827-4721; www.woodsvalleyskiarea.com

Two double chairlifts, T-bar; patrol, snowmaking, school, rentals; bar, cafeteria. Longest run 4,000 feet, vertical drop 500 feet. December-March, Tuesday-Sunday; closed holidays. Some evening rates.

SPECIAL EVENT

WORLD SERIES OF BOCCE

1412 E. Dominick St., Rome, 315-339-3609; www.worldseriesofbocce.org

The big event for aficionados of Italian lawn bowling. Mid-July.

HOTELS

★★INN AT THE BEECHES

7900 Turin Road, Rome, 315-336-1775, 800-765-7251; www.thebeeches.com

75 rooms. Three restaurants. 52 acres with pond. Complimentary morning coffee. Pool. Business center. $

★★QUALITY INN

200 S. James St., Rome, 315-336-4300; www.qualityinnrome.com

103 rooms. Restaurant. Pool. Wireless Internet access. Outdoor pool. Business center. Fitness center. Pets accepted. $

RESTAURANTS
★★THE BEECHES
7900 Turin Road, Rome, 315-336-1700; www.thebeeches.com
Lunch, dinner, Sunday brunch. Closed Monday. Bar. Children's menu. **$$**

★★SAVOY
255 E. Dominick St., Rome, 315-339-3166; www.romesavoy.com
American and, Italian menu. Lunch, dinner. Closed holidays. Bar. Children's menu. **$$**

ROSCOE
Dutch settlers conquered the wilderness in this Catskill area, but in the process did not destroy it, and the area has been well preserved. Small and large game abounds, and the Willowemoc and Beaverkill rivers provide excellent trout fishing. Four unusual and interesting covered bridges are located in the surrounding countryside.
Information: Roscoe-Rockland Chamber of Commerce, Roscoe, 607-498-6055; www.roscoeny.com

WHAT TO SEE AND DO
CATSKILL FLY FISHING CENTER & MUSEUM
1031 Old Route 17, Roscoe, 914-439-4810; www.cffcm.net
Demonstrations, programs, events and interpretive exhibits showcase the heritage, science and art of the sport. Explore the lives of legendary characters who made angling history. Displays of rods, reels, flies; video room, library, hall of fame. April-October: 10 a.m.-4p.m. (daily), November-March: 10 a.m.-4 p.m. (Saturday), 10 a.m.-1 p.m. (Tuesday through Friday).

SPECIALTY LODGING
THE GUEST HOUSE
408 Debruce Road, Livingston Manor, 845-439-4000; www.theguesthouse.com
Visit this 40-acre estate on the Willowemoc River for the nearby outdoor activities and the comfortable rooms, some of which feature fireplaces and whirlpool tubs. Seven rooms. Complimentary full breakfast. Airport transportation available. **$$**

ROSLYN
More than 100 historic sites dot this village in Nassau County in Long Island.
Information: www.historicroslyn.org

WHAT TO SEE AND DO
NASSAU COUNTY MUSEUM OF ART
One Museum Drive, Roslyn, 516-484-9337; www.nassaumuseum.com
This museum is housed in a mansion that was once owned by poet William Cullen Bryant and later lived in by steel tycoon Henry Clay Frick. Temporary exhibits have covered a wide range of topics, from Napoleon, the Civil War and American Revolution, to the surrealist art of Dali. The museum's permanent collection showcases works of many 19th- and 20th-century American and European artists. Art lovers will also enjoy the museum's outdoor sculpture garden, which features works by such artists as Auguste Rodin and Roy Lichtenstein. Tuesday-Sunday 11 a.m.-5 p.m.

RESTAURANTS

★★★BRYANT & COOPER STEAK HOUSE

Two Middleneck Rd., Roslyn, 516-627-7270; www.bryantandcooper.com

Have a drink at the bar or feast in the dark wood and marble-accented dining room at this classic steakhouse. The filet mignon is particularly good. Steak menu. Lunch, dinner. Closed holidays. Bar. Valet parking. $$$

★★★GEORGE WASHINGTON MANOR

1305 Old Northern Blvd., Roslyn, 516-621-1200; www.georgewashingtonmanor.com

This historic building was once the home of Roslyn founder Hendrick Onderdonk, host to President George Washington during his 1790 Long Island visit. American continental cuisine is served in a colonial room complete with six fireplaces, original wood beams and antique furnishings. American menu. Lunch, dinner, Sunday brunch. Closed holidays. Bar. Valet parking. $$

RYE

Rye is a quiet village on a harbor that opens into Long Island Sound. John Jay, the nation's first Supreme Court chief justice, lived in and is buried in Rye.

Information: www.ryeny.gov

RESTAURANT

★★★LA PANETIERE

530 Milton Road, Rye, 914-967-8140; www.lapanetiere.com

Set in a charming 19th-century house in lower Westchester County, La Panetiere serves stunning, contemporary French fare. The kitchen focuses on local, seasonal ingredients, searching out nearby farmers for fish, poultry and produce. The dining room has its original wood-beamed ceiling which gives it a rustic warmth that is balanced with elegant tapestries and beautiful 19th-century furnishings. French menu. Lunch, dinner. Bar. Valet parking. $$$

SACKETS HARBOR

This is a lakeside resort area for the eastern Lake Ontario region. Two major battles of the War of 1812 occurred here. In the first skirmish, the British warships invading the harbor were damaged and withdrew. A landing force was repulsed in the second battle.

Information: www.sacketsharborny.com

WHAT TO SEE AND DO

SACKETS HARBOR BATTLEFIELD STATE HISTORIC SITE

505 W. Washington St., Sackets Harbor, 315-646-3634;
www.nysparks.state.ny.us/sites/info.asp?siteid=25

War of 1812 battlefield; Federal-style Union Hotel (1818); Commandant's House (1850); US Navy Yard (1812-1955); visitor center, exhibits; demonstrations; tours. Admission: adults $3.00, students 13-21 $2.00, NYS seniors over 62, military with I.D., children 12 years and under free, Groups: $2.00 minimum group 15 people. Mid-May-early September: Tuesday-Saturday 10 a.m.-5 p.m., Sunday from 11 a.m.; late September-Columbus Day: Friday-Saturday 10 a.m.-5 p.m., Sunday from 11 a.m.

WESTCOTT BEACH STATE PARK

12224 Route 3, Sackets Harbor, 315-938-5083;
ww.nysparks.state.ny.us/parks/info.asp?parkID=161

Swimming beach, bathhouse, fishing, boating, hiking and nature trails, cross-country skiing, snowmobiling, picnicking, playground, concession, tent and trailer sites. Open from early May through Columbus Day. Waterfowl hunting is permitted in season.

HOTEL
★ONTARIO PLACE HOTEL

103 General Smith Dr., Sackets Harbor, 315-646-8000, 800-564-1812;
www.ontarioplacehotel.com

38 rooms. Coffee Bar. Pets accepted. **$**

SAG HARBOR

This great whaling town of the 19th century provided prototypes from which James Fenimore Cooper created characters for his sea stories. Sheltered in a cove of Gardiner's Bay, the economy of Sag Harbor is still fueled by the sea, attracting wealthy New Yorkers who come to retreat and relax in this chic summertime community by the beach.

Information: Chamber of Commerce, Sag Harbor, 631-725-0011;
www.sagharborchamber.com

WHAT TO SEE AND DO
CUSTOM HOUSE

161 Main St., Sag Harbor, 631-692-4664; www.splia.org

This building served as a custom house and post office during the late 18th and early 19th centuries. Antique furnishings. July-August: Tuesday-Sunday; May-June and September-October: Saturday-Sunday.

ELIZABETH A. MORTON NATIONAL WILDLIFE REFUGE

784 Noyac Road, Sag Harbor, 631-286-0485; www.refuges.fws.gov

At one time, Native American tribes inhabited this area. Today, a variety of birds—some endangered—call this 187-acre refuge home at different times of the year. Daily, ½ hour before sunrise to ½ hour after sunset.

SAG HARBOR WHALING AND HISTORICAL MUSEUM

200 Main St., Sag Harbor, 631-725-0770; www.sagharborwhalingmuseum.org

Listed on the National Register of Historic Places, this museum, housed in a mansion, celebrates Sag Harbor's long history of whaling. It features items such as the tools used to capture whales, a replica of a whaleboat, whale teeth and bones and other materials associated with whaling. May-October, daily 10 a.m.-5 p.m., Sunday 1-5 p.m.

RESTAURANTS
★★★AMERICAN HOTEL

49 Main St., Sag Harbor, 631-725-3535; www.theamericanhotel.com

Located in the atmospheric American Hotel is an elegant and romantic restaurant filled with Empire and Victorian antiques and furnishings. The menu offers American and French classics, and an excellent wine list. American, French menu. Lunch, dinner. Closed holidays. Bar. Business casual attire. Reservations recommended. Valet parking. Outdoor seating. **$$$**

★★IL CAPUCCINO

30 Madison St., Sag Harbor, 631-725-2747; www.ilcapuccino.com
Italian menu. Dinner. Closed holidays. Bar. Children's menu. Casual attire. **$$**

★★ESTIA'S LITTLE KITCHEN

1615 Sag Harbor, Sag Harbor, 631-725-1045; www.eatshampton.com/LittleKitchen.htm
American menu. Breakfast, lunch, dinner. Closed Tuesday. Casual attire. Reservations recommended. **$$**

★★SPINNAKER'S

63 Main St., Sag Harbor, 631-725-9353
American, International menu. Lunch, dinner, Sunday brunch. Closed holidays. Bar. Children's menu. Casual attire. Reservations recommended. Valet parking. **$$**

SAINT JAMES

This community in Smithtown (on Long Island) attracts power players from professional sports, media and entertainment.
Information: www.smithtownchamber.org

RESTAURANTS

★★LOTUS EAST

416 N. Country Road, Saint James, 631-862-6030
Chinese menu. Lunch, dinner. Bar. Casual attire. **$$**

★★★MIRABELLE

404 N. Country Road, Saint James, 631-584-5999; www.restaurantmirabelle.com
With a seasoned French chef and former food writer as proprietors, this Long Island restaurant rivals many in the city. Menu items are a twist on classical French fare, accented with the freshest herbs, and the wine list highlights local vintners. Standout dishes on the menu include the shredded braised rabbit leg with kimchee and the seared organic salmon with a ragout of flageolet beans and pearl onions. French menu. Lunch, dinner. Closed Monday; holidays. Bar. Business casual attire. Reservations recommended. Valet parking. **$$$$**

SARANAC LAKE

Surrounded by Adirondack Park, the village of Saranac Lake was first settled in 1819 when Jacob Moody, who had been injured in a sawmill accident, retired to the wilderness, built a log cabin at what is now Pine and River Streets and raised a family of mountain guides. The qualities that attracted Moody and made the town a famous health resort in the 19th century continue to lure visitors who come for the fresh, mountain air and a relaxing environment.
Information: Chamber of Commerce, 9 Main St., Saranac Lake, 518-891-1990,
800-347-1997; www.saranaclake.com

WHAT TO SEE AND DO

MOUNT PISGAH VETERANS MEMORIAL SKI CENTER

Highway 86, Saranac Lake, 518-891-0970; www.saranaclake.com/pisgah.shtml
Five slopes, T-bar; patrol, school, snowmaking; snacks. Longest run 1,800 feet, vertical drop 300 feet. Mid-December-mid-March, Thursday-Sunday.

ROBERT LOUIS STEVENSON MEMORIAL COTTAGE

11 Stevenson Lane, Saranac Lake, 518-891-1462; www.adirondacks.com/robertlstevenson

Where Robert Louis Stevenson lived while undergoing treatment for what is believed to have been tuberculosis, 1887-1888. July-mid-September: Tuesday-Sunday 9:30 a.m.-noon, 1-4:30 p.m.; daily by appointment.

SIX NATIONS INDIAN MUSEUM

Adirondack Park, Buck Pond Road, Onchiota, 518-891-2299

Indoor and outdoor exhibits portray the life of Native Americans, with a council ground, types of fires, ancient and modern articles; lecture on Native American culture and history. July-Labor Day: daily 10 a.m.-6 p.m.; May-June, September-October: by appointment.

SPECIAL EVENTS

ADIRONDACK CANOE CLASSIC

Adirondack Marina, Saranac Lake, 518-891-2744, 800-347-1992; www.saranaclake.com

A ninety-mile, three-day race from Old Forge to Saranac Lake embarked upon by roughly 250 canoes, kayaks and guideboats. Early September.

WINTER CARNIVAL

30 Main St., Saranac Lake, 518-891-1990; www.saranaclakewintercarnival.com

Skating, ski, snowshoe and snowmobile racing and a parade are all part of this seasonal festival. Early February.

HOTELS

★★★★★THE POINT

Highway 30, Saranac Lake, 518-891-5674, 800-255-3530; www.thepointresort.com

Exceptionally well-heeled travelers seeking a glamorous version of roughing it head straight for the Point. This former great camp of William Avery Rockefeller revives the spirit of the early 19th-century Adirondacks, when the wealthy came to rusticate in this sylvan paradise. No signs direct visitors to this intimate camp, and a decidedly residential ambience is maintained. The resort has a splendid location on a 10-acre peninsula on Upper Saranac Lake. Rooms feature Adirondack twig furnishings, stone fireplaces, elegant bathrooms and luxe antiques. From snowshoeing and cross-country skiing to water sports, trail hikes and croquet, you'll find a variety of outdoor activities. Guests have the run of the place and no request is too much. Champagne and truffled popcorn at 4 a.m.? No problem. Gourmet dining figures largely in the experience and with a nod to the patrician past, guests don black-tie attire twice weekly at the communal dining table in the resort's great room. 11 rooms. No children allowed. Restaurant, bar. Spa. Beach. Tennis. $$$$

★★HOTEL SARANAC

100 Main St., Saranac Lake, 518-891-2200, 800-937-0211; www.hotelsaranac.com

86 rooms. Wireless Internet access. Two restaurants, bar. $

★★SARANAC INN GOLF & COUNTRY CLUB

125 County Route 46, Saranac Lake, 518-891-1402; www.saranacinn.com

10 rooms. Closed Columbus Day-April. Restaurant, bar. Golf. $

SARATOGA SPRINGS

Saratoga Springs is a resort city that is rural yet decidedly cosmopolitan. Much of the town's Victorian architecture has been restored. The city boasts the natural springs, geysers and mineral baths that first made the town famous, as well as internationally recognized harness and thoroughbred racing and polo, respected museums and the Saratoga Performing Arts Center.

Information: Saratoga County Chamber of Commerce, 28 Clinton St.,
Saratoga Springs, 518-584-3255; www.saratoga.org

WHAT TO SEE AND DO

HISTORIC CONGRESS PARK
Canfield Casino and Union Ave., Saratoga Springs, 518-584-6920
The Museum of the Historical Society and the Walworth Memorial Museum are housed in the old 1870 casino. The museums trace the history of the city's growth. Museums Memorial Day-Labor Day: daily; rest of year: call for hours. Park daily.

LINCOLN AND ROOSEVELT BATHS
65 S. Broadway, Saratoga Spa State Park, 518-226-4790
Relax and savor treatments with mineral waters, baths, massages and hot packs. Roosevelt all year, Wednesday-Sunday; Lincoln July and August, daily.

NATIONAL BOTTLE MUSEUM
76 Milton Ave., Ballston Spa, 518-885-7589; www.nationalbottlemuseum.org
Glass of all shapes and purposes, including antique bottles, jars, stoneware and related items, are on display. Research library on bottle collecting. June-October: daily; rest of year: Monday-Friday.

NATIONAL MUSEUM OF DANCE
99 S. Broadway, Saratoga Springs, 518-584-2225; www.dancemuseum.org
Dedicated to American professional dance. Exhibits, hall of fame, museum shop. Late May-Labor Day: Saturday-Sunday, from 10 a.m.-4:30 p.m.

NATIONAL MUSEUM OF RACING AND HALL OF FAME
191 Union Ave., Saratoga Springs, 518-584-0400, 800-562-5394;
www.racingmuseum.org
Exhibitions on the history and mechanics of Thoroughbred racing include the stories of racing champs Man o' War, Secretariat, Seattle Slew and Affirmed. Also contains exhibits on Saratoga's gambling heydey. Training track tours in summer. Monday-Saturday 10 a.m.-4 p.m., Sunday from noon to 4 p.m.; closed holidays.

SARATOGA GAMING AND RACING
Crescent Avenue, Saratoga Springs, 518-584-2110; www.saratogaraceway.com
Video gaming machines; harness racing February-November.

SARATOGA PERFORMING ARTS CENTER
108 Avenue of The Pines, Saratoga Springs, 518.587.3330; www.spac.org
A setting for diverse art and theater performances, this amphitheater in natural setting seats 5,000 under cover with space for more on the lawn. The Little Theatre is a 500-seat indoor showcase for chamber music.

★
★
★
★
☆

SARATOGA SPA STATE PARK

19 Roosevelt Drive, Saratoga Springs, 518-584-2535; www.saratogaspastatepark.org

This 2,200-acre park is home to the performing arts center, mineral bath houses, golf and many other recreational facilities. Daily.

YADDO GARDENS

Union Ave., Saratoga Springs, 518-584-0746; www.yaddo.org

An artists' retreat since 1926, this Victorian Gothic mansion's famous residents have included Flannery O'Connor, Leonard Bernstein and John Cheever. The mansion is closed to the general public, but landscaped gardens are open to all. Daily.

SPECIAL EVENTS

POLO

Saratoga Polo Association, Whitney Field, Bloomfield and Denton Road,
Saratoga Springs, 518-584-8108; www.saratogapolo.com

Polo ponies and riders face off on these historic grounds each summer. June-August.

SARATOGA PERFORMING ARTS CENTER

108 Ave. of the Pines, Saratoga Springs, 518-587-3330; www.spac.org

New York City Opera, June; New York City Ballet, July. The Philadelphia Orchestra and Saratoga Chamber Music Festival, August. Jazz festival, summer.

SARATOGA RACE COURSE

Union Ave. and Highway 9P, Saratoga Springs, 518-584-6200;
www.saratogaracetrack.com

Thoroughbred racing. Late July-Early September.

HOTELS

★★GIDEON PUTNAM RESORT AND SPA

24 Gideon Putnam Road, Saratoga Springs, 518-584-3000; www.gideonputnam.com

120 rooms. High-speed Internet access. Three restaurants, bar. Spa. Golf. Tennis. **$$$**

★GRAND UNION MOTEL

120 S. Broadway, Saratoga Springs, 518-584-9000; www.grandunionmotel.com

64 rooms. Spa. Pool. **$**

★★HOLIDAY INN

232 Broadway, Saratoga Springs, 518-584-4550; www.spa-hi.com

168 rooms. High-speed Internet access. Restaurant, bar. Pets accepted. Pool. **$$**

★★THE INN AT SARATOGA

231 Broadway, Saratoga Springs, 518-583-1890, 800-274-3573;
www.theinnatsaratoga.com

42 rooms. Complimentary full breakfast. Wireless Internet access. Restaurant, bar. **$**

SARATOGA NATIONAL HISTORICAL PARK

In two engagements, September 19 and October 7, 1777, American forces under General Horatio Gates defeated the army of General John Burgoyne in the Battles of Saratoga. This brought France into the war on the side of the colonies. The battle is regarded as the turning point of the Revolutionary War. The scene of this historic event is the rolling hill country between Highways 4 and 32, five miles north of Stillwater. Open season: April 1-November 30. April 7-September 30: 9 a.m.-7 p.m.: October 1-Daylight Savings Time: 9 a.m.-5 p.m., Daylight Savings Time November 30: 9 a.m.-4 p.m. Information: 648 Route 32, Stillwater, 518-664-9821; *www.nps.gov/sara*

★★ROOSEVELT INN & SUITES

2961 Highway 9, Saratoga Springs, 518-584-0980, 800-524-9147;
www.rooseveltsuites.com

51 rooms. Complimentary continental breakfast. Restaurant, bar. Spa. Whirlpool. Pool. Tennis. **$$**

★★THE SARATOGA HILTON

534 Broadway, Saratoga Springs, 518-584-4000, 888-866-3591;www.thesaratogahotel.com
242 rooms. Wireless Internet access. Restaurant, bar. **$$**

SPECIALTY LODGING

WESTCHESTER HOUSE BED & BREAKFAST

102 Lincoln Ave., Saratoga Springs, 518-587-7613, 888-302-1717;
www.westchesterhousebandb.com

Master carpenter Almeron King built this gracious 1885 Queen Anne, Victorian style, Saratoga Springs Inn for his family home. King's skill and imagination abound throughout this NY bed and breakfast inn. The handcrafted chestnut moldings and elaborately carved fireplace mantles within the Inn reflect a strong Eastlake influence. The whimsical roofline, complete with cupola and balcony, soars skyward. Seven rooms. Closed January. Complimentary continental breakfast. **$$$**

RESTAURANTS

★★★CHEZ PIERRE

979 Route 9, Gansevoort, 518-793-3350, 800-672-0666;
www.chezpierrerestaurant.com

Joe and Pierrette Baldwin's romantic French restaurant serves inspired cooking—like the throwback steak au poivre flambé and veal Oscar, a veal cutlet topped with crabmeat, asparagus and hollandaise sauce—in a setting accented with murals painted by a local artist and framed pictures of the owners' homeland. French menu. Dinner. Closed Sunday-Monday; holidays. Bar. Business casual attire. Reservations recommended. **$$$**

★OLDE BRYAN INN

123 Maple Ave., Saratoga Springs, 518-587-2990; www.oldebryaninn.com
American menu. Dinner. Closed holidays. Bar. Children's menu. Casual attire. Outdoor seating. **$$**

NEW YORK

★
★
★
★
☆

★★PRIMO'S RESTAURANT

231 Broadway, Saratoga Springs, 518-583-1890, 800-274-3573;www.theinnatsaratoga.com
American menu. Dinner. Closed holidays. Bar. Casual attire. Reservations recommended. Outdoor seating. **$$**

SAUGERTIES

At the confluence of Esopus Creek and the Hudson River, Saugerties was a port of call for riverboats. The town was famous for building racing sloops and for the production of fine paper, leather and canvas.

WHAT TO SEE AND DO

OPUS 40 & QUARRYMAN'S MUSEUM

50 Fite Road, Saugerties, 845-246-3400; www.opus40.org
Environmental sculpture rise out of this abandoned bluestone quarry. More than six acres of fitted bluestone were constructed over 37 years by sculptor Harvey Fite. Site of Sunset Concert series and other programs. Quarryman's Museum houses collection of tools of quarry workers and others. Memorial Day-Columbus Day, Friday-Sunday; some Saturday reserved for special events.

HOTEL

★COMFORT INN

2790 Route 32 N., Saugerties, 845-246-1565, 877-424-6423; www.choicehotels.com
65 rooms. Complimentary continental breakfast. Pets accepted. **$**

RESTAURANTS

★★CAFE TAMAYO

89 Partition St., Saugerties, 845-246-9371; www.cafetamayo.com
American menu. Dinner. Closed Monday-Wednesday; holidays. Bar. Casual attire. Reservations recommended. Guest rooms available. **$$$**

★★NEW WORLD HOME COOKING

1411 Route 212, Saugerties, 845-246-0900; www.ricorlando.com
American, International menu. Lunch, dinner. Closed holidays. Casual attire. Reservations recommended. Outdoor seating. **$$**

★★RED ONION

1654 Route 212 at Glasco Turpike, Saugerties, 845-679-1223;
www.redonionrestaurant.com
American, International menu. Dinner, brunch. Closed Wednesday; holidays. Bar. Business casual attire. Reservations recommended. Outdoor seating. **$$**

SAYVILLE

On the Great South Bay of Long Island, Sayville is the point of departure for ferries taking vacationers to Fire Island.
Information: Chamber of Commerce, Montauk Highway and Lincoln Ave.,
631-567-5257

LONG ISLAND MARITIME MUSEUM

86 West Ave., West Sayville, 631-854-4974; www.limaritime.org

Local maritime exhibits include oyster cull house (circa 1870), tug boat *Charlotte* (1888), oyster vessel *Priscilla* (1888) and the oyster sloop *Modesty* (1923). Monday-Saturday 10 a.m.-4 p.m., Sunday noon-4 p.m.; closed holidays.

HOTELS

★COMFORT INN

2695 Route 112, Medford, 631-654-3000, 877-424-6423; www.choicehotels.com

75 rooms. Wireless Internet access. Complimentary continental breakfast. Pool. Fitness center. Pets accepted. **$**

★★HOLIDAY INN

3845 Veterans Memorial Highway, Ronkonkoma, 631-585-9500, 888-465-4329; www.holiday-inn.com

289 rooms. High-speed Internet access. Restaurant, bar. Airport transportation available. **$$**

SCHENECTADY

Schenectady offers a unique blend of the old and the new, from row houses of the pre-Revolutionary War stockade area to the bustle of the downtown area.

Information: Schenectady County Chamber of Commerce, 306 State St., Schenectady, 518-372-5656, 800-962-8007

261

WHAT TO SEE AND DO

THE HISTORIC STOCKADE AREA

32 Washington Ave., Schenectady, 518-374-0263; www.historicstockade.com

Privately owned houses, some dating to colonial times, many marked with historic plaques. Schenectady County Historical Society offers guided tours of their building and folder describing walking tour. The society also maintains a historical museum with a collection of Sexton and Ames paintings; also 19th-century dollhouse, Shaker collection, genealogical library. Monday-Saturday, afternoons.

NEW YORK

★
★★
★★
★

PROCTOR'S THEATRE

432 State St., Schenectady, 518-346-6204; www.proctors.org

Former movie/vaudeville palace is a regional performing arts center hosting Broadway touring shows, dance, opera and plays. 1931 Wurlitzer theater organ. Seats 2,700. Free tours by appointment.

THE SCHENECTADY MUSEUM AND PLANETARIUM AND SCHENECTADY HERITAGE AREA

15 Nott Terrace Heights, Schenectady, 518-382-7890; www.schenectadymuseum.org

Exhibits and programs on art, history, science and technology. Tuesday-Friday 10 a.m.-4:30 p.m., Saturday-Sunday noon-5 p.m.; closed holidays. Planetarium shows and children's planetarium shows summer: Tuesday-Sunday; rest of year: Saturday-Sunday.

UNION COLLEGE

807 Union St., Schenectady, 518-388-6000; www.union.edu

Country's first planned campus; original buildings (1812-1814) by French architect Joseph Jacques Rame. Nott Memorial (1875) is the only 16-sided building in the Northern Hemisphere. Also on campus is Jackson Garden, eight acres of landscaped and informal plantings.

HOTELS

★★★GLEN SANDERS MANSION INN

1 Glen Ave., Scotia, 518-688-2138; www.glensandersmansion.com

The inn is a 1995 addition to the Glen Sanders Mansion restaurant, which is housed in the original historic residence. Rooms feature comfortable, elegant furnishings and make for the perfect weekend retreat. Complimentary fresh fruit, cookies and coffee are served throughout the day. 22 rooms. Complimentary continental breakfast. Restaurant. $

★★HOLIDAY INN

100 Nott Terrace, Schenectady, 518-393-4141; www.holiday-inn.com

183 rooms. High-speed Internet access. Complimentary full breakfast. Restaurant, bar. Airport transportation available. $

SENECA FALLS

The first convention of the U.S. Women's Suffrage Movement met in July 1848, in Seneca Falls. The town was the home of Amelia Jenks Bloomer, who drew international attention to women's rights by advocating and wearing the costume that bears her name. The two great leaders of the movement, Elizabeth Cady Stanton and Susan B. Anthony, also worked in Seneca Falls.

Information: Seneca County Chamber of Commerce, Highways 5 and 20 W., Seneca Falls, 315-568-2906; www.senecachamber.org

★
★
★
★
☆

WHAT TO SEE AND DO

CAYUGA LAKE STATE PARK

2678 Lower Lake Road, Seneca Falls, 315-568-5163, 800-456-2267; www.nysparks.state.ny.us

Swimming, beach, bathhouse, fishing, boating, picnicking, playground, tent and trailer sites, cabins late April-late October.

ELIZABETH CADY STANTON HOUSE

32 Washington St., Seneca Falls; www.nps.gov/wori/historyculture

In Women's Rights National Historical Park. House where Stanton worked and lived from 1847 to 1862. Artifacts include original china, books and furniture. Changing exhibits. Tours daily.

MONTEZUMA NATIONAL WILDLIFE REFUGE

Highway 20, Seneca Falls, 315-568-5987; www.fws.gov/r5mnwr

Federal wildlife refuge; visitor center. Peak migration for shorebirds (fall), Canada geese and ducks (spring and fall). Refuge, daily daylight hours.

NATIONAL WOMEN'S HALL OF FAME

76 Fall St., Seneca Falls, 315-568-8060; www.greatwomen.org

Museum and education center honors famous American women, past and present. May-September: Monday-Saturday 10 a.m.-5 p.m., Sunday from noon; October-April, Wednesday-Saturday 11 a.m.-5 p.m.

SENECA FALLS HISTORICAL SOCIETY MUSEUM

55 Cayuga St., Seneca Falls, 315-568-8412; www.sfhistoricalsociety.org

A 19th-century, 23-room Victorian/Queen Anne mansion with period room, local history exhibits; research library and archives. Tours. July-August, daily.

WOMEN'S RIGHTS NATIONAL HISTORICAL PARK

136 Fall St., Seneca Falls, 315-568-2991; www.nps.gov/wori

Visitor center with exhibits and film; talks scheduled daily during summer.

SPECIAL EVENT
CONVENTION DAYS CELEBRATION

115 Fall St., Seneca Falls, 315-568-2906; www.conventiondays.com

Commemorates first women's rights convention, held July 19 and 20, 1848. Weekend closest to July 19 and 20.

SHANDAKEN

This Catskill Mountain town carries the Iroquois name meaning "rapid waters." Shandaken is a town in the Catskills with easy access to New York City—a rare combo. It is home of the highest peak in the Catskills, Slide Mountain and is also the home of Esopus Creek, one of the finest wild trout fisheries in the East. Skiing, hiking and hunting are popular in this area of mountains and streams.

Information: www.shandaken.us

WHAT TO SEE AND DO
BELLEAYRE MOUNTAIN

Route 28, Shandaken, 845-254-5600, 800-942-6904; www.belleayre.com

Two quad, triple, two double chairlifts; three-handle tows; 41 runs; patrol, school, rentals; snowmaking; cafeterias; nursery. Longest run 2¼ miles; vertical drop 1,404 feet.November-early April, daily. Half-day rates. More than five miles of cross-country trails.

HOTEL
★★★THE COPPERHOOD INN & SPA

70-39 Route 28, Shandaken, 845-688-2460; www.copperhood.com

This European-style oasis with elegant, inviting rooms and helpful staff overlooks the rushing waters of the Esopus Creek. Guests can take advantage of an extensive range of spa services and recreational activities or simply lounge and enjoy nature. The inn's menu includes such dishes as free-range chicken with sun-dried tomatoes and tarragon purée. 20 rooms. Spa. Pool. Fitness center. Tennis. $$$

SHELTER ISLAND

Quakers, persecuted by the Puritans in New England, settled Shelter Island in Gardiner's Bay off the east end of Long Island. The island is reached by car and

★
★
★
★

pedestrian ferry from Greenport, on the North fork of Long Island, or from North Haven (Sag Harbor), on the south. There is a monument to the Quakers and a graveyard with 17th-century stones. Two museums recount the area's history: the 18th-century Havens House and the 19th-century Manhanset Chapel. Also here is the 2,200-acre Nature Conservancy's Mashomack Preserve, with miles of trails for hiking and educational programs. The island offers swimming, boating off miles of sandy shoreline, biking, hiking, tennis and golfing.

Information: www.shelterislandtown.us

HOTEL

★★PRIDWIN BEACH HOTEL AND COTTAGES

81 Shore Road, Shelter Island, 631-749-0476, 800-273-2497; www.pridwin.com

40 rooms. Closed mid-October-April. Complimentary full breakfast. Restaurant, bar. Pool. Tennis. $$

RESTAURANTS

★★★CHEQUIT INN

23 Grand Ave., Shelter Island, 631-749-0018; www.shelterislandinns.com

This casual Victorian inn was originally built (circa 1870) around a maple tree that, now enormous, still shades the terrace that overlooks Dering Harbor. Try the home-style Atlantic cod fish and chips with fresh tartar sauce, a proprietary specialty. Continental menu. Lunch, dinner. Bar. Children's menu. Casual attire. Reservations recommended. Outdoor seating. $$

★★★RAM'S HEAD INN

108 Ram Island Drive, Shelter Island, 631-749-0811; www.shelterislandinns.com

At this inn tucked away at a far corner of Shelter Island, meals include fare like roast loin rack of lamb with garlic pommes Anna and wild salmon with wilted spinach and morels. Continental menu. Dinner, brunch. Closed November-April. Bar. Children's menu. Casual attire. Reservations recommended. Outdoor seating. $$$

SKANEATELES

Skaneateles (skany-AT-les) was once a stop on the Underground Railroad. Today it is a quiet resort town at the north end of Skaneateles Lake.

Information: www.skaneateles.com

WHAT TO SEE AND DO

MID-LAKES NAVIGATION BOAT TRIPS

11 Jordan St., Skaneateles, 315-685-8500, 800-545-4318; www.midlakesnav.com/

A 32-mile cruise along shoreline of Skaneateles Lake. July-August, Monday-Saturday. Lunch cruise Monday-Friday, dinner cruises nightly; three-hour excursion Sunday, sightseeing cruise daily.

SPECIAL EVENT

POLO MATCHES

Skaneateles Polo Club Grounds, 813 Andrews Road, 315-685-7373

Sunday July-August.

HOTELS

★THE BIRD'S NEST

1601 E. Genesee St., Skaneateles, 315-685-5641
30 rooms. Whirlpool. Pets accepted. $

★★★★MIRBEAU INN & SPA

851 W. Genesee St., Skaneateles, 315-685-5006, 877-647-2328; www.mirbeau.com
This 12-acre Finger Lakes country estate, filled with ponds, gardens and woodlands, seems to have leapt off the canvases of Claude Monet. Delightful Provençal fabrics and French country furnishings make the rooms cozy and comfortable while fireplaces and soaking tubs add romance. The friendly staff is available when you need them, unobtrusive when you don't. With winsome views of the lily pond and footbridge and the fresh-from-the-garden taste of the dishes, the restaurant truly transports diners. The European-style spa is both modern and charming. 34 rooms. High-speed Internet access. Restaurant, two bars. Fitness room, fitness classes available, spa. Whirlpool. $$$

★★★SHERWOOD INN

26 W. Genesee St., Skaneateles, 315-685-3405, 800-374-3796; www.thesherwoodinn.com
Beautifully furnished with an aura of refinement, this 1807 inn, a former stagecoach stop, has fantastic views of the lake. The staff, cuisine and common and guest rooms are terrific. 24 rooms. Complimentary continental breakfast. Wireless Internet access. Two restaurants, bar. $$

SPECIALTY LODGINGS

THE ARBOR HOUSE INN AND SUITES

41 Fennell St., Skaneateles, 315-685-8966, 888-234-4558; www.arborhouseinn.com
This country inn has rooms decorated with antiques and oriental rugs. Some come complete with Jacuzzi tubs or fireplaces. Eight rooms. Complimentary full breakfast. $$

HOBBIT HOLLOW BED AND BREAKFAST

3061 W. Lake Road, Skaneateles, 315-685-2791; www.hobbithollow.com
This colonial revival building with country décor is set on 300 acres in the Finger Lakes region. The region's many wineries are a short drive away. Five rooms. Children over 18 years only. Complimentary full breakfast. $$$

LADY OF THE LAKE

2 W. Lake St., Skaneateles, 315-685-7997, 888-685-7997; www.ladyofthelake.net
The Lady of the Lake, a beautiful 1899 Queen Anne Victorian house located across from Skaneateles Lake, boasts a large front porch, décor that includes period furnishing and antiques and rooms named after the ladies who previously owned the house. Plenty of modern comforts are offered, including high-speed Internet access as well as a refrigerator stocked with complimentary soft drinks, bottled water and beer. Three rooms. Children over 8 years only. Complimentary full breakfast. $$

RESTAURANT

★★★★GIVERNY

851 W. Genesee St., Skaneateles, 315-685-1927, 877-647-2328; www.mirbeau.com
Named after painter Claude Monet's French country home, this elegant dining room, under the confident direction of executive chef Edward Moro, delivers the best of

Provençal cooking in a cozy, romantic setting. Try the four- or five-course tasting menu or dine à la carte on dishes such as butter-braised Maine lobster with squash risotto or sautéed foie gras with caramelized pear. The wine list includes selections from around the world, and around the corner, with local Finger Lakes wineries highlighted. American, French menu. Breakfast, lunch, dinner. Bar. Business casual attire. Reservations recommended. Outdoorseating. **$$$**

SPA

★★★★SPA MIRBEAU

851 W. Genesee St., Skaneateles, 315-685-1927, 877-647-2328; www.mirbeau.com

Fourteen-thousand square feet of tranquility await at the Spa Mirbeau, whose beautiful natural surroundings serve as the inspiration for everything from the herbal-infused steam rooms to body wraps and facials. After some pre-treatment relaxation in the resting area—complete with heated foot pools—you're ready to head to one of 18 treatment rooms. More than just a massage, the Monet's Favorite Fragrance massage blends essential oils of herbs and flowers from the Finger Lakes region to create an aromatherapy treatment that stimulates the senses. The expansive fitness center offers everything from meditation to Pilates.

SMITHTOWN

Smithtown includes six unincorporated hamlets and three incorporated villages and is situated near several state parks.

Information: www.smithtowninfo.com

HOTELS

★★★MARRIOTT ISLANDIA LONG ISLAND

3635 Express Drive, Islandia, 631-232-3000, 800-228-9290; www.marriott.com

This convenient hotel is located just off the Long Island Expressway near Islip McArthur Airport. Guests will find a wide range of comforts including cable TV, coffee and tea makers and luxurious bedding with down comforters and pillows and plush cotton linens. Bistro Five-Eight, the hotel's elegant restaurant, offers American fare for breakfast, lunch and dinner while the Atrium Piano Bar is a more casual spot. 278 rooms. High-speed Internet access. Restaurant, bar. Airport transportation available. Fitness center. Pool. **$**

★★★SHERATON LONG ISLAND HOTEL

110 Motor Parkway, Hauppauage, 631-231-1100, 800-325-3535;
www.sheraton.com/longisland

Comfortable guest rooms, contemporary-styled public spaces and amenities like an indoor pool and fitness center attract both business and leisure travelers to this comfortable hotel. After visiting nearby beaches, relax at the Piano Bar for a cool cocktail or dine at the Fountain Grille. 209 rooms. High-speed Internet Access, Two restaurants, bar. Children's activity center. Airport transportation available. **$$**

SOUTHAMPTON

Southampton is the most formal of the fabled Hamptons, attracting the blue-blood set who summer here in their vast mansions overlooking Lake Agawam and the Atlantic dunes. The village center boasts terrific shopping in the form of Saks Fifth Avenue,

Ralph Lauren and more. And the town's Parrish Art Museum is a terrific spot to browse the ever-changing collections.

Information: Chamber of Commerce, 76 Main St., Southampton, 631-283-0402; www.southamptonchamber.com

WHAT TO SEE AND DO

CONSCIENCE POINT NATIONAL WILDLIFE REFUGE

North Sea Road, Southampton, 631-286-0485; www.fws.gov/northeast/longislandrefuges/consciencepoint.html

With 60 acres, this refuge is known for its maritime grasslands. A host of birds and fowl call this area home in the colder months, and a different variety migrate here in the warmer season. The refuge opened in 1971 and over the years has played host to many guests, both feathered and non-feathered. Conscience Point overlooks the North Sea Harbor and is a quiet area. This refuge is for those who want such peace and quiet while they are touring. Hours vary.

OLD HALSEY HOUSE

249 S. Main St., Southampton, 631-283-2494

This 1648 structure is the oldest English frame house in the state. Furnished with period furniture; colonial herb garden. Mid-July-mid-September, Tuesday-Sunday.

PARRISH ART MUSEUM

25 Jobs Lane, Southampton, 631-283-2118; www.parrishart.org

Includes collection of 19th- and 20th-century American paintings and prints focused on local artists; Japanese woodblock prints; collection of Renaissance works; changing exhibits; arboretum; performing arts and concert series; lectures; research library. Mid-June-mid-September: Monday-Tuesday and Thursday-Saturday, also Sunday afternoons; rest of year: Monday and Thursday-Sunday; closed holidays.

SHINNECOCK INDIAN OUTPOST

Old Montauk Hwy., Southampton, 631-283-8047; www.shinnecocktradingpost.com

This funky shop sells Native American crafts, clothes and glassware. There is also a deli, where you can get your morning coffee and a bagel. Summer, Monday-Sunday 6:30 a.m.-7 p.m., to 6 p.m., rest of year.

SOUTHAMPTON HISTORICAL MUSEUM

17 Meeting House Lane, Southampton, 631-283-2494; www.southamptonhistoricalmuseum.org

This mansion, built in 1843, depicts Southampton's colorful history. It has some original furnishings, photos and quilts. The museum's grounds include a one-room schoolhouse, drugstore, paint shop, blacksmith shop and carpentry store. There are also special exhibits at different times of the year. Tuesday-Saturday 11 a.m.-5 p.m., Sunday 1-5 p.m.

WATER MILL MUSEUM

41 Old Mill Road, Water Mill, 631-726-4625; www.watermillmuseum.org

Restored gristmill, 18th-century tools, other exhibits; craft demonstrations. Monday, Thursday-Saturday 11 a.m.-5 p.m., Sunday from 1 p.m.

★
★
★
★
★

SPECIAL EVENTS

HAMPTON CLASSIC HORSE SHOW

240 Snake Hollow Road, Bridgehampton, 631-537-3177; www.hamptonclassic.com
Horse show jumping event features celebrity spectators, food, shopping and family activities. Last week of August.

POWWOW

Shinnecock Indian Reservation, Southampton, 631-283-6143
Dances, ceremonies, displays. Labor Day weekend. Admission: adults $10, children and seniors $7.

HOTEL

★★SOUTHAMPTON INN

91 Hill St., Southampton, 631-283-6500, 800-732-6500; www.southamptoninn.com
90 rooms. Breakfast, lunch, dinner, Restaurant, bar. Children's activity center. Pets accepted. Pool. Tennis. $$

SPECIALTY LODGING

THE VILLAGE LATCH INN

101 Hill St., Southampton, 631-283-2160, 800-545-2824; www.villagelatch.com
67 rooms. Complimentary full breakfast. Pool. Tennis. $$$

RESTAURANTS

★GOLDEN PEAR

99 Main St., Southampton, 631-283-8900; www.goldenpearcafe.com
American menu. Breakfast, lunch. Casual attire. $$

★★COAST GRILL

1109 Noyack Road, Southampton, 631-283-2277
American, seafood menu. Dinner. Closed Monday-Thursday. Bar. Casual attire. $$

★★JOHN DUCK JR.

15 Prospect St., Southampton, 631-283-0311
American, German menu. Lunch, dinner. Closed Monday; holidays. Bar. Children's menu. Casual attire. $$

★★LE CHEF

75 Jobs Lane, Southampton, 631-283-8581; www.lechefbistro.com
French menu. Lunch, dinner, brunch. Bar. Casual attire. $$

★★LOBSTER INN

162 Inlet Road, Southampton, 631-283-1525
American, seafood menu. Lunch, dinner. Closed holidays. Bar. Children's menu. Casual attire. Outdoor seating. $$

★★MIRKO'S

Water Mill Square Water Mill, 631-726-4444
American menu. Dinner. Bar. Casual attire. Reservations recommended. Outdoor seating. $$$

SOUTHOLD

This community on Long Island is close to more than a dozen vineyards and countless museums and cultural activities.

Information: Greenport-Southold Chamber of Commerce, 631-765-3161; www.greenportsoutholdchamber.org

WHAT TO SEE AND DO

GREENPORT POTTERY

64725 Main Road, Southold, 631-477-1687; www.greenportpottery.com

For a great selection of homemade pottery, this is the place to go on the North Fork. The owner creates beautiful lamps, vases, mugs, dishes, decorative plates and other items in his shop. You can custom order items, and he will ship just about anywhere. In addition to the fine craftsmanship, the pottery is extremely reasonably priced—just a fraction of what comparable shops in the tonier Hamptons would charge. Daily 10 a.m.-5 p.m.; closed Tuesday.

HORTON POINT LIGHTHOUSE AND NAUTICAL MUSEUM

Lighthouse Park, 54325 Main Road, Southold, 631-765-5500

Memorial Day-Columbus Day, Saturday-Sunday limited hours.

THE OLD HOUSE

Cases Lane and Route 25, Cutchogue, 631-734-7122; www.cutchoguenewsuffolkhistory.org

This 1649 house is an example of early English architecture; 17th- and 18th-century furnishings. Also on the Village Green are the Wickham Farmhouse and the Old Schoolhouse Museum. July-Labor Day: Saturday-Monday; September-October: by appointment.

SOUTHOLD INDIAN MUSEUM

1080 Bayview Road, Southold, 631-765-5577; www.southoldindianmuseum.org

This museum celebrates Long Island's Native American history and features displays of artifacts such as weapons, tools and pottery, as well as other items used by the Long Island Algonquins. Sunday 1:30-4:30 p.m.; also Saturday in July-August; other times by appointment.

HOTEL

★★SANTORINI BEACHCOMBER RESORT MOTEL

3800 Duck Pond Road, Cutchogue, 631-734-6370; www.santorinibeach.net

50 rooms. Closed mid-October-Memorial Day. Beach. $

RESTAURANT

★★SEAFOOD BARGE

62980 Main Road, Southold, 631-765-3010; www.seafoodbarge.com

Seafood menu. Lunch, dinner. Bar. $$

SPRING VALLEY

This quaint village is about 35 miles due north of New York City.

Information: www.villagespringvalley.org

★
★★
★★★
★★★★
★★★★★

HISTORICAL SOCIETY OF ROCKLAND COUNTY

20 Zukor Road, New City, 845-634-9629; www.rocklandhistory.org/home.php

Museum of county history located in the Jacob Blauvelt House, a circa 1832 Dutch farmhouse and barn. Tuesday-Sunday afternoons; closed holidays.

HOTELS

★FAIRFIELD INN SPRING VALLEY NANUET

100 Spring Valley Marketplace, Spring Valley, 845-426-2000, 800-228-2800; www.marriott.com

105 rooms. Complimentary continental breakfast. High-speed Internet access. $

★★HOLIDAY INN

3 Executive Blvd., Suffern, 845-357-4800; www.holiday-inn.com

241 rooms. Restaurant, bar. Fitness center. High-speed Internet access Pool. $

★★★HILTON PEARL RIVER

500 Veterans Memorial Drive, Pearl River, 845-735-9000; www.hilton.com

Only 20 miles from Manhattan, the Hilton Pearl River boasts a relaxed, country park-like setting on 17 verdant acres overlooking the adjacent links of the Blue Hill golf course. Guest rooms are spacious and feature French country-styled décor along with high-thread-count sheets and toiletries from Crabtree & Evelyn. The hotel's restaurant, La Maisonette, serves contemporary American cooking with a French twist. 150 rooms. Restaurant, bar. Pool. Fitness center. $$

STAMFORD

Stamford, located along the west branch of the Delaware River, has a large historic district dating from the Victorian era including numerous former inns from the town's heyday. The nearby hamlet of Hobart is chock full of antique bookstores. And close-at-hand Andes bustles with terrific galleries, shops and restaurants.

Information: www.delawarecounty.org

WHAT TO SEE AND DO

LANSING MANOR

Highways 30 and 23, North Blenheim, 607-588-6061, 800-724-0309

A 19th-century manor house depicting life of an Anglo-Dutch household of the mid-1800s. Memorial Day-Columbus Day, Monday, Wednesday-Sunday.

MINE KILL STATE PARK

161 Mine Kill State Park, North Blenheim, 518-827-6111; www.nysparks.state.ny.us/parks/info.asp?parkID=117

Swimming pool (late June-early September), bathhouse, fishing, boating; hiking and nature trails, cross-country skiing, snowmobiling, picnicking, playground.

ZADOCK PRATT MUSEUM

1828 Homestead, Prattsville, 518-299-3395; www.prattmuseum.com

Period furnishings and memorabilia. Tours, exhibits. Memorial Day-Labor Day, Thursday-Sunday 1-4 p.m.

STATEN ISLAND (NEW YORK CITY)

Staten Island, twice the size of Manhattan with less than four percent of the population, is the most removed, in distance and character, from the other boroughs. At one time, sightseers on the famous Staten Island Ferry rarely disembarked to explore the almost rural character of the island. The completion of the Verrazano Bridge to Brooklyn, however, brought growth and the beginning of a struggle between developers and those who would preserve the island's uncrowded appeal.

Information: Staten Island Chamber of Commerce, 130 Bay St., Staten Island, 718-727-1900; or the NYC Convention & Visitors Bureau

WHAT TO SEE AND DO

CONFERENCE HOUSE

7455 Hylan Blvd., Staten Island, 718-984-6046; www.theconferencehouse.org

Built in the mid-1680s by an English sea captain, this was the site of an unproductive meeting on September 11, 1776, between British Admiral Lord Howe, Benjamin Franklin, John Adams and Edward Rutledge to discuss terms of peace to end the Revolutionary War. The meeting helped to produce the phrase the "United States of America." Rose, herb gardens; open-hearth cooking; spinning and weaving demonstrations. April-November, Friday-Sunday.

THE GREENBELT/HIGH ROCK

200 Nevada Ave., Egbertville, 718-667-2165

An 85-acre nature preserve in a 2,500-acre park. Visitor center, trails. Environmental programs, workshops. Self-guided tours. Urban park ranger-guided tours by appointment. Daily.

HISTORIC RICHMOND TOWN

441 Clarke Ave., Staten Island, 718-351-1611; www.historicrichmondtown.org

This outdoor museum complex depicts three centuries of history and culture of Staten Island and the surrounding region. Daily life and work of a rural community is shown in trade demonstrations and tours of shops and buildings. Among the restoration's 27 historic structures are the Historic Museum; Voorlezer's House (circa 1695), the oldest surviving elementary school in the United States; general store; and tradesmen's shops. Wednesday-Sunday afternoons; extended hours July-August; closed holidays.

★
★★
★★★
★★★★
★★★★★

JACQUES MARCHAIS MUSEUM OF TIBETAN ART

338 Lighthouse Ave., Staten Island, 718-987-3500; www.tibetanmuseum.com

Perched on a steep hill with views of the Atlantic Ocean, this museum houses the collection of Jacqueline Norman Klauber, who became fascinated with Tibet as a child. Highlights of the exhibits include a series of bright-colored masks and a large collection of golden *thangkas* or religious images, plus terraced sculpture gardens and a koi pond. Wednesday-Sunday 1-5 p.m.

SNUG HARBOR CULTURAL CENTER

1000 Richmond Terrace, Staten Island, 718-448-2500; www.snug-harbor.org

Founded in 1833 as a seamen's retirement home, Snug Harbor is now a performing and visual arts center with 28 historic buildings featuring Greek Revival and Victorian architecture; art galleries; children's museum; botanical garden, sculpture, 83 acres of parkland. Daily; closed holidays.

STATEN ISLAND ZOO
614 Broadway, Staten Island, 718-442-3100; www.statenislandzoo.org
Maintained by the Staten Island Zoological Society. Large collection of native and exotic reptiles, varied species of rattlesnakes, amphibians, marine reef fishes, mammals, birds. Children's center includes a miniature farm. Daily 10 a.m.-4:45 p.m.; closed holidays.

STONY BROOK
Originally part of the Three Village area first settled by Boston colonists in the 17th-century, Stony Brook became an important center for the shipbuilding industry on Long Island Sound in the 1800s.
Information:www.stonybrookvillage.com

WHAT TO SEE AND DO
THE MUSEUMS AT STONY BROOK
1200 N. Country Road, Stony Brook, 631-751-0066; www.longislandmuseum.org
Complex of three museums. The Melville Carriage House exhibits 90 vehicles from a collection of horse-drawn carriages. The Art Museum features changing exhibits of American art. The Blackwell History Museum has changing exhibits on a variety of historical themes as well as exhibits of period rooms and antique decoys. Blacksmith shop, schoolhouse, other period buildings. Wednesday-Saturday 10 a.m.-5 p.m Sunday noon-5 p.m. and Monday holidays; closed other holidays.

STALLER CENTER FOR THE ARTS
Nicholas Road and Route 347, Stony Brook, 631-632-7235; www.staller.sunysb.edu
On the SUNY campus, this venue houses a 1,049-seat main theater, three experimental theaters, an art gallery, a 400-seat recital hall and an electronic music studio. Summer International Theater Festival. Events all year.

HOTEL
★★★THREE VILLAGE INN
150 Main St., Stony Brook, 631-751-0555, 888-384-4438; www.threevillageinn.com
This harborside inn has elegant rooms overlooking the water. Enjoy village shopping and museums. Stonybrook University and Hospital are both nearby. 26 rooms. Restaurant, bar. $$

RESTAURANTS
★★★COUNTRY HOUSE
Route 25A, Stony Brook, 631-751-3332; www.countryhouserestaurant.com
This restaurant serves elegant dishes such as roasted salmon with spinach, saffron risotto and orange balsamic or sautéed sweet sea scallops with key line beurre blanc. Delicious chops, chicken and steak are on the menu, too. The romantic and elegant setting is perfect for special-occasion dining. American menu. Lunch, dinner. Closed holidays. Bar. Business casual attire. Reservations recommended. $$$

★★THREE VILLAGE INN
150 Main St., Stony Brook, 631-751-0555; www.threevillageinn.com
American menu. Breakfast, lunch, dinner, brunch. Closed holidays. Bar. Business casual attire. Reservations recommended. **$$$**

SYRACUSE

Syracuse began as a trading post at the mouth of Onondaga Creek. Salt from wells was produced here from 1796 to 1900. Industry began in 1793, when Thomas Wiard began making wooden plows. Shortly after 1800, a blast furnace was built that produced iron utensils and, during the War of 1812, cast shot for the Army. When the Erie Canal reached town in the late 1820s, Syracuse's industrial future was assured. Today the city has many large and varied industries.

Information: Convention and Visitors Bureau, 572 S. Salina St., Syracuse,
315-470-1910; www.syracusecvb.org

WHAT TO SEE AND DO

BEAVER LAKE NATURE CENTER
8477 E. Mud Lake Road, Baldwinsville, 315-638-2519
A 600-acre nature preserve with 10 miles of trails and boardwalks, a 200-acre lake that serves as a rest stop for migrating ducks and geese and a visitor center. In the winter the preserve is also used for cross-country skiing and snowshoeing. Other programs include maple sugaring and guided canoe tours. Daily 7:30 a.m.-dusk.

ERIE CANAL MUSEUM
318 Erie Blvd. E., Syracuse, 315-471-0593; www.eriecanalmuseum.org
Indoor and outdoor exhibits detail the construction and operation of the Erie Canal, including a 65 foot reconstructed canal boat from which exhibits are seen; research library and archives. Tuesday-Saturday 10 a.m.-5 p.m., Sunday to 3 p.m.

EVERSON MUSEUM OF ART
401 Harrison St., Syracuse, 315-474-6064; www.everson.org
The first I. M. Pei-designed museum houses a permanent collection of American art and a collection of American ceramics, with changing exhibits. It's the home of the Syracuse China Center for the Study of American Ceramics. Tuesday-Friday, Sunday noon-5 p.m., Saturday from 10 a.m.; closed holidays.

LANDMARK THEATRE
362 S. Salina St., Syracuse, 315-475-7980; www.landmarktheatre.org
Built in 1928 as Loew's State Theatre in the era of vaudeville-movie houses. The interior architecture is filled with carvings, chandeliers and ornate gold decorations. Theater houses concerts, comedy, plays, dance and classic movies.

ONONDAGA HISTORICAL ASSOCIATION MUSEUM
321 Montgomery St., Syracuse, 315-428-1864; www.cnyhistory.org
Changing and permanent exhibits illustrate history of central New York including exhibits on sports history, transportation, military history and industry.

NEW YORK

★
★
★
★
☆

ROSAMOND GIFFORD ZOO AT BURNET PARK

1 Conservation Place, Syracuse, 315-435-8511; www.rosamondgiffordzoo.org

Zoo traces origin of life from 600 million years ago, with exhibits on animals' unique adaptations and animal/human interaction. Gift shop. Daily 10 a.m.-4:30 p.m.; closed holidays.

ST. MARIE AMONG THE IROQUOIS

Syracuse, 315-453-6767; onondagacountyparks.com/parks/sainte-marie

A 17th-century French mission living history museum. Blacksmithing, cooking, carpentry and gardening. May-November: Wednesday-Sunday; December-April: Tuesday-Sunday.

SYRACUSE HERITAGE AREA VISITOR CENTER

Weighlock Building, 318 Erie Blvd. E., Syracuse, 315-471-0593;
www.eriecanalmuseum.org/urban

Video presentation and exhibits here introduce visitors to area attractions.

SYRACUSE UNIVERSITY

University Ave. at University Place, Syracuse, 315-443-1870; www.syr.edu

Prvivate research university noted for the Maxwell School of Citizenship and Public Affairs, Newhouse School of Public Communications, College of Engineering and 50,000-seat Carrier Dome.

SPECIAL EVENTS

BALLOON FESTIVAL

Jamesville Beach Park, Apulia Road, Jamesville, 315-435-5252

Mid-June.

NEW YORK STATE FAIR

State Fairgrounds, 581 State Fair Blvd., Syracuse, 315-487-7711; www.nysfair.org

Over 375 acres of rides, food, entertainment and midway games appear here every summer. 12 days in late August-early September.

SYRACUSE STAGE

820 E. Genesee St., Syracuse, 315-443-3275; www.syracusestage.org

Hosts original, professional theatrical productions. September-May.

HOTELS

★★BEST WESTERN TULLY INN

5779 Highway 80, Tully, 315-696-6061; www.bestwestern.com

44 rooms. Restaurant, bar. Complimentary breakfast. High-speed Internet access. $

★★COURTYARD BY MARRIOTT

6415 Yorktown Circle, East Syracuse, 315-432-0300; www.marriott.com

149 rooms. High-speed Internet access. Restaurant. $

★★★DOUBLETREE HOTEL SYRACUSE

6301 Highway 298, Syracuse, 315-432-0200; www.doubletree.com

This comfortable hotel caters to the business travelers who visit the corporate park in which it is located and the area's surrounding businesses. Amenities include luxury bedding, high-speed Internet and MP3 docking stations. 250 rooms. High-speed Internet access. Restaurant, bar. Whirlpool. Airport transportation available. Fitness center. Pool. **$**

★★EMBASSY SUITES

6646 Old Collamer Road, Syracuse, 315-446-3200, 800-362-2779;
www.embassy-suites.com
215 rooms, all suites. Complimentary full breakfast. Restaurant, bar. Children's activity center. Airport transportation available. **$**

★★★GENESEE GRANDE HOTEL

1060 E. Genesee St., Syracuse, 315-476-4212, 800-365-4663;
www.geneseegrande.com
Befitting its name, the Genesee Grande is a luxurious hotel in the University Hill section of downtown Syracuse. Rooms have soft, comfortable beds and flatscreen televisions. Gracious service complements the grand surroundings. 159 rooms. Complimentary continental breakfast. Wireless Internet access. Restaurant, bar. Airport transportation available. **$**

★★HOLIDAY INN

6555 Old Collamer Road S., East Syracuse, 315-437-2761, 800-465-4329;
www.holiday-inn.com
203 rooms. Complimentary full breakfast. High-speed Internet access, Restaurant, bar. Children's activity center. **$**

★★HOLIDAY INN

441 Electronics Parkway, Liverpool, 315-457-1122, 800-465-4329; www.holiday-inn.com
280 rooms. Restaurant, bar. High-speed Internet access. Airport transportation available. **$**

★★★THE MARX HOTEL AND CONFERENCE CENTER

701 E. Genesee St., Syracuse, 315-479-7000, 877-843-6279; www.marxsyracuse.com
Located in downtown Syracuse, this chic, contemporary hotel has rooms featuring desks with ergonomic seating and high-speed Internet access. There's also a fully equipped fitness center. Those on a working vacation can order room service for breakfast, lunch or dinner and the complimentary van service transports sightseers to and from points of interest in the downtown area. 280 rooms. Wireless Internet access. Restaurant, two bars. **$**

★QUALITY INN

6611 Old Collamer Road, East Syracuse, 315-432-9333, 800-228-2800;
www.qualityinn.com
134 rooms. Wireless Internet access, Outdoor heated pool Complimentary continental breakfast. **$**

★★★SHERATON UNIVERSITY HOTEL AND CONFERENCE CENTER

801 University Ave., Syracuse, 315-475-3000, 800-395-2105;
www.sheratonsyracuse.com
Bordering Syracuse University and hospitals, this hotel is within walking distance of downtown civic centers, restaurants, entertainment arenas and other attractions.

NEW YORK

★
★
★
★
★

Service is friendly, and rooms have been updated with plush beds. 236 rooms. High-speed Internet access. Restaurant, bar. Airport transportation available. **$$**

RESTAURANTS

★BROOKLYN PICKLE
2222 Burnet Ave., Syracuse, 315-463-1851
Deli menu. Lunch, dinner. Closed Sunday; holidays. Casual attire. Outdoor seating. **$**

★★COLEMAN'S
100 S. Lowell Ave., Syracuse, 315-476-1933; www.colemansirishpub.com
American menu. Lunch, dinner, late-night. Bar. Children's menu. Casual attire. Outdoor seating. **$**

★★GLEN LOCH MILL
4626 North St., Jamesville, 315-469-6969; www.glenloch.net
Seafood, steak menu. Dinner, Sunday brunch. Closed Monday. Bar. Children's menu. Outdoor seating. **$$**

★★★PASCALE
204 W. Fayette St., Syracuse, 315-471-3040
Centrally located in Armory Square, a revitalized sector of downtown Syracuse, this restaurant features eclectic international food served in a contemporary setting. The menu changes with the seasonally. American menu. Lunch, dinner. Closed Sunday; holidays. Bar. Children's menu. Casual attire. Valet parking. Outdoor seating. **$$**

★PLAINVILLE FARMS
8450 Brewerton Road, Cicero, 315-699-3852; www.plainvillefarms.com
American menu. Lunch, dinner. Children's menu. **$**

TARRYTOWN

The village of Tarrytown and the neighboring villages of Irvington and Sleepy Hollow were settled by the Dutch during the mid-1600s. The name Tarrytown was taken from the Dutch word "Tarwe," meaning wheat. On September 23, 1780, the British spy Major John Andre was captured while carrying the detailed plans for West Point given to him by Benedict Arnold. The village and the area were made famous by the writings of Washington Irving, particularly *The Legend of Sleepy Hollow*, from which this region takes its name.

Information: Sleepy Hollow Chamber of Commerce, 54 Main St., Tarryown,
914-631-1705; www.sleepyhollowchamber.com

WHAT TO SEE AND DO

KYKUIT, THE ROCKEFELLER ESTATE
Highway 9 N. and N. Broadway, Sleepy Hollow, 914-631-3992; www.hudsonvalley.org
This six-story stone mansion was home to three generations of the Rockefeller family. Principal first-floor rooms open to the public. Extensive gardens with spectacular Hudson River views feature an important collection of 20th-century sculpture acquired by Governor Nelson A. Rockefeller; carriage barn with collection of antique cars and horse-drawn vehicles. Scheduled tours lasting 2½ hours and depart

approximately every 15 minutes from Philipsburg Manor, mid-April-October, Monday and Wednesday-Sunday.

LYNDHURST

635 S. Broadway, Tarrytown, 914-631-4481; www.lyndhurst.org

Gothic Revival mansion built in 1838 for William Paulding, mayor of New York City in the 1830s. Approximately 67 landscaped acres overlooking the Hudson. Contains books, art and furnishings. Tours. Mid-April-October: Tuesday-Sunday 10 a.m.-5 p.m.; rest of year: Saturday-Sunday 10 a.m.-4 p.m.

MUSIC HALL THEATER

13 Main St., Tarrytown, 914-631-3390; www.tarrytownmusichall.org

One of the oldest remaining theaters in the county, this 1885 structure now serves as a center for the arts.

OLD DUTCH CHURCH OF SLEEPY HOLLOW

42 N. Broadway, Tarrytown, 914-631-1123

This 1685 Church building of Dutch origins was built on what was the Manor of Frederick Philipse. Restored, includes a replica of the original pulpit. Tours by appointment. May-October, Tuesday-Sunday.

PHILIPSBURG MANOR

381 N. Broadway, Sleepy Hollow, 914-631-8200; www.hudsonvalley.org

Colonial farm and trading site (1720-1750) is also the departure point for tours of Kykuit. Manor house, barn, animals; restored operating gristmill, wooden millpond bridge across Pocantico River. March-December, Monday, Wednesday-Sunday; closed holidays.

SLEEPY HOLLOW CEMETERY

540 N. Broadway, Sleepy Hollow, 914-631-0081; www.sleepyhollowcemetery.org

Grounds contain graves of Washington Irving, Andrew Carnegie and William Rockefeller. Monday-Friday 8 a.m.-4:30 p.m., Saturday-Sunday 8:30 a.m.-4:30 p.m.

SUNNYSIDE

W. Sunnyside Lane, Tarrytown, 914-631-8200; www.hudsonvalley.org

Washington Irving's Hudson River estate contains much of his furnishings, personal property and library. March-December: Monday and Wednesday-Sunday; rest of year: weekends; closed holidays.

VAN CORTLANDT MANOR

500 S. Riverside Ave., Croton on Hudson, 914-631-8200; www.hudsonvalley.org

Post-Revolutionary War estate of prominent Colonial family. Elegantly furnished manor house; ferry house inn and kitchen building on old Albany Post Road; "Long Walk" with flanking 18th-century gardens; picnic area. Frequent demonstrations of open-hearth cooking, brickmaking, weaving. April-December, Monday and Wednesday-Sunday; closed holidays.

277

NEW YORK

★
★
★
★

THOUSAND ISLANDS

This group of more than 1,800 islands on the eastern U.S.-Canadian border, at the head of the St. Lawrence River, extends 52 miles downstream from the end of Lake Ontario. Slightly more than half the islands are in Canada. Some of them are five miles wide and extend more than 20 miles in length. These rocky slivers of land are noted for their scenery and numerous parks, including St. Lawrence Islands National Park. The Thousand Islands Bridge and highway (seven miles long) between the New York and Ontario mainlands crosses several of the isles and channels. Many of the Islands were settled during the early 1900s by American millionaires, whose opulent summer residences and private clubs made the area renowned throughout the world.

The Seaway Trail, a 454-mile national scenic byway, runs through the Thousand Islands region along the southeastern shore of Lake Ontario and beside the St. Lawrence area.

Uncluttered villages, boat tours, museums, walks, water sports and abundant freshwater fishing make the Islands a popular vacation center. *Information: www.thousandislands.com*

SPECIAL EVENTS

CANDLELIGHT TOURS

150 White Plains Road, Tarrytown, 914-631-8200; www.hudsonvalley.org
At Sunnyside, Philipsburg Manor and Van Cortlandt Manor. English Christmas Celebration. December.

HERITAGE AND CRAFTS WEEKEND

Van Cortlandt Manor, South Riverside Ave., Croton-on-Hudson, 914-271-8981; www.hudsonvalley.org
Demonstrations and hands-on exhibits of 18th-century crafts and activities. Columbus Day weekend.

SUNSET SERENADES

635 S. Broadway, Tarrytown, 914-631-4481
On Lyndhurst grounds. Symphony concerts Saturdays, July.

HOTELS

★★★CASTLE ON THE HUDSON

400 Benedict Ave., Tarrytown, 914-631-1980, 800-616-4487; www.castleattarrytown.com
Built between 1897 and 1910, this hotel has panoramic views of the Hudson River and the historic Hudson Valley. The rooms and suites are romantically furnished with four-poster or canopied beds. The grounds are meticulously maintained and feature tennis courts and a pool. Equus restaurant is a destination in its own right, and its three rooms suit a variety of moods. The Tapestry and Oak rooms resemble a European castle with stone fireplaces and beamed ceilings while the conservatory style of the Garden Room has scenic river views. 31 rooms. Restaurant, bar. Whirlpool. Airport transportation available. Spa. Pool. Fitness center. $$$

★★COURTYARD BY MARRIOTT

475 White Plains Road, Tarrytown, 914-631-1122, 800-589-8720; www.courtyard.com

139 rooms. High-speed Internet access. Restaurant, bar. Pool. Fitness center. $$

★★★DOUBLETREE HOTEL TARRYTOWN

455 S. Broadway, Tarrytown, 914-631-5700; www.doubletree.com

This hotel features comfortable rooms (with complimentary wireless Internet access) and grand, Adirondack-styled public rooms. 247 rooms. Wireless Internet access. Restaurant, bar. Whirlpool. Airport transportation available. Fitness center. Tennis. Business center. $$$

★★★TARRYTOWN HOUSE ESTATE AND CONFERENCE CENTER

49 E. Sunnyside Lane, Tarrytown, 914-591-8200, 800-553-8118;
www.tarrytownhouseestate.com

Located only 24 miles from Manhattan, this lovely estate was built in the late 1800s and has views overlooking the Hudson River Valley. The comfortable rooms mix country touches with a modern sensibility. Sup in the hotel's Sleepy Hollow Pub with its billiards table and fireplace and numerous wines by the glass. 212 rooms. Complimentary full breakfast. High-speed Internet access. Restaurant. Whirlpool. Pool. Tennis. Business Center. $

RESTAURANTS

★★★★BLUE HILL AT STONE BARNS

630 Bedford Road, Pocantico Hills, 914-366-9600; www.bluehillstonebarns.com

An extension of Blue Hill restaurant in Manhattan set in the Pocantico Hills, Blue Hill at Stone Barns is not only a restaurant but a working farm and educational center dedicated to sustainable food production. The dining room is a former dairy bar that has been converted to a lofty, modern space with vaulted ceilings, dark wood accents and earthy tones. Diners can choose three-, four- or five-course meals from a variety of dishes such as pancetta wrapped trout or lamb with local rapini, chickpeas and chorizo. Desserts are freshly made and hard to resist, like the chocolate torte with salted peanuts, caramel, and coffee ice cream. American menu. Dinner, Sunday lunch. Closed Monday-Tuesday. Bar. Business casual attire. Reservations recommended. $$$$

★★CARAVELA

53 N. Broadway, Tarrytown, 914-631-1863; www.caravelarestaurant.com

Brazilian, Portuguese menu. Lunch, dinner. Closed holidays. Bar. Casual attire. Reservations recommended. Outdoor seating. $$

★★★EQUUS

400 Benedict Ave., Tarrytown, 914-631-3646; www.castleattarrytown.com

Choose from three charming dining rooms at this restaurant within the Castle on the Hudson. The menu includes standouts such as bacon-wrapped chicken roulade with sweet corn pudding and pistachio-crusted tuna with grape tomatoes and arugula. French, American menu. Lunch, dinner. Bar. Jacket required. Valet parking. $$$

★★SANTA FE

5 Main St., Tarrytown, 914-332-4452; www.santaferestaurant.com

Mexican, Southwestern menu. Lunch, dinner. Closed holidays. Bar. Casual attire. $$

TICONDEROGA

This resort area lies on the ancient portage route between Lake George and Lake Champlain. For almost 200 years, it was the site of various skirmishes and battles involving American Indians, French, British, Canadians, Yankees and New Yorkers.
Information: Ticonderoga Area Chamber of Commerce, 94 Montcalm St.,
Ticonderoga, 518-585-6619; www.ticonderogany.com

WHAT TO SEE AND DO
FORT TICONDEROGA
Route 74, Ticonderoga, 518-585-2821; www.fort-ticonderoga.org
This fort was built in 1755 by the Quebecois, who called it Carillon, and was successfully defended by the Marquis de Montcalm against a more numerous British force in 1758. It was captured by the British in 1759 and by Ethan Allen and the Green Mountain Boys in 1775 (known as the first victory of the Revolutionary War). The stone fort was restored in 1909. The largest collection of cannons in North America is assembled on the grounds. The museum houses weapons, paintings and articles of daily lives of the soldiers garrisoned here during the Seven Year and Revolutionary wars. Costumed guides give tours; cannon firings daily; fife and drum corps parade July and August. Scenic drive to the summit of Mount Defiance for 30-mile view. Early May-mid-October, daily.

HERITAGE MUSEUM
Montcalm St. and Tower Ave., Ticonderoga, 518-585-2696;
www.ticonderogaheritagemuseum.org
Displays of civilian and industrial history of Ticonderoga. Children's workshop. Late June-Labor Day: daily; Labor Day-mid-October: weekends.

REPLICA OF HANCOCK HOUSE
6 Moses Circle, Ticonderoga, 518-585-7868; www.thehancockhouse.org
The home of the Ticonderoga Historical Society is a replica of the house built for John Hancock on Beacon Street in Boston. It is maintained as a museum and research library. The rooms display various period furnishings as well as exhibits presenting social and civil history from the 1700s through the present.

HOTEL
★CIRCLE COURT
440 Montcalm St. W., Ticonderoga, 518-585-7660; www.circlecourtmotel.com
14 rooms. Wireless Internet access. Pets accepted. $

RESTAURANTS
★CARILLON RESTAURANT
872 Route 9N., Ticonderoga, 518-585-7657; www.carillonrestaurant.com
American menu. Dinner. Closed Wednesday. $

★HOT BISCUIT DINER
14 Montcalm St., Ticonderoga, 518-585-3483; www.hotbiscuitdiner.com
American menu. Lunch, dinner, brunch. Closed holidays. Children's menu. Casual attire. $$

TIVOLI

This village is on the Hudson River near the Catskill Mountains.
Information: www.tivoliny.org

RESTAURANTS

★★MILAGROS

73 Broadway, Tivoli, 845-757-5300

American menu. Breakfast, lunch, dinner, brunch. Bar. Children's menu. Business casual attire. Reservations recommended. Outdoor seating. **$$**

★★THE BLACK SWAN

66 Broadway, Tivoli, 845-757-3777

American menu. Dinner. Bar. Business casual attire. Reservations recommended. **$$**

TROY

This town has a reputation for having beautiful Victorian architecture. Visitors searching for a one-of-a-kind treasure will enjoy Troy's downtown antique district.

WHAT TO SEE AND DO

CHILDREN'S MUSEUM OF SCIENCE AND TECHNOLOGY

250 Jordan Road, Troy, 518-235-2120; www.cmost.org

Science, natural history, Iroquois and art are some of the subject covered in this diverse array of exhibits. Standouts includes a settlers' cabin, a marine aquarium, animals, a diorama of a beaver pond environment and planetarium shows. September-June, Thursday-Sunday 10 a.m.-5 p.m.; closed holidays.

GRAVE OF SAMUEL WILSON

Oakwood Cemetery, 50 101st St., Troy, 518-272-7520; www.oakwoodcemetery.org

By an act of the 87th Congress, a resolution was adopted that saluted meat supplier Samuel Wilson as the originator of the national symbol of "Uncle Sam."

RENSSELAER COUNTY HISTORICAL SOCIETY

57 Second St., Troy, 518-272-7232; www.rchsonline.org

An 1827 town house, the Hart-Cluett Mansion, has period rooms furnished with decorative and fine arts. Tuesday-Saturday noon-5 p.m.; closed holidays; late December-late January.

TROY SAVINGS BANK MUSIC HALL

32 Second St., Troy, 518-273-0038; www.troymusichall.org

Victorian showplace in Italian Renaissance building. Presents a wide variety of concerts. Tours by appointment. September-May.

SPECIAL EVENT

STARS AND STRIPES RIVERFRONT FESTIVAL

Troy, 518-458-0547

Concerts, fireworks, carnival rides, military equipment displays, arts and crafts, food. Mid-June.

NEW YORK

★
★
★
★
★

HOTEL
★FAIRFIELD INN ALBANY EAST GREENBUSH
124 Troy Road, East Greenbush, 518-477-7984, 800-228-2800; www.marriott.com
105 rooms. Wireless Internet access. Complimentary continental breakfast. **$**

TUPPER LAKE
In the heart of the Adirondack resort country and surrounded by lakes, rivers and mountains, Tupper Lake offers hunting, fishing, boating, mountain climbing, skiing, camping, snowmobiling, golf, tennis and mountain biking amid magnificent scenery.
Information: Chamber of Commerce of Tupper Lake and Town of Altamont,
121 Park St., Tupper Lake, 518-359-3328; www.tupperlakeinfo.com

WHAT TO SEE AND DO
HISTORIC BETH JOSEPH SYNAGOGUE
Miller and Lake St., Tupper Lake, 518-359-7229;
www.tupperlakeinfo.com/historic_beth_joseph_synagogue
This restored version of the area's first synagogue is itself based on the Eastern European synagogues familiar to early Jewish settlers. Gallery features Adirondack art and artists. Daily 11 a.m.-3 p.m. Building tours Tuesdays and Fridays. Sunday evening programs begin at 8 p.m.

RAQUETTE RIVER OUTFITTERS
1754 State Route 30, Tupper Lake, 518-359-3228; www.raquetteriveroutfitters.com
Canoe and kayak outfitting, sales and rentals in the Adirondack Mountains; guided tours.

★
★
★
★

SPECIAL EVENTS
FLATWATER WEEKEND
Highways 3 and 30, Tupper Lake
Annual canoe races. Mid-June.

TINMAN TRIATHLON
60 Park St., Tupper Lake, 518-359-3328
Mid-July.

WOODSMEN'S DAYS
14 Second St., Tupper Lake, 518-359-9444; www.woodsmendays.com
Logging demonstrations, chainsaw carving and axe throwing are some of the events that dominate this annual outdoor event. Second weekend in July.

HOTELS
★SHAHEEN'S
314 Park St., Tupper Lake, 518-359-3384, 800-474-2445; www.shaheensmotel.com
31 rooms. Complimentary continental breakfast. High-speed Internet access. Pool. **$**

★TUPPER LAKE MOTEL
255 Park St., Tupper Lake, 518-359-3381, 800-944-3585; www.tupperlakemotel.com
18 rooms. Complimentary continental breakfast. High-speed Internet access. Pool. **$**

UNADILLA

Play year-round in this village. Its location—at the foot of the Catskills, near the Susquehanna River—makes it a prime spot for boating, rafting, hiking, mountain biking and (after a short drive) skiing.

Information: www.unadillachamber.org

RESTAURANT

★UNADILLA HOUSE

188 Main St., Unadilla, 607-369-7227, 866-640-9713;
www.unadillahouserestaurant.com

American menu. Lunch, dinner. Closed Sunday; holidays. Bar. Children's menu. $$

UTICA

Near the western end of the Mohawk Trail, Utica has been a manufacturing and trading center since its early days. By 1793 there was stagecoach service from Albany. The opening of the Erie Canal brought new business. The first Woolworth "five and dime" opened here in 1879.

Information: Oneida County Convention and Visitors Bureau, Utica;
www.oneidacountycvb.com

WHAT TO SEE AND DO

CHILDREN'S MUSEUM

311 Main St., Utica, 315-724-6128; www.museum4kids.net

One of the nation's oldest children's museums includes hands-on exhibits teaching history, natural history and science. Iroquois exhibit includes section of Long House; local history displays; dress-up area; Playspace; outdoor railroad display; special weekend programs. Monday-Tuesday, Thursday-Saturday 9:45 a.m.-3:45 p.m.; closed holidays.

F.X. MATT BREWING COMPANY

Court and Varick Streets, Utica, 315-642-2480

Includes plant tour, trolley ride and visit to the 1888 Tavern. Free beer or root beer. Daily; closed holidays. Children only with adult.

MUNSON-WILLIAMS-PROCTOR INSTITUTE

310 Genesee St., Utica, 315-797-0000; www.mwpai.org

Museum of Art has collection of 18th- to 20th-century American and European paintings and sculpture; European, Japanese and American prints; American decorative arts. Adjacent is Fountain Elms, a Victorian house museum, with five mid-19th-century rooms; changing exhibits. Tuesday-Sunday; closed holidays. Also School of Art Gallery featuring exhibits by visiting artists, faculty and students. Monday-Saturday; closed holidays.

ONEIDA COUNTY HISTORICAL SOCIETY

1608 Genesee St., Utica, 315-735-3642; www.oneidacountyhistory.org

Museum traces Utica and Mohawk Valley history; reference library; changing exhibits. Tuesday-Friday; closed holidays.

UTICA ZOO
99 Steel Hill Road, Utica, 315-738-0472; www.uticazoo.org
More than 250 exotic and domestic animals roam this 80-acre zoo. Children's zoo April-October, daily; included with admission. Main zoo, daily 10 a.m.-5 p.m.; closed holidays.

HOTELS
★BEST WESTERN GATEWAY ADIRONDACK INN
175 N. Genesee St., Utica, 315-732-4121; www.bestwestern.com
89 rooms. Complimentary continental breakfast. High-speed Internet access. Business center. Fitness center. Pets accepted. $

★★HOLIDAY INN
1777 Burrstone Road, New Hartford, 315-797-2131; www.holiday-inn.com
100 rooms. High-speed Internet access. Restaurant, bar. Whirlpool. Pets accepted. Pool. Fitness center. $

★★RADISSON HOTEL-UTICA CENTRE
200 Genesee St., Utica, 315-797-8010; www.radisson.com
158 rooms. High-speed Internet access. Restaurant, bar. Pets accepted. Pool. $

RESTAURANT
★★★HORNED DORSET
Highway 8, Leonardsville, 315-855-7898
Apple orchards and farmland create a bucolic backdrop for the first-class New American cooking and impeccable European service found at this historic inn with its charming, expansive dining rooms. There are rooms in the inn should you wish to stay longer and savor the rural setting. French menu. Dinner. Closed holidays. $$$

VICTOR
A suburb of Rochester, Victor is a small town with pretty homes and a beautiful rural setting.
Information: www.victorny.org

WHAT TO SEE AND DO
VALENTOWN MUSEUM
7370 Valentown Square, Victor, 585-924-4170; www.valentown.org
A three-story structure built as a community center and shopping plaza in 1879. General store, harness maker and cobbler shops, bakery, schoolroom; Civil War artifacts. It contains thousands of artifacts, objects and heirlooms that represent the local 19th-century history of the Victor and Rochester, New York area. May-October, Wednesday-Sunday.

HOTEL
★HAMPTON INN
7637 Highway 96, Victor, 585-924-4400, 800-426-7866; www.hamptoninn.com
123 rooms. Complimentary continental breakfast. Pool. Fitness center. $

WARRENSBURG

Near Lake George, Warrensburg is an old-time village in the heart of a year-round tourist area and is a center for campgrounds, dude ranches and antiques shops. Activities include canoeing, fishing, golf, swimming, tubing, skiing, horseback riding and biking, among others. The fall foliage here is especially beautiful.

Information: Chamber of Commerce, 3847 Main St., Warrensburg, 518-623-2161; www.warrensburgchamber.com

WHAT TO SEE AND DO
WARRENSBURG MUSEUM OF LOCAL HISTORY
47 Main St., Warrensburg, 518-623-2928
Exhibits detail the history of Warrensburg from the time it became a town to the present. Artifacts of livelihood, business, industry and general living of the residents. July-August, Tuesday-Saturday.

SPECIAL EVENTS
ARTS & CRAFTS FESTIVAL
Main St. and Stewart Farrar Ave., Warrensburg, 518-623-2161
July 4 weekend.

WORLD'S LARGEST GARAGE SALE AND FOLIAGE FESTIVAL
Warrensburg, 518-623-2161; www.warrensburggaragesale.com
Everything from vintage treasures to old junk can be found at this massive sale.

HOTEL
★★★FRIENDS LAKE INN
963 Friends Lake Road, Chestertown, 518-494-4751; www.friendslake.com
A stay at this restored 19th-century inn offers cross-country skiing, a private beach and canoeing on Friends Lake. Many of the Adirondack-styled rooms feature soaring ceilings, river rock-enclosed fireplaces and whirlpool tubs. The inn's New American menu features dishes such as braised Chilean sea bass with a tomato fennel broth and ancho-rubbed lamb chops with a minted pea purée. There's also a great wine bar for less hearty fare. 17 rooms. Restaurant. Pool. **$$$**

RESTAURANTS
★★FRIENDS LAKE INN
963 Friends Lake Road, Chestertown, 518-494-4751; www.friendslake.com
American, seafood menu. Lunch, dinner. Bar. Children's menu. Casual attire. Reservations recommended. Outdoor seating. Built in 1860. **$$**

★★★MERRILL MAGEE HOUSE
3 Hudson St., Warrensburg, 518-623-2449; www.merrillmageehouse.com
Situated in the Adirondack Mountains, the Merrill Magee offers comfortable, relaxed accommodations—and delicious dining. The inn's dinner menu includes New York strip steak with mushroom and tomato ragu and shrimp Florentine, and jumbo shrimp sautéed with bacon, garlic and spinach. Continental menu. Dinner. Closed holidays. Bar. Casual attire. Reservations recommended. Outdoor seating. Overnight stays available. **$$**

NEW YORK

★
★
★
★
★

WATERLOO

The Church of Jesus Christ of Latter-Day Saints (Mormons) was founded by Joseph Smith and five other men in a small log cabin here on April 6, 1830. The site is commemorated at the Peter Whitmer Farm.

Information: www.waterloony.com

WHAT TO SEE AND DO

MCCLINTOCK HOUSE

14 E. Williams St., Waterloo, 315-568-2991

Home of the McClintocks, a Quaker family who were active in the planning of the first Women's Rights Convention. Tours Saturday-Sunday.

PETER WHITMER FARM

1451 Aunkst Road, Waterloo, 315-539-2552

The site where the Church of Jesus Christ of Latter-Day Saints (Mormons) was organized in 1830; period furnishings. Daily.

TERWILLIGER MUSEUM

31 E. Williams St., Waterloo, 315-539-0533; www.waterloony.com/library

Historical museum housing collections dating from 1875; Native American displays; authentic full-size vehicles and a replica of a general store provide a glimpse of life as it was in the 1920s. Recently restored Fatzinger Hall on the Library's second floor seats 140, and hosts Spring and Fall programs featuring dance, theater productions, music and public lectures. Also five rooms, each furnished to depict a specific era. Tuesday-Friday afternoons.

WATERLOO MEMORIAL DAY MUSEUM

35 E. Main St., Waterloo, 315-539-9611; www.waterloony.com/MdayMus.html

Mementos of Civil War, World War I, World War II, the Korean conflict, Vietnam and the first Memorial Day in this 20-room mansion furnished to depict the 1860-1870 period. Mid-May-Mid-November, Tuesday-Saturday 1-4 p.m.; closed July 4. Under 12 years only with adult.

HOTEL

★★HOLIDAY INN

2468 Mound Road, Waterloo, 315-539-5011; www.holidayinn.com

148 rooms. Restaurant, bar. Whirlpool. Pets accepted. High-speed Internet access. Pool. Tennis. $

WATERTOWN

Watertown lies along the Black River, 11 miles east of Lake Ontario and 22 miles south of the St. Lawrence. Within the city, the river falls more than 100 feet, which makes for great whitewater rafting. During a county fair in 1878, young Frank W. Woolworth originated the idea of the five- and ten-cent store.

Information: Chamber of Commerce, 1241 Coffeen St., Watertown, 315-788-4400; www.watertownny.com

AMERICAN MAPLE MUSEUM

9753 Main St., Croghan, 315-346-1107; www.lcida.org/maplemuseum.html

Displays of maple syrup production; equipment; history of maple production in North America; lumberjack display. July-mid-September, Monday-Saturday 1-4 p.m.; mid-May-June and mid-September-mid-October, Friday-Monday 11 a.m.-4 p.m.; mid-October-November by appointment.

JEFFERSON COUNTY HISTORICAL SOCIETY MUSEUM

228 Washington St., Watertown, 315-782-3491

Paddock mansion; Victorian mansion with period rooms, military rooms; Native American artifacts, changing and regional history exhibits; Victorian garden. Monday-Friday; closed holidays.

ROSWELL P. FLOWER MEMORIAL LIBRARY

229 Washington St., Watertown, 315-788-2352; www.flowermemoriallibrary.org

Neo-Classic marble building houses murals of local history, French furniture; miniature furniture; genealogy and local history. Daily; closed holidays.

SCI-TECH CENTER

154 Stone St., Watertown, 315-788-1340

Hands-on science and technology museum for families houses more than 40 exhibits, including laser display and discovery boxes; science store. Tuesday-Saturday; closed holidays.

287

HOTELS

★★BEST WESTERN CARRIAGE HOUSE INN

300 Washington St., Watertown, 315-782-8000; www.bestwesternwatertownny.com

160 rooms. Restaurant, bar. Pool, sauna. Fitness center. High-speed Internet access. **$**

★DAYS INN

110 Commerce Park Drive, Watertown, 315-782-2700; www.daysinn.com

135 rooms. Restaurant, bar. Fitness center. Pool. High-speed Internet access. Business center. **$**

★THE INN

1190 Arsenal St., Watertown, 315-788-6800, 800-799-5224

96 rooms. Pets accepted. Pool. **$**

RESTAURANT

★★PARTRIDGE BERRY INN

26561 Highway 3, Watertown, 315-788-4610; www.partridgeberryinn.com

American menu. Lunch, dinner, brunch. Closed Monday. Bar. Children's menu. **$$**

NEW YORK

WATKINS GLEN

Watkins Glen is situated at the southern end of Seneca Lake, where the famous tributary gorge for which it is named emerges in the middle of the town. Several estate wineries offering tours and tasting are located near town on the southern shores of the lake.

Information: Schuyler County Chamber of Commerce, 100 N. Franklin St., Watkins Glen, 607-535-4300, 800-607-4552; www.schuylerny.com

WHAT TO SEE AND DO

FAMOUS BRANDS OUTLET

412 N. Franklin St., Watkins Glen, 607-535-4952; www.famousbrandsoutlet.com
This is a popular spot for finding deals on such brand names as Carhartt, Docker's and Woolrich. Monday-Saturday 9 a.m.-8 p.m., Sunday 10 a.m.-5 p.m.

INTERNATIONAL MOTOR RACING RESEARCH CENTER AT WATKINS GLEN

610 S. Decatur St., Watkins Glen, 607-535-9044; www.racingarchives.org
The center features a wonderful display of all things racing, including cars. The broad collection also includes books, films, fine art, photographs, documents, magazines, programs and memorabilia with a motor sports theme. Monday-Saturday 9 a.m.-5 p.m.; also some Sunday race days.

MONTOUR FALLS

408 W. Main St., Montour Falls, 607-535-7367; www.villageofmontourfalls.com
Small community with seven glens nearby; fishing for rainbow trout in Catharine Creek. Chequaga Falls plunge into a pool beside the main street. Municipal marina, north of town, has access to barge canal system.

SENECA LAKE WINE TRAIL

Watkins Glen; www.senecalakewine.com
Twenty-two wineries dot the hillsides of Seneca Lake. Follow Highways 14 or 414 for tasting and tours. Contact the Seneca Lake Wine Trail for more information.

SENECA LODGE

State Route 329, Watkins Glen, 607-535-2014; www.senecalodge.com
This place is very popular with race fans, many of whom reserve a year in advance. On site is the historic Seneca Lodge Restaurant. The bar has NASCAR memorabilia; the mechanics hang out here. Cabins, A-frames and motel rooms available.

WATKINS GLEN GORGE

Route 14, Watkins Glen, 607-535-4511; www.nysparks.state.ny.us/parks
The gorge features 19 waterfalls. Park in town to avoid the fee at the entrance on Franklin. Guided walks by naturalists.

WATKINS GLEN STATE PARK

Route 14, Watkins Glen, 607-535-4511; www.nysparks.state.ny.us/parks
Stairs and bridges lead upward through Watkins Glen Gorge, past cataracts and rapids, rising some 600 feet in 1½ miles.

★
★
★
★
★

NASCAR RACE DAY

2790 County Road 16, Watkins Glen, 607-535-2481; www.theglen.com
Contests, drivers, entertainment. Early August.

WATKINS GLEN INTERNATIONAL

2790 County Road 16, Watkins Glen, 607-535-2481; www.theglen.com
IMSA and NASCAR Winston Cup racing. Late May-September.

RESTAURANTS

★★CASTEL GRISCH

3380 County Road 28, Watkins Glen, 607-535-9614; www.castelgrisch.com
Alpine, American menu. Dinner. Wine tasting room, Closed January-March. Outdoor seating. Guest rooms available. **$$**

★★WILDFLOWER CAFÉ

301 N. Franklin St., Watkins Glen, 607-535-9797; www.roosterfishbrewing.com
American menu. Restaurant, lunch, dinner. Closed holidays. Bar. **$$**

WEST POINT

West Point has been of military importance since Revolutionary days when it was one of four points on the mid-Hudson River fortified against the British. In 1778, a great chain was strung across the river to stop British ships and links can still be seen today. The military academy was founded by an act of Congress in 1802. The barracks, academic and administration buildings are closed to visitors, but there is still plenty to see and do.

Information: www.usma.edu

WHAT TO SEE AND DO

BATTLE MONUMENT

Thayer and Washington Roads, West Point, 845-938-4011; www.usma.army.mil
Memorial dedicated to the 2,230 officers and men of the Regular Army who died in action during the Civil War. Nearby are some links from the chain used to block the river from 1778 to 1782.

CADET CHAPEL

Ruger Road and Cadet Drive, West Point, 845-938-4011; www.usma.army.mil
On hill overlooking the campus. Large pipe organ and stained glass. Daily.

MICHIE STADIUM

700 Mills Road, West Point, 845-938-4011
Seats 42,000 fans for Army home football games.

WEST POINT MUSEUM

Pershing Center, West Point, 845-938-2638; www.usma.edu/Museum
Exhibits on history and ordnance. Daily; 10:30 a.m.-4:15 p.m. closed holidays.

289

NEW YORK

★
★
★
★
★

HOTEL

★★THE THAYER HOTEL

674 Thayer Rd., West Point, 845-446-4731, 800-247-5047; www.thethayerhotel.com
161 rooms. National Historic Landmark. Restaurant, bar. Fitness center. **$**

SPECIALTY LODGING

CROMWELL MANOR INN

174 Angola Road, Cornwall, 845-534-7136; www.cromwellmanor.com
Elegant gardens surround the historic Cromwell Manor Inn. Rooms are situated in both the Manor House that dates to the 1820s and the 1764 Chimneys Cottage. Antiques, fireplaces, claw-foot tubs, four-poster beds and rich upholsteries fill the elegant accommodations. 13 rooms. Complimentary full breakfast. Airport transportation available. **$$**

RESTAURANTS

★★CANTERBURY BROOK INN

331 Main St., Cornwall, 845-534-9658; www.thecanterburybrookinn.com
American menu. Lunch, dinner. Closed Sunday; holidays. Bar. Casual attire. Outdoor seating. **$$**

★PAINTER'S

266 Hudson St., Cornwall-on-Hudson, 845-534-2109; www.painters-restaurant.com
American, International menu. Lunch, dinner, Sunday brunch. Closed holidays. Bar. Children's menu. Casual attire. Reservations recommended. Outdoor seating. **$$**

WESTBURY

On Long Island, Westbury and its surrounds offer opportunities to enjoy the great outdoors, learn about American history, shop for antiques and dine on delicious food.
Information: www.villageofwestbury.org

WHAT TO SEE AND DO

CLARK BOTANIC GARDEN

193 I. U. Willets Road, Albertson, 516-484-8600; www.clarkbotanic.org
The 12-acre former estate of Grenville Clark. Includes Hunnewell Rose Garden; ponds, streams; bulbs, perennials, annuals; wildflower, herb, rock, rhododendron, azalea and day lily gardens; children's garden; groves of white pine, dogwood and hemlock. Daily 10 a.m.-4:30 p.m.

OLD WESTBURY GARDENS

71 Old Westbury Road, Old Westbury, 516-333-0048; www.oldwestburygardens.org
This historic mansion dates back to 1906. The 66-room house features paintings, magnificent furniture and trinkets of all kinds. The gardens have a variety of flora and fauna that change with the seasons. The estate has been featured in such films as *The Age of Innocence*. Monday, Wednesday-Sunday 10 a.m.-5 p.m.; winter hours vary.

WESTBURY MUSIC FAIR

960 Brush Hollow Road, Westbury, 516-334-0800; www.musicfair.com

This concert series offers a unique chance to see performances in a theater-in-the-round style. Most of the stars are a bit from yesteryear and have included Paul Anka, Ringo Starr, Aaron Neville and Tony Bennett.

RESTAURANTS

★★BENNY'S RISTORANTE

199 Post Ave., Westbury, 516-997-8111; www.bennysristorante.com

Italian menu. Lunch, dinner. Closed Sunday; holidays; also the last two weeks in August. Reservations recommended. **$$$**

★★CAFE BACI

1636 Old Country Road, Westbury, 516-832-8888;
www.cafebacirestaurant.com

Italian, American menu. Lunch, dinner. Bar. Casual attire. **$$**

★★GIULIO CESARE RISTORANTE

18 Ellison Ave., Westbury, 516-334-2982

Italian menu. Lunch, dinner. Closed Sunday; holidays. Bar. **$$$**

WHITE PLAINS

In October 1776, General George Washington outfoxed General Lord Howe here. Howe, with a stronger, fresher force, permitted Washington to retreat to an impregnable position. He never could explain why he had not pursued his overwhelming advantage.

Information: Westchester County Office of Tourism, 222 Mamaroneck Ave., White Plains, 914-995-8500, 800-833-9282; www.cityofwhiteplains.com

WHAT TO SEE AND DO

MILLER HILL RESTORATION

Dunlap Way and White Plains

Restored earthworks from the Battle of White Plains (Oct 28, 1776). Built by Washington's troops. Battle diagrams.

MONUMENT

S. Broadway and Mitchell Place, White Plains

The Declaration of Independence was adopted at this site on July 1776, and the state of New York was formally organized.

WASHINGTON'S HEADQUARTERS

140 Virginia Road, North White Plains, 914-949-1236;
www.westchestergov.com/parks/NatureCenters05/WashintonsHeadquarters.htm

Revolutionary War relics; demonstrations, lectures. By appointment.

HOTELS

★LA QUINTA INN AND SUITES

94 Business Park Drive, Armonk, 914-273-9090; www.lq.com

179 rooms. High-speed Internet access. Fitness center. Business center. Pets accepted. Restaurant, bar. Airport transportation available. **$**

★★★HILTON RYE TOWN

699 Westchester Ave., Rye Brook, 914-939-6300; www.hilton.com

Spacious and well-appointed guest rooms await at this hotel in suburban Rye Brook. Accommodations feature Hilton's signature Serenity Beds, with plush mattress toppers and down comforters and pillows, as well as CD players, alarm clock radios with MP3 docks, mini-bars and work desks with lamps. A fitness center and pool help keep guests fit, and three on-site restaurants provide dining options for every palate. 437 rooms. High-speed Internet access. Three restaurants, bar. Whirlpool. Tennis. Business center. Fitness center. **$$**

★★★RENAISSANCE WESTCHESTER HOTEL

80 W. Red Oak Lane, White Plains, 914-694-5400, 800-891-2696; www.marriott.com

Rooms at this hotel offer both comfort and luxury, with rich fabrics, down comforters, plush pillows and views of the surrounding countryside. An indoor pool, whirlpool and Jacuzzi, as well as indoor tennis courts, volleyball courts and a fitness center with cardio equipment and free weights offer onsite recreation. 350 rooms. High-speed Internet access. Restaurant, bar.

★★★THE RITZ-CARLTON, WESTCHESTER

3 Renaissance Square, White Plains, 914-946-5500; www.ritzcarlton.com

As one of the newest notches in the Ritz-Carlton belt, opened in December 2007, this elegant hotel is only a short jaunt from Manhattan but feels miles removed in suburban White Plains. Whether it's to avoid the 24-hour honking of New York City or to get closer to nature with nearby bike trails and forest preserves, you'll find plenty to reasons to extend a stay here. The guest rooms are spacious and contemporary with neutral tones and modern amenities including flat-screen TVs and wireless Internet. If you can, opt for a room on the club level, which awards you a personal concierge, decadent treats throughout the day and access to a complimentary business center. No need to go into the city for dinner; just book a table at BLT, where famed chef Laurent Tourondel whips up tasty French bistro fare in a chic urbane setting. 118 rooms. Wireless Internet access. Restaurant, bar. Fitness center. Spa. Business center. **$$$$**

SPA

★★★★THE RITZ-CARLTON SPA, WESTCHESTER

3 Renaissance Square, White Plains, 914-467-5888, 800-241-3333; www.ritzcarlton.com

This gorgeous spa offers a getaway from your New York City escape. The 10,000-square-foot complex also features a gym and indoor rooftop pool, but if you want to really relax, head for one of the four massage rooms. Opt for seasonal signature services, such as summertime's Liquid Gold treatment, which includes a cleanse of lemon and chamomile, a warm wrap of jojoba butter and a massage. Or if you want to put your best face forward when you get back home, get the Derma Lift Facial, which uses a skin-lifting massage and marine-based products to brighten the skin. Wrap up your trip to the spa with the half-hour New York Minute manicure—the closest you'll get to the hustle and bustle of the Big Apple at this sactuary.

WHITEHALL

Whitehall is one of Mother Nature's favorite children. Nearby are the Adirondack Mountains, Vermont's Green Mountains and both Lake George and Lake Champlain—all offering beautiful backdrops for any outdoor activity.
Information: 124 Main St., Whitehall, 518-499-1535

RESTAURANT

★FINCH & CHUBB RESTAURANT AND INN

82 N. Williams St., Whitehall, 518-499-2049; www.visitwhitehall.com
American menu. Lunch, dinner. $

WILLIAMSVILLE

This village has worked hard to preserve its historic buildings, making it a great place for history and architecture buffs to spend an afternoon.
Information: www.amherst.org

RESTAURANTS

★★★DAFFODIL'S

930 Maple Road, Williamsville, 716-688-5413
Fireplaces, paintings and book-lined walls create a library-like atmosphere at this long-standing restaurant which serves American cooking heavy on the seafood. The live piano adds a festive touch. Lunch, dinner. Bar. Children's menu. Victorian décor. Valet parking. $$$

★★RED MILL INN

8326 Main St., Williamsville, 716-633-7878; www.redmillinn.com
American menu. Lunch, dinner, Sunday brunch. Closed holidays. Bar. Children's menu. Casual attire. Reservations recommended. Valet parking. Outdoor seating. $$

WILMINGTON

Gateway to Whiteface Mountain Memorial Highway, Wilmington is made-to-order for skiers and lovers of scenic splendor.
Information: Whiteface Mtn. Regional Visitors Bureau, Highway 86, Wilmington, 518-946-2255, 888-944-8332; www.whitefaceregion.com

WHAT TO SEE AND DO

HIGH FALLS GORGE

Route 86, Wilmington, 518-946-2278; www.highfallsgorge.com
Deep ravine cut into the base of Whiteface Mountain by the Ausable River. Variety of strata, rapids, falls and potholes can be viewed from a network of modern bridges and paths. Photography and mineral displays in main building. Memorial Day-mid-October, daily.

WHITEFACE MOUNTAIN MEMORIAL HIGHWAY

Highway 431, Wilmington, 800-462-6236
A five-mile toll road to top of mountain (4,867 feet). Trail or elevator from parking area. Views of St. Lawrence River, Lake Placid and Vermont.

NEW YORK

★
★
★
★
★

WHITEFACE MOUNTAIN SKI CENTER
Highway 86, Wilmington, 518-946-2223, 877-754-3223; www.whiteface.com
Gondola; two triple, seven double chairlifts; snowmaking; patrol, school, rentals; cafeteria, bar, nursery. Longest run 2½ miles; vertical drop 3,350 feet. Chairlift mid-June-mid-October. Lift-serviced mountain biking center; rental, repair shop, guided tours late June-mid-October. Skiing, mid-November-mid-April, daily.

HOTELS
★HUNGRY TROUT MOTOR INN
5239 Route 86, Wilmington, 518-946-2217, 800-766-9137; www.hungrytrout.com
22 rooms. Closed April, November. Bar. Wireless Internet access. Pets accepted. $

★LEDGE ROCK AT WHITEFACE
5078 NYS Route 86, Wilmington, 800-336-4754; www.ledgerockatwhiteface.com
18 rooms. Wireless Internet access. Bar. Pets accepted. $

RESTAURANT
★WILDERNESS INN II
Highway 86, Wilmington, 518-946-2391; www.lakeplacid.net/wildernessinn
American menu. Dinner. Closed Wednesday (in winter, Bar). Children's menu. Outdoor seating. Guest cottages available. $$

WINDHAM

Windham's keepers call it "the land in the sky," and for good reason. This community in the Catskills is located on the aptly named Windham Mountain, which offers skiing in the winter and hiking, backpacking and mountain biking in the summer.
Web site www.windhamchamber.org

WHAT TO SEE AND DO
SKI WINDHAM
33 Clarence D. Lane Road, Windham, 518-734-4300; www.skiwindham.com
High-speed detachable quad, double, four triple chairlifts; surface lift; patrol, ski school, rentals; snowmaking; nursery, ski shop, restaurant, two cafeterias, bar. Snowboarding. Longest run 2¼ miles; vertical drop 1,600 feet. Early November-early April, daily.

WHITE BIRCHES CAMPSITE
Princess Navoo Road, Windham, 518-734-3266; www.whitebirchescampsites.com
Summer activities include lake swimming, canoeing, camping, mountain biking, archery.

HOTEL
★HOTEL VIENNA
107 Route 296, Windham, 518-734-5300; www.thehotelvienna.com
29 rooms. Closed April-mid-May. Indoor Pool. Complimentary continental breakfast. $

ALBERGO ALLEGRIA

Route 296, Windham, 518-734-5560; www.albergousa.com

This Victorian inn, furnished with antiques, has 16 bedrooms with down comforters, full private baths and TVs with VCRs. There are 12 guest rooms named after the months of the year and four suites named after the seasons. 16 rooms. Complimentary full breakfast. **$$**

WOODSTOCK

Woodstock has traditionally been known as an art colony. In 1902 Ralph Radcliffe Whitehead, an Englishman, came from California and set up a home and handicraft community (Byrdcliffe, north of town). The Art Students' League of New York established a summer school here a few years later, and in 1916 Hervey White conceived the Maverick Summer Music Concerts, the oldest chamber concert series in the country. Woodstock was the original site chosen for the famous 1969 Woodstock Music Festival. When the event grew bigger than anyone imagined, it was moved 60 miles southwest to a farmer's field near Bethel, New York. Nevertheless, the festival gave Woodstock much notoriety.

Information: Chamber of Commerce and Arts, Woodstock, 845-679-6234; www.woodstockchamber.com

WHAT TO SEE AND DO

WOODSTOCK ARTISTS ASSOCIATION GALLERY

28 Tinker St., Woodstock, 845-679-2940; www.woodstockart.org

Center of the community since 1920. Changing exhibits of works by regional artists. Nationally recognized permanent collection. Friday-Saturday noon-6 p.m., Monday and Sunday noon-5 p.m.; closed Tuesday-Thursday.

295

SPECIAL EVENT

MAVERICK CONCERTS

120 Maverick Road, Woodstock, 845-679-8348; www.maverickconcerts.org

Maverick Concerts, America's oldest continuous summer chamber music festival and winner of the Chamber Music America/ASCAP Award for Adventurous Programming, thrives on the love of great music and the spirit of its unique site in the unspoiled woods. June-August.

SPECIALTY LODGINGS

LA DUCHESSE ANNE

1564 Wittenberg Road, Mount Tremper, 845-688-5260; www.laduchesseanne.com

The building that housed it was originally a boarding house dating from the mid 1800's. 13 rooms. Complimentary continental breakfast. Restaurant, bar. Built as a guest house in 1850. **$**

TWIN GABLES OF WOODSTOCK

73 Tinker St., Woodstock, 845-679-9479; www.twingableswoodstockny.com

Nine rooms. **$**

NEW YORK

★
★
★
★
☆

RESTAURANTS

★★BEAR CAFÉ
295A Tinker St., Woodstock, 845-679-5555; www.bearcafe.com
American menu. Lunch, dinner. Closed Tuesdays. Bar. Casual attire. Outdoor seating. $$$

★★BLUE MOUNTAIN BISTRO
1633 Glasco Turnpike, Woodstock, 845-679-8519; www.bluemountainbistro.com
French, Mediterranean menu. Dinner. Closed Monday; holidays. Bar. Casual attire. Reservations recommended. Outdoor seating. $$

★★VIOLETTE RESTAURANT & WINE BAR
85 Mill Hill Road, Woodstock, 845-679-5300; www.violettewoodstock.com
American menu. Lunch, dinner, Sunday brunch. Closed Wednesday; holidays. Bar. Casual attire. Reservations recommended. Outdoor seating. $$

YONKERS

Yonkers, on the New York City line, was originally purchased by Adriaen van der Donck in the early 1600s. His status as a young nobleman from Holland gave him the nickname "DeJonkeer," which underwent many changes until it became "the Yonkers land" and finally, Yonkers.

Information: Chamber of Commerce, 55 Main St., Yonkers, 914-963-0332; www.yonkerschamber.com

WHAT TO SEE AND DO

BILL OF RIGHTS MUSEUM
897 S. Columbus Ave., Mount Vernon, 914-667-4116
Exhibits include a working model of an 18th-century printing press and dioramas depicting John Peter Zenger, whose trial and acquittal for seditious libel in 1735 helped establish freedom of the press in America.

THE HUDSON RIVER MUSEUM OF WESTCHESTER
511 Warburton Ave., Yonkers, 914-963-4550; www.hrm.org
Includes Glenview Mansion (1876), an Eastlake-inspired Hudson River house overlooking the Palisades; Andrus Planetarium; regional art, history and science exhibits; changing exhibits of 19th- and 20th-century art in the Glenview galleries and contemporary wing. Changing exhibits, planetarium shows, lectures, jazz festival in summer. Wednesday-Sunday noon-5 p.m., Friday noon-8 p.m.; closed Monday, Tuesday and holidays.

ST. PAUL'S CHURCH NATIONAL HISTORIC SITE
897 S. Columbus Ave., Mount Vernon, 914-667-4116; www.nps.gov/sapa
Setting for historical events establishing basic freedoms outlined in the Bill of Rights Building was completed after the war and served not only as a church but also as a meeting house and courtroom where Aaron Burr practiced law on at least one occasion. Tours Monday-Friday open 9 a.m.-5 p.m., by appointment; closed holidays.

INDEX

297

INDEX

★
★
★
★
★

★
★
★
✩

300

INDEX

★
★
★
★
★

303

INDEX

★
★
★
★
★

INDEX

★
★
★
★
★

309

INDEX

★
★
★
★

311

INDEX

★
★
★
★
★

INDEX

★
★
★
★
★

314

INDEX

★
★
★
★
★

INDEX

★
★
★
★
☆